Social Work at the Level of International Comparison

Cinur Ghaderi · Kristin Sonnenberg ·
Luqman Saleh Karim ·
Niyan Namiq Sabir ·
Zhiya Abbas Qader ·
Lisa Marie Dünnebacke
Editors

Social Work at the Level of International Comparison

Examples from Iraqi-Kurdistan and Germany

Springer VS

Editors
Cinur Ghaderi
Evangelische Hochschule Bochum RWL
Bochum, Germany

Kristin Sonnenberg
Evangelische Hochschule Bochum RWL
Bochum, Germany

Luqman Saleh Karim
University of Sulaimani
Slemani, Iraq

Niyan Namiq Sabir
University of Sulaimani
Slemani, Iraq

Zhiya Abbas Qader
University of Sulaimani
Slemani, Iraq

Lisa Marie Dünnebacke
Evangelische Hochschule Bochum RWL
Bochum, Germany

ISBN 978-3-658-30393-8 ISBN 978-3-658-30394-5 (eBook)
https://doi.org/10.1007/978-3-658-30394-5

Responsible Editor: Stefanie Laux
This Springer VS imprint is published by the registered company Springer Fachmedien Wiesbaden GmbH part of Springer Nature.
The registered company address is: Abraham-Lincoln-Str. 46, 65189 Wiesbaden, Germany

Acknowledgement

Behind us lies a very special period of cooperation, which began in 2015. We are grateful that we traveled this path together with colleagues, friends and families.

We would like to thank the authors represented in this book for their willingness to participate in this long and adventurous process. The result is a wonderful composition of topics and perspectives.

This compilation of the diverse contributions and perspectives on the project and the international comparison would not have been possible without the support of the participating universities, the Protestant University of Applied Sciences in Bochum (EvH) and the University of Sulaimani (UoS), the teachers of the faculties of Social Work, the International Offices, the practice partners (especially Haukari e. V.), the students, including the culinary cooperation of the families of the project team in both countries. For this, thanks from the editors.

In the end it was our English editor who actively supported us in the realization of this book project. Therefore, special thanks go to James Brown for his thorough and reflective accompaniment of our texts. His cautious work has added to the precision of the texts in many places that we would not have been able to achieve as non-native speakers. We would like to thank our student assistant Marie Müller-Handrejk, who has always supported us reliably, flexibly and very thoroughly in checking English texts and editing the final layout.

Representing all editors,

Düsseldorf
Bonn
Slemani
July 2021

Cinur Ghaderi
Kristin Sonnenberg
Luqman Saleh Karim

Contents

Editors and Contributors

About the Editors

CINUR GHADERI, Prof. Dr., Professor of Psychology in the Faculty of Social Work at the Protestant University of Applied Sciences (EvH RWL Bochum). She is Vice-President for Research, Transfer and Internationalization. After her post-graduate education in psychological psychotherapy (behavioral therapy), she worked in the "Psychosocial Centre for refugees" (PSZ) in Düsseldorf. She received her PhD at the faculty of Social Sciences of the Ruhr University Bochum. She is a member of the steering committee of DTPPP (transcultural psychiatry, psychotherapy and psychosomatics). Main academic interests: International Social Work, Refugee Studies, Transcultural Psychotherapy, Psychotrauma, Identity, Diversity and Gender. She is the initiator of the DAAD-cooperation project CoBoSUnin 2016–2019 between the University of Sulaimani and Bochum. Contact: ghaderi@evh-bochum.de

KRISTIN SONNENBERG, Prof. Dr., Professor of Social Work at the Protestant University of Applied Sciences Bochum. She studied Social Pedagogy in Germany, completed an M.A. in Comparative European Social Studies at the University of North London and her PhD at the University of Cologne in Germany 2004 in the Faculty of Educational Science. She is a qualified psychodrama trainer. Since 2011 she is specialized in the field of methods and conceptualizing social work. Her main research projects are social inclusion of people with disabilities and international social work. She is member of the German Association of Social Workers (DGSA). Since 2016 she has been head of the BA Social Work

Studies and, together with Prof. Ghaderi, she was leader of the DAAD cooperation project CoBoSUnin 2016–2019 between the University of Sulaimani and Bochum. Contact: sonnenberg@evh-bochum.de

LUQMAN SALEH KARIM, Ass. Prof., Assistant Professor in the Social Work Department. He holds a PhD in Social Work from the University of Sulaimani, Kurdistan Region of Iraq. He was head of the Social Work Department from 2014–2017. He is a researcher and has conducted a large body of academic and organizational research on gender-based violence, environment policy, honor killing, child marriage, GBV assessments of needs, impact evaluation and COVID-19. He also worked with the United Nations Population Fund (UNFPA) and the Women's Refugee Commission (WRC) as a research consultant from 2018–2019, and as a child marriage research co-investigator in the Johns Hopkins University (USA); from 2016–2019 he was a University of Sulaimani coordinator of the DAAD cooperation project CoBoSUnin between the University of Sulaimani and the University of Applied Sciences in Bochum. Currently he works as lecturer at the University of Sulaimani, as a supervisor in the Khanzad women's organization, and as a research consultant for the Civil Development Organization (CDO). Contact: loqman.karim@univsul.edu.iq

NIYAN NAMIQ SABIR, Prof. Dr., Professor in the Social Work Department / College of Humanities at the University of Sulamani. She has a PhD in Philosophy of Education, an M.A. in Education and a Bachelor in Education and Psychology from Baghdad. She worked in Baghdad, Libya and Yemen. Since 2004 she has been working at the University of Sulaimani. From 2011–2015 she participated in the Delphi program of capacity building with the University of Bristol and she is one of the founders of the Gender and Violence Study Centre. From 2016–2019 she participated in the CoBoSUnin project with the Protestant University of Applied Sciences in Bochum. She has worked with most of the NGOs in Slemani. She taught and supervised MA & PhD students. She has about 20 published research articles in international, Arabic and local scientific journals. Contact: nian.sabir@univsul.edu.iq

ZHIYA ABBAS QADER, Ass. Prof., Assistant Professor, Lecturer and since 2021 head of the Social Work Department, College of Humanities, University of Sulaimani. Her specialty and major is in gender. She was a member of the delegation of the social work department in the shared project between the University of Sulaimani and the University of Applied Sciences in Bochum, Germany. Furthermore, in 2017–2018, she was Director of Center for Gender and Development Studies at the University of Sulaimani. Since 2018, she has been in charge of the Higher Education Department at the College of Humanities, University of Sulaimani. She has thus researched widely on gender, violence, woman and LGBTQI with publications in academic journals. So far, she has participated actively in many international and local conferences. Moreover, she is Iraq Coordinator of the Arab Association for Research and Communication Sciences and she is a member of many local and international organizations. Finally, she has a great deal of interests in gender studies, violence and related matters. Contact: zhiya.qader@univsul.edu.iq

LISA MARIE DÜNNEBACKE, M.A., B.A., in German Philology and Comparative Education (2010); M.A. in Social Inclusion (2014). From February 2017 to December 2019 she was scientific associate and lecturer at the EvH, Bochum, and a freelance Social Justice and Diversity trainer. Since January 2020 she has been Head of Education in the Martinswerk e.V. Dorlar child and youth service near Schmallenberg in the Upper Sauerland District, parallel to which she has been preparing her PhD thesis [projected thematic focal point: masculinity constructions in Kurdistan-Iraq]; Contact: l.duennebacke@outlook.com

Contributors

Kwestan Ali Abdalla Slemani, Iraq

Jwan Bakhtiar Bahaulddin Slemani, Iraq

Kamil Basergan Düsseldorf, Germany

Karen Bossow Bochum, Germany

Renate Dieterich Bonn, Germany

Lisa Marie Dünnebacke Schmallenberg, Germany

Thomas Eppenstein Frankfurt, Germany

Chro Mohammed Faraj Slemani, Iraq

Najat Mohamed Faraj Slemani, Iraq

Frank Fechter Bochum, Germany

Cinur Ghaderi Düsseldorf, Germany

Kale Jamal Hamasalih Slemani, Iraq

Shatw Farhad Hassan Slemani, Iraq

Aurfa Hassan Husen Slemani, Iraq

Luqman Saleh Karim Slemani, Iraq

Karzan Ghafur Khidhir Slemani, Iraq

Tobias Klug Bochum, Germany

Hildegard Mogge-Grotjahn Bochum, Germany

Briska Mariwan Mustafa Slemani, Iraq

Shnya Shwan Omer Slemani, Germany

Zhiya Abbas Qader Slemani, Iraq

Niklas Rokahr Bochum, Germany

Julika Laura Rundnagel Velbert, Germany

Niyan Namiq Sabir Slemani, Iraq

Fraidoon Arif Saeed Slemani, Iraq

Johannes Sczyrba Bonn, Germany

Helene Skladny Bochum, Germany

Kristin Sonnenberg Bonn, Germany

Jan Gerrit Weweler Bochum, Germany

Insights into International Cooperation and Social Work in Germany and Kurdistan-Iraq

Cinur Ghaderi and Kristin Sonnenberg

Abstract

In this article, insights into international cooperation and social work in Germany and Kurdistan-Iraq are given and, above all, clarified: Socio-political challenges such as violence, traumatization, (religious) fundamentalism, ethnicization, changing gender relations, flight and migration are necessitating a professional examination of social work as a human rights profession in international comparison.

Socio-political challenges such as violence, traumatization, (religious) fundamentalism, ethnicization, changing gender relations, flight and migration are necessitating a professional examination of social work as a human rights profession in international comparison.

The book opens up the possibility of dealing with international social work theoretically and practically, using the example of a region (the Kurdistan Region of Iraq) that is in a pioneering phase in teaching social work and at the same time is in a highly explosive situation in global politics.

These topics are not only perceptible in Iraq, where social work studies are in a pioneering phase, but are also highly relevant in Europe and specifically in Germany. An academic dialogue on teaching, research and further education on

C. Ghaderi (✉)
Düsseldorf, Germany
E-Mail: ghaderi@evh-bochum.de

K. Sonnenberg
Bonn, Germany
E-Mail: sonnenberg@evh-bochum.de

C. Ghaderi et al. (eds.), *Social Work at the Level of International Comparison*,
https://doi.org/10.1007/978-3-658-30394-5_1

common topics such as ethics, gender, counselling, aesthetic education, which are prominent in the fields of action of psychosocial work, is indispensable. This book gives insight into the results of a research project 'CoBoSUnin', which was dedicated to exactly these aspects.

What is the Meaning Behind the Word 'CoBoSUnin'?
CoBoSUnin means in Kurdish '*Get together for a knowledge acquisition*'. It is the acronym for the name of the project: "Cooperation between Bochum and Sulaimani Universities nowadays" – a multidimensional project on the internationalization of science and research within the Faculties of Social Work of the cooperating universities.

This volume is also part of a collection of several publications and a multilingual film:

1. A documentary film presents the international cooperation project between the Departments of Social Work at the Protestant University of Applied Sciences Rhineland Westphalia Lippe (EvH RWL) and the University of Sulaimani (UoS). It provides an insight into social work in Kurdistan-Iraq and Germany, for example in the areas of migration and flight, gender and violence, and international social work. In the second part, the film shows excerpts from the International Conference.[1]
2. In addition, a first textbook, *Introduction to Social Work*, in Kurdish-Sorani has been published, in which the majority of the authors are lecturers from the Faculty of Social Work at the University of Sulaimani (College of Humanities). The aim is to promote the development of indigenous teaching materials and research in accordance with local communities and their conditions.
3. A volume entitled *Social Work in Post-War and Political Conflict Areas. Examples from Iraqi-Kurdistan and beyond*, covers core topics from the International Conference in 2019 in Slemani, Kurdistan Region of Iraq. It offers unique access to theoretical approaches and practical examples for international social work in the context of war and conflicts from different countries such as Switzerland, Sierra Leone and South Africa. This book has already been published: Sonnenberg, K. & Ghaderi, C. (Eds.) (2021). Social work in post-war and political conflict areas. Wiesbaden: Springer VS.

[1] A documentation about the CoBoSUnin-project. The film offers insights into social work in the Kurdistan Region of Iraq and Germany. A Film by Ernst Meyer, SMIDAK Filmproduktion, Berlin: https://www.youtube.com/watch?v=wEkW9v51fps.

4. Several more conference articles, written in Kurdish or Arabic, will be published in a special edition of the UoS Journal.
5. And this book as another joint editorial volume focuses on the topic of *Social Work at the Level of International Comparison: Examples from Iraqi-Kurdistan and Germany* and was prepared by an editorial board from the CoBoSUnin project team. It presents the results of the project, with about 40 contributions from both participating countries.

It should be noted that the original plan was to publish all contributions jointly in three languages, which turned out not to be practicable. The international dialogue, however, will continue.

Explanation of the Naming 'Slemani'
After a long reflection of the different versions and options of how to write the name of the town where the University of Sulaimani is located, we decided to use the Kurdish version *Slemani* in our texts, as used for example in the city of Slemani. In Fig. 1 you can see a writing of Slemani from the perspective of e.g. arriving airplanes (see Fig. 1). We think with regard to de-colonizing processes and the empowerment of the people concerned, the best solution is to take the version the citizens themselves use and not an English or Arabic or German interpretation. Within our research we found the following versions:

Anglophone texts:

1. Sulaimaniya
2. Sulaimaniyah
3. Sulaymaniyah
4. Sulaymaniyyah
5. Sulaimani

Other versions:

6. Sulaimania (German language, English texts of NGOs, e.g.: Haukari)
7. As- Sulaymaniyyah (Arabic pronunciation, Arabic authors using English language.)

The justification for this decision is not essentialist in the sense that the real, original Kurdish version would be called. For this would indeed be a classic 'identity trap' (Sen 2007) that ignores the historical interactions and is oriented towards singular

Fig. 1 The City of Slemani – View of the Mountains

reduced explanations. The city of Slemani was founded in 1784 by Ibrahim Pashai Baban. He named the city 'Sleman Pasha' after his father, with the aim of establishing a capital of the Kurdish principality of Baban. The name Sleman comes from Arabic, is probably derived from Salam and means peace. The variants of this name alone fill an entire Wikipedia page.[2] The Arabic name Sleman in turn is related to or a derivation of the Hebrew name 'Solomon', from which the word 'shalom' (peace) is also derived. Solomon was the son of David in the Old Testament and, according to biblical reports, he was the builder of the first Jewish temple in Jerusalem and the third king of Israel. These brief notes should suffice to make it clear that '(…) the decolonization of the Spirit requires that we say goodbye to the temptation of exclusive identities.' (ibid., p. 111).

[2] https://de.wikipedia.org/wiki/Suleiman, accessed December 15, 2020.

In Which Political Context Do We Talk About Social Work in Kurdistan-Iraq? Iraq is one of those countries that has a long history of conflict and has been continuously involved in wars and military operations, both nationally and internationally. Most of the political systems that have been active between its formal foundation in 1920 and the overthrow of Saddam Hussein in 2003 came to power in the context of military coups. Accordingly, they have violently ruled the people of Iraq and Kurdistan with an "iron fist". As a result, large parts of the population become IDPs in their own country or refugees outside of the country's borders. When, in 2003, the U.S. troops pulled down a statue of Saddam Hussein in central Baghdad, a profound symbolic image turned the world around and introduced changes and developments with many facets. On the on hand, it was a war that created new wars and conflicts, and at the same there were several challenges like coping with the consequences of war, post-war shaping and preventive conflict management.

Currently, Iraq is facing simultaneous crises: a high number of refugees and political instability. Both aspects are proving to be relevant to social work in different ways and both have implications for the higher education system and therefore for teaching social work.

Refugees The Kurdistan Region of Iraq, which according to its official website has 5.2 million inhabitants, has become a safe haven for refugees. This figure is mainly made up of approximately 250,000 Syrian and 1.5 million internally displaced persons (IDP)[3] from southern and central Iraq, who have taken refuge in the Kurdistan Region of Iraq.[4] These include IDPs from other regions of Iraq who have escaped the IS war, including 300,000 Yazidis, 100,000 Assyrians, Shabak, Sunnis who have fled the Shiite militias and other religious minorities.

The context of flight, armed violence, increasing poverty, and human rights violations not only pushes the infrastructure, communities and authorities to their limits, it also causes significant social challenges and changes. Traditional social networks and protective mechanisms are disrupted. The traditional family structures and existing systems of solidarity have been shaken by the wars in different ways and women and girls become specifically vulnerable to gender-based violence (GBV). GBV is

[3] https://reporting.unhcr.org/iraq, accessed December 15, 2020.

[4] Concerning Iraq as whole, it should be mentioned that more than 3 million Iraqis have been displaced across the country since the start of 2014 and over 260,000 are refugees in other countries. In addition, there are 4.7 million returned refugees living in Iraq. Often, their entire livelihoods are destroyed upon return. They have no housing, no jobs and limited access to basic supplies. It is estimated that over 11 million Iraqis are currently in need of humanitarian assistance. https://www.unhcr.org/iraq-emergency.html, accessed December 15, 2020.

the manifestation of a hierarchical system of gendered domination and exploitation. It has been proven that acts of violence and especially gender-based violence after fleeing from war and conflict have not ended, but represent a continuum of the painful experiences. At the same time, it should be noted that there has always been a strong women's movement for women's rights in Iraq and the Kurdistan region.

Considering the chronic crises and wars in this region, the question is whether social work with these uncertain social and political conditions is even possible? In particular, given the humanitarian disasters that have led to a significant number of refugees in Iraq and from Iraq, a need for professional social work has been created. The current practice of cooperation between international non-governmental organizations and local organizations and actors, is that which provides humanitarian assistance to refugees and IDPs. In this context, the political and practical role of social work is challenged.

Political Instability The people in Kurdistan and Iraq are still facing the threat of violence, social disintegration, the fragility of society, economic tension and political instability, significant social challenges which still affect Iraq to the present day. The major current problems affecting all of Iraq are a lack of state authority, sectarianism and related corruption and clientelism, the close intertwining of political power and military power, and more continuous influence from external states, such as the neighboring countries of Iran and Turkey or from the United States, which in turn affect the ability to govern.

There have certainly been democratic achievements by the Iraqi Kurds over the past two decades. Iraqi Kurdistan exhibited many characteristics of an independent state. The Iraqi constitution of 2005 recognizes the KRI as an autonomous region with far-reaching executive and legislative rights, with its own regional parliament and its own regional government and its own armed forces, the Peshmerga. The Kurdistan Region of Iraq has long been known as the relatively safe and stable part of the country and considered one of the safest regions of Iraq.

But at the time of writing (December 2020), Slemani is beset by violent clashes. Predominantly young people are holding protests against the government. The cause is frustration over delayed payments of public sector salaries, decades of mismanagement and a growing wealth gap. In the town of Slemani, security forces used tear gas, rubber bullets and live ammunition against protesters. Kurdish leaders have portrayed the protests as a conspiracy, imposed a curfew and travel ban, had journalists arrested and harassed, and throttled the Internet.

The Kurdish Region in Iraq is essentially ruled by two major parties, the Democratic Party of Kurdistan (KDP) from Erbil and the Patriotic Union of Kurdistan (PUK) from Slemani. Protesters accusing politicians of corruption, embezzlement and nepotism set fire to the headquarters of various political parties. The political crisis of confidence in the government, the parties and the politicians, which finds expression in the ongoing protests, is clear. Moreover, they highlight the frustration with the extent of economic and political dysfunction that has long characterized both the Kurdistan Region of Iraq and Iraq as a whole.[5]

The core conflicts that have accompanied the KRI and Iraq in recent years are as follows:

(1) The threat of IS, starting with the invasion of Mosul in 2014, which led to fear among the population in existential, psychological, political and economic ways.
(2) The ongoing disputes between the federal government of Iraq and the Kurdistan Region, and Intra-Kurdish power struggles that characterize the political situation in the Kurdistan Region of Iraq.
(3) The Iraqi government's dependence on oil and natural gas revenues. The distribution of oil revenues plays a central role in Iraq's democratic processes and regularly causes discord. Oil was already the central economic factor in the Baath regime. As a so-called rentier state, the regime did not collect taxes and was thus not dependent on its population, for which it functioned more as a distributor. Even today in Iraq, a country with comparatively little private enterprise, the government is the largest employer. Salaries and benefits are estimated to account for about 80 percent of total government spending. In KRI, two-thirds of households are on the public payroll. Regional government budgets are insufficient to cover the consequential costs of falling oil prices since 2014, the Corona pandemic and demographic change.[6] This is because the population is young and looking for work. Without financial security, many are motivated to flee.[7] There is a lack of a functioning, decision-making (regional) government that implements constructive, sustainable political measures, such as a consistent fight against corruption, or the development of alternative sources of income to oil through investments in agriculture, industry, education and youth.

[5] Loveluck, Louisa and Salim Mustafa Salim (2020): Protests flare in Iraq's Kurdish north, adding new front in national crisis.

[6] Demographic survey Kurdistan Region of Iraq. International Organization for Migration (IOM), 2018.

[7] Interview with Kamil Basergan, Journalist, accessed December 10, 2020.

Influences of the Political Instability on Higher Education The political and economic problems mentioned influence students, lecturers and the higher education system. Young people are demotivated because they see no chance of being hired after graduating from college, and if even they found a job, the paychecks remain uncertain. Many earn their living as day laborers or work as support staff despite having a university degree. Lecturers also have to find secure part-time jobs or assignments, e.g., through international NGOs, to bridge the periods without a salary. Motivation for good teaching and research is a challenge under these circumstances. The disappointed hopes do not remain without consequences: many young people, including many highly qualified lecturers, flee and leave the country. This brain drain is a major problem for Iraq and the Kurdish regions in Iraq, and it affects the development of the region.

It is a fact that the region has experienced a rapid expansion of the higher education sector in the last two decades: until 1992 there was only one university, meanwhile there are 14 public universities and 16 private universities. In particular, the government has invested heavily in opening new universities. However, under the aforementioned conditions of political instability, higher education institutions are challenged, especially by 'an increasing number of students seeking places in H.E.; a high rate of graduate unemployment; and low quality of H.E.' (Atrushi and Woodfield 2018, p. 4). According to Issa and Jamil (2010), the main factors responsible for the decline in the quality of H. E. are as follows: the low level of financing, lack of minimum standards in the form of teaching-learning materials (such as textbooks, libraries, laboratories), deteriorating infrastructure, outdated curricula, and overcrowding.[8]

This book, as well as the books mentioned above, which were created in the context of this bi-national university project, can certainly also be read or understood as an attempt to provide further learning materials. Investing in the education of future generations ensures social stability in the long term.

And Why Does It Matter in Germany, for German Social Work?

Social work as a human rights profession is called upon to contribute to overcoming historical Western colonialism and Western hegemony. In our understanding, this includes reflecting on the relationship between colonial power and colonized territories, transgenerational transmission of roles with a view to powerful hierarchical positions. In other words, we assume that a postcolonial perspective in the sense of

[8] Issa, H. & Jamil, H (2010): 'Overview of the Education System in Contemporary Iraq', European Journal of Social Sciences, 14 (3) (2010), pp. 360–368.

a power-critical analysis of past and present (here in the form of global interdependencies and unequal relations between Germany and the Kurdish Region in Iraq) is relevant for both countries. Here, a postcolonial perspective means looking at the long-term effects of colonialism,[9] perceiving and questioning one's own, in our case Eurocentric, perspective, as Midgley suggested in the 1980s on the subject of *professional imperialism* (Midgley 1981). At the same time, it means a critical reflection of historiography with a view to the interconnections of German and Kurdish-Iraqi history. To critically draw attention and perceive in the sense of giving a voice to those who have not yet come up for discussion, and to deal with the phenomenon of subalternity (cf. Spivak 2016) or to make visible knowledge that was previously invisible (Ammann 2021). This is certainly a project for the next decades.

An example for invisible knowledge derives from an encounter and a narration within the project, which took place in a refugee camp and moved us a lot. It is the story of a Yezidi tribal leader, a member of the Council of Elders in a refugee camp in the north of the Kurdish Region of Iraq. We met him during our visit in 2016. He identified us as outsiders from Europe, made contact and invited us to join him in his tent in the refugee camp, creating space and hospitality in this restricted and poverty-stricken place where he had found shelter with his family. He recounted his flight from the IS in 2014, his experiences in the Sinjar Mountains, and the air strikes that followed. An extermination strike on the Yezidi population, violence, death, hunger, panic, the flight with his children, while people worldwide looked on inactively, no one helped:

'Listen to me…, I ask you only one thing: tell my version of the story, tell what happened here in Europe…, be a representative for us, and make our story visible. That's all I ask of you,' we recall his words from our memory. We are sad, silent, affected and moved, by the narrative, the situation, what we experience and feel at that moment. Telling the story from the perspective of those affected, making the suppressed visible, giving a voice to those made invisible, making different perspectives on history visible. These are significant and challenging concerns.

A critical reflection of historiography includes, on the one hand, a critical academic dialogue in the form of reflection and exchange, and on the other hand, considerations about integrating an international perspective into teaching and practice. This demand is increasing in the current discourse and can be found in the central international documents on the profession and science of social work, e.g.

---

[9] The German perspective on colonialism as a former colonial power, especially in the colonies in Southwest and East Africa from 1884–1914/1915 and the genocide of the Herero and Nama (cf. do Mar Castro Varela and Dhawan 2015, p. 31) is fundamentally different from the long history of the oppression experienced by various occupying powers in Iraq and the Kurdish region in Iraq.

- Global Definition of Social Work (IFSW and IASSW 2014 and comments)
- Global Social Work Statement of Ethical Principles (IFSW and IASSW 2018)
- A scientific discourse about postcolonial theory (Frantz Fanon, Eward W. Said, Homi K. Bhabha, Gayati Chakravorty Spivak, cf. Kerner 2012; do Mar Castro Varela and Dhawan 2015).
- The importance of indigenous knowledge: Knowledge, visualization and integration of indigenous knowledge, approaches and methods (Straub 2020)

At a global institutional level, we observe a shift towards the acknowledgement and integration of alternative knowledge systems, such as eco-social-spiritual approaches. The topic of the Global Agenda for Social Work & Social Development Framework for 2020–2030 is 'Co-building Inclusive Social Transformation'. As a first theme, the partners announced 'Ubuntu: Strengthening Social Solidarity and Global Connectedness'. It will run from 2020 to 2022:

'Ubuntu: Strengthening Social Solidarity and Global Connectedness'

> (…) Ubuntu as a principle for enhancing social solidarity and recognizing global connectedness is central to shared and sustainable futures that highlight responsibility between all peoples and the environment. (…) It lays the foundation for the promotion of an inclusive process of developing new social agreements between governments and the populations they serve. The new social agreement to emerge is aimed at facilitating universal rights, opportunities, freedom and sustainable well-being for all people nationally, regionally and globally.
>
> Ubuntu has been popularised across the world by Nelson Mandela and is generally interpreted as meaning 'I am because we are'. A word, concept and philosophy that resonates with the social work and social development perspectives of the interconnectedness of all peoples and their environments. Ubuntu also highlights indigenous knowledge and wisdom and we invite all nations and populations to use an equivalent word or concept that speaks to your culture in promoting this theme: 'Ubuntu: I am because we are'. (IFSW 2020a)

Its significance can be seen as it is also the chosen topic for the World Social Work Day in 2021 (IFSW 2020b). For us, the focus on connectedness is central, as is taking responsibility for this aspect within our international cooperation work. This strengthening of social and human rights at the global level very much changes the perspective of human rights within social work. The view taken of social development has to be wide and integrative, sensitive to different voices from around our globe.

For our cooperation, we tried to realize a respectful and attentive approach to each other as well as a continuous reflection on communication, language and the creation of knowledge. We tried to include different perspectives in the creation of new knowledge, including local actors on the spot such as Haukari e.V. and people working in the social fields,[10] in order to integrate their knowledge and to stimulate a theory-practice transfer and to make access to knowledge visible and available in the form of literature, workshops and lectures. This book is intended to make a contribution to this; a second book, which is being developed in parallel, is an introduction to social work in Kurdish-Sorani for teachers, students and practitioners in the Kurdish Region of Iraq.

The Topics of the Book in Detail

The book at hand is divided into five larger thematic blocks Part I–V.

We have decided to start with a theoretical location (Part I), and then in a second part to give space to the project CoBoSUnin, which is the reason for the publication (Part II). A third part is an introduction to the teaching of social work (Part III), which leads into the thematic content we have dealt with in the project and beyond. These include the aspects: Professional identity, ethics, counselling, aesthetical education, gender, general and practical support (Part IV). Finally, the last part provides theoretical and practical perspectives on internationalization in a university context.

The authors are from the circle of project participants, teachers from the Faculties of Social Work in Slemani and Bochum, trainers who have offered workshops in the project, the external supporters of the DAAD, the internal supporters from the Internal Offices and students who were involved in the project in the years 2016–2019.

Part I: Theoretical Approaches

A first theoretical thematic block introduces the scientific landscape.

It begins with the article *Introduction to International Social Work* by Kristin Sonnenberg, which gives an overview of the scientific debate (definitions, theories, topics and approaches to international social work) as well as an insight into important international organizations in a historical context and current fields. The integrated perspective approach is introduced and postcolonial thinking with its relevance for critical and culture sensitive social work discussed. The author follows the assumption that social work as a truly global profession deals with social problems with global relevance. International social work brings together the dimensions of individual well-being and social justice in the context of challenging global interdependencies. The contribution points out possible fields of work, special skills and concrete working places in NOSs. It concludes with a reflection of the meaning of

[10] Experts by experience.

international social work for social work studies and summarizes challenges, tasks and open questions and makes a connection to the international perspective of the CoBoSUnin project.

In the second article with the title *Postcolonial and Transcultural Perspectives on Communication in International Cooperations*, Cinur Ghaderi critically and reflexively deals with the topics of communication and knowledge production in international cooperation. To this end, she chooses a theoretical and empirical approach by placing examples from the concrete cooperative project CoBoSUnin in the context of theoretical discourse and analysis. This is based on the assumption that intercultural communication does not take place in an ahistorical space. To shed light on this, she first introduces the theoretical constructs of trust and understanding as well as difference and similarity. This is supplemented by reflections on the concept of relational foreignness experience and considerations of global colonial histories. Thus, among other things, she provides an insight into the history of Iraq and the Kurdish region in Iraq in order to analyze how this history can be classified from a postcolonial perspective and investigates whether KRI can be described as a former colony. Based on the three themes of communication, language and understanding and knowledge, she critically and reflexively derives important insights into international cooperation using examples from the project. Particularly noteworthy are the high standards of self-reflection and attentiveness of the participants, the view of postcolonial and global interdependencies of the participating regions or countries, and current power-critical analyses that may influence cooperation, including through transgenerationally conveyed messages.

Within the third contribution, *Assumptions for International Social Work in the Kurdistan Region of Iraq*, Luqman Saleh Karim outlines a brief history of globalization and the emergence of international social work. He explores the opportunities and challenges through which international social work passes. Furthermore, he gives a brief overview of gaps and challenges in working with international organizations in the Kurdistan Region of Iraq (KRI). At the end he summarizes the most important points, why social services can fail to meet the needs of the target groups adequately and gives concrete examples.

Part II: The Scientific Project CoBoSUnin

A compilation of essential assumptions, methods and findings concerning the research project is presented in the second part of this edition.

In the first article, *The History of the CoBoSUnin-Project - From the Beginning to Realization*, Cinur Ghaderi outlines the development of the research project from the beginning. History, preliminary considerations, motivations, course and some challenges are outlined in this article. In retrospect, three project phases can be identified: from Dialogue to Cooperation, from Cooperating to Functioning and from Functioning to Producing. The political instability of Iraq is highlighted as a challenge. Despite the obstacles, a positive summary remained that many goals have been achieved, including publications, symposia, the international conference, cooperative research projects and hopefully a contribution to the international dialogue in social work and the development of social work as a human rights discipline.

The second article, *Evaluation and Results of the Scientific Research Project*, by Kristin Sonnenberg, covers the research methodology, introduces the goals of the project and the planning of measures. Central results of the scientific research are presented on different levels and the findings are made visible for international cooperation. The presentation of the results of a comprehensive analysis of educational opportunities in the form of joint workshops provides insight into joint learning processes. The results are highlighted in their context and their significance for international and intercultural learning processes and important findings are summarized.

A special feature in the research design of the project was a focus group discussion of the project team at the end of 2018, which was conducted according to four core categories: a) Experiences and expectations, b) Personal and technical learning and change processes, c) Institutional change processes, d) Evaluation of the usefulness, opportunities and risks of the bi-national cooperation project. The results after conducting a semantic content analysis are summarized and presented in the contribution *Analysis of the Results of the Bi-National Project from the Point of View of the Lecturers* by Cinur Ghaderi.

The fourth article, *Challenges in International Cooperation – Reflections on the Development and Research Project CoBoSUnin*, by Kristin Sonnenberg and Lisa Marie Dünnebacke, concludes the conference. The authors reflect on their time in the project from the perspective of two women who grew up in Germany and have no experience in the Middle East. The focus is on the question of security and stability based on the main challenges they experienced during the project, such as 'supposed secureness is getting unsafe'. They finish with a presentation of solutions found for these challenges within the project.

Part III: Teaching Social Work

This section of the book addresses the central theme of teaching and provides an insight into the content and organization of the Bachelor's programs in Social Work. From the perspective of the course director, Kristin Sonnenberg presents the BA Social Work course at the Protestant University of Applied Sciences RWL in Bochum in her article *Teaching Social Work in Germany*. Luqman Saleh Karim and Cinur Ghaderi then present the Kurdish counterpart *Teaching Social Work in the Kurdistan Region of Iraq*. Both articles place the development of the study programs in the historical context of their origin (Bochum, Kurdish Region of Iraq: Erbil and Slemani). In addition to the central objective, they provide an insight into the module structure, outline the current situation and address current challenges. Central topics in Germany are, for example, the lack of skilled workers, but also the increasing economization of science and the difficulty of demanding critical, emancipatory and participatory approaches. In KRI, for example, a current challenge is the demarcation of the young academic profession from the other human sciences (sociology and psychology) and, in the longer term, the establishment of a professional association.

Part IV: Topics of Social Work in Teaching and Practice

Part IV.1: Professional Identity

Two articles introduce the question of professional identity. In the first contribution, *Professional Identity in Social Work*, by Kristin Sonnenberg and Fraidoon A. Saeed, the authors try to clarify a basic professional theoretical framing and include perspectives on social work from a scientific and educational level.

In the second contribution, *Professional Identity of Teachers*, by Kwestan Ali Abdullah, the focus lies on the requirements for successful teaching and the corresponding criteria for professional behavior. It offers insights and examples from the BA Social Work lecturers at the University of Sulaimani, concerning the role, attitude and attributes.

Part IV.2: Ethics

With the contribution on *Ethics and Ethical Values in Social Work and their Meaning for International Social Work* by Kristin Sonnenberg, in a first step ethics and values in professional social work are summarized and explained within their theoretical backgrounds. Key documents on an international level are introduced, examples from the Middle East area that are members of IFSW (2019) and Kurdistan-Iraq are presented with regard to social work values and professional status. As a conclusion, the relevance of shared values and reflection for everyday work within international social work is summed up.

In the second contribution entitled *The Ethics of Social Work in Kurdistan – The Curriculum Implementation on the Local Level* by Chro Mohammed Faraj, the author discusses how the roots of social work or helping people in need and life improvement are a unit and an integral part of Kurdish society. She analyses the meaning of ethics and values as part of the academic preparation from university (knowledge, skill, ethic and value, process) as well as part of society's culture, norms, values, religion, policy, law, and human rights, and the policy of the institutions or the organizations. The chapter includes a general overview on social work, the social work departments at universities, the meaning of ethics and its different levels in social work, practicing ethics within social work, and ethical roles and responsibilities according to clients, colleagues, institutions, society, practitioners, and the profession of social work.

Part IV.3: Counseling

'Counseling', especially in teaching academic studies of social work, was one focus within the framework of the international 'CoBoSUnin' project ('Cooperation between Bochum and Sulaimani Universities nowadays'). The *Importance of Integration and Implementation of Psycho-Social Counseling in Social Work* as an intervention method within social work is introduced by Cinur Ghaderi. She outlines the multifactorial conditions framing the requirements of counseling skills in teaching and in practice, including the reflection of theoretical and methodical approaches as well as the consideration of historical and sociocultural circumstances.

Thereafter, the precise conversion and changes of teaching counseling at the University of Sulaimani are described by Niyan Namiq Sabir in her contribution *The Realization and Changes in the Teaching of Counseling at the University of Sulaimani.* The analysis is orientated towards the development of counseling as a professional method in teaching, the choice of theoretical approaches, the changes of the module during the course of the project and the conversion in teaching and practice in that region which is embedded by political instability.

The contribution entitled *Counseling Processes – Experiences as Trainer in a Workshop of the CoBoSUnin Project* about the experiences of Hildegard Mogge-Grotjahn as an expert concerning a workshop in line with the internationally and interculturally aligned dialog of counseling completes this chapter.

Part IV.4: Aesthetical Education

This section begins with the contribution *Fine Arts Meet Social Work, from First Observations to Realization* by Luqman Saleh Karim, in which he attempts to answer the question 'What is art?' In addition, the text aims to reveal the importance of art in social work, in general as well as specifically in the Iraqi Kurdistan region.

The second contribution is called *Where Language Fails, the Image Begins – Aesthetic Education and Social Work: Insights into the Cooperation between Bochum and Slemani* by Helene Skladny. It deals with the significance of aesthetic education as part of the study of social work. Based on insights into the workshop activities of the CoBoSUnin project, possible perspectives, approaches and suggestions for professional practice are presented.

Part IV.5: Gender

Modern societies have a gendered structure, so gender is a cross-cutting theme in social work and is relevant in the teaching, practice and research of this subject – whether in Germany or in Kurdistan. In the CoBoSUnin project, this was one of the topics inherent to the concept of the project and was desired by the participants as a focus for exchange, practice visits and workshops with experts. The participating lecturers of the UoS were gender-moved, for example Niyan Sabir was involved in the founding phase of Gender Studies and Zhiya Abbas is active in gender issues at the university.

In this chapter on 'Gender', Cinur Ghaderi's contribution, *Gender – A Topic for Social Work and in Higher Education in the Kurdistan Region of Iraq*, begins by outlining the fundamental relevance of gender in social work, then relates it to the project and thus to the dimension of higher education policy issues. These are to be categorized taking into account the gender discourses in the respective region; this chapter focuses on the Kurdistan Region Iraq. The initial activities on gender studies at the University of Sulaimani are presented by Niyan N. Sabir, Najat M. Faraj and Jwan B. Bahaddin in their contribution *Gender – Founders' Perspective.* Zhiya Abbas Qader describes the current implementation of the topic Gender in the Department of Social Work at the University of Sulaimani in her contribution *Realization of Teaching Gender as a Subject in Kurdistan.* In a transcultural comparison, the common ground can be found that early women's studies have changed from women's studies to gender studies, and especially in recent times explicit masculinities have been taken into consideration. It is in this sense that Kamil Basergan's contribution on *Gender and masculinity in Kurdistan in Transition – some images of Change* can be read, which expands the gender question by the perspective of a male Kurdish social worker and journalist.

Part IV. 6: Teaching Meets Practice

In her chapter, *'Rahenani Maidani' – the Kurdish Version of Social Work Internships at UoS*, the author Chro Mohammed Faraj describes the internship education of social work students in Kurdistan. She focusses on a definition of internship and the structure it has at the UoS, which includes the participating institutions, the general program, the role of the supervisors and the evaluation of the students.

The German legal ground and structure of practical phases in studies of social work is presented in the contribution *'Praxisbegleitung' – The German System of*

Social Work Internships at EvH by Frank Fechter, Tobias Klug and Kristin Sonnenberg. It mentions the concept to achieve professional and personal competences and the main methods with which to reach these aims. In addition, the aims and the philosophy of practical phases are mentioned.

The contents and experiences of a bilateral workshop between the University of Sulaimani and the Protestant University of Applied Sciences in Bochum are presented in *Exchange of Experiences about the Practical Phases in the Study of Social Work – A Workshop Report* by Frank Fechter and Tobias Klug. This concerns the historical and theoretical background of the Kurdish and German education of socials workers and different concepts of the practical phases.

Part V: Internationalization in Higher Education – Different Perspectives on Opportunities and Boundaries

Perspectives on internationalization can differ depending on position, and they are guided by multiple motivations and interests and playable depending on the instruments available. This polyphony of perspectives is given space in this chapter by being heard in its broad variance: in the first part the perspective of universities as educational institutions in general is outlined in the contribution *Internationalization in Higher Education – The Universities' Definitions, Motivations, Concepts, and Perspectives* by Cinur Ghaderi, which emphasizes the connection between the task of the internationalization of the global university community and the social-political responsibility for society and the global production of knowledge.

The other contributions each share their professional perspective within the binational CoBoSUnin project. In their text entitled *German Academic Exchange Service (DAAD) Perspective. Academic Cooperation with Iraq: Chances and Challenges*, Renate Dietrich and Johannes Sczyrba describe the German-Iraqi Partnership Program, in which the CoBoSUnin project was funded, as an example of 'efforts towards nations in a transformative or crisis state', and they recognize it as positive with the words: 'an example of how a project can be successfully implemented in a challenging environment'.

This is followed by the *Perspectives from the International Offices of the Universities* by Karzan Ghafur Khidir and Karen Bossow of the respective International Offices, who place the CoBoSUnin project in the history of the internationalization of their universities. These approaches from an institutional point of view are followed by descriptions and analyses by the teachers.

In his contribution as a trainer in a workshop in the project, Thomas Eppenstein critically reflects in his contribution *International and intercultural perspectives: Shared perspectives?* on learning processes that cannot be thought of without 'power effects of the production, dissemination, and exchange of knowledge' and advocates a consistent dialogue and participatory orientation.

With their contribution, *'Teaching International Social Work'*, Kristin Sonnenberg and Luqman Saleh Karim introduce the specific BA/MA programs of the participating universities and explicitly focus on the potential of international and intercultural education through teaching.

In the final part, students describe what they have learned and researched from their perspective of the internationalization of the university and the concrete project experience. This is complemented by a selection of posters that give an insight into the collaborative work of the students involved in the project (Jan Wewler, Shatw Farhad Hassan, Julika Rundnagel, Kale Jamal Hama Salih, Niklas Rokahr) and in a seminar in preparation for the conference, where they were presented. They give an insight into the BA topics of the Kurdish students Shnya Shwan Omer, Aurfa Hassan Husen and Briska Mariwan Mustafa.

We hope that, after reading this volume, insights may have been given on the issues of the bi-national project and the transnational dialogue. On the way to 'Strengthening Social Solidarity and Global Connectedness', perhaps new questions have arisen and preliminary tentative answers have been given. We would be pleased if the contributions stimulate you.

References

Ammann, B. (2021). Soziale Arbeit zwischen lokalem und westlichem Wissen. In *Zeitschrift für soziale und sozialverwandte Gebiete, 4*(2021), 144–150. Berlin: Soziale Arbeit.

Atrushi, D., & Woodfield, S. (2018). The quality of higher education in the Kurdistan Region of Iraq. *British Journal of Middle Eastern Studies, 45*, 1–16. 10.1080/13530194.2018.1430537.

Demographic survey Kurdistan Region of Iraq (2018). International organization for migration (IOM), https://reliefweb.int/sites/reliefweb.int/files/resources/KRSO_IOM_UNFPA_Demographic_Survey_Kurdistan_Region_of_Iraq.pdf. Accessed 14 Dec 2020.

do Mar Castro Varela, M., & Dhawan, N. (2015). *Postkoloniale Theorie. Eine kritische Einführung* (2nd fully revised ed.). Bielefeld: Transcript.

IFSW & IASSW (2014). Global Definition of Social Work. https://www.ifsw.org/what-is-social-work/global-definition-of-social-work/. Accessed: 27 Aug 2019.

IFSW & IASSW (2018). Global Standards. https://www.iassw-aiets.org/wp-content/uploads/2018/08/Global-standards-for-the-education-and-training-of-the-social-work-profession.pdf. Accessed: 10 Mar 2020.

IFSW (2020a). 2020 to 2030 Global agenda for social work and social development framework: 'Co-building inclusive social transformation'. https://www.ifsw.org/2020-to-2030-

global-agenda-for-social-work-and-social-development-framework-co-building-inclusive-social-transformation/. Accessed 4 Dec 2020.

IFSW (2020b). The world social work day poster for 2021 is now available. https://www.ifsw.org/the-world-social-work-day-poster-for-2021-is-now-available/. Accessed 4 Dec 2020.

Issa, H., & Jamil, H. (2010). Overview of the education system in contemporary Iraq. *European Journal of Social Sciences, 14*(3), 360–368.

Kerner, I. (2012). *Postkoloniale Theorie zur Einführung*. Hamburg: Junius.

Loveluck, L., & Salim, S. M. (2020, December 12). Protests flare in Iraq's Kurdish north, adding new front in national crisis. https://www.washingtonpost.com/world/middle_east/iraq-kurdistan-protests-north/2020/12/12/72e75066-3be4-11eb-aad9-8959227280c4_story.html. Accessed 14 Dec 2020.

Midgley, J. (1981). *Professional imperialism: Social work in the third world*. London: Wm. Heinemann Educational Books.

Sen, A. (2007). *Die Identitätsfalle. Warum es keinen Krieg der Kulturen gibt*. München: Beck.

Spivak, G. C. (2016). *Can the Subaltern Speak? Postkolonialität und subalterne Artikulation* (Unaltered reprint, 2008). Vienna: Turia + Kant.

Straub, U. (2020, August 5). *Indigene Ansätze in der Sozialen Arbeit* [online]. *socialnet Lexikon*. Bonn: socialnet. https://www.socialnet.de/lexikon/Indigene-Ansaetze-in-der-Sozialen-Arbeit. Accessed 23 Oct 2020.

Cinur Ghaderi, Prof. Dr., Professor of Psychology in the Faculty of Social Work at the Protestant University of Applied Sciences (EvH RWL Bochum). She is Vice-President for Research, Transfer and Internationalization. After her post-graduate education in psychological psychotherapy (behavioral therapy), she worked in the "Psychosocial Centre for refugees" (PSZ) in Düsseldorf. She received her PhD at the faculty of Social Sciences of the Ruhr University Bochum. She is a member of the steering committee of DTPPP (transcultural psychiatry, psychotherapy and psychosomatics). Main academic interests: International Social Work, Refugee Studies, Transcultural Psychotherapy, Psychotrauma, Identity, Diversity and Gender. She is the initiator of the DAAD-cooperation project CoBoSUnin 2016–2019 between the University of Sulaimani and Bochum. Contact: ghaderi@evh-bochum.de

Kristin Sonnenberg, Prof. Dr., Professor of Social Work at the Protestant University of Applied Sciences Bochum. She studied Social Pedagogy in Germany, completed an M.A. in Comparative European Social Studies at the University of North London and her PhD at the University of Cologne in Germany 2004 in the Faculty of Educational Science. She is a qualified psychodrama trainer. Since 2011 she is specialized in the field of methods and conceptualizing social work. Her main research projects are social inclusion of people with disabilities and international social work. She is member of the German Association of Social Workers (DGSA). Since 2016 she has been head of the BA Social Work Studies and, together with Prof. Ghaderi, she was leader of the DAAD cooperation project CoBoSUnin 2016–2019 between the University of Sulaimani and Bochum. Contact: sonnenberg@evh-bochum.de

Part I Theoretical Approaches

Introduction to International Social Work

Kristin Sonnenberg

Abstract

The aim of this article is to give an introduction to international social work. Access was given to German and English language-based literature and other resources. The structure includes an overview of the scientific debate (definition, theories, dimensions, topics) and of the practical level (organizations, associations, social work practice). It concludes with a reflection of the meaning of international social work for social work studies and summarizes challenges, tasks and open questions. It is connected to the experience gained from a four-year international project.

Keywords

International social work • Transnational • Postcolonial • Indigenous social work

1 International Social Work: History and Associations

The question of what international social work includes and means can be answered from different perspectives; in short definitions, more detailed definitions, broad approaches; by core topics, practical fields and scientific debate. This article tries to structure the knowledge that was accessible for the author for a concentrated introduction by taking into consideration current debates and also to lay a

K. Sonnenberg (✉)
Bonn, Germany
E-Mail: sonnenberg@evh-bochum.de

C. Ghaderi et al. (eds.), *Social Work at the Level of International Comparison*,
https://doi.org/10.1007/978-3-658-30394-5_2

basis for answering the question of what international social work is and its meaning for social work studies and the profession and, finally, to indicate challenges as well as open questions.

The topic of international social work invites those involved in it to think and act beyond national borders. Cross-national cooperation is needed to tackle global social-economic and political problems within a global dialogue. International social work brings together the dimensions of individual well-being and social justice in the context of challenging global interdependencies. This seems to be an important argument as to why international social work is important and it gives first indications of what it can be. It deals with all levels from the individual to the institution and from community to the societal level, which is why Healy argues that a definition has to be dynamic, based on action-oriented conceptualization (2008, p. xiv). The three major areas of social work practice are social control and protection – mostly within state-run agencies –, the enhancement of the social functioning or well-being of individuals or families, and community or social development that seeks to promote healthy, cohesive and enabling communities (Cox and Pawar 2013, p. 15).

There are at least four main international publications about international social work that function as handbooks or overviews (Healy 2008; Cox and Pawar 2013; Healy and Link 2012; Lyons et al. 2012). By slightly changing the order and depth of topics, these focus on social problems with global relevance such as worldwide poverty, social development, flight aid, migration, post-conflict reconstruction and unemployment (Healy 2008; Cox and Pawar 2013) or offer a wide range of global social issues (Healy and Link 2012; Lyons et al. 2012). Some of these are typical social work topics at the local level but, due to global interdependencies, they have to be addressed at the international level as well, for example by international associations and organizations. Cox and Pawar point out a strong linkage between international social work and social development practice. In explaining this, they take into consideration different parts of the world and address development workers and members of helping professions in addition to social workers: 'One focus is particularly on the programs and strategies that are being applied to a range of situations involving needy individuals in developing countries, but also to similarly marginalized and deprived situations in developed countries' (2013, p. x).

Taking a historical approach to defining international social work results in a history of international social work stretching back more than 150 years because, from its very beginning, social work can be described within an international perspective. This is to be seen in the establishment of the three main associations of international social work and their tasks and targets. They represent the framework that strengthens the social work profession and they are the ones who coordinate and publish the global statements. In 1856, first steps of exchange started with the first congress in Brussels (Belgium, Europe) focused on social questions. Around the turn of the century – in 1898 and 1901 – the first comparable research into poverty was conducted (Kruse 2009, p. 16 in Straub 2018, p. 22). Healy also refers to the 1893 World's Fair as evidence of international communication and the aim 'to remodel charity work as scientific philanthropy' (2008, p. ix). The year 1928 is also significant and is frequently mentioned and discussed in the literature (for example Straub 2018, p. 23; Friesenhahn and Kniephoff-Knebel 2011, pp. 103) as a starting point for professional and institutionalized exchange, networking and cooperation. A result of the Paris International and World Congress was the foundation of the three central associations of social work and/or their precursor organizations: the International Federation of Social Workers (IFSW), the International Council of Social Welfare (ICSW) and the International Association of Schools of Social Work (IASSW). *IASSW* consists of Universities (of Applied Sciences) with Social Work Studies and Schools of Social Work as national members. Current controversies include value dilemmas, diversity within social work and debates about the Global Agenda for Social Work and Social Development. In 2004, the first ever Global Standards for Social Work Education and Training were published by IASSW and IFSW. These aims and guidelines for universities have recently been revised in 2020. The *IFSW* is the federation where social workers from all over the world fight for social justice, human rights and social development. One aim is to strengthen the profession at an international level. This is done, for example, in the form of critical papers that focus on (socio-) political topics. Another task is to mandate the profession with legal representation. As a non-governmental organization, the *ICSW* is focused on '(…) advocacy, knowledge-building and technical assistance projects in various areas of social development carried out at the country level and internationally (…).' (ICSW). At its core are matters of social development and transnational advocacy. Since the 1980s, a stronger involvement of the (so-called) Global South can be observed with a stronger focus on development movements and an interdisciplinary orientation which means non-professionals can be included within the field of social work (Straub 2018, p. 26).

All three associations have a consultative, advisory status in United Nations bodies, for example the World Health Organization (WHO), the High Commissioner for Refugees as the Refugee Agency (UNHCR) and the United Nations Children's Fund (UNICEF). An important publication is the journal 'International

Social Work',[1] another core document is the 'Ethics in Social Work, Statement of Principles' (2018), recently revised at the World Conference in Dublin. The revision of the 'Global Definition of Social Work' in 2014 shows a change of paradigms as it represents an outcome of the discussion concerning the conflicts within the context of post-colonialism and globalization. Social cohesion, social development and indigenous knowledge have been integrated into the definition. This is described as gaining more diversity at a global level (Straub 2018, p. 27). The latest definition summarizes the main tasks of social work as agreed on an international level:

> 'Social work is a practice-based profession and an academic discipline that promotes social change and development, social cohesion, and the empowerment and liberation of people. Principles of social justice, human rights, collective responsibility and respect for diversities are central to social work. Underpinned by theories of social work, social sciences, humanities and indigenous knowledge, social work engages people and structures to address life challenges and enhance wellbeing.' (IFSW and IASSW 2014)

The definition points to social change and development, social cohesion, and the empowerment and liberation of people to improve their well-being. This has to be done by following the principles of social justice, human rights, collective responsibility and respect for diversities. International social work has the task to identify diverse ways of living and to bring together various forms of knowledge (theories, indigenous approaches, narrative access), methods and practical fields. It is also the task to point to conflicts within current discourses about the reflection and reprocessing of (post-) colonial influences.

2 Definitions, Dimensions and the Integrated Perspective Approach of International Social Work

A short definition can be found in Healy: '(…) *international social work* is defined as international professional action and the capacity for international action by the social work profession and its members.' (2008, p. 10). International action is further explained with four dimensions: internationally related domestic practice and advocacy; professional exchange, international practice and international

[1] In the 1950s, the journal 'International Social Work' was founded to strengthen scientific exchange. It is the official journal of the three main international social work associations IASSW, ICSW and IFSW. Abstracts of articles are translated into French, Spanish, Russian, Chinese and Arabic. https://www.ifsw.org/journal/. Accessed: October 14, 2019.

policy development and advocacy. She suggests a second definition taking this into account: '(…) international social work is values driven action aimed at promoting human rights and human well-being globally.' (ibid., p. 16). A third version of a definition links it to core concepts of international social work: '*International social work* can also be defined as a composite of the major concepts that inform its practice.' (ibid., p. 16) and 'The practice is international social work if it involves bilateral, multilateral, or global relationships, social policies, or problems.' (Healy 2008, p. 369). For Healy, international social work includes four main concepts: globalization, development, human rights, and transnationalism (p. 17).

Cox and Pawar combine their definition with their idea of an integrated perspective approach. They suggest this very long and broad version:

> 'International social work is the promotion of social work education and practice globally and locally, with the purpose of building a truly integrated international profession that reflects social work's capacity to respond appropriately and effectively, in education and practice terms, to the various global challenges that are having a significant impact on the well-being of large sections of the world's population. This global and local promotion of social work education and practice is based on an integrated-perspective approach that synthesizes global, human rights, ecological, and social development perspectives of international situations and responses to them.' (Cox and Pawar 2013, pp. 29–30)

The key emphasis of this definition is that social work should engage in response to the significant global challenges that are consistent with the essential nature of social work and in responses that are effective within the context of these global challenges (2013, p. 30).

In a next step, *dimensions and topics* of international social work shall be looked at. To clarify the meaning and range of international social work, Straub,[2] with reference to Healy[3] (2001) and Cox and Pawar (2006), structures it into the following five dimensions in one of her recent publications (Straub 2018, p. 23):

a) internationally related domestic practice and advocacy: due to globalization, local practice and global perspectives should be connected

---

[2] Ute Straub has been a member of the extended board of the IASSW since 2016; she is head of the professional group International Social Work of the German Association of Social Work and professor for International and Transnational Social Work in Frankfurt, Germany.

[3] Lynne M. Healy is a key UN representative for IASSW from the University of Connecticut, USA.

b) professional exchange: global interdependencies need good structures of exchange
c) international practice: spread and compare aims and methods
d) international policy development and advocacy: political intervention to realize social justice
e) promoting social work around the world as an integrated international profession

The last point seems to have been added by Straub. These five dimensions show very well the areas where international social work is involved. All five dimensions are relevant for future social work. Healy, who introduced the dimensions, herself originally mentions four dimensions (2008, pp. 10).

Within the scientific debate, an *integrated-perspectives approach* is being discussed and recommended (Cox and Pawar 2013; Straub 2018). It covers current fields and debates in which international social work should be involved. These include the diversity of the profession, the integration of human rights (e.g. values and principles), globalization (e.g. interdependence, global citizenship), ecology (e.g. sustainability) and social development (e.g. proactive intervention, multilevel). The model is described as multi-perspective and can be applied to international social work practice (Friesenhahn and Kniephoff-Knebel 2011, pp. 98). The integrated-perspectives approach derives from Cox and Pawar. They describe it as an analytical tool or model for social work practice to clarify which levels are relevant and have to be analyzed (2013, p. 53). This model should be applied for analysis, planning of interventions and implementation. It encourages thinking globally and should be applied in addition to responding immediately to need in order to overcome an exclusively remedial focus.

3 Theoretical Approaches and Discussions

The early development of social work in the Global North, that was embedded in processes such as industrialization, leads to the problematization of influence during (post-) colonial times and is connected to oppression of groups of people and indigenous knowledge, '(…) the export of welfare systems held back the emergence of an indigenous profession in the former colonies.' (Cox and Pawar 2013, p. 7). Social work was spread through colonization. This is heavily criticized, because a 'Western stamp' (ibid., p. 9) was imposed. Cox and Pawar argue that it is a matter of judgment whether this is on the whole negative or positive. It might be an inappropriate form of social work education and practice, but it laid the foundation for modern, in the sense of state-run, social work, that others among the least developed countries do not have at all. They highlight one argument from the Asian scene that totally doubts whether a liberal Judeo-Christian capitalist foundation has any relevance to Asia. For the African context, there is still a gap between Western theory of social sciences and social work practice in Africa. It is a question of re-defining social work by analyzing what resources and skills are available, what processes can be borrowed from others and to identify knowledge, a philosophy and value base of the profession (Osei-Hwedie 1993, p. 27 in Cox and Pawar 2013, pp. 12). This idea is summarized as follows: 'Indeed in most regions, the need for culturally sensitive social work education and practice is increasingly recognized by those who are involved at grassroot level.' (Cox and Pawar 2013, p. 12). Cox and Pawar suggest ten very concrete steps for developing indigenous social work education (2013, p. 14 with reference to Pawar 1999).

Representatives of postcolonial theories and social movements in countries of the Global South address critically the implications of colonialization and the unreflective copying of social work concepts from the Global North with a demand for critical analysis of unjust power relations. One aim is to find or re-discover hidden indigenous resources in former colonized countries. Such movements can be observed in Africa, Asia and Latin-America (Wagner and Lutz 2018, p. 18). For international social work at the local and global level, it would mean not only searching for a joint identity, but at the same time reflecting on colonial influences and restraints to overcome hegemonial attitudes. Three strategies are identified: heterogenization, decentralization and indigenization: 'Following critical African theorists, the last of these means the process of reformulation of imported ideas and practice to match them with the local and cultural context of specific (colonial) experiences.' (Wagner and Lutz 2018, p. 18[4]). This way, new concepts can emerge that relate local and global social work. Within the social work literature, a new word is making the rounds: 'glocal', interlinking the global and the local perspectives. Another expression Wagner and Lutz (2018) use is 'international entanglement or interwovenness'.[5] Interwovenness is explained as follows: 'The social work transferred from colonial interdependence and power structures as a northern import has developed in an independent way in the South, each with its own and other social work structures,

[4] Translation by the author, KS.

[5] Original German version: 'Die aus kolonialen Verflechtungs- und Machtstrukturen als Nordimport transferierte Soziale Arbeit hat sich in eigenständiger Weise im Süden entfaltet, dabei wurden je eigene bzw. auch indigene Traditionen neu belebt.'

also revived indigenous traditions.' (ibid., p. 10). Thus, each of them creates its own designs in different places and contexts, which can be reflected on a global level. This means that human beings and problems cross national borders and these transgressions of boundaries should be identified and analyzed.

The processes of de-colonialization may back away from a so-called Eurocentric view and interpretation of social work concepts. A variety of social work theories and approaches seem to be useful with the above described critical approaches: liberation, empowerment, capabilities, reflexivity and justice (ibid.).

Other (German) authors thinking about the global interlacing of knowledge and the reciprocal influence name their approach 'Transnational Studies'. They agree with the assumption that globally caused problems and conflicts such as flight and war cannot be solved within national borders. Concluding that social work connects over borders, they call the discipline a 'world science'. They ask for an analytical and comparative approach to search for similarities and causes between national states and regions and discuss differences in theory and practice (Wagner and Lutz 2018, p. 11 with reference to Graßhoff et al. 2016).

4 Topics

After analyzing the current debate about international social work, there seems to be unity about themes. The core topics identified for international social work are social development (e.g. poverty), human rights and globalization (Healy 2008 p. 25; p. 52) in harmony with social work ethics (p. 76). More specifically global social issues with relevance for social work mentioned by Healy are: poverty, status of women (health, reproduction issues, gender violence and human trafficking), children in difficult circumstances (mortality, labor, street children, soldiers, orphans), aging, natural and man-made disasters. These are analyzed in Healy's work (2008, pp. 80). Furthermore, she mentions conflicts, post-conflict reconstruction and recovery, substance abuse, child abuse and challenges of people with disabilities (p. 102). Cox and Pawar have a structure of four main fields that include social development, poverty, conflicts and post-conflict reconstruction and migration (2013, pp. 145). They identify a few needy groups that they sum up as *specific population*, these are: street children, child laborers, orphans and the HIV/AIDS crisis, child soldiers and, in developing countries, the groups of youth, elderly and persons with disability (ibid., pp. 473).

Another huge influence on the rise of social conflicts is the process of globalization (Wagner and Lutz 2018, p. 10). These can be fights, conflicts and war over resources such as oil in the Middle East Region. War and postcolonial conflicts are important topics that should be further discovered for social work (Seifert 2004, 2018). In 2019, the final conference of the CoBoSUnin project organized an international conference on the topic of '*Social Work in Post-War and Political Conflict Areas*' that brought together scientists and researchers from various countries all over the world, local and international NGOs, teachers, students and practitioners from Iraqi-Kurdistan and representatives from the local government.[6]

5 International Social Work – Practical Level, Jobs

Alongside other development and human services professionals, social workers play important roles within international organizations. Cox and Pawar structure these into five categories: The United Nations (UN) with regional bodies and global programs such as UNICEF and UNHCR; governments with their departments for international development; nongovernmental organizations mostly concerned with development and humanitarian work (OXFAM, Amnesty International); multinational corporations (Shell, British Gas Group) and global civil society organizations (2013, pp. 517). The roles social workers can have are: within research and development, special skills, managerial and administrative, coordination and liaison. Internships are seen as stepping stones to other positions, the entry level is mostly field program staff (p. 534). Requirements are international experience, multi-language skills and, as a core aspect, a knowledge of the local language. Cox and Pawar argue that it is necessary to prepare social workers for international social work, because they observe of 'a rapidly growing interest globally in social workers engaging in the international field' (2013, p. xiii). They suggest an elaborated concept of how to prepare for an international career. This is, for instance, the development of cross-cultural communication skills and socio-cultural sensitivity. The attitude of flexibility seems important: 'Learning occurs all the time. Cultivating flexibility and adaptability attributes will also facilitate better learning.' (p. 539), which is something we can share from our experience in the project.

Looking at the practical level, some of these ideas already seem to be reality. By using a global digitalized access to search for jobs via the internet, a list of the '10 Best International Social Work Job Opportunities' appears, published by one of the US social work degree centers. It starts with the following description:

[6] The project and the conference are documented in film by Ernst Meyer, SMIDAK Filmproduktion, Berlin: https://www.youtube.com/watch?v=wEkW9v51fps.

> 'International social work is a vast profession with growing demand to address injustices faced across the globe, especially third-world countries. (…) Poverty, disease, war, natural disaster, trafficking, and forced labor are just a few of the problems international social workers strive to eradicate. They work mostly for non-government organizations (NGOs) to coordinate human service projects across borders. It's their mission to alleviate suffering for the world's most vulnerable and oppressed civilians. (…)'[7]

The guiding principle introduced here is to fight injustice across the globe. It is the center of this description and matches with the aspect of social justice within the Global Definition of Social Work. Furthermore, it points out specific problems, such as poverty and war that have been identified as core topics within the literature. A qualification of a BA in Social Work or Human Sciences, sometimes a Master's degree, is required for working as an international social worker. Special qualifications that are demanded are: respect for diversity and language fluency, bilingual ability in local languages and 2–5 years' experience in human services.

To give an example, organizations where international social workers can find jobs will be introduced briefly here.

- The United Nations (UN), established in 1945, 'is one of the foremost social work organizations striving to maintain international peace and human rights across 193 member countries. In 2001, the United Nations received the Nobel Peace Prize for their public service. The UN's global workforce consists of over 41,000 altruistic staff at field offices from Baghdad and Nairobi to Port-au-Prince. Worldwide job opportunities are listed for social workers on political, humanitarian, emergency relief, or peacekeeping missions.'[8] The focus here lies on peace and human rights and emergency relief. Staff is described as 'altruistic'.
- Another NGO with a long history that is focused on the issues around war and crisis is the International Rescue Committee (IRC): 'In over 40 nations, the International Rescue Committee provides lifesaving assistance to refugees forced to flee from war, natural disaster, or other humanitarian crises. Since 1933, IRC's passionate post-conflict network has grown to 8000 + staff. Currently, there are 320 job openings, such as protection coordinator, refugee youth advocate, resettlement manager, and emergency health officer.'[9]

---

[7] https://www.socialworkdegreecenter.com/best-international-social-work-job-opportunities/ accessed September 5, 2019.

[8] Ibid. For further information see: https://www.un.org/en/, accessed January 24, 2020.

[9] Ibid. For further information see: https://www.rescue.org/, accessed January 24, 2020.

- A third NGO that is also based in Slemani in Kurdistan-Iraq is Save the Children, which is '(...) working in 120 nations to protect the welfare of over 55 million youth annually. Recent missions have included delivering hygiene kits to Ebola-stricken Liberia and repairing classrooms destroyed in the typhoon Haiyan. (...) Social workers could work full-time as child protection managers, migration advisers, nutrition advocates, and more.'[10] Save the Children has a 100-year history. It was set up in 1919 after World War I: 'After seeing how children in Austria and Germany were starving in the aftermath of the First World War, our founder, Eglantyne Jebb, launched the Save the Children Fund to raise money to help them.'[11] Save the Children conducts important research as well. Recent reports include the Global Childhood Report 2019 and the Report 'Stop the War on Children'.

This shows that, besides practical work, NGOs realize the fourth dimension of international social work by political interventions based on scientific research to realize social justice. They strive for all others dimensions as well, if methods are exchanged, structures can be built and the professional status can be promoted. Within the project CoBoSUnin, it was possible to conduct interviews with members of Save the Children Kurdistan. Information about child protection methods in Kurdistan could be accessed by those means by a German BA Social Work student and were explored and analyzed at different levels: local, bi-national, international.

A fourth example of an NGO that operates at the international level is the German-based Association for International Cooperation HAUKARI e.V.[12] Since the mid-1990s, HAUKARI has been supporting projects in Iraq, especially within the Kurdistan Region, in the realm of assistance given to women survivors of violence and women and youth empowerment. One of the partners is the social and cultural center for women KHANZAD, based in Slemani, in the Kurdistan Region of Iraq. Established in 1996 by a group of Kurdish women in cooperation with HAUKARI e.V., it was the first center with access only for women, independent of any political party. It aims at giving some space for social exchange for women that is accepted by society.[13] They work on broader projects that

[10] Ibid. For further information see: https://www.savethechildren.net/.

[11] https://www.savethechildren.net/about-us/100-years-children

[12] https://www.haukari.de/Home.html, accessed September 11, 2019. The website is in German. The English information was kindly given by Karin Mlodoch, board member and project coordinator of HAUKARI in July 2019 and summarized by the author for this article. HAUKARI was a partner for organizing the international conference in 2019.

[13] https://www.haukari.de/Khanzad_Frauenzentrum.html, accessed September 16, 2019.

aim to strengthen local sustainability, with counseling structures for women survivors of gender-based, social and political violence. They work with governmental (Kurdistan Regional Government) and civil society partners and in IDP[14] camps and host communities. HAUKARI offers training to governmental and civil society counselors (social, psychosocial and legal counselors). The training aims to encourage local counselors to systematize and further elaborate locally developed and contextualized practices of (psycho-) social work rather than teaching concepts developed in other contexts. Indeed, not only trained social workers and psychologists, but also men and women activists for women and human rights have developed sophisticated and creative methods and tools of (psychosocial) counseling and family and community mediation in the context of gender-based violence in Kurdistan-Iraq in the last 25 years.

This last organization is a very good example for the theoretical approach for integrating local resources and knowledge, with a sustainable strategy to empower local staff and at the same time facilitate global scientific professional standards and discuss these with the local staff. Two students who finished their education as pioneers of the first BA Social Worker Studies at the University of Sulaimani in 2018 started working after their studies at KHANZAD.

6 Reflections and Conclusions

This final paragraph aims at summarizing the main points, structured in consequences for social work education, future development of the profession and open question.

Social Work Education: The topics and theories presented above should be integrated in social work studies, at the bachelor level as an introduction to develop the ability to see the interdependencies of local and global topics and, at master's level, there should be specialized programs on international social work. At the BA level at the EvH, there are, for example, already good links within modules that deal with the history and theories of social work. They include concepts and theories of critical social work, empowerment, capability approaches. During the studies of social work, there is a stable base that covers topics of social policy and law, social development and global change, social justice and human rights.

[14] "Internally displaced people (IDPs) have not crossed a border to find safety. Unlike refugees, they are on the run at home." https://www.unhcr.org/internally-displaced-people.html, accessed September 11, 2019.

Reflexivity and critical awareness are core abilities for social workers to gain and train. Cox and Pawar suggest changing the curriculum (at least this should be considered) and integrating cross-cultural understanding, comparative social policy with regard to global social problems (as written down in the Millennium Goals).

Within the *Global standards for education and training of the social work profession*, international standards are laid down that include a description of standards with regard to core curricula. Within paragraph 4.1.1: 'Domain of the Social Work Profession', schools should aspire toward: 'A critical understanding of how social-structural inadequacies, discrimination, oppression, and social, political and economic injustices impact human functioning and development at all levels, including the global.' (IFSW and IASSW 2018, p. 3). The document is strongly linked to the international social work code of ethics and the global definition. As one of the domains of the social work professional, the following statement is laid down: 'The development of the social worker who is able to conceptualize social work wisdom derived from different cultures, traditions and customs in various ethnic groups, insofar that culture, tradition, custom and ethnicity are not used to violate human rights.' (ibid., p. 4). To support this wisdom and to realize an awareness about injustice (especially Western) universities and schools of social work should add and integrate knowledge about central associations and NGOs as well as non-Western studies or theories to break a hegemonial postcolonial thinking and to raise awareness about unjust power relations and interlinked influences. This can be done by adding as much knowledge as possible from directly involved persons in need.

At the academic and scientific level, Universities of Applied Sciences and Schools of Social Work can act on different international dimensions: They can develop strategies for internationalization and build networks with partners from other countries.[15] Researchers and scientists can design international research projects and build up sustainable cooperation and networking to meet the dimensions of international social work.[16]

Professional Status and Role of Social Work: Supporting global changes for social justice around the world and interfering with a political mandate is seen as valuable. It is still necessary to spread knowledge of social work topics, to strengthen

---

[15] *The Directorate of International Academic Relations at the University of Sulaimani (UoS)* by Karzan Ghafur Khidhir & *Internationalization at the EvH RWL and the Contribution of CoBoSUnin. An International Office Perspective* by Karen Bossow in this volume.

[16] See for example the research design within the chapter *Evaluation and Results of the Scientific Research Project* by Kristin Sonnenberg in this volume.

the profession and to show the added contribution social work makes to civil society and social justice (Straub 2018, p. 31).

Demands and visions for social work for the new decade and in the twenty-first century are that it should become a truly global profession, reflecting a truly global response to international needs (Cox and Pawar 2013, p. 547).

Theoretical Discourse: Open questions with regard to processes of professionalization in the South and East by re-conceptualization of existing Western and Northern concepts (as well as the necessity to add non-Western knowledge within the latter as described above):

- *Global standards of education and possible interpretations*: Maybe different levels of education (should) exist, depending on national service conditions, salaries and validations of the profession (IFSW and IASSW 2018, p. 10). Some argue that local social work should be established and react to local needs and requirements, especially if a 3–4-year academic education and training is not available or too cost-intensive (Straub 2018, p. 31). What about educational models, with different levels: social assistants, social workers and senior social workers? Where is the border to de-professionalization? Cox and Pawar suggest a model with a tertiary level of preparation and deployment with different degrees of professionalism: social work senior professionals acting as supervisors and within social administration, social work professionals with a university degree and paraprofessionals as social assistants with a short period of training and supervision offered for the kind of frontline workers. This differentiation offers a comprehensive and integrated strategy of response to needs, '(…) the numerical balance between the three levels of recruitment and education will reflect the socioeconomic and development realities and need profiles prevailing in any country or region.' (2013, p. 23)
- *Theories and methods*: To what extent is it possible to work with theoretical approaches that have been developed in individualized societies and to develop these further? Are methods from the North suitable for communities in the South, with more traditional and family-oriented support systems? How can indigenous concepts (local and traditional approaches) be considered and added in the variety of social work (Straub 2018, p. 30)?

This first question seems to aim at an analysis of formation conditions of social problems within a society using approved methods and theories of explanation that have been developed in similar circumstances such as post-war experience or post-conflict societies. The dimension of international social work of exchanging professional knowledge and comparing specific methods can lead to a reflective development with regard to local solutions and global standards that are needed for professional high-quality answers and strengthening the status of the social work profession. The second question seems more rhetorical or provoking and leads to a critical awareness not to import models without modification or adaptation to local contexts. Local solutions or re-conceptualizations with regard to local knowledge might be more successful for different reasons already discussed. The third question seems to be of high relevance with regard to integrating indigenous knowledge and an empowerment of local welfare structures and resources. Additionally, it postulates including the critical voices and voices of representatives of the Global South in international scientific discourses. For the Global North and West, it means an ongoing critical reflection and analysis of the postcolonial heritage (Straub 2018, p. 31). As Healy states: 'Through dialogue and exchange, international social work may well reduce Western dominance that has long been expressed in social theory and practice models, as suggested by Noble (2004).' (Healy 2008, p. 369).

Similar to national neoliberal developments threatening the welfare states in the Global North since the 1990s, Straub advises against 'a tendency of neoliberal development that threatens social work in its function of being an advocate for social justice in many countries of the world' (Straub 2018, pp. 31) and asks for a political mandate as well as political independence for social work as a profession. This includes not being part of and participating in political strategies that are exclusive and discriminating.

Future Social Work: In 2008, Healy already wrote: 'The profession's attention can now turn to efforts to strengthen its role in international action as a force for humane social change and development.' (Healy 2008, p. 357). Concepts for social work dialogue and theory development are needed in the areas of development and human rights. These are still not fully realized, new threats to civil liberties have emerged as a result of war and terrorism: the widening rich-poor gap, poverty, unemployment, personal violence.

The linkage between human rights and social work is laid down in the Ethical Principles of the IFSW (2018).[17] Dilemmas that arise at practical level are in balancing cultural rights with universal human rights. War and terrorism lead to concepts of multi-culturalism and cultural competence, for example preventive diplomacy, discouraging hostilities, reconciliation and reconstruction (Healy

[17] See also chapter: *Ethics and Ethical Values in Social Work and their Meaning for International Social Work* by Kristin Sonnenberg in this volume.

2008, p. 363). Inter-ethnic dialogues are needed in migration processes and their impacts.

Cultural diversity and approaches to it will play an important role within international social work, which also means social work in national context concerned with international topics, for example flight and migration. Cultural pluralism and multiculturalism are two recently discussed approaches that need to be acknowledged. Other current topics Healy mentions are social exclusion and inclusion (inadequate social participation), security (cutbacks of welfare states, terrorism), sustainability (environmental limits and resource scarcity).

A core aspect that should be integrated in future (international) social work is cultural diversity:

> 'While universalism may contest indigenization or multiculturalism, internationalism does not necessarily do so. In fact, successful international social work must embrace multiculturalism, while it struggles with tensions between localism and standards of human rights and well-being' (Healy 2008, p. 369)

In social work, especially in international social work, a multi-perspective or integrated perspective approach offers the ground for complex problem analysis and intervention. The local contexts and influences of colonial history to the specific countries or regions and their influence in establishing or developing social work has to be thought of.

The theory and practice of social work have to cross borders. This includes thinking without limits and crossing national as well as cultural borders. It is necessary to bring an openness of mind for new solutions and learning processes based on partnerships. The construction of reciprocal learning within our CoBoSUnin cooperation project aimed at deconstructing power relations, or at least at making them transparent. It was an attempt to work together on one level without hierarchies by accepting each other's different expertise.

Social work has to find a position between being a world science and a specific interweaved social work based on indigenization. Maybe there are theories and methods that have universal significance, independent of time and space. Thanks to comparative research, critical reflection and interaction, these can be approved in different contexts, modified or rejected and newly discovered.

References

Cox, D., & Pawar, M. (2013). *International social work. Issues, strategies, and programs* (2nd ed.). Los Angeles: SAGE.

Friesenhahn, G. J., & Kniephoff-Knebel, A. (2011). *Europäische Dimensionen Sozialer Arbeit*. Schwalbach am Taunus: Wochenschau.

Graßhoff, G., Homfeldt, H.-G., & Schröer, W. (2016). *Internationale Soziale Arbeit. Grenzüberschreitende Verflechtungen, globale Herausforderungen und transnationale Perspektiven*. Weinheim: Belz Juventa.

Healy, L.M. (2008). International social work. Professional action in an interdependent world (2nd edn). Oxford University Press.

Healy, L.M., & Link, R.J. (Eds.). (2012). Handbook of international social work. Human rights, development, and the global profession. Oxford University Press.

IASSW (2018). Global social work statement of ethical principles. Long version, April 27, 2018. https://www.ifsw.org/wp-content/uploads/2018/07/Global-Social-Work-Statement-of-Ethical-Principles-IASSW-27-April-2018-1.pdf. Accessed 27 Aug 2019.

ICSW (n.d.). About ICSW. https://www.icsw.org/index.php/about-icsw. Accessed 14 Oct 2019.

IFSW & IASSW (2018). Global Standards for the Education and Training of the Social Work Profession. https://www.iassw-aiets.org/wp-content/uploads/2018/08/Global-standards-for-the-education-and-training-of-the-social-work-profession.pdf. Accessed 10 Mar 2020.

IFSW & IASSW (2014). Global Definition of Social Work. https://www.ifsw.org/what-is-social-work/global-definition-of-social-work/. Accessed 27 Aug 2019.

Kruse, E. (2009). Zur Geschichte der internationalen Dimension in der Sozialen Arbeit. In L. Wagner & R. Lutz (Eds.), *Internationale Perspektiven Sozialer Arbeit. Dimensionen. Themen. Organisationen* (pp. 15–32). Wiesbaden: VS Verlag.

Lyons, K., Hokenstadt, T., Pawar, M., Huegler, N., & Hall, N. (Eds.). (2012). *The SAGE handbook of international social work*. London: SAGE.

Seifert, R. (2018). Armed conflict and social work. In L. Wagner, R. Lutz, C. Rehklau, & F. Ross (Eds.), *Handbuch Internationale Soziale Arbeit. Dimensionen – Konflikte – Positionen* (pp. 181–193). Weinheim: Beltz Juventa.

Seifert, R. (2004). Kriegerische Konflikte und Soziale Arbeit. Eine Skizzierung der Problemlage. In R. Seifert (Ed.), *Soziale Arbeit und kriegerische Konflikte* (pp. 20–49). Münster: LIT.

Straub, U. (2018). Definitionen Internationaler Sozialer Arbeit. In L. Wagner, R. Lutz, C. Rehklau, & F. Ross (Eds.), *Handbuch Internationale Soziale Arbeit. Dimensionen – Konflikte – Positionen* (pp. 22–34). Weinheim: Beltz Juventa.

Wagner, L., & Lutz, R. (2018). Internationale Soziale Arbeit zwischen Kolonialisierung und Befreiung. Eine Einleitung. In L. Wagner, R. Lutz, C. Rehklau, & F. Ross (Eds.), *Handbuch Internationale Soziale Arbeit. Dimensionen – Konflikte – Positionen* (pp. 7–20). Weinheim: Beltz Juventa.

Kristin Sonnenberg, Prof. Dr., Professor of Social Work at the Protestant University of Applied Sciences Bochum. She studied Social Pedagogy in Germany, completed an M.A. in Comparative European Social Studies at the University of North London and her PhD at the University of Cologne in Germany 2004 in the Faculty of Educational Science. She is a qualified psychodrama trainer. Since 2011 she is specialized in the field of methods and conceptualizing social work. Her main research projects are social inclusion of people with disabilities and international social work. She is member of the German Association of Social Workers (DGSA). Since 2016 she has been head of the BA Social Work Studies and, together with Prof. Ghaderi, she was leader of the DAAD cooperation project CoBoSUnin 2016–2019 between the University of Sulaimani and Bochum. Contact: sonnenberg@evh-bochum.de.

Postcolonial and Transcultural Perspectives on Communication in International Cooperations

Cinur Ghaderi

Abstract

This chapter examines communication and knowledge production in international collaborations at universities – such as the Kurdish-German CoBoSUnin project – by placing them in a broader political and historical context of relations. The basic assumption is that intercultural communication does not take place in an ahistorical space. This communication and exchange is framed by the current conditions of transnational cooperation and is based on historical interlinkages between Germany and Kurdistan, or rather Kurdistan-Iraq. Among other things, the following are informative: Concepts of trust and understanding, difference and similarity in intercultural communication. Concrete experiences of the German-Kurdish CoBoSUnin project will be used for the communicative negotiations (on trust, partnership, hierarchy, cultural practices, language policy, etc.) by way of illustration. Knowledge of transnational historiography, of one's own history and history of relationships within the colonial fabric is considered as a factor that can influence partnership communication and cooperation.

Keywords

Intercultural communication • International cooperation • Trust • Postcolonial • Kurdistan • Germany • Social work • Higher Education

C. Ghaderi (✉)
Düsseldorf, Germany
E-Mail: ghaderi@evh-bochum.de

C. Ghaderi et al. (eds.), *Social Work at the Level of International Comparison*,
https://doi.org/10.1007/978-3-658-30394-5_3

1 Introduction

Ignorance:

Who is Saddam?

Where's the desert?

Oh, they don't like to be called Aryans?

Normative knowledge:

Did you hear that? He thinks homosexuality is a deviation?

Did you hear that? She seems crazy, what does she want here alone in Kurdistan?

Racified knowledge:

He has developed well! (German student on Kurdish lecturer)

They are not to be joked with, they are clever and differentiated, sometimes complicated.

International and bi-national projects create a space for exchange at different levels. According to Kruse (2018), the following forms of exchange can be differentiated: reception of literature, cooperation at conferences, cross-border research projects, exchange of persons in university collaborations (e.g. guest semesters and professorships) and research on the exchange itself with a reflexive intention. This exchange will be partly influenced by hierarchical patterns of communication that have grown out of postcolonial contexts.

In the 'CoBoSUnin' project too, some of these exchange dimensions were part of the work. Particularly in the accompanying evaluation research, effects were recorded and evaluated.[1] In principle, exchange experiences can be directly or indirectly profitable in different ways: for the individuals in their biography as self-referential, intercultural and specialist competencies and for the further development of the discipline in the teaching and/or practice of social work in the respective countries (cf. Kruse 2018, p. 93).

What this yields or produces has an effective impact on the content of teaching, on the structures and on the travelers and hosts taking part, whereby the word

[1] The multi-layered personal and technical processes of change in this project from the perspective of the participating teachers and students can be found described in many ways in this book. The view of the teachers comes into play in the topics, but is above all the core of the evaluation chapter, also in the analysis of the results of the project from the point of view of the lecturers and the reflections on the project. The view of the students can be found in the chapter on internationalization in this publication.

'yield' is to be used with caution. Change and perhaps learning processes may be more appropriate. The encounters and experiences lead to new knowledge. They take place in a hierarchical space with specific culture, history, etc. and as an encounter between 'representatives' of the Global North and the Global South, or of the West and the East. They are intercultural encounters and it is an exchange on transnational knowledge. The latter is the subject of this article.

First of all, questions about space, time and context are to be asked, i.e. an analysis of the framing (nation state, financing, interculturality, internationality), which have effects in the encounters and the communication. The analysis of the framing leads to the questions: To what extent does the analysis of the (standard and/or automatic) associated images of the other in the transnational encounter expose colonial history?

How can these intercultural and transnational experiences be evaluated from the postcolonial perspective (Wagner and Lutz 2018) that is generally sought in international social work?

This goes hand in hand with further questions: To what extent is the high standard of a dialogical, partnership communication with the aim of a decolonial knowledge production in the context of an East-West exchange possible? In which direction does the knowledge flow (directionality)? Is social work an 'import good' for Kurdistan, as knowledge from the Global North is accepted because of the many international NGOs on the ground? Is there an indigenization process in the sense of a re-/new-formulation of imported concepts? Is the term indigenous knowledge or decolonial knowledge accurate or appropriate, if applied to Kurdistan? How should the concept of decolonization of knowledge for Kurdistan be discussed in the context of historical circumstances?

What conclusions can be drawn from these ideas for the teaching, practice and research of social work in Kurdistan Region of Iraq and Germany?

2 Analysis of the Framing and Direction of the Communicative Exchange Relationship

2.1 National Financing: Openness and Boundaries

Every bilateral or international university cooperation has a financial and national side. It is made possible by monetary contributions (capital) and social relations, which are governed by legal and political structures of states, i.e. there are no depoliticized encounters between individuals, but they are at the same time a mirror and expression of the relations between national economies. In this project, the funds came from the German Federal Foreign Office and the prerequisites for the application were to be submitted via a DAAD project application and approved by an expert panel. The official objective was the establishment and expansion, as well as the development and modernization of the Iraqi higher education landscape, i.e. it primarily addresses changes in Iraq and is thus intrinsically hierarchical. Only employees of the participating German university were allowed to be employed within the project framework. The financing was made possible by the German side, which also opened up the space for exchange. This affects the structure and objectives and decides who can participate and under what conditions (relevance of nationality and statehood, visa issuance, language skills). The project enabled the mobility of all participants and status groups, creating an extended sphere of action. At the same time, the Iraqis are required to apply for a visa, for which they, as scientists, need an invitation from the official German authorities. This means that citizenship, legal requirements and financial resources[2] also regulate mobility. Visa requirements for German travelers varied during the project phase due to political situations. As the conflicts between the central government and the Kurdish regional government intensified, the fragility of Iraq as a state structure increased, with the consequence that it was uncertain for German travelers whether they now required an Iraqi visa for entry or whether it could be interpreted as an affront by the Kurdish side if, for good measure, passports were adorned with an Iraqi visa as well.

In this section we will take a look at the directions of resource exchange in bi-national cooperation: capital flows, mobility conditions and expected changes[3] in universities. This is sometimes relevant when we talk about partnership-based dialogue[4] and communication as well as knowledge transfer.

A practical prerequisite for the dialogue was linguistic understanding, which became increasingly easier over time – even if there were always situations in which the participants were 'lost in translation'. The languages and the permanent translations led to a deeper understanding of the respective cultures (multiple

[2] The costs of the project were covered by the DAAD. This relieved the Iraqis of the burden of having to prove that they had additional financial resources. As a rule, Iraqis are required to provide proof of financial resources when applying for a visa.

[3] Sections in the DAAD tender text talk of the 'Development of Iraqi universities and thus of Iraqi society' and 'Modernization of higher education in Iraq'; but development and modernization are quite evaluative terms that also have their colonial prehistories.

[4] See also Sonnenberg 'Introduction to International Social Work' in this volume; see also Rehklau and Lutz (2009): Partnerschaft oder Kolonisation.

translation function). Linguistic competence in English (absolute minimum requirement B2/Ils 5) became the criterion for participation in the project. Interpreter costs were not budgeted for.

In addition to these harsh primary criteria, there were more open aspects, almost a secondary framework, in which the bi-national cooperation and communication took shape. This concerns the exchange of resources, which was not directly financed by the project: the time spent together, the willingness to pay attention to each other, the provision of social capital, access to the respective host country and persons, and finally the development of group cohesion, which gave to common goals and visions an emotional and trusting side in addition to strategic aspects.[5]

2.2 Intercultural Communication and Its Symptoms: Trust and Understanding, Difference and Similarity

Trust and mutual understanding grew, among other things, through the exchange of history and stories[6]: The history of social work in the regions and the visit of mutual places of practice, personal professional and private history, the history of the countries and their historical places, the shared history of the project and the shared discipline established an anticipated similarity.[7] Similarity does not mean the same, because differences and differentiations were visible, whether

---

[5] 'As a result of this week, we have not only built a bridge between East and West or between two countries, but also internally, for a ... bridge has been built in the team, trust has been built ... because otherwise they would never have had the time nor taken the time to talk and work together intensively and to engage in exchange.' (Transcript Conversation 4/2016 in Slemani, p. 11); 'that it is the beginning of a project and we are the core group and there was some sort of loyalty to the team.' (Transcript Conversation 11/2016 in Bochum, p. 8); similarly, also Transcript 5/2017 p. 2: 'have the feeling that we are not only colleagues now, it is kind of friendly'; ibid., p. 4, 'a third thought, I was impressed how quickly we were familiar with each other... thank you... for the trust... so it can really be a good cooperation.'

[6] Straub (2020) describes among other things relationship building and community building as well as the organization of historical realities as important socio-cultural and psycho-social functions of storytelling.

[7] E.g. from the transcription Interview 2016, p. 11: 'Then it would have become clear to him again that humanity is somehow such a piece of a broken mirror and we all carry a piece of it and anyway they always put it together so and in such situations everyone carries such a splinter that he carries to the image; and it would have become clear to him that we are all humans and, anyway, no different religions, languages, regional places can alienate us from this humanity anyway and therefore, in spite of all the strangeness, this remains the commonality of all.'

in the subject-related issues (see e.g. Chapter Topics), or in the knowledge and evaluation of and the impact of historical and political events.

The terms ‘trust’, ‘understanding’, ‘difference’ and ‘similarity’, which are often used for intercultural communication, are by no means self-evident. Understanding needs to be understood and trust explained.

Understanding. There is the assumption that, in intercultural communication situations, understanding begins in the dialogue between the own (i.e. the individual or collective self) and the stranger. This means, however, that the stranger and the difference are presupposed to understanding. But precisely this assumption has been criticized for some years in the cultural sciences, in particular in the works of Anil Bhatti. He advocates a paradigmatic change by highlighting the ‘concept of similarity’ (Bhatti and Kimmich 2015).

Difference and Similarity. In my opinion, differences cannot be eliminated and the criticism here refers more to automated othering processes and to the ‘focus on cultural differences, concepts of the own and the foreign, of identity and alterity’ (Schirilla 2018, p. 126). This criticism is justified by the fact that, among other things, in current migration research, diverse identities and cultural hybridity have long been debated, which ‘question concepts such as identity or alterity and refer to the mutual interdependencies and intermingling also in a historical perspective’ (ibid.). They continue to build on postcolonial approaches ‘of ‘entangled’ or ‘shared’ history’ (ibid.), which call into question dichotomous opposites between the poles of the world or modernity and their forerunners. They argue that ‘thinking of differences in the global context requires dealing with them and with the concept of understanding, which in turn can be criticized as violent, engaging and instrumentalizing, as shown by numerous examples from the scientific accompaniment of colonialism’ (ibid.). This cultural-theoretical suggestion of thinking assumes that the logic of difference of colonial thinking can only be escaped by understanding going beyond traditional hermeneutic concepts of understanding. It aims at similarity thinking that takes more account of simultaneities in pluricultural and complex societies. Thus, while thinking in (partly constructed) differences presupposes the alienation and alteration of the opposite, similarity opens up the option of dialogical understanding. The focus is on ‘overlapping fields, similar practices, interconnected lifeworlds and networks’ (ibid.).

‘Polyvalent thinking’ facilitates thinking ‘cultural differences more openly, fluently or blurredly’ and linking them to ‘interdependencies, shared and joint history and/or stories and their mutual interdependencies’ (ibid.). The aim in outlining this philosophical investigation is to illustrate how, besides the concept of the (cultural) difference between own-foreign or self-stranger, it can also be conceived of in terms of similarity, in terms of not-only-but-also or as ongoing. The cultural scientist Dorothee Kimmich assumes that similarity provokes and irritates heuristic separations of modernity as well as nature-culture, since no contradiction and no boundary marking of opposites is assumed (Bhatti and Kimmich 2015, p. 21). Moreover, the concept of similarity can 'substitute or complement the well-known oppositions such as those of homogeneity and heterogeneity or also identity and alterity... It acts as a corrective in both directions, both against processes of othering and against a violent homogenization of one's own self and the formation of a hegemonic obligatory identity' (Bhatti et al. 2011, p. 247). Thus, it can be an opener of thought for the requirements of time as 'a flexible conceptual approach and an openness to an asymmetric narrative of modernity' (Bhatti et al. 2011, p. 233).

Trust is discussed as a multifaceted phenomenon, depending on one's point of view as a moral, mechanistic-functional, rationalistic or ethical concept (cf. e.g. Endres 2002). Sociologists such as Luhmann, Giddens, and Sztompka, among others, have different ways of reading, analyzing and locating the concept of trust. According to Luhmann, trust is a 'hinge between different systems that is capable of reducing complexity, stabilizing expectations and thereby increasing systemic options for action. Trust bridges knowledge boundaries' (Schäfer 2004, p. 5 with reference to Luhmann 2000). While in private relationships familiarity is unquestionably assumed, the boundaries between familiar and unfamiliar at the social level are blurred and require clarification and mediation. It is precisely for this mediation that trust is fundamental, as a 'mechanism of the social dimension, that solves problems on the factual dimension (information deficits, risks, uncertainties) and on the time dimension (sequentiality, i.e. asynchronism)' (Schäfer 2004, p. 6 with reference to Luhmann 2000, p. 34). Giddens embeds trust in the context of modernity, in which social relationships are singled out from place, space and time. For Giddens, too, trust acts as a mediating hinge, but above all as a belief in symbolic signs and expert systems, in addition to trust in unknown persons. Since modern institutions are closely linked to trust in abstract systems, it is precisely the 'faith in the correctness of principles that one does not know oneself' (Giddens 1995, p. 33 f.) that is important. Sztompka places confidence in the context of the transformation processes of Central Eastern European countries. He sees trust as a cultural resource for the realization of a societal potential for action in conditions of complexity, uncertainty and insecurity – a resource that creates room for maneuver, makes control unnecessary and saves costs (Schäfer 2004, p. 6 with reference to Sztompka 1999). Endress defines the concept of 'functional trust' (2010, p. 95) in contrast to reflexive trust, which he perceives as ambivalent and as a mode 'that in the sense of a resource implicitly accompanying in the core, i.e. as the undisputed background precondition for social action and social relations' (ibid., p. 6). It conceptualizes trust as a relational or connecting term the subject of which is the 'irreversible tension between implicitness and non-implicitness' (ibid., p. 7). Each of the authors mentioned refers to different facets of the concept of trust. There is unanimity on the count that the genesis of trust is related to the control of expectations in fragile communications and serves to generate security.

Trust and Intercultural Communication Competence. There is no universally valid concept of intercultural competence,[8] but some counter-concepts in the debate such as 'incompetency competence' (Mecheril 2002, p. 15) describe the criticism of a technological understanding and refer to the communicative fragility and ambivalent tension (cf. Eppenstein 2015, p. 61), which must be floated in a similar way to 'trust'. Weidemann et al. (2010) describe intercultural competence as 'an ability to consciously relate to an alienating experience and to implement this interactively in such a way that a communication system that tends to be fragile remains functional. It requires – and presupposes – that the questioning of the system of one's own certainties caused by difference does not have the effect of fundamentally shattering one's own self-assurance'. Gaining control over the unexpected expectations in intercultural communication thus serves to re-establish confidence with all its described important social functions as well as security and orientation.

In his multidimensional concept of intercultural communications, Georg Auernheimer (2002) has identified four levels of expectation from a communication and social psychological perspective: power dimensions, collective experiences, mutual images and cultural dimensions. It is noteworthy that Auernheimer only mentions possible cultural differences in fourth place as a cause of uncertainty in communication, more importantly he considers the other three dimensions. In doing so, he assumes that a variety of intercultural situations are characterized by power asymmetries, in the sense of unequal possibilities for action, such as economic, political or discursive power or power through information advantages. The second dimension of collective experience refers to historical events, which are usually painful and contain a real historical core. When representatives of two groups meet, who share a serious (painful) collective experience, it must be assumed that the communication is influenced by it.

[8] The controversial concept of competence is not the subject of this paper.

In everyday life, collective experiences and images of others are often difficult to distinguish sharply, but they produce a respective and mutual image of the 'other' and fuel prejudices and stereotypes. Images of the other are often shaped topically and are linked to personal experiences and representations in the media. They influence feeling and social action.

Thereby, images of others are subject to a context-specific construction process. The foreign is not of the essence, not a given aspect; it is not a categorical characteristic of things, cultures or the other. The production of foreignness as cultural foreignness is fragile in modern societies, since foreignness can also be caused, among other things, by different life worlds and milieus, with the consequence that foreignness has long been observable as a regular generalized experience (Ghaderi 2017, p. 9). Thus, experiences of foreignness are an omnipresent experience of modern societies, which can be given by the interaction between different milieus, but also between genders or generations, and can only be experienced in relation. The imagination of the stranger as a historical-social-political construction is transformable. Thus, during the Nazi period, Jews, Roma or people with disabilities were the strangers in the imagined racial or national corpus (the so-called 'Volkskörper'). These concrete examples make it clear that the talk of the construction of the stranger denies the experience that proves to be a reality beyond scientific deconstruction. It is no coincidence that Birgit Rommelspacher, in 2006, called for an examination of the stories of mutual relations: 'In our encounter with strangers, we encounter not only our own self-conflict and individual narrow-mindedness but also real history, a story of conquest, of racism and Anti-Semitism, which is inscribed in our thinking and feeling. In this respect, psychological analysis only captures half the truth when it perceives in the stranger, above all, the proper state of mind and excludes the history of the relationship with these strangers from its field of view' (Rommelspacher 2006, p. 147). The stranger is not only the product of my self-awareness; it is not just repressed self. Such a reduced understanding would be equivalent to a functionalization of the stranger for the psychological stabilization of the self. It is important that the 'relationship with these strangers and the history of the relationship and the associated power relations are also addressed' (ibid.).

For the context of international university cooperation, this would mean actively dealing with the histories. In the specific case of the binational CoBoSUnin project, to think about German history and Kurdish history with their respective wounds, as well as their possible interlinkages and effects on transmission relations in intercultural communication.

This can be an opportunity to deal with the hierarchy of one's own thinking and feeling and to realize that they are not accidental. They reproduce social norms and orders. These feelings are neither temporal nor natural, but connected with the respective societies, respective families and other groups in which we live and in which we grew up. Thus, children learn that they are better or stranger, ruler or ruled, guilty or victim; they learn to fit into the systems of order that are not free from ambivalences and ambiguities.

2.3 Historicity: Kurdish-German Interdependencies and Adhesions

The Kurdish and German, or the Kurdish-German history cannot be presented here and is also not relevant in detail. Rather, it is a question of associated images (of the other) in the encounters, which may have arisen against the background of current media representations or historical-political events. The formation of these images of each other is neither sharp nor unambiguous.

2.3.1 Pictures of the Germans and Germany in Kurdistan

There is hardly any research on the topic of how Kurdish people perceive Germans and Germany, but in the following I will use, among other things, historical cornerstones and try to draw an outline: The pictures of Germany and the Germans in Kurdistan are diverse and include, among other things, the following facets: at first traditional images such as the land of poets and thinkers; football; the country in which Hitler and National Socialism ruled; the land of freedom and of liberality for women; a democratic, secure, peaceful and economically stable country and a country (cf. Ghaderi 2014, pp. 226), which belongs to Europe and the Western world. In the 1980s, some engineers working in the oil industry were in Kurdistan-Iraq. Later, when the first elections were held in May 1992, Germans became visible as journalists and as employees of NGOs, few also as spouses of Kurds who re-migrated or traveled from migration. The exposure of the violence of the 1980s and the involvement of German companies in the Halabja poison gas tragedy was another piece of the mosaic in the picture. In addition, the 2010–2020s saw the delivery of German Milan missiles, further arms exports (also for Turkey) and the support of the Peshmerga in training by the Bundeswehr and in the fight against the Islamic State. The framing, in which media images and texts of the Germans are constructed and are often read in Kurdish-language media, what tips the scales in the Kurdish perception of 'the Germans' is the question of whether a political act represents support of or a rejection of the Kurdish question.

2.3.2 Pictures of Kurds and Kurdistan in Germany

What images of Kurds and Kurdistan have existed and still exist in Germany? The depiction of Kurds in the German media has been little researched. One of the few publications is the anthology 'Kurds and Media' (2004). In it, the publicist Ulrich Pätzold provides an insightful analysis of the image of Kurds in the German media, which he divides into chronological stages: Initially transported as deep-rooted romanticizing cultural images through the books 'West-Eastern Divan' by Johann Wolfgang von Goethe and 'Im wilden Kurdistan' by Karl May. 'But in this imaginary world Kurds were not present as real experience … Kurds remained something mythical, an existence between fairy tale and reality. Kurdistan had a rough geographical classification, but no state identity to be marked by borders … The 'wild Kurdistan' remained a metaphor in the self-image of the Germans' (Pätzold, p. 15). As real people, the Kurds only entered the history of the Germans in the 1960s with the immigration movements, when they came to Germany as so-called 'guest workers' with Turkish passports or as refugees.[9] In this phase Kurds were perceived as Turks. This perspective of perception shaped German media coverage, especially since German-Turkish relations played a formative role (ibid., p. 16).

A differentiation and expansion of the Kurdish image could be observed at the end of the 1980s and in the 1990s 'as a result of a general sensitization to human rights that was now also supported by the media' (ibid., p. 17), when the human catastrophes of the Kurds in Iraq and Turkey became apparent. The visibility of the Kurds increased and the political discussions about the Kurds in Iraq, Turkey, Syria and Iran and beyond that in the diaspora gained momentum. At the same time, polarizations arose in the media images of Kurdish fate 'in the role of the helpless victim, and later in that of the murdering and suicidal perpetrator' (Ghaderi 2004, p. 242). The media images of the criminal stranger in the absence of political facts gave reason to investigate the reporting and develop a so-called 'Kurdish model' (cf. Scheufele and Brosius 2002, p. 117). This model examined an interaction between the objective problem of PKK violence, the perceived threat of Kurds in public consciousness and political discourse, mass media reporting, and the propensity to violence of xenophobically motivated persons. These negative effects by the media were probably not intended by the journalists, but they did lead to increased hostility toward Kurds and to xenophobic acts of violence against Kurds (Weber-Menges 2005, p. 172). These effects are confirmed by recent studies. 'The image of the Kurds that the media produces is at best

[9] Since the 1950s, there were a few thousand people who had migrated as students and educational elites, some of whom lived and remained in the GDR (cf. Engin 2019, p. 9).

incomplete and characterized by an overrepresentation of violence, police, justice and the PKK. Reports from everyday life hardly ever occur, and if they do, they too are at least in part charged with potential for conflict (for example, between 'their' and 'our' culture)' (Nowaki 2018, p. 58).

In recent years, Kurds have been placed in the context of the war in Syria (since March 2011). The struggle of the Syrian and Iraqi Kurds against the so-called Islamic State (IS) (since summer 2014), especially the image of the female fighters of the YPG and PKK, the political developments in Turkey (since 2015), as well as the numerous demonstrations of Kurdish citizens in the course of Turkey's invasion of Afrin (January 2018), Kobane and Rojava (October 2019) continued to be present in the media. In the process, parallel diverging images emerged, at times enemy and terrorist, at times 'victim people' and those affected by genocide (in the case of the Yezidi Kurds), and at times Peshmerga, ally and hero.[10] The respective images of and themes about Kurds are placed in the context of the interest of 'German' themes, such as integration or the imminence or legitimization of participation in the war. Thus, the images of the poison gas victims of Halabja were increasingly broadcast before the 2nd/3rd Gulf War to document the brutality of Saddam Hussein. 'The use of poison gas necessarily deeply affected Germans with the memory of their own history' (ibid., p. 20). The Kurdish public had a hard time bringing their issues to the newsrooms 'if they did not pay sufficient attention to German self-images and related feelings' (ibid., p. 18). Depending on the context, it is not 'the Kurdish' that is relevant to the German public, but rather its classification as Muslim, Oriental, migrant, etc. Places of articulation were redefined with the age of globalization, the Internet and satellite TV, and the possibilities of Kurdish broadcasters and media were expanded. Not infrequently, there are converging interests in the representation of others and oneself. An example from the recent past is mentioned here: The image of Kurdish anti-IS fighters illustrates a specific representation of Kurdish women as warriors and freedom fighters. This image is very popular with both Kurdish and Western audiences. For some, it symbolizes secular, self-confident feminism against Islamization. For others, it combines the vision and longing for a modern Kurdish nationalism recognized by the world public. Against this background, the glossy magazines and fashion labels' liking for the Kurdish anti-IS fighters in 2014 does not seem to be exclusively an expression of appreciation. The images not only say something about the fighters, but also about their image makers.

[10] Oliver Welke parodied this circumstance in a Heute Show program with the title 'Gute Kurden-Schlechte Kurden' ('Good Kurds-Bad Kurds'). https://www.youtube.com/watch?v=1lvS8BSaD_k (Accessed October 19, 2020).

It nurtured their normative self-assurance. In any case, the folkloristic attributes of the Kurdish image have meanwhile been exchanged for political questions at home and abroad; they have changed, are sometimes victims, sometimes perpetrators, sometimes heroines. These images are, as can be easily seen, connected with the political (collective) experiences. The political relations between Germany and the Kurds are always embedded in Germany's foreign policy relations with Turkey, Iraq, Syria, and Iran (see Gürbey 2019, p. 131). There is a historically evolved continuity of German-Turkish relations, which is important 'for the stability in the EU's southeastern neighborhood, European migration policy, the fight against IS, and for the energy policy supply of Germany and the European Union' (ibid., p. 133). Kurds play a secondary role in this interstate network of relations and in Germany's politics of interests. The way Kurds are treated is guided by a security policy approach that leads to their being perceived as a 'security problem' and encourages their criminalization (ibid., p. 134). Furthermore, the historical conflict over the rights of Kurds is negated and seen as a human rights and minority issue, with the result that demands for autonomy are rejected per se. 'For example, the military support of the Kurdish Peshmerga in Iraqi Kurdistan, which is only due to the battle against the common enemy IS, did not automatically lead to a benevolent review of the independence referendum in Iraqi Kurdistan in September 2017' (ibid., p. 135). This view in turn irritates Kurdish perceptions (see framing above). In addition, Kurds are one of the largest migration groups in Germany (see Engin 2019, p. 8). The largest Kurdish community outside the original settlement area lives in Germany, and most of them are based in North Rhine-Westphalia. The Kurdish communities and identities in Germany can be described as heterogeneous and hybrid, with the younger generation in particular creating new imaginary reference spaces and collective narratives that do not necessarily have to be linked to the region or language of origin (cf. Ammann 2019, p. 36). This text focuses on the Kurdistan region of Iraq. In the Kurdish images in Germany, there is not always a distinction between Kurds from different countries of origin, especially since Kurds in Germany were not perceived separately from Turks for a long time – as described. An important factor connected with the construction of these images, the reality of the different historical experiences of Kurds in their respective countries of origin, as well as the relationship of these countries of origin with Germany, is colonial history, which continues through development and foreign policy to the present day.

2.3.3 Entanglements with Global Colonial History from Various Positions

The relationship between Germany and the Kurds is based on historical facts. But to what extent is global colonialism significant in this context? To what extent do the entanglements with colonial history from different positions play a role or even co-construct current power asymmetries in in the relationship and communication to this day? Are we actually dealing here with colonized and colonialists? Germany neither identifies itself primarily as a colonial state,[11] nor do Kurds, in their self-descriptions, consider themselves first and foremost as colonized. The self-classification within a power matrix based on colonialism is not a standardized, associated way of reading Kurdish and German self-images.

As a reminder, in this text I would like to reflect on the possibility of binational partnerships and the question of the need for decolonization of knowledge in social work in Kurdistan. Decolonization of knowledge requires knowing what is to be decolonized and how, and what it means to unravel the production of knowledge from a mainly Eurocentric episteme. A post- and/or decolonial perspective implies 'a critical view of oneself in the context of colonial and global interdependence' (Schirilla 2018, p. 4). And only in this way can social work theory and practice explicate, discuss and overcome colonial contexts.

It is precisely this more critical view that is to be begun here with a historical review: Is Kurdistan a former colony? Did Germany play a role at all in the region? Are there transnational historical connections?

For the historical sketch I have chosen the period beginning with the Paris Peace Conference, which was relevant for Germany and Kurdistan and which was a political caesura for global colonial history:

Interestingly, the Paris Peace Conference of 1919 is in the German historical consciousness primarily associated with the Versailles Treaty as the author of the high reparation payments. According to this treaty, the German colonies were ceded and thus the German colonial empire (1884–1914), which had lasted about thirty years, came to an end. In 1914, the German colonies were the third largest colonial empire after the British and French. However, the end of the German colonial empire was primarily a formal one and was continued in a policy of 'colonialism without colonies' (Gründer & Hiery 2019, p. 161). 'Foreign rule in the former colonies continued under the status of League of Nations mandates,

[11] In recent years there has been an increased confrontation with German colonial history, see for example Gründer, H / Hiery, H (2019): Die Deutschen und ihre Kolonien (Eds.).

and colonially influenced patterns of thought and perception survived even beyond colonial revisionist discourses.'[12]

However, the Paris Peace Conference of 1919 not only had the function of negotiating the interests of the warring parties after the First World War, but also had wider global and world-political significance. Representatives from all over the world were gathered to establish a new international order to secure long-term peace. The League of Nations, the predecessor organization of the UN, was founded to guarantee peace. In addition, European colonialism was to be reformed. 'During the negotiations at the Paris Peace Conference, the mandate system was developed to bring about a solution between the old colonial policy and the fulfillment, the freedom promised by the Allies for the oppressed peoples. The official justification for this was that most of the new states to be created cannot stand on their own feet, neither economically nor politically' (Asadi 2007, p. 82). Consequently, the Treaty of Versailles institutionalized the system of mandates, whereby the former German colonies as well as the former provinces of the Ottoman Empire were to fall under the supervision of the new international organization. As early as 1916, the Sykes-Picot Treaty established a secret agreement between the governments of Great Britain and France, which defined their colonial areas of interest in the Middle East after the expected defeat of the Ottoman Empire in World War I. Until the end of the First World War, the Kurdish territory, which today belongs to Iraq, was part of the Ottoman Empire, i.e. until the British Empire brought Southern Kurdistan – as British diplomacy called today's Iraqi Kurdistan during this period – under its control in 1917. In World War I, British troops invaded Baghdad and occupied the country in 1917 against the resistance of coalition of Turkish and German troops. Their aim was to create a pro-British state in the region to enforce their own interests. Finally, in San Remo, 'the Allies met again in April 1920. There they divided the mandate areas among themselves: Great Britain received the mandate over Iraq including the Wilayat Mosul'. In 1920, France concluded the Sèvres Peace Treaty, which provided for the possibility of founding an independent Kurdish state. But historical developments prevented this from happening; the treaty was never ratified, and Great Britain lost interest in an independent Kurdish state (see Ghaderi 2014). It is worth mentioning that, in early July 1920, Kurdish activists handed over a memorandum to the responsible British High Commissioner Wilson 'which bore the signatures of all 62 tribal chiefs and notables of the Kurdish areas' (Asadi 2007, p. 86). In it, they called for the establishment of the independent Kurdish

[12] https://www.bpb.de/apuz/297589/deutsche-kolonialgeschichte, Accessed October 19, 2020.

state of Kurdistan under British protectorate in accordance with British promises during wartime. But Britain's main aim was to form a pro-British-Arabia state, thus securing control over resources in the region, as was laid down, among other things, in the Cairo Conference in March 1921, which was called by British colonial minister Winston Churchill (ibid., p. 92). The sovereign and territorial relationships in the region were finally determined by contract in Lausanne in 1923. In Iraq, Great Britain established a Hashemite monarchy under Faisal Ibn Hussein, a main ally from the First World War. In 1932, the British mandate was revoked and Iraq joined the League of Nations as an independent state. Britain, however, secured a special economic position and retained a strong political influence. From then on, the Kurds' settlement area was located in four states: Turkey, Iraq, Iran and Syria.

In 1930, an 'Anglo-Iraqi Treaty' was signed. This treaty was intended to enable local self-government and at the same time give the British control over foreign and military affairs. The 1930 treaty was based on an earlier Anglo-Iraqi treaty of 1922, but took into account the increasing importance of Iraq for British interests in the face of new oil discoveries in 1927. There were demonstrations against this British policy on September 6, 1930, in Slemani (Saleh 2017, p. 5). Resistance to British domination is complex in the history of Slemani and Kurdistan-Iraq, and is particularly associated with the name of Shaikh Mahmud Barzinji (for more details, see Asadi 2007, p. 34–55).

These historical annotations remain sketches, they illuminate the effects of the First World War and global colonial histories. Germany and Kurdistan have no direct relationship. Perhaps it can be said that entangled histories exist (see also Castro Varela and Dhawan 2015, p. 14).

Can Kurdistan be called a colony?

In the case of Kurdistan, one cannot speak of a classical colony. Classical colonies are characterized by the fact that a metropolis occupied a peripheral country, dominated it politically and economically, and exploited it. In this process, 'clear' boundaries were drawn.

In the search movements for a Kurdish perspective on colonialism or postcolonial readings, the terms 'international colony' (Beşikçi) and 'internal colonies' (Bozarslan)[13] can be found. The term 'internal colonies' is used to describe structural political and economic inequality between individual regions within a state (Castro Varela and Dhawan 2015, p. 15).

With the term 'international colony' Beşikçi conceptualizes the fact that Kurdistan is a colony without names and borders and differs in this respect from

[13] Cf. Skubsch 2002, p. 129 with reference to Bozarslan 1995.

'classical' colonies. Kurdistan would be colonized by countries that were either colonized themselves (Syria, Iraq, behind which France and Great Britain stood as 'mandated powers') or were in a colonial dependency relationship with the Western powers (Turkey, Iran). Inherent to the definition of a classical colony are its spatial characteristics, namely its territorial unity within fixed borders. Kurdistan's borders have never been marked by a colonial power. Beşikçi draws the conclusion from these characteristics that Kurdistan cannot be described as colonial and its population consequently does not have any kind of political status with associated rights. For this reason, the Kurdish question would be treated internationally as a 'minority question' or internal affair. Non-recognition as a colonial people would also mean the deprivation of rights as subjects of international law (Beşikçi, 1991, p. 16 f.). Beşikçi assesses the territorial character of the colonization of Kurdistan as crucial in its analysis. For example, during the colonization of Africa at the Berlin Conference of 1885, the boundaries of the African colonies were drawn. In contrast to the colonies of Africa, Kurdistan has never experienced the formation of such a territory, with consequences up to the current political situation: 'Even in Southern Kurdistan, Kurdistan Regional Government [in Iraq], it is a federation but we do not know where exactly the borders fall. It is your territory, your rule will reign there, but where? That is an issue of drawing boundaries that is why we say, Kurdistan is not even a colony, as colonies have established borders' (Beşikci quoted from Duruiz 2020). According to Beşikçi, this difference in the territorial character of the colonization of Kurdistan had an influence on the specific logics of resistance, oppression and destruction and led to specific effects on power relations on the international stage. While in most anti-colonial national liberation struggles the colonized people had to fight against a single state, in Kurdistan the struggle is being fought against four states, each of which has different relations and interests in the international arena.

Terms of *international colony* and *internal colonies* refer to political-economic-territorial aspects. Colonialism, however, had its effects beyond that for the formation of subjectivities of the colonialists and colonized. Beşikçi emphasizes this point – in a way comparable to Frantz Fanon's analysis of the colonization of Algeria – of humiliation and shame on the subjectivities of the colonized, which goes beyond material exploitation, political rule and state violence directed against Kurds. On a psychological level, colonialism influenced self-images in the sense of colonial internalizations and identities.[14]

[14] Cf. Bocheńska et. al. (2018) conceptualizes a postcolonial approach by making visible different themes and methodological approaches. With her volume 'Rediscovering Kurdistan's Cultures and Identities,' she makes an attempt to go beyond the dominant narratives regarding

These colonial internalizations are reproduced in intercultural communication situations, and internalized colonialized-racialized knowledge can also be demonstrated in relation to Kurdish-German communicative interactions, in terms of ethnic hierarchization, processes of drawing ethnic boundaries, etc. (see Ghaderi 2014, p. 255 f. for Kurdish self-images). This internalized relationship is being revitalized by political events, for example: the responsibility of German companies for the use of poison gas in Halabja in 1988; economic interdependencies and current arms supplies; as well as the 'good' side[15] in the development aid policy of the second half of the twentieth century, with which influence on societal and social structures is secured and shaped.

Thus, a colonial history in the classical sense cannot be proven, but a global historical interdependence between Germany and Kurdistan can be proven. The extent to which the various positions in these historical interrelationships could be heard in the communicative interactions in the bi-national project is the subject of further analysis.

3 Classification of Communicative Negotiations in the CoBoSUnin Project

In the following, bi-national cooperation is to be reflected upon with regard to its potential to be analyzed from a postcolonial – in the sense of power-critical – perspective. In particular the intercultural-transnational experiences from the project process and the communicative negotiations observed in the process (around trust, understanding, respect, partnership, similarity, difference, hierarchization, cultural practices, language policy, etc.) are taken as the starting point. The empirical basis is, among other things, the transcriptions from the formative evaluation.

Kurdistan that focus on wars, politics, and conflicts, and explore the little-known and less popular aspects of Kurdistan's reality.

[15] See also the image of the 'good German colonial ruler and his faithful Askari' (Gründer and Hiery 2019, p. 24).

3.1 Language Policy Negotiations

In this project there was a willingness to engage in dialogue from the very beginning, but there was not always a common language of understanding.[16] At the beginning, in the initiation phase (CoBoSUnin I), the only solution was translation[17] in order to participate constructively in this project and its goals.[18] For the project approval of CoBoSUnin II, the DAAD (German Academic Exchange Service) required a 'Concept for Linguistic Communication', which excluded translation costs. At the official start of the project in 2017, those who could not prove a minimum level of competence in English were excluded. Thus, one of the established selection criteria became good English language skills for both Bochum and Slemani students. In the course of the project, all lecturers of the Department of Social Work in Kurdistan attended English courses, at the beginning in order to prove their participation in the project, later on as it was set as a part of the University of Sulaimai's internationalization strategy. The 'Concept for Linguistic Communication' for the 2017–2018 phase was designed to optimize the previously partly intuitive and partly formalized communication concepts (e.g. through strategic recruitment of project participants in the selection phase, preparatory courses with students, parallel study programs, English as a language of communication during the stays). The pragmatic solution described here bore fruit and improved the language skills of all participants.

Language policy plays an essential role in the internationalization of universities, both in Germany and in Kurdistan. At German universities there are language policy issues, such as the relationship between German and English as a language of science and communication, and the promotion of multilingualism and language diversity. The aim is to achieve receptive multilingualism[19] for European universities. Similarly discussed concepts are models of 'parallel language use' and 'functional multilingualism' (HRK 2019, p. 5 f.).

---

[16] 'For me, the week is also an absolute success, I didn't think that despite the language barriers we would be able to get so incredibly detailed into the technical discussions anyway' (Quote from Transcript Interview 4/2016; p. 8).

[17] We would like to sincerely thank Ari Saeed for his assistance with the translation during the visits in Germany.

[18] During the workshops and discussions, the language of communication aimed at was English, otherwise we practiced a pragmatic multilingualism, i.e. the communication participants switched between languages (primarily English, but also German, Sorani) until the relevant content was conveyed.

[19] Receptive multilingualism is a form of intercultural communication in which the participants can understand each other's language sufficiently, but speak their own.

(American) English is gaining ground as a language at Kurdish universities and throughout the educational system in the Kurdistan region of Iraq. This is especially true for the teaching and practice of social work, which has been shaped from the beginning by a nexus of local traditional practices and the presence of international humanitarian organizations and NGOs.

The topic of language policy and internationalization is an ambivalent venture, in which the dominance of the English-speaking context plays an essential role. In Kurdistan, the dominance of English replaces the previous dominance of Arabic as an elitist language.[20]

Depending on the historical perspective, these developments can have a bad aftertaste. Language is an expression of identity and belonging, it has physical, emotional, and historical-political dimensions. Social, ethnic, national and other affiliations are constructed and formed through language ideologies (cf. Butler and Spivak 2007). For example, Kurds in Turkey have had the biographical experience that their first language Kurdish (Kurmanci or Zaza) was forbidden and that they had to speak Turkish when they entered school. For an entire generation, Turkish is associated with violence by state institutions such as schools, authorities, the military, etc., in which they have been degraded, if not traumatized (Van Keuk and Ghaderi 2013, p. 37 f.) Language policy also plays a fundamental role in the history of colonization. 'The introduction of colonial languages – such as Spanish, English or French – was presented as a way to bring the 'backward' communities in the colonies out of the darkness and into the light of economic progress and intellectual development' (Castro Varela and Dhawan 2015, p. 38). In addition, such language policies served as a cover to prevent internal communication among the colonized and to ensure control over them. Through language policy, colonized people were silenced in their thoughts, their community was made insecure in their solidarity, and their knowledge was robbed, even to the point of epistemicide. Not to forget that articulation in languages that are less mastered makes people appear less expressive, intelligent and educated and/or feel this to be the case.

The biographical requirements for being able to speak English were different in this project as well, depending on the country of origin, generation, gender, etc., and accordingly, the efforts and resistance to make oneself understood and to be understood in spoken and written communication were unequal.

[20] Interestingly, in 2011 the Arab-Lebanese scholar Haytham Ahmad Mouzahem titled an article 'Will Kurdistan be an American Colony?'

These phenomena are all to be acknowledged as critical, according to Philippe Van Parijs, but in his book on 'Language Justice' he presents a sober counter-thesis. He asks what actually speaks against it when we observe that English (primarily American English) is developing underhand as lingua franca of communication. This informal language regime may sometimes feel unfair, but in his view it is fair. In doing so, he distinguishes three ways of reading linguistic justice: 'Namely as fair cooperation when it comes to producing a shared language, as equalization of those opportunities for which a certain language competence is required, and as equal appreciation between linguistically defined collective identities' (Van Parijs 2013, p. 397). The predominance of English in transnational communication is therefore to be welcomed in the sense of justice, especially when solutions are to be sought together globally, and it would give a voice to those who would not be heard without a common language. In this project, the common third language for both sides was not the mother tongue. With the participation of English-speaking researchers this would have been unfair again.

These remarks may suffice that the pragmatic solution to linguistic communication in this project was accompanied by a multi-layered background music.

3.2 Normative Negotiations

There are expectations in transnational relations that are the result of historical and current images of the outside world (see Auernheimer 2002) and that influence the process.

Gender norms were repeatedly a trigger for amazement and discussions,[21] to which the examples at the beginning point exemplarily. Another topic was the division of roles and responsibilities in the joint book editions. The distribution of roles, who takes on which responsibility, was mutually determined. On the German side, there are formulations in the transcripts that classify one's own professionalism as the norm, e.g., a team member from Bochum says of the Kurdish colleagues: 'That they believe that they are not so far along in the practical areas, um, but I personally think that they are incredibly far along..., um, just maybe scientifically that simply hasn't been written down yet'.[22]

[21] Example: In the survey of the students, the UoS colleagues did not agree to enter 'diverse' on the question of gender in the evaluation sheet.

[22] Transcript 4/2016, Interview Slemani, p. 9.

Also, internalized hierarchical positioning can be seen in the dialogical negotiations about the tasks, because the Kurdish colleagues first of all assign the 'donor' side to the German side, which irritates them: 'They imagine that we somehow have a fund or somehow money to finance the print, but we don't have that either ... they wonder why we are so poor, they thought we are very rich and so I said, no, (laughter).'[23]

The misunderstandings about mutual expectations about who gives money and who contributes to the book with what knowledge dissolve into laughter and one of the Kurdish colleagues makes the compromise proposal that 'everyone writes one page in English and one in Kurdish', where 'page' is meant here as part or article (ibid., p. 6) and a German colleague promises to look for sources of funding for the printing (ibid., p. 5). The concept for three books was already developed in 2016 during this conversation, the concretizations followed in 2017.

A productive approach was the attentiveness of all participants to norms and hierarchies, to talk about them and to position themselves in relation to each other. This led to the insight that it is less about cultural differences than about the ability to perceive, formulate and reflect one's own needs, norms and attitudes. This ability was classified by a project member as 'an area which, in my view, also belongs in the teaching of social work'.[24] The impressive experiences that transnational cooperation can bring and the complexity and multifaceted nature of this requires time and space for self-reflection.[25] To develop a culture of self-reflection and mindfulness is seen as a chance for all participants in the transnational exchange.[26]

3.3 Epistemic Negotiations

As a result of the epistemic negotiations, I refer, among other things, to the books and articles that illustrate what the participants in the bi-national project agreed on with regard to relevant stocks of knowledge and what specific topics were set. The

[23] Transcript 4/2016, Interview Slemani, p. 2, 3.

[24] Transcript 11/2016, Interview Bochum, p. 15.

[25] '*I think there must be more time for reflection and it was a very short time for*' (Transcript 9/2018, p. 6).

[26] 'And this aspect of mindfulness and self-reflection I would find important in the teaching, in the – such an overall program, which also includes having in between room for exchange, for one's own state of mind, in other words a more mindful approach to one another. This is what I want in terms of programming, but also in terms of theory and practice.' (Transcript 11/2016, p. 15).

formulation and articulation originated in part developed from individual authors, in part out of cooperation between two or more authors. The texts are written in English and, in the case of the introductory book on social work, in Kurdish. None of this is or was self-evident; it took numerous personal conversations during the trips, visits in the fields of social work, telephone calls, virtual meetings, e-mails, etc. to reach consensus on formulations, weightings, on the what and the how of the content. Being aware of their own location in the geopolitics of knowledge and the repeated willingness to question standardized, dominant knowledge and to reconstruct the constitution of the respective knowledge stocks was the basis of the joint work. Without the trust mentioned at the beginning, the disclosure of thoughts, the willingness to make cultural patterns and modes of action comprehensible to the other person and not only to translate them linguistically, but also to decode them in terms of social meaning, the bi-national university cooperation would not have been productive.

For the entire team, self-confidence was a constant companion in order to avoid any kind of centrist faux pas that might have occurred in the structure of the project framework: This was already the case when the application was submitted with the goal of 'developing' and 'modernizing' the Iraqi university landscape; the recent founding of the Department of Social Work and the fact that the application was submitted by a university in the Global North in order to enable the improvement of the educational system of a country in the Global South; the invitation of speakers from the North who, as experts, passed on knowledge to 'natives'; the premise that it was necessary to learn and speak English, all of this committed the Kurdish side to the role of catching up – that means there was much potential to follow colonial continuities and many communicative messages in this respect. In other words, the different historical contexts – i.e. the experiences as an occupied country and as an occupying power – can influence the present with regard to the danger of continuing these roles (transgenerationally) even independently of a common colonial history.

One way to achieve more equality and justice in the global production of knowledge was the goal set from the beginning to write a Kurdish language textbook. The asymmetries were to be changed by the fact that the book was mainly written by the lecturers of the University of Sulaimani and addressed to students.

The intention was to make a knowledge archive available to those being spoken about whom it will serve. Not only people who are English speakers should benefit from the new lust for and production of knowledge regarding social work in Kurdistan. In the course of the project, the communication and articulation of expectations became clearer and clearer, and ultimately a more self-confident positioning, as Luqman Saleh Karim's words testify: 'Certainly, we can learn and benefit from more than hundred years of standards and experience of social work in Europe and America. But probably this dress does not really fit for us. Our cultural codes are different, our religion is different, our history is different, our social and family problems are different. Maybe in your country the topic of individuality and freedom have priority. In our country the priority is hunger, poverty and conflict. Therefore, we need codes of social work that address our specific challenges and pains'.[27]

4 Thoughts in Conclusion

Certainly, the ideas presented here can only be a beginning to reflect on the high standard of a dialogical, partnership-based communication with the goal of decolonial-oriented and power-critical knowledge production.

Long-term, result-oriented transnational partnerships in social work can hardly flourish without an awareness of local, global, colonial and interwoven histories – because it seems impossible for all participants to 'steal themselves out of history'. To recognize one's own positioning and to adopt it in a relational perspective conveys security and knowledge in intercultural dialogues.

Since transnational university partnerships are embedded in specific funding structures of nation states that are not free of colonial continuities, historical and political knowledge is relevant for the classification of communicative relationships. Aram Ziai (2007, p. 22) puts forward the hypothesis that there are continuities between colonial and developmental thinking.

He makes a historical reference to the Versailles Peace Treaty 1919 Art. 22,[28] in which the basic structure of colonial discourse is documented and in which it is assumed that there are groups of peoples 'who are not capable of governing themselves' (Ziai 2007, p. 25), i.e. there would be developed, advanced and backward nations with low levels of development. Even if real political conditions are different, the worldwide reactions to the independence referendum 2017 in the Kurdistan region of Iraq can be read in this sense.

Some of the texts that were written in the context of the project deal with the classification of social work in Kurdistan. The genesis and history of the departments in Erbil and Slemani, for example, show that knowledge has always flowed

[27] Original sound (time: 50:00–51:00) in the film documentation: 'CoBoSUnin - Coming Together for Acquiring Knowledge'. A Film by Ernst Meyer, SMIDAK Filmproduktion, Berlin: https://www.youtube.com/watch?v=wEkW9v51fps (Accessed October 11, 2020).

[28] Versailles Peace Treaty 1919, Art. 22, Online: https://www.documentarchiv.de/wr/vv01.html (Accessed October 11, 2020).

multi-directionally and not as 'imported goods' in which theoretical knowledge and methods have been adopted in social work without reflection. The lecturers in Slemani had participated in various training courses of different international NGOs and at the same time had knowledge of the local social structure. In addition, there was a lively exchange with people who were active in the field. These had not studied social work at all, their successes in their work testified to a high degree of habituated professionalism. The extent to which the term indigenous knowledge or decolonial knowledge is correct with reference to Kurdistan remains debatable in my opinion against the background of the historical circumstances. An intensive examination of postcolonial approaches to social work in the Kurdistan region of Iraq is still pending. It can have identity-political consequences for Kurdish areas. It can mean re-conceptualizing knowledge productions between the nation, culture and ethnicity complex and questioning common dominant narratives of Kurdish identity constructions. This would have far-reaching political and cultural implications beyond the theory and practice of social work.

References

Ammann, B. (2019). Das kurdische Identitätsprojekt und seine Entwicklung. In K. Engin (Ed.), *Kurdische Migration in Deutschland* (pp. 23-41). Kassel: Kassel University Press.

Asadi, A. (2007). *Der Kurdistan-Irak-Konflikt. Der Weg zur Autonomie seit dem Ersten Weltkrieg*. Berlin: Hans Schiler Verlag.

Auernheimer, G. (2002). Interkulturelle Kompetenz und pädagogische Professionalität. Opladen.

Beşikçi, I. (1991). Kurdistan - Internationale Kolonie. Frankfurt a. M.

Bhatti, A., & Kimmich, D. (Eds.). (2015). *Ähnlichkeit. Ein kulturtheoretisches Paradigma*. Konstanz: Konstanz University Press.

Bhatti, A., Kimmich, D., Koschorke, A., Schlögl, R., & Wertheimer, J. (2011). Ähnlichkeit. Ein kulturtheoretisches Paradigma. In *Internationales Archiv für Sozialgeschichte der deutschen Literatur (IASL), 36*(1), 233–247. https://doi.org/10.1515/iasl.2011.018.

Bocheńska, J. (2018). Rediscovering Kurdistan's cultures and identities: The call of the cricket. https://doi.org/10.1007/978-3-319-93088-6.

Butler, J., & Spivak, G. C. (2007). *Sprache, Politik, Zugehörigkeit*. Zürich: Diaphanes.

Castro Varela, Md. M., & Dhawan, N. (2015). *Postkoloniale Theorie. Eine kritische Einführung* (2nd ed.). Bielefeld: Transcript.

Duruiz, D. (2020). Tracing the conceptual genealogy of Kurdistan as international colony. Middle East Report 295 (Summer 2020). https://merip.org/2020/08/tracing-the-conceptual-genealogy-of-kurdistan-as-international-colony/.

Endreß, M. (2002). *Vertrauen*. Bielefeld: Transcript.

Endreß, M. (2010). Vertrauen – soziologische Perspektiven. In *Vertrauen – zwischen sozialem Kitt und der Senkung von Transaktionskosten*. Karlsruhe: KIT Scientific Publishing. https://books.openedition.org/ksp/2566.

Engin, K. (2019). Kurdische Migrant_innen in Deutschland. In K. Engin (Ed.), *Kurdische Migration in Deutschland* (pp. 5–23). Kassel: Kassel University Press.

Eppenstein, T. (2015). Interkulturelle Kompetenz. In I. Zacharaki, T. Eppenstein, & M. Krummacher (Eds.), *Interkulturelle Kompetenz. Handbuch für soziale und pädagogische Berufe*. Frankfurt a. Main: Debus Pädagogik Verlag.

Ghaderi, C. (2004). *Das Bild der Kurden im öffentlich-medialen Diskurs und ihre Wirkung auf die Integration. In: Kurden und Medien. Navend Schriftenreihe* (Bd. 14. pp. 239–255). Bonn.

Ghaderi, C. (2014). *Politische Identität – Ethnizität – Geschlecht. Selbstverortungen politischer aktiver MigrantInnen. Reihe: Studien zur Migrations- und Integrationspolitik*. Wiesbaden: VS Verlag.

Ghaderi, C. (2017). Postmigrantische Gesellschaft: Identität und Kultur im Wandel. In I. Graeff-Callies & M. Schouler-Ocak (Eds.), *Migration und Transkulturalität* (pp. 3–20). Stuttgart: Schattauer.

Giddens, A. (1995). *Die Konsequenzen der Moderne*. Frankfurt a. M.: Suhrkamp.

Gründer, H., & Hiery, H. (Eds.). (2019). *Die Deutschen und ihre Kolonien*. Zentralen für politische Bildung ZpB. Berlin-Brandenburg: be.bra Verlag.

Gürbey, G. (2019). Gibt es eine eigenständige deutsche Kurdenpolitik? Eine kritische Bilanz. In K. Engin (Ed.), *Kurdische Migration in Deutschland* (pp. 131–141). Kassel University Press.

Hochschulrektorenkonferenz HRK (Eds.). (2019). Institutionelle Sprachenpolitik an Hochschulen – Fortschritte und Herausforderungen. Beiträge zur Hochschulpolitik 1/2019.

Kruse, E. (2018). Erst der Vergleich öffnet … die Augen. In L. Wagner, R. Lutz, C. Rehklau, & F. Ross (Eds.), *Handbuch Internationale Soziale Arbeit. Dimensionen – Konflikte – Positionen* (pp. 80–97). Weinheim: Beltz Juventa.

Kurden und Medien (2004). Ein Beitrag zur gleichberechtigten Akzeptanz und Wahrnehmung von Kurden in den Medien, Navend, Schriftenreihe Bd. 14.

Luhmann, N. (2000). *Vertrauen. Ein Mechanismus der Reduktion sozialer Komplexität*. Stuttgart: UTB. Lucius & Lucius. (Orig.: 1968).

Mecheril, P. (2002). Kompetenzlosigkeitskompetenz. Pädagogisches Handeln unter Einwanderungsbedingungen. In *Interkulturelle Kompetenz und pädagogische Professionalität* (pp. 15–34). Opladen: Leske u. Buderich.

Nowaki, A. (2018). Opfer – Täter – Helden? KurdInnen in der deutschen Diaspora: Eine Themenfrequenz- und Diskursanalyse deutscher Tageszeitungen. https://f.hypotheses.org/wp-content/blogs.dir/3830/files/2019/07/KurdInnen-und-%C3%96ffentlichkeit_FINAL.pdf. Accessed 12 Oct 2020.

Rehklau, C., & Lutz, R. (2009). Partnerschaft oder Kolonisation? Thesen zum Verhältnis des Nordens zur Sozialarbeit des Südens.

Rommelspacher, B. (2006). *Dominanzkultur. Texte zu Fremdheit und Macht* (2nd edn). Orlanda Frauenverlag.

Saleh, M. (2017). Wer hat warum am 6.4.1930 demonstriert? In J. Lolo (Ed.), *Die Demonstration bar darki sara am 6.4.1930*. Slemani: Sivan.

Schäfer, M. S. (2004). Rezension zu: Martin Endress (2002). Vertrauen [29 Absätze]. Forum Qualitative Sozialforschung/Forum: Qualitative Social Research, Art. 8. https://nbn-resolving.de/urn:nbn:de:0114-fqs040285.
Scheufele, B., & Brosius, H.-B. (2002). Die Qualität der Kurden-Berichterstattung. Gibt es einen Zusammenhang mit fremdenfeindlicher Gewalt? In A. Baum & S. J. Schmidt (Eds.), *Fakten und Fiktionen. Über den Umgang mit Medienwirklichkeiten.* (Schriftenreihe d. Dt. Gesellschaft für Publizistik und Kommunikationswissenschaft) (pp. 114–126). Konstanz: UVK-Verlagsgesellschaft.
Schirilla, N. (2018). Diversität in einer postkolonialen Perspektive. In M. Pfaller-Rott, E. Gómez-Hernández, & H. Soundari (Eds.), *Soziale Vielfalt.* Wiesbaden: Springer VS.
Schirilla, N. (2015). Von Differenz zu Ähnlichkeit – ein kulturwissenschaftlicher Paradigmenwechsel? Zeitschrift für interkulturelles Philosophieren. https://www.polylog.net/fileadmin/docs/polylog/38/38_rez_Schirilla_Bhatti.pdf. Accessed 15 Sept 2020.
Skubsch, S. (2002). *Kurdische Migranten und deutsche (Bildungs-)Politik. Beiträge zur Kurdologie* (Vol. 5). Münster: Unrast-Verlag.
Straub, J. (2020). Erzähltheorie/Narration. In G. Mey & K. Mruck (Eds.), *Handbuch Qualitative Forschung in der Psychologie.* Wiesbaden: Springer.
Sztompka, P. (1999). *Trust: A sociological theory.* Cambridge University Press
Van Keuk, E., & Ghaderi, C. (2013). Dolmetschereinsatz in der Psychotherapie. In Reddemann et al. (Eds.), *Mehrsprachigkeit und Trauma. Zeitschrift für Psychotraumatologie* (Vol. 3/2013, pp. 37–45). Asanger Verlag.
Van Parijs, P. (2013). *Sprachengerechtigkeit.* Berlin: Suhrkamp.
Wagner, L., & Lutz, R. (2018). Internationale Soziale Arbeit zwischen Kolonialisierung und Befreiung. Eine Einleitung. In L. Wagner, R. Lutz, C. Rehklau, & F. Ross (Eds.), *Handbuch Internationale Soziale Arbeit. Dimensionen – Konflikte – Positionen* (pp. 7–20). Weinheim: Beltz Juventa.
Weber-Menges, S. (2005). Die Wirkungen der Präsentation ethnischer Minderheiten in deutschen Medien. *Massenmedien und die Integration ethnischer Minderheiten in Deutschland* (pp. 127–184). Bielefeld: Transcript.
Weidemann, A., Straub, J., & Nothnagel, S. (Eds.) (2010). *Wie lehrt man interkulturelle Kompetenz? Theorien, Methoden und Praxis in der Hochschulausbildung. Ein Handbuch.* Bielefeld: transcript Verlag. https://doi.org/10.14361/9783839411506
Ziai, A. (2007). Rassismus und Entwicklungszusammenarbeit. Die westliche Sicht auf den Süden vom Kolonialismus bis heute. In Berliner Entwicklungspolitischer Ratschlag (Eds.), *Von Trommlern und Helfern. Beiträge zu einer nicht-rassistischen entwicklungspolitischen Bildungs- und Projektarbeit* (pp. 12–19). Berlin: BER.

Cinur Ghaderi, Prof. Dr., Professor of Psychology in the Faculty of Social Work at the Protestant University of Applied Sciences (EvH RWL Bochum). She is Vice-President for Research, Transfer and Internationalization. After her post-graduate education in psychological psychotherapy (behavioral therapy), she worked in the "Psychosocial Centre for refugees" (PSZ) in Düsseldorf. She received her PhD at the faculty of Social Sciences of the Ruhr University Bochum. She is a member of the steering committee of DTPPP (transcultural psychiatry, psychotherapy and psychosomatics). Main academic interests: International

Social Work, Refugee Studies, Transcultural Psychotherapy, Psychotrauma, Identity, Diversity and Gender. She is the initiator of the DAAD-cooperation project CoBoSUnin 2016–2019 between the University of Sulaimani and Bochum. Contact: ghaderi@evh-bochum.de

Assumptions for International Social Work in the Kurdistan Region of Iraq

Luqman Saleh Karim

Abstract

The aim of this article is to reveal and present a brief history of globalization and the emergence of international social work; at the same time, it explores the opportunities and challenges through which international social work passes. Furthermore, it gives a brief overview of gaps and challenges in working with international organizations in the Kurdistan Region of Iraq (KR-I). It gives particular attention to the international exchange of knowledge, skills and experiences in order to create a common ground for international social work.

Keywords

Globalization • International social work • Indigenous social work • Kurdistan Region of Iraq

1 An Introduction to Globalization

Due to its interconnection between them, it is important to shed light on globalization concepts as an introduction to international social work. On the other hand, international social work can be regarded as a part of the process of globalization (Hugman 2010, p. 11). Globalization can be defined as a 'complex economic, political, cultural and geographic process in which the mobility of capital, peoples,

L. S. Karim (✉)
Düsseldorf, Germany
E-Mail: loqman.karim@univsul.edu.iq

C. Ghaderi et al. (eds.), *Social Work at the Level of International Comparison*,
https://doi.org/10.1007/978-3-658-30394-5_4

organization, movements, ideas, and discourse takes on an increasingly transnational or global form.' (Moghadam 2009, p. ix). This concept is manifested at times as social theory, at other times as a political ideology and last but not least as a status quo (Fadhli 2008, p. 22). There is a difference between 'global imagination' and 'global reality'. Global imagination is an old and ancient phenomenon and it is a component part of human imagination, while global reality – like political, social and cultural reality – is new and modern (Kanie 2012, p. 46).

The term 'globalism' was used for the first time in 1944, but globalization as a noun was used for the first time in a magazine in 1961 (Rauf 2009, p. 96). There are various forms of use of the term globalization: sometimes it is used to describe internationalization; in other usages, the word has the meaning of liberalization, that is, the removing of state limits and restrictions on movement among countries so as to achieve an open and integrated global economy. The third concept of globalization has been regarded as 'universalization' in the sense of widening things and experiences. Its fourth usage is the one which most people, especially critics of imperialism, use to define American-style 'globalization' and 'westernization' (Rauf 2009, p. 97). Most people using this meaning say that we are no longer fellow citizens of a specific city or country, but we live in global civilization (Daarder 2003, p. 498).

The United Nations was founded in 1945 after the Second World War. The Preamble to the UN Protocol opens with the words: 'We the peoples of the United Nations' (Hatam 2005, p. 33), thereby expressing its conviction of the equality of the nations of the world in their rights and duties towards humanitarian issues. One of the significant characteristics of globalization is diversity and interconnection among societies and countries that lead to the formation of various institutions in the world (Kamal 2007, p. 2) and shape life within the nations. This mutual life is not only to be seen in factories and financial markets which have become globalized, but also in political movements, women's organizations, children's groups, human rights teams, environmental activists. In brief, a global civil society is emerging that goes beyond borders and enters the respective geographies, shaping cultures, political visions, knowledge and diverse information (Kanie 2005, p. 26). This globalization is not without its problems, and it has some negative effects, such as rising joblessness, the pollution and destruction of the environment, ethnical, national and religious struggles and the distribution of drugs and addictive substances, the spreading of contagions and lethal diseases, including the current spreading of Coronavirus disease (COVID-19),[1] which is now recognized as a global contagion. All of this has revealed the truth that we have the same destiny and fate, and we are in the same boat. It has also revealed that no borders could have prevented this negative phenomenon. This new world and its challenges need new minds that have the ability to understand this new reality, its problems and how to deal with them according to the concept or paradigm: 'Think Globally and Act Locally' (Hatam 2005, p. 376).

2 Brief History of International Social Work

The history of internationalization in the social work profession is connected to the rise of social problems resulting from global interactions around the world (Estes, DSW 2010, p. 5). The interdependence of the world and the need for the development of international collaboration have necessitated the introduction of international concepts and global competence to the social work profession (ibid: p. 5).

Historically and in the initial stages, the international exchange of examples of social work forms moved from Britain to the United States of America, especially with regard to professional values of social work. This stage lasted from 1880 to 1940, the countries cooperating and collaborating with each other in this area. When the first international conference of social work convened in Paris in 1928, there were delegations from 42 different countries (Hugman 2010, p. 2). The next stage in the internationalization of social work lasted from the 1940s to the 1970s. This stage was called the professional imperialism stage. During this period, individual social work modules, social work with groups and organizing society moved from America to Europe, England and other places in the world. It was emphasized that harmful traditions and the local culture of the respective countries prevented the development of the profession (craft) of good practice in professional social work. American examples and models of social work were seen as paradigms to be imitated.

The third stage of international social work took place from the 1970s to the 1990s. During this stage, a revision and evaluation of western examples and models of social work was undertaken, and it was revealed that this paradigm cannot respond to the needs of social work in developing countries. International

[1] A pneumonia of unknown cause detected in Wuhan, China, was first reported to the WHO Country Office in China on December 31, 2019. https://www.who.int/emergencies/diseases/novel-coronavirus-2019/events-as-they-happen, accessed April 11, 2020.

social work became increasingly aware that local and traditional as well as indigenous knowledge together are essential for drafting theories and practice methods in particular (Lutz et al. 2018, p. 4), and the question arose of how to combine international social work with local social work. In the twenty-first century, the developing countries have realized that the western model in the area of clinical social work and methods of treatment somehow does not fit for developed countries and needs to be revised (Ali 2012, pp. 18–19). This long development of international social work means that international social work includes a variety of stages; however, there are many more fields than this, which Lynn Healy has condensed into the following main areas:

- International social work practice, which focuses on nationality and relationship with internationality.
- International professional exchange, for the purpose of concentrating on an international system, which urges professional exchange internationally.
- Collaboration between countries in which social workers exchange ideas or work together on projects that cross national borders.
- International practice of the social work profession (craft).
- Developing international policy concerning protecting human rights and securing heightened quality of life (Ali 2012, p. 198). Hugman also talks about an important area of social work which is
- Working with international organizations, such as INGOs, like the International Social Service (ISS) or Save the Children Fund (SCF) or UN agencies (Hugman 2010, pp. 18–20).

The intention of international social work is irreconcilable with egocentrism, ethnocentrism, and xenophobia, and is unable to do without 'compound eyes' or eyes from the outside (Akimoto 2008, p. 2). This leads to the fact that social workers are aware of global changes in social work as well as having critical vision and deep understanding of politics, social services, economic systems and practicing their profession (Ali 2012, p. 77). Finally, it enables the social workers to respond to the challenges of globalization, to confront the social problems of society and to have influence on social service issues and the quality of composing social care policy (Fahmi 2013, pp. 75–76). On the other side, international social work faces some challenges as listed below:

- There is no international curriculum in the social work area.
- Lack of international or global perspective for social work.
- Weak contribution of social workers in international activities and programs.

- The influence of international organizations in the social work area is not at the required level (Fahmi 2013, p. 84).

International social work with its chances and challenges creates the opportunity to understand international social work better, as well as dealing properly with it. At the same time, it is also considered as an opportunity to broaden perspectives and clarify general perceptions, so that it can potentially be a new window from which to view and understand the experience of developed countries better as well as how to respond to and solve local problems.

3 Gaps and Challenges in Working with International Organizations in KR-I

After most international organizations had come to KR-I, especially those working in the field of social work, i.e. working with internally displaced people 'IDPs' and/or the refugee and host community, providing multiple services to them, there were many gaps between the society and the services provided by international organization, as listed below:

- Most of the international organizations focused on providing psychosocial services, while most IDPs and refugees are in dire need of the provision of basic needs, such as foods and health services.
- There was often little understanding of the Kurdistan context, especially of legal enforcement, legal inconsistence and concentrating more on the role of law, especially with regard to gender-based violence issues, and ignoring the main role of subculture and local contexts that leads to social work having with less effect.
- Most of the international organizations offer their services to IDPs and refugees, and fewer offer them to the host community, even though the host community is in need of all types of services. As a result, this could lead to hostility and allergic reactions among all three components.
- Many of the international organization focus more on women and girls, while in a humanitarian setting men and boys also become vulnerable. As a result, this might be a type of gender discrimination.
- Few of the international organizations conducted research to understand the need assessment, but a large number of them offer programs and services according to funder agendas or desires. All these gaps mean that the services fail to meet the needs of the target group adequately.

References

Akimoto, T. (2008). What is international social work? Its contribution to social work in the global society. https://www.ash-berlin.eu/100-Jahre-ASH/symposium/akimoto.htm, PDF Version: https://www.ash-berlin.eu/100-Jahre-ASH/symposium/doc/3_5_akimoto.pdf. Accessed: 1. Sep. 2020.

Ali, M.A.A.-M. (2012). *New dimensions of international social work*. Alexandria: Al-Hadith University Office.

Fahmi, M. S. (2013). *General function of social work practical areas*. Alexandria: Al-Hadith University Office.

Fadhli, N. (2008). *Culture and university*. Tehran. Third Edition: No place of publication.

Gaarder, J. (2003). *Sophie's world*. Translated by Bahroz Hassan. Slemani: Sardam Publishing House.

Hatam, M. A. (2005). *Globalization*. Cairo: General Egyptian Board for Books.

Hugman, R. (2010). *Understanding international social work. A critical analysis*. China: Palgrave Macmillan.

Kamal, M. (2017). *Sulaimani. Philosophy of art*. Sardam Publishing House.

Kanie, M. W. (2005). *Nationalism and migration. Kurds in diaspora*. Slemani: Rahand Center, Ranj Publishing.

Kanie, M. W. (2012). *Identification and complicate, Sulaimani*. Andesha for Publishing.

Lutz, R., Sachau, I., & Stauss, A. (2018). *Border thinking*. Center of International Social Work (Working Papers 05–17).

Moghadam, V. M. (2009). *Globalization and social movements*. USA: Rowman and Littlefield Publishers Inc.

Rauf, L. (2009). *Third world and modern world through hint vision*. Slemani: Yanay Qalam.

Richard J. E., & DSW. (2010). United states-based conceptualization of international social work education. https://repository.upenn.edu/cgi/viewcontent.cgi?article=1185&context=spp_papers. Accessed: 1. Sep. 2020.

LUQMAN SALEH KARIM, Ass. Prof., Assistant Professor in the Social Work Department. He holds a PhD in Social Work from the University of Sulaimani, Kurdistan Region of Iraq. He was head of the Social Work Department from 2014–2017. He is a researcher and has conducted a large body of academic and organizational research on gender-based violence, environment policy, honor killing, child marriage, GBV assessments of needs, impact evaluation and COVID-19. He also worked with the United Nations Population Fund (UNFPA) and the Women's Refugee Commission (WRC) as a research consultant from 2018–2019, and as a child marriage research co-investigator in the Johns Hopkins University (USA); from 2016–2019 he was a University of Sulaimani coordinator of the DAAD cooperation project CoBoSUnin between the University of Sulaimani and the University of Applied Sciences in Bochum. Currently he works as lecturer at the University of Sulaimani, as a supervisor in the Khanzad women's organization, and as a research consultant for the Civil Development Organization (CDO). Contact: loqman.karim@univsul.edu.iq

Part II The Scientific Project CoBoSUnin

The History of the CoBoSUnin Project – Project Description from the Beginning to Realization

Cinur Ghaderi

Abstract

This article traces the history of the origin and development of the university cooperation project 'CoBoSUnin' (Cooperation between Bochum and Sulaimani Universities nowadays), an international collaboration in the Social Work Department of the EvH RWL and the University of Sulaimani (UoS). The project was funded by the German Academic Exchange Service (DAAD) from 2016 to 2019 with funds from the Federal Foreign Office. History, preliminary considerations, motivations, course and some challenges are outlined in this article.

Keywords

Project development • Cooperation • International dialogue • Higher Education

1 Introduction

How did it all begin? The description of the beginning has a subjective-personal and an objective-formal variant. The subjective beginning and its importance have different variations for different actors in this project: whether as an initiator, as a project leader, or as a lecturer, employee or student. During this journey of collaboration, more and more people have joined over time, have been hired or have

C. Ghaderi (✉)
Düsseldorf, Deutschland
E-Mail: ghaderi@evh-bochum.de

C. Ghaderi et al. (eds.), *Social Work at the Level of International Comparison*,
https://doi.org/10.1007/978-3-658-30394-5_5

been invited. The technical intensity increased steadily. The first year involved initiation, personal acquaintance and visits to practical institutions, while last year the focus was on organizing an international conference, publishing a scientific journal and publishing science-based books. The description of this quantitative and qualitative development from the beginning to the realization is the subject of this text.

2 Preliminary Considerations and Explanations: Why Such a Project?

2.1 Political, Academic and Disciplinary Considerations

The study course Social Work in Kurdistan-Iraq is a young subject under construction and has been at the University of Sulaimani (UoS) since the 2014/15 winter semester. The UoS was founded in 1968 as the oldest university in the Kurdish territory of Iraq. With around 24,500 students in eight faculties and two colleges, it is one of the largest universities in Kurdistan-Iraq. Social work has been and is more necessary in Iraq than ever before as a profession that is oriented towards the minimization of social inequality and human rights violations in a value- and needs-oriented manner and provides preventive and intervention knowledge. Iraq was and is in a volatile political situation with contradictory social developments: violence and patriarchal ideals are present in everyday life, at the same time freedom has developed and numerous civil society organisations have been formed. Further factors are the war with the so-called Islamic State, the consequences of the enslavement and ill-treatment of Êzîdî women and the murder of Christians and other minorities. These socio-political challenges such as violence, traumatization, (religious) fundamentalism, ethnicization, changing gender relations, flight and migration force the need for a professional discussion. These issues were not only perceptible in Iraq, but also of great relevance in Europe and specifically in Germany; they were 'closer'. In this context, the practice of social work raises questions about an appropriate attitude and practice in Iraq as well as in Germany. There was and still is a need for exchange in an international and intercultural comparative perspective. An exchange in teaching, research and practice on common topics, which are prominent in the fields of action of psychosocial work, seemed to be useful and necessary. Based on these considerations, the application was submitted by the EvH RWL with the intention of developing a long-term cooperation and exchange with the University of

Sulaimani. Both universities were interested in an internationalization of teaching and research with the aim of knowledge and competence transfer.

2.2 Personal Motivations, Views and Insights

As mentioned, personal motivations vary. Many perspectives at the beginning and in the course of the project can be found in the entire book as part of the evaluation or with direct individual or personal articulation. The beginning of the project depends on the motivation of the project leaders who have been involved since the beginning, so they are briefly presented here, specifically Cinur Ghaderi as initiator and project manager, Kristin Sonnenberg as second project manager and Luqman Saleh Karim as project manager at the UoS. For the initiator, it seemed obvious to synthesize the presumed need, the biographical connection, the institutional and technical possibilities. She formulates her memories of the beginnings as follows:

> 'I wrote down the beginnings of the project in my travel notes from 2015 when Germany became the heart of a refugee protection crisis. My trip to Kurdistan was in the spring, i.e. before the summer of migration. Since the complexity and speed of the impressions were barely tangible, this time I had taken a notebook to capture my thoughts. Although I had already travelled to my family's hometown several times, I spoke Kurdish and had been well informed in Germany about the formal possibilities of the DAAD, I only knew the president of the university from conversations on the phone. I had never seen the university from the inside and the customs were new to me as someone who is foreign-born but educated in Germany. What I had in mind was the will, as long as possible, not to let family and political relations play, but ideas, to let the thing work in itself, as an experiment against all the demotivating statements that I had heard from my surroundings: You can do nothing there, nothing works without corruption, nepotism in the parties. Fortunately, I met many people (in both countries) with whom a relationship of trust became possible as a basis for joint action'.

Luqman Saleh Karim, then head of the study programme at FB in UoS, recalls the first conversation in 2015 with these words:

> 'I remember that at UoS we had only reopened the department in 2014 and many things were still unclear. We had no experience, hardly any materials, we were not sure whether enough students would enroll in the next semester for social work, this still unknown subject. The visit from Germany gave me hope: Will we really be given international access? Will a window really open for new experiences and knowledge in the future? Are we going to travel to Germany and to the university in Bochum? But it was also said that the initial implementation would ideally take a year. In my heart,

I thought that if she only talks about next year, the conversation will not have a result. I was between anxiety and hope'.

Kristin Sonnenberg, too, looks back on the early days of 2015, when the DAAD launched the tenders for Iraq and the project was being considered:

'When Cinur asked me and told me about this project… I was curious, I wanted to learn in what was, for me, another atmosphere, because Iraq and Kurdistan are regions I don't know and I had no connection to. I thought it might be very important for me in rethinking German concepts and developing methods with which to learn and to develop intercultural competences.'

In the following, the individuals became a 'we', and we made the request. In 2016, the DAAD approved the proposed initiation project called 'CoBoSUnin' (Cooperation between Bochum and Sulaimani Universities nowadays). The genesis, or the prehistory at the formal level included the following steps: an official discussion with the then rector with the result of a letter of intent took place, followed by discussions with the faculty. During these discussions, common key topics for teaching and research were identified and, as the first concrete opportunity for collaboration, the EvH extended an invitation to participate in the International Forum at the November 2015 conference.[1]

The 'CoBoSUnin' project aimed – in the spirit of a sustainable development policy measure – to promote the knowledge society in Iraq by strengthening teaching and research at the Faculty of Social Work at the University of Sulaimani. The intention of the requested DAAD initiation project (2016) was to open up a framework for further discussions and opportunities for developing joint projects and to intensify and institutionalize these existing contacts in the context of the 'CoBoSUnin' project. This was done successfully, so that a follow-up application for 2017-18 was first submitted and approved, and finally an extension application for 2019.

[1] At the heart of the International Forum, which was held from June 2 to 5 at the EvH RWL, the question was raised of what significance - in a cross-cultural perspective – 'successful life' has as a guiding perspective in social professions. Cf. an article in the Journal for Women's and Gender Studies; see: https://doi.org/10.17185/duepublico/72446.

3 Project Progressions: CoBoSUnin I, II, III

3.1 The Initiation Project 'CoBoSUnin 2016': From Dialogue to Cooperation

This initation project had three main objectives: in the short term to analyze the supply of teaching material in order to explore the need for teaching materials and, if necessary, to identify the need for training materials, to optimize the training of students of social work by means of new teaching materials; in the medium term to promote the cooperation of the two universities in teaching and research to promote the processes of sustainable structural formation; in the long term to contribute at a socio-political level to the constructive dialogue of the participants.

In order to achieve the first short-term objective, reciprocal visits were carried out by members of the university. A first dialogue took place in April 2016 in Slemani. Students from both universities were also involved. The project partners on site had prepared a comprehensive and detailed programme, in which a variety of insights were possible: attending the teaching, discussions with lecturers and students, processes at the university and intensive workshops in which the curricula were compared and standards and methods in social work were discussed. In order to gain an insight into the practical fields, visits were made to facilities such as workshops for disabled people, a school for deaf children, a refugee camp, a prison, a women's house (Consolation Center) and the children's protection center of the NGO Save the Children Kurdistan.

The return visit of a delegation of teachers and students from the University of Sulaimani was hosted by the Protestant University of Applied Sciences RWL Bochum in November 2016. The members of the delegation were given an insight into practical social work. This was realized by means of a tour through the Rhine-Ruhr area and its fields of practice. The delegation dedicated a day of work to the Diakonie as a welfare association and visited facilities of the Diakonie Düsseldorf: a nursing home, a youth centre, the youth migration service and the refugee counselling. In Dortmund there was an opportunity to deal with the topic of poverty during a tour of the district in the Nordstadt; in Bochum they visited the drug counselling center, the emergency overnight accommodation and Pro Familia, and in Gelsenkirchen the prison. One focus was the integration of aesthetic education in the Social Work degree programme. These meetings and dialogues were not only informative and a good basis for long-term cooperation, but also strengthened the participants in the goal of continuing the dialogues on the theory and practice of social work and learning from each other from an international and intercultural comparative perspective. These efforts were then institutionalized through a

Fig. 1 Project Team in front of the UoS Presidency

five-year cooperation agreement / Memorandum of Cooperation (MoC) with the aim of establishing and expanding a long-term partnership between the EvH and the UoS.

Personal and professional dialogues led to an understanding of different developments in Germany and Kurdistan-Iraq, and the problems of the addressees of social work were contextualized historically, politically and culturally. In the workshops and during the practical visits, controversial discussions were held at both theoretical and practical levels. The first research projects were the visible first fruits of the commitment of the students. The openness of the rectors and deans and, above all, the commitment of the International Offices contributed to the success of this cooperation. By the end of 2016, we were looking forward to Act 2 of CoBoSUnin. The following picture (Fig. 1) shows the project team in its first year on the UoS campus.

3.2 The Follow-Up Project 'CoBoSUnin II': From Cooperating to Functioning

After the start-up phase, a core team of both universities was formed, consisting of the team of colleagues and the academic staff. The students switched. The criteria of belonging were qualification, interest and commitment as well as English language skills.

This core team worked on the objectives of the follow-up project defined by the DAAD: Improvements in the field of teaching, training and research at the partner institution, developing university management, modernizing higher education, promoting young researchers/students and networking. In addition, the presentation of an appropriate language concept was required[2], convincingly demonstrating how communication is ensured in the long term without the involvement of interpreters in the cooperation. During these two years, there were further meetings at both cooperating universities and the content work was shaped. The focus of this phase was on higher education in social work in order to explore opportunities for sustainable modernization. In concrete terms, the modules were compared in workshops on teaching analysis and commonalities and needs were identified. The lecturers of the UoS set their plans, measures, possibilities and limits with regard to: the enhancements and new concepts of the modules Gender, Gender and Violence, Ethics, International Social Work, Aesthetic Education, Advice and Practical Instructions. Mutual visits to teaching and discussions with students opened up new perspectives. Then the project teams of both countries started to plan and implement the further education and training opportunities.

During this project phase, various training courses were carried out on the module topics 'Consulting and Gender', 'Practical Support/Guidance', 'Introducing/Deepening into International Social Work', 'Aesthetic Education', 'Trauma-Sensitivity in Social Work' and 'Consulting Techniques in Practice Support/Guidance' in order to ensure the continuous further training of the Kurdish-Irakian teachers and, partant, the modernisation of the Iraqi higher education. At the same time, the formative evaluation process was initiated, so that the support for the implementation of the UoS curriculum expansion and revision could take place continuously by the EvH project team. The following pictures (Fig. 2) show impressions from the workshops and working meetings.

Creating networks was a permanent task. For this purpose, formal and informal opportunities have been created, e.g. with other interested colleagues at the EvH, the Women's and Gender Research Network NRW or with people from the field.

Research by the students was explicitly funded and supervized bi-nationally; opportunities for mutual field research on relevant issues were made possible, so that the research assistant was supported in her doctoral project, having previously completed her MA work on 'Gender-Structures in Comparison' within the scope of the project (cf. Dünnebacke 2018). The first cooperative scientific publication entitled 'Social work with refugees in Kurdistan Region in Iraq' (Ghaderi/Luqman 2019) was written during this time and further scientific publications were designed, such as an introductory book to social work in Sorani. The content, and formal and financial foundations were established for the planned International

---

[2] On the aspect of language in detail, see chapter *Postcolonial and transcultural glances on communication* in this volume.

Fig. 2 Work Impressions in Bochum (left) and Slemani (right)

Conference and discussions were held with representatives from the Rectorate, Administration, Practice, Teaching and Research.

3.3 Project Progression CoBoSUnin III: From Functioning to Producing

While the first three years of the project were more like a quiet, steadily flowing stream, the last year of the project extension saw a strong flow: work and travel density increased and the visibility of international cooperation increased.

There have been a number of important and sustainable measures. The project results were transferred via a public event on July 8, 2019, entitled 'Insights of Social Work in Kurdistan-Iraq - an international dialogue within the context of the project CoBoSUnin I-III in Bochum'. The following picture (Fig. 3) shows the Kurdish project members after their lecture in Bochum.

In addition to the core team, more and more colleagues from the Department of Social Work were able to take part in the project. They participated more visibly in the process of modernizing teaching and research, internationalization and networking than in previous years. Almost all faculty members took part with great commitment in the training courses offered on the topics 'Trauma sensibility in Social Work' and 'Counseling techniques in practice attendance/entourage'. They actively participated as authors in the book projects, in particular in the book Introducing Social Work in Sorani for UoS students, and they were actively involved in the International Conference and much more.

Fig. 3 Dr. Zhiya, Dr. Luqman and Dr. Niyan in Bochum, EvH

Throughout the year, intensive work from the project team and other stakeholders from both universities was required to prepare and implement the International Conference. Starting with the conclusion of the contract between the two universities on the tasks and responsibilities during the International Conference on October 21–22, 2019[3] on 'Social Work in post-war and conflict areas' – with the involvement of the further cooperation partner for the conference, the NGOs Haukari e. V. and Khanzad – up to the agreement on content, form and timeline for 'call for papers' and pre-review procedure of the submitted contributions for the conference (trilingual English, Kurdish/Sorani, Arabic) and finally the implementation of the conference. During the conference, the existing cooperation agreement between the two participating universities was delimited in order to give a clear signal that the partnership in teaching, research, promotion of young researchers, etc. will continue beyond the project period. The Commission will continue its work on the subject. The Figs. 4, 5 und 6 show Impressions from the conference.

Intensive press and public relations work accompanied and animated the entire course of the project: reports on the homepages of both universities, radio interviews in both countries, newspaper articles, press releases, in-house dialogues and information events on the project in both locations, and lastly a professional

[3] Conference report in German: https://www.evh-bochum.de/artikel/konferenz-cobosunin-team-schliesst-kooperation-ab.html; Kurdish: https://univsul.edu.iq/en/news/1968/34---u-u and https://univsul.edu.iq/en/event/1965/34; English: https://www.haukari.de/files/pdf/HAUKARI_KHANZAD_Invitation_Conference_SocialWorkOctober2019.pdf.

Fig. 4 Banner (left), Press conference before the start of the conference (right)

Fig. 5 Last consultations before the conference (left); Start of the conference with a minute of silence for war victims (right)

Fig. 6 At the Conference: Final Panel International Social Work

film documentation[4]. Intensive work was put into the publications, such as the contributions to the conference, which are to be published, and the textbook mentioned above. The objective of the textbook is to create materials that combine international and local knowledge, in a language accessible to the students, with the involvement of the faculty's lecturers, and with the inclusion of the modules of the UoS Social Work Curriculum (like International Social Work, Aesthetic Education).

4 Challenges

The fact that a 'success story' can be told here is one side of the coin. Certainly, there was always the other side of the coin, which required time and patience from all the people and institutions involved. The challenges often concerned communicative and political processes (see chapter on Evaluation). Purposeful and transparent communication on measures, actions and decisions at different levels within the project has formed the fundamental foundation for achieving the defined project goals. This would not have been possible without the willingness to be open, appreciative and willing to learn. Without the political contextualization, the activities carried out by the project cannot be classified. Because it was a turbulent political period, starting with the referendum (September 2017), the youth protests, Iraqi parliamentary elections in July 2018, then elections in the Autonomous Region of Kurdistan in September and presidential elections for all of Iraq in October 2018. These developments had an impact on the activities of the project at different levels: on the fundamental question of what sense social work makes in such a fragile situation, in which neither continuous study nor jobs and salaries are stable and the universities were temporarily paralysed, all the way to practical challenges, such as the feat of complying with visa requirements, which were at times tightened, without the state structures being able to cope with this requirement in Iraq or in foreign consulates.

There was repeated uncertainty with regard to when and from what airport of departure flights to both countries could be operated; at times the Kurdish airspace was closed. After a period of solidification and stagnation, the political process picked up speed again at the end of 2018, and the colleagues and students at the partner university spoke of cautious optimism in the region plagued by wars and

[4] A film documentation about the CoBoSUnin-project offers insights into social work in Kurdistan Region of Iraq and Germany. A Film by Ernst Meyer, SMIDAK Filmproduktion, Berlin: https://www.youtube.com/watch?v=wEkW9v51fps.

crises. The first signs of normalization were observed at the universities at the end of 2018. In the winter semester 2018/19, regular teaching and learning took place there for the first time in four years without interruption due to economic and political crises, strikes and salary losses. The politically explosive and unpredictable situation in Kurdistan-Iraq described here gave rise to challenges[5]. In the end, however, many goals could be achieved, including: publications, symposia, the international conference, cooperative research projects and, hopefully, a contribution to the international dialogue in social work and to the development of the subject of social work as a human rights discipline.

Cinur Ghaderi, Prof. Dr., Professor of Psychology in the Faculty of Social Work at the Protestant University of Applied Sciences (EvH RWL Bochum). She is Vice-President for Research, Transfer and Internationalization. After her post-graduate education in psychological psychotherapy (behavioral therapy), she worked in the "Psychosocial Centre for refugees" (PSZ) in Düsseldorf. She received her PhD at the faculty of Social Sciences of the Ruhr University Bochum. She is a member of the steering committee of DTPPP (transcultural psychiatry, psychotherapy and psychosomatics). Main academic interests: International Social Work, Refugee Studies, Transcultural Psychotherapy, Psychotrauma, Identity, Diversity and Gender. She is the initiator of the DAAD-cooperation project CoBoSUnin 2016-2019 between the University of Sulaimani and Bochum. Contact: ghaderi@evh-bochum.de

[5] On the aspect of uncertainty in detail, see chapter *Reflections on the Project* by Sonnenberg and Dünnebacke in this volume.

Evaluation and Results of the Scientific Research Project

Kristin Sonnenberg

Abstract

This chapter offers a broad approach to the scientific research of the CoBOSUnin project from 2016 until 2019. It covers the aims and the different levels of research questions as well as the planning of the formative evaluation in its different steps. In a second part, the methodology for the research instruments is laid down and explained. The third part introduces a summary of the results and their illustration followed by an analysis, interpretation and contextualization. A focus is set on the seven workshops conducted during the project.

Keywords

International cooperation • Research • Evaluation

1 Project Aims and Research Questions

CoBoSUnin was a research project aimed at professional exchange, development of curricula and an evaluation of the process. The main questions at the beginning were: How can professional exchange be successfully organized? What do both universities want to change or newly introduce? What can fruitful international cooperation look like? The aims of transferring knowledge and competence to

K. Sonnenberg (✉)
Bonn, Deutschland
E-Mail: sonnenberg@evh-bochum.de

C. Ghaderi et al. (eds.), *Social Work at the Level of International Comparison*,
https://doi.org/10.1007/978-3-658-30394-5_6

the science society in Kurdistan-Iraq and developing existing concepts in Bochum, Germany, can be structured like this:

1. In the short term: teaching analysis and exploration of the need for teaching materials to optimize the training of students of social work, to strengthen teaching and research at the University of Sulaimani (UoS) within the Faculty of Social Work and reflect upon existing concepts of teaching and research at Bochum Protestant University of Applied Science (EvH), that is, to work on concrete modules.
2. In the medium term: the promotion of cooperation between the two universities in teaching and research and the support of processes of sustainable structure formation. This includes intensifying internationalization at both universities and the promotion and encouragement of junior scientists.
3. In the long term: on a socio-political level, to make a contribution towards constructive dialogue between the parties involved and to support regional, national and international networking and dialogue.

During the project, a variety of measures were planned and realized to meet the targets. These and the means to reach them will be introduced in the next paragraph.

2 Methodology of the Research

The methodology of the research will be presented in two parts: first, the stages of the project with respect to milestones and their target clusters and, second, the concrete methodological approaches and instruments.

2.1 Stages of the Project – Detailed Targets and Milestones

As can be seen in Table 1, the four years are divided into three stages of the project in chronological order. Each of the three stages had a different financial application, different aims and tasks and different measures to reach them.

The first stage was called CoBoSUnin I. As an initiation phase, the first year in 2016 aimed at building trust in a cooperation, finding a team and themes for further exchange and collecting ideas for the main project. At the end of the first year, the evaluation concept was developed and laid the ground for the second application. This led to the second stage CoBoSUnin II, which is the core of the

Table 1 Stages of the Project (own representation based on project application)

CoBoSUnin I (2016)	CoBoSUnin II (2017 & 2018)						CoBoSUnin III (2019)
Phase 0	*Phase I*	*Phase II*	*Phase III*	*Phase IV*	*Phase V*	*Phase VI*	*Phase VII*
Beforehand	Planning stage	Evaluation of the situation	Workshops 1 & 2	Integration/ development	Transfer	Evaluation & analysis	Stabilization
March 1, 2016 until February 28, 2017	March & April 2017	May 13–22	July 20–29	Starting in August 2017	October 2017–April 2018	May 2018	2019
T 0 Initiation, analyze first data	Develop survey instruments	T 1 Formative evaluation	T 2/ 3 Interviews trainers 1st/2nd workshops	Implementation, review of material	Implementation in science and teaching	T 4 Analysis; outcome 'action plan'	T 5 Final evaluation, publication, new material, conferences in Germany and Kurdistan-Iraq

scientific evaluation as well as the concrete action within the project. It is subdivided into phases I–VI as can be seen in Table 1: We started with the planning (Phase I) and did a first survey to evaluate the situation (Phase II), and detected the needs in terms of content in the form of core modules for the project. Methods used were group discussions, brainstorming, a document analysis and comparison of the curricula of both universities. During the core evaluation and developmental part, we realized that we would not manage to reach stability and transfer within CoBoSUnin II. We therefore applied for a duration of one year to realize these goals. The application succeeded.

In 2019 the project reached stage three: CoBoSUnin III. This is described above as Phase VII 'stabilization'. We defined two milestones for this last period. For the first half of 2019, we planned the continuation of open processes such as finding two new students, continuing the evaluation processes of stage two, planning two events: one small conference in Germany in July 2019 and the huge international conference in October 2019 in Kurdistan-Iraq. The second milestone was the realization of the two conferences, the documentation of the conferences and the publication of the international conference in the official scientific journal of the UoS and two book publications at the beginning and middle of 2020 in the so-called 'stability phase'. A third milestone was added for reaching the goals of stability and transfer of knowledge: the production of a documentary film about the project that was finalized at the beginning of 2020.

The following target clusters were identified for CoBoSUnin II:

Target Cluster 1: Curriculum Social Work

1 Re-conceptualization and further development of the curriculum, BA studies of social work at the University of Sulaimani. Emphasis: working out the core modules:
   - current state; needs, wishes, concrete targets of further development within the project,
   - evaluation of the targets during the project (milestones),
   - evaluation of the process,
   - allocation of responsible lecturers for the modules and their content.

   Modules:

   (1) Gender Studies.
   (2) International Social Work.
   (3) Aesthetic Education.

(4) Counseling.
(5) Practical Skills (supervised experiences in practical fields, internships).
(6) Ethics.

Modules 1–4 were identified as important during CoBoSUnin I. An application to change the curriculum was submitted to the Ministry of Education in Erbil. It contained, for example, the introduction of a module called 'Aesthetic Education' as a new module, the integration of 'International Social Work' within an existing module and a revision of 'Practical Skills/Internship' as well as a revision of 'Counseling' as an existing component within the existing module of Psychology.

2. **Evaluation of Workshops and Training** (in Germany and Kurdistan; e.g. questionnaire for the trainers; group discussion/feedback)
3. **Developing (new) Teaching Material** in Kurdish (that fits the national, cultural conditions and knowledge within Kurdistan). *For further criteria see:* Graßhoff et al. 2016).
4. **Sustainability** within the university development.

Target Cluster 1 meets the first core aim: strengthening the teaching at the UoS. These targets were differently met, for example in introducing Phase III to conduct the concrete workshops for all participants of the project (Kurdish and German staff). The method of conducting workshops had been chosen as a good opportunity for learning and exchanging ideas together. The trainers had been asked to conduct the workshops in English and to use a format that combines theoretical input, practical exercises and time for reflection and discussion. The workshops should partly be carried out at the EvH and partly at the UoS. The experts were all suggested by the German team because they could use their networks as these topics already existed in German Social Work Studies.

A second important core aim was strengthening the networks around the UoS, that is, at local, national and international levels. To reach these goals, we developed Target Cluster 2:

Target Cluster 2: Networking

1 **Regional Networking: University with practical fields** (e.g. HAUKARI, center for families, training for practitioners without a university degree.)

2 **Regional and International Scientific Networking:** [international congress IFSW in Dublin 2018, Bochum, Essen, Berlin], Uni Sulaimani (interdisciplinary approach and exchange with the Faculty of Arts), Center for Kurdish Studies in Berlin, Germany.
3 **Interdisciplinary Regional Networking** with other universities: Dohuk — Center for Psychotherapy Studies, founded by the federal state Hessen, Germany; traumatized persons (Yeziden)

The method for achieving the targets described was the planning of a joint international conference with different actors (→ see the chapter *Project Description from the Beginning to Realization* by *Cinur Ghaderi*). Some of the conference contributions could already be published in English (Sonnenberg and Ghaderi 2021), another publication is planned for the Kurdish and Arabic contributions.

Such a project is ambitious and gives new insights into international cooperation. Consequently, we were interested in identifying the criteria for good international cooperation and thought of a third target cluster:

Target Cluster 3: International Cooperation
1 **Evaluation** of the international cooperation between Bochum und Slemani (e.g. language and cultural understanding), that could be based on the evaluation of CoBoSUnin I, II, III

2.2 Methodological Approaches

We decided on the methodology of a formative evaluation that allows changes and a feedback process during the project's duration. The main methods used within the evaluation were of a qualitative nature with a few quantitative data such as small scales for rating, for example for the quality of the workshops. The instruments applied were:

- *Evaluation rounds at the milestones of the project:* this systematically included all members of the project, especially within Phases IV-VI, at the end of each journey (that is 10 times; 2 × 2016, 3 × 2017, 2 × 2018, 3 × 2019), these were recorded and transcribed. The direct aim was a continuous project evaluation to analyze what aims and progress could be reached and what next steps are necessary. [Target Cluster 1]

- *Written standardized interview questions with internal project members as experts:* standardized questionnaires for process evaluation at the beginning of 2016 and at the end of 2019 with the possibility of drawing comparisons. [Target Cluster 1]
- *Analysis of documents:* changes within the curriculum: Emphasis on the above-mentioned modules and the overall themes such as ethics and gender, starting with a description of the current status, a definition of targets and an evaluation at the end. Targets should be measurable and as concrete as possible. Definition of criteria such as: What kind of material (lectures, notes) is used in May 2017? Is there something new in May 2018? etc. [Target Cluster 1]
- *Written standardized interview questions for trainers and workshop participants:* [Target Cluster 3]

The analysis of the interview transcripts and the transcripts of the team discussions followed the classical qualitative content analysis – with criteria and categories as described in the target clusters – deductively, as Mayring suggests, as well as inductively with the addition of new topics arising (cf. Mayring 2015). Additionally, the following steps of evaluation for international comparative research were applied (Friesenhahn and Kniephoff-Knebel 2011, p. 53; Graßhoff et al. 2016, p. 31):

1. Determination of the core item of comparison and the main research question aiming at empirical cognition: What will I compare exactly and why did I chose the comparison as a method?
2. Selection of relevant categories of comparison with regard to the research question.
3. Collection of country specific data and facts for a status quo and description.
4. Juxtaposition: comparison and systematization of data; finding of similarities and differences.
5. Interpretation of context conditions with regard to the core item of comparison, assessment of results considering the research questions.

The interest is in relating and checking for equality (congruence), similarity (affinity) and difference (discrepancy): ‘Comparing is thinking in relationships’ (Friesenhahn and Kniephoff-Knebel 2011, p. 37), so the aim of comparison is to work out similarities and differences between two or more systems or perspectives to be compared and to relate them to each other. These methods were applied mainly for the evaluation of the workshops.

The core interest was to gain specific insights with regard to mutual perception and learning processes, specific empirical findings to gain knowledge about conducting workshops within international cooperation. Another aim was to evaluate how satisfied the trainers and participants had been with the concrete workshops and to give feedback to the trainers. The following comparison options would have been theoretically available for the collected material:

- Identification of differences and similarities between the perspective of the trainers and the participants.
- ... between lecturers and students.
- ... between participants from Kurdistan and Germany.
- Evaluation of individual workshops (impression of all or group-specific).
- Overall view of the training courses conducted and the core findings, thematically bundled.

The decision was only to focus on the latter point, because the groups were really small. If there were interesting aspects that should be discussed due to different roles (being a student or German ...), this would be pointed out during the analysis.

In the evaluation, it should be noted that, with such a small number of participants, anonymity can hardly be maintained if such attributions are made and therefore this can only be done in individual cases with consent. It must also be borne in mind that the German project participants knew the trainers largely from collegial contexts.

The selection of categories will be introduced and explained in the next paragraph. These were the basis for the systematization and of the comparison (see presentation of the results).

In order to ensure a good standard of objectivity in the evaluation, 2–3 researchers did the systematization of the data independently (classification in categories as part of the qualitative content analysis), and compared and discussed the results before summarizing and interpreting the data. The data was rendered anonymous. Only one person knew the code. The data could in that case be traced back to the persons, due to the very small sample and the different languages (English and German) in which the answers were written. This has advantages and disadvantages. The advantages are a possible classification to the concrete perspective in relation to a national form or statement of a role (teachers, students) in the context of other nationally developed structures and patterns of action (Treptow 2006, p. 23 in Friesenhahn and Kniephoff-Knebel 2011, p. 37).

3 Results: Illustration, Interpretation and Contextualization

This section is divided into two parts: First the results to the main questions and aims of the project are presented, followed by a deep analysis of the results of the workshops in the years 2017–2018.

3.1 Results of the Main Questions and Aims

This paragraph offers a summary of the three main levels of aims.

(1) Short term: The aim of strengthening teaching and research at the universities and its realization within lectures and curriculum changes.
Workshops, expert interviews and analysis of documents formed a starting point to frame requirements and potential for development for modernizing the studies of social work at the UoS and reflect upon existing concepts at the EvH. At the beginning of the project in 2016, lecturers of both universities presented their curricula for the BA Social Work Studies. As a result, the Kurdish colleagues identified changes and a need for deepening the topics of International Social Work (Dr. Luqman), Gender (Dr. Zhiya), Counseling and Internships (Dr. Nihan). From the German perspective, the lecturers identified a need for an exchange on ethics of social work within an international comparison (Dr. Kristin, Dr. Cinur). International social work was a new topic for Kurdistan-Iraq as well as aesthetical education, which is a part of the social work curriculum at the EvH and was added as needing to be established at the UoS (Dr. Luqman). Concerning these chosen topics, both universities developed new concepts of teaching such as input, methods, literature. One focus at the EvH in Germany was discussing social work in areas of conflict and war, theoretical foci on postcolonial theories, and social work as a human rights discipline. Another topic was the integration of intercultural, transnational and international perspectives on social work within the existing curriculum. During the project there was an intense exchange and discourse with the group of lecturers and students from both countries, e.g. about what a global definition of social work means and whether it is possible to agree on shared standards (approaches, methods, theories) for social work as framing

concepts. A second group of workshops in Kurdistan-Iraq and Germany followed, to intensify knowledge bases, exercises and exchange. The workshops especially intensified the cooperative work of the bi-national team. The main results from the perspectives of trainers and participants can be found below.

With respect to the promotion and encouragement of junior scientists, there have already been joint BA theses and first empirical work based on comparative research supervised by lecturers from both countries in pairs of one Kurdish and one German supervisor. An MA thesis has been completed and published (Dünnebacke 2019) with the support for research in preparing a PhD, teaching and conducting workshops at the UoS.

It proved possible to realize this aim due to the changed and accepted curriculum of the BA Social Work Studies by the Ministry of Education in Kurdistan-Iraq. This has secured a sustainable structure within the Kurdish-Iraqi scientific landscape and can be applied within lectures (→ for more details see the chapter *Teaching Social Work in Kurdistan-Iraq* by *Luqman Saleh Karim and Cinur Ghaderi* in this publication).

(2) Medium term: the promotion of cooperation between the two universities in teaching and research and the support of processes of sustainable structure formation.

The strategies for international cooperation were discussed, analyzed and further developed at the university level, for example thanks to a structured dialogue between the international offices and the presidencies. The realization of two huge results – the international conference and the international book publication – is described in the following paragraph.

The next step was conceptualizing the new ideas arising for the existing curriculum (see above) and developing concrete measures for teaching, further cooperation, for example with the College of Arts at the UoS, and joint publications in the future. One aim was to publish a first textbook for social work in the Kurdish-Sorani language. This was realized in 2021. The book covers topics such as: an introduction to social work practice, theory and research methods; framing conditions such as law, ethical values and policy; a focus on central topics that are relevant for all fields of practice such as counseling, supervision and trauma; and a selection of practical fields: gender and violence, child and youth welfare, prison, empowering disabled people, working with refugees, school social work and drugs.

(3) Long term: socio-political level and the aim of supporting regional, national and international networking.
Exchanging knowledge, building networks, and integrating local actors to strengthen social work in Kurdistan-Iraq can be seen in the following central results: the international symposium in July 2019 at the EvH in Bochum; the international conference in October 2019 at the UoS in Slemani, involving, for example, speakers from different countries and disciplines, local actors and representatives from the Ministry of Education. Concerning the sustainability of the international cooperation, a documentation of the latter in the scientific journal of the UoS in 2020 along with a film documentation are facilitating the results of the conference at local, national and international levels. Last but not least, this book presents one result of the project in being a contribution within the field of international comparative research and discourse.

3.2 Results of the Workshops 2017–2018

The core research question was: What distinguishes successful workshops in international cooperation? What is special about workshops in an international context?

These are the coding instructions for the three researchers who analyzed the data:

a. Which topics occur more frequently per question or cluster? (multiple answers, identify topics that are repeated) [concrete level].
b. Which topics / responses stand out in the series? (especially interesting, surprising, deviant) [concrete level].
c. What was typical for the workshop? (1–2 sentences, if there is a particularity to be noted, special characteristic) [meta-level].
d. Is there something that stands out about all workshops? If so, how can it be explained? [meta-level].

A total of five workshops were held in 2017 and two workshops were offered in 2018 as internal training courses. The duration of the workshops was 0.5 – 1.5 days. Workshops W1 to W5 were conducted by external trainers. An overview can be seen in Table 2.

Table 2 Overview of the workshops held (own representation)

Code 1	Code 2	Topic/Title of workshop	Period of time	Number of participants and trainers P (T)
W1	F1, F2	Internships I	July 2017	8 (2)
W2	F3	Intercultural social work	July 2017	9 (1)
W3	F4	Counseling	July 2017	9 (1)
W4	F5	Aesthetical Education	September 2017	6 (1)
W5	F6a, F6b	International social work	September 2017	6 (2)
W6	F7	Internships II (methods)	April 2018	8 (1)
W7	F8	Trauma I	April 2018	6 (1)

The questionnaire contained the following questions and topics:

- I: Satisfaction with the workshop (question 1, see Table 2).
- II: Expectations (question 2) and their fulfillment (question 3).
- III: Surprising, unexpected moments that were experienced or observed (question 4) and their classification (question 5).
- IV: Perceived learning processes among oneself and the others (question 6a, 6b).
- V: Development needs identified on the basis of experience for the study program of social work in Slemani/Kurdistan (question 7) and Bochum/Germany (question 8).

3.2.1 Presentation of the Results: Description, Analysis and Interpretation

In this section, selected results of the surveys concerning the workshops will be presented for subsequent interpretation, evaluation and discussion. It is divided content-wise into sections called *clusters.*

As described within the theory and design of this research, the methods applied are of a qualitative nature. Three researchers from the project team analyzed the written material from the single workshops, the main themes and the focus questions. In a second step, the structure for discussing, analyzing and presenting the results was developed from the material and the feedback of the evaluators and at the end discussed again, to approve or disapprove the presented data in different steps of validation. The transcriptions of the seven workshops, the single qualitative coding and the summarizing process are not presented here; instead core quotations identified by the researchers will be given from the material as examples.

In this paragraph, the results will be described and discussed according to different kinds of results:

- Results that are related to a certain topic, that could be identified as core codes by all researchers or have been selected as results with an overall special significance.
- Results with regard to conducting workshops in an international context. In this case that means a group of participants from different countries, who, at the same time, are members of the research team.
- Results that are specific to one workshop. This last point was not of high relevance for the leading question and is neglected in this analysis.

The order of presentation of the results follows the structure of questions 2–8 and their cluster complex. The conclusion will be presented at the end.[1]

Cluster 1: Satisfaction with the Workshops

Cluster Complex I covers the overall satisfaction with the respective workshop. It also offers the possibility of comparison and provides information about the self- and external assessment of the overall satisfaction with the workshops. Two trainers did not fill in a sheet, so that no information is available there. The results can be found in Table 3.

The data in Table 3 shows that a high level of satisfaction was found in almost all workshops, with the exception of W5 on the topic of 'International Social Work'. W3 on the topic 'Counseling' and W7 on 'Trauma' achieved the highest value with a score of 9.8. For Workshop W1-3, the self and external assessments are very close to each other (or individually they deviate by one point even for W1). A deviation of 1 and 2 points is present at W6 and W7 (in one case more satisfied, in the other more critical).

Cluster 2: Expectation and their Fulfillment

The first two questions are condensed into Cluster Complex 2 (questions 2 & 3), offering the opportunity to learn more about the satisfaction of the participants using the example of one's own expectations and their fulfillment. This summary contains the analysis of all seven workshops.

---

[1] The abbreviations used are W = Workshop; P = Participant; T = Trainer.

Table 3 Satisfaction with the Workshop (own representation based on the evaluation results)

Question 1: How satisfied are you with these training days on a scale of 0–10? (0 = dissatisfied and 10 very satisfied)		
Code	Self-assessment of trainers	External assessment by participants, average
W1	10 and 8 (9)	8.9
W2	8	7.8
W3	10	9.8
W4	-	8.7
W5	-	6
W6	10	8.8
W7	7.7	9.8

Empathic attitude, openness, exchange and dialogue
The criteria of openness, openness of exchange, dialogue, of getting involved with each other and with all members was found in answers given in Workshops 1–5.

Knowledge and methods
The topic *knowledge* was named in the variation of knowledge sharing, gaining new knowledge, new ideas, new methods, concepts and learning about practical examples in all workshops (W1-7). Another focus was the development process and concrete ideas for profitable implementation (W1, W2, W3). Concerning more methodological answers, a combination and relation of theoretical and practical aspects was named (W6, 7) and the space given for reflection (W6).

Cultural aspects and language
Language was seen as an obstacle, especially in the first years of the project (W1, W2, W3 in 2017), as could be seen in answers from trainers and participants. As an example, the answers of one trainer can demonstrate this;

- 'that my language skills would not be sufficient to express everything that is important to me precisely and in a differentiated way' (T3)
- 'that the language skills of the guests would not be sufficient to enable a real exchange' (T3)
- 'that the guests and I would remain strangers to each other - less because of the linguistic, than because of the cultural and professional hurdles' (T3)

In this case, the trainer reflected that not all of her fears were realized:

- 'The positive expectations have been fulfilled throughout, the negative ones have not been fulfilled throughout.' (T3)

The expectations seem to be fully met in nearly all workshops, except W5, where they are partly met. The participants justify this with the openness of exchange:

- 'It was better than I expected and more useful. And we got more information from each other.' (P4/W1)
- 'The mixture of long experiences of T2 and the short and experiences of T1′ (P5/W1)
- 'I see all thing going well as I believed. I think now I have more experience than before and more than my teachers by the way.' (P6/W1).

Cluster 3: Surprising and Unexpected Moments

The results of Cluster Complex 3 open up the possibility of comparing surprising, unexpected moments and their classification (questions 4 & 5) and thus focus on the subjectively experienced.

Openness, reciprocal recognition
With regard to the frequency of certain topics within the contributions, there is a repetition of openness, reciprocal recognition, together with observations on discussions on an equal footing, described by one evaluator as 'mutual touching and recognition of professionalism; balance, experience with *another society* and constructive *university dialogue'*.

Methods and their meaning, exchange and language
Again, there are answers about methods and their meaning together with the topics exchange and language. With regard to language, there are different observations: positive exchange despite language barriers (fun, wit, fast, profound), e.g.:

- 'Image viewing [as a method, KS] was good to have a basis for phenomena, language does not have to be a hurdle; facial expressions, gestures, personality remain authentically conveyed' (P1/W2)

New are the words *courage* and *surprise* within the answers. Especially the latter was used in the context of language, e.g.:

- 'Everything is a surprise for me, but the big surprise is I don't know how, I can act by English' (P3/W3)
- 'That it all worked in English' (P9/W3)
- 'the English language of the speaker worked uncomplicatedly' (P9/W4)

Language was not a burden, which is described as a surprise, because none of the participants was a native speaker. The explanations are, for instance, the positive group dynamics within the project team (W3), openness, and mutual understanding (W4).

The assessment was very positive concerning the knowledge of trainers as very good, open and understanding the group, as well as the role of the participants and their willingness to contribute within the process of training: 'Professional and personal competence of the participants is essential for the success of transnational learning processes' (P9/W4).

Within Workshop 6, a reflection of the process of the project was included to introduce a specific method. This was recognized and described as the use of active methods to start professional exchange: 'It was really useful for me, because we could talk about our self and the project' (P4/W6) and it shows 'that the participants are a team with typical dynamics' (P9/W6). An important context factor has to be added: At that moment the context conditions of the project had been difficult (due to political circumstances), the energy was lost and that workshop has been a good intervention for opening the next stages of cooperation.

The answers to question 4 & 5 within Workshop 7 (and in some aspects Workshop 5) show the importance of the connectedness of topics offered by the trainers and the relevance for social work as well as the relevance for Kurdish society. This can be connected to the expectations (Questions 2 & 3) of gaining knowledge and expertise for development of the curricula and the introduction of new ideas.

Cluster 4: Learning Processes

The results of Cluster Complex 4 (Questions 6a & 6b) are about learning processes that were perceived personally, but also by other participants or trainers. The results can be summarized as:

Self-reflection, learning processes

Self-reflective learning processes were on the level of relevance of changing perspectives, making new experiences, challenges and chances of a pioneer status, reflection of clichés, to explain oneself to the other and to make one's own perspective plausible. Other answers focused on concrete learning process, e.g. supervision and counseling or the role of emotion in learning processes. The answers show an interest in exchange and openness amongst participants.

Knowledge and methods

Learning processes depend on new, creative methods (example of picture cards), the relevance of the topic, the personality of the lecturer or trainer as well as the honesty of the individual and the effects of representation. An internal and external factor was identified in balanced learning processes with regard to cognition and emotion. Some participants described processes of expansion of their consciousness.

An obstructive factor was identified: Educators who do not respond to participants generated anger, annoyance and frustration. This illustrates the need for a careful selection of external trainers.

Cultural aspects and language

Cultural awareness was described among the participants and towards cultural differences:

- 'Going with the process of the group is always a good decision, it needs more attention with a foreign language (…)' (T7)

The foreign language was addressed as developing in a positive direction during the project to safe handling.

The following perspective is interesting and relevant for both aspects of learning: 'You cannot and should not always classify and analyze everything' (T6b), there was understanding within the group that there is not a single true concept of international social work that is transferable, but that examination of the contextual space and time is necessary.

Cluster 5: Needs for Further Development

Cluster Complex 5 (questions 7 & 8) contains development needs, which could be proposed on the one hand for one's own study program and university, but also for the other university. The results can be summarized in the categories of content-related issues, conclusions and new perspectives.

Citations of content-related discussions include concrete ideas, suggestions and measures as well as a perception of the other university, curriculum and persons. Most of the answers were reserved and avoided suggestions with regard to one's own expertise on site. Representatives of both universities identified further education and training needs.

It also became clear that different concepts are used, for example in the practical internships. Some terms could be identified which have different connotations for representatives from the two different countries: reflection, case, client and grass-root movement, the difference between local and indigenous. The exchange about this was valued and described as enriching.

With a view to the future, there was a suggestion to develop joint research questions and to combine international experience with local experience.

The Iraqi-Kurdish colleagues provided the following specific answers and recommendations:

- 'Iraqi art is very rich, you might benefit from it' (P5/W4)
- 'expand the module [intercultural social work, KS] and add more international knowledge, e.g. Kurdish local experience' (3 similar versions of the statement in W2)

These answers point to greater cooperation and awareness with partners from the Middle East. Another special observation was that some Kurdish colleagues finished their questionnaire with a 'Thank You' to the trainers.

3.2.2 Conclusions

A rich variety of results was presented in the previous paragraph. In this chapter, the conclusions are presented, structured according to the core coding. This is done in full knowledge that these are not strictly delimitable from each other, but that there are overlaps and connections.

(1) Conclusions with respect to openness, exchange and dialogue

It seems that a basic fundament and a necessary precondition for international cooperation – and, in this case, joint workshops and training for a project team – is an empathic attitude on the part of trainers and participants. Openness and reciprocal recognition as well as mutual understanding lay the ground for successful learning processes and cooperation.

Openness and reciprocal perception also includes making each other's motivation and interests transparent and supporting each other in achieving the goals.

This can be described as not only empathy, but also as strategic exchange relationships, for example each time a little trip to other cities, countries, etc. was planned and realized from both partners.

One possible recommendation would be to plan the training within a project following the phases of group dynamics, to take into consideration the group process and influence it in a positive way. Maybe – although that would be different in character – supervision and counseling for the project team should be included in the process.

(2) Conclusion with respect to knowledge, methods, trainers and participants

With respect to the trainers, their personality, skills and experience were clearly identified as positive factors. At the same time, the results show how one workshop proved unsatisfactory because of the strongly hierarchical attitude of one external instructor; this led to a negative atmosphere and silence amongst the participants. A careful selection process for trainers is important.

The role and personality of participants and trainers are important. One researcher put it as follows:

- 'It was very obvious who had said what, beyond Kurdish, German, teachers, trainers. The answers are often mirrors of the attitude of the people, their typical thinking and language game and they put their stencil on the situation, workshop, they judge, so I believe that personal aspects are also very relevant.'

(3) Conclusion with respect to language, cultures, special observations

At the end, one question addressed the impulses that can be found for development at both universities. The Kurdish project members sometimes made suggestions for the German context, but more often they instead thanked the trainer in this section. This raises open questions for which there are different interpretation options: Are the colleagues too polite to give recommendations? Is it a kind of special awareness? Would it be impolite to give suggestions or critical feedback? Maybe the aim of the question was not clear? A discussion about this with the Kurdish colleagues would be needed to validate these interpretations.

The findings also reveal variations in self- and external images. In 2017, one statement listed amongst the expectations was: 'We need any information from a country like Germany to be a source to our project' (P5/W1) and, a few months later that same year, the suggestion was made of integrating more from the rich Kurdish culture into the German curriculum.

An interesting aspect was the surprise of one trainer that the conversations could be on an equal footing, because of the quality of the questions and the second statement about the fact, that *they* (the Others) are on the right track:

- 'I am positively surprised by the quality of the questions and contributions of the participants. These were conversations on eye.' (T2)
- 'I suspect that they have perceived that they are on the right track.' (T2):

Even if this seems like an empathic description, from a researcher's perspective a paternalistic evaluation is possible and, if this is taken to mean a standardization of German knowledge as orientation, it should be critically reflected. Who says or decides what is the right way or track?

Besides this, there are many indicators to show the cultural awareness among the participants and among trainers and participants. This is a central aspect to keep in mind for international training and cooperation.

It had been decided to use English as the working language for the project. Some colleagues had to train their skills during the project and participated in English language courses. This was a very good decision, because at the beginning English was described as a barrier and hurdle. During the project, the participants talked about the language in the context of various questions and showed surprise, relief and pride that they were able to use the language successfully. Another phenomenon is that, as of the beginning of 2018 (the third year of the project), all members wrote in English and translation was no longer needed during the discussions.

(4) Conclusion with respect to the realization of the workshops

Creative methods and openness on the part of trainers and participants as well as a careful observation of group dynamics lay the ground for constructive dialogue, which should be one important goal. With regard to different preconditions of the participants, it should be taken into consideration that teaching methods might differ. Additionally, due to cultural awareness, extended times and space for exchange are needed. This values professional exchange and the combination of cognition, emotion and action-based methods, as well as recognizing the fact that the exchange in another foreign language needs more time and is more exhausting.

Concerning the framing conditions, it is important to recognize that all of the project members participated in the workshops, although the students did vary. Two German lecturers from the project team offered a workshop themselves. This decision was mainly made topic-wise. The three Kurdish lecturers who stayed within the project until the end instead took responsibility for a seminar lecture that was attended. The participating students held presentations on their BA topics. Four workshops were offered by lecturers from the EvH, one from another German university. These decisions were made because of their given expertise and context. With a reflective distance, a consideration for a new concept could be to share the responsibility of offering a workshop amongst all project members.

With respect to power relations, there were observations of power disparities between countries and positions (lecturers to lecturers and lecturers to students); sometimes this illustrates emotions such as uncertainty and pride. For international training, workshops and cooperation social and power-sensitive competences are of high relevance.

(5) The project team as a learning group

The joint participation within the workshops was an asset with regard to positive group dynamics and developing a stage of intense cooperation and trust. The project members, in this case the participants of the workshops, gradually grew into a learning group. This can be shown with different references to psycho-social group dynamics within the workshops and the time spent together in the four years of the project. For example, in Workshop 3 on counseling in July 2017, the trainer strengthened the trust in processes and the group grew together. It was a good process through a combination of the speaker's personality, setting preparation and the group dynamic aspects from contact to trust phase. Courage to take part in the processes and cultural diversity also played a role. That was already referred to before as the personality and attitude of participants.

The participants trained and developed skills in interacting intercultural sensitivity by working together as a learning group.

Another important combination of workshop and project process was made in April 2018 in Workshop 6, when the reflection and evaluation of the project with respect to one's own role was chosen as a topic to work with.

Final remark

The success of transnational learning processes, the technical and – at the same time – the personal competences of the participants are of significant importance. There is certainly a need for preparations for seminars, but the fact that actors in this field must be flexible and process-oriented in every aspect seems more important.

References

Dünnebacke, L. M. (2019). *Soziale Arbeit in Kurdistan-Irak und Deutschland – ein Vergleich am Beispiel von Genderstrukturen. Empirische Zugänge im internationalen Dialog. Gender Studies – Interdisziplinäre Schriftenreihe zur Geschlechterforschung*, Band 32. Verlag Dr. Kovac: Hamburg.

Friesenhahn, G. J., & Kniephoff-Knebel, A. (2011). *Europäische Dimensionen Sozialer Arbeit*. Schwalbach am Taunus: Wochenschau Verlag.

Graßhoff, G., Homfeldt, H.-G., & Schröer, W. (2016). *Internationale Soziale Arbeit. Grenzüberschreitende Verflechtungen, globale Herausforderungen und transnationale Perspektiven*. Belz Juventa: Weinheim, Basel.

Mayring, P. (2015). *Qualitative Inhaltsanalyse. Grundlagen und Techniken*. Beltz Verlag: Weinheim, Basel.

Sonnenberg, K., & Ghaderi, C. (Eds.). (2021). *Social work in post-war and political conflict areas*. Wiesbaden: Springer VS.

Kristin Sonnenberg Prof. Dr., Professor of Social Work at the Protestant University of Applied Sciences Bochum. She studied Social Pedagogy in Germany, completed an M.A. in Comparative European Social Studies at the University of North London and her PhD at the University of Cologne in Germany 2004 in the Faculty of Educational Science. She is a qualified psychodrama trainer. Since 2011 she is specialized in the field of methods and conceptualizing social work. Her main research projects are social inclusion of people with disabilities and international social work. She is member of the German Association of Social Workers (DGSA). Since 2016 she has been head of the BA Social Work Studies and, together with Prof. Ghaderi, she was leader of the DAAD cooperation project CoBoSUnin 2016–2019 between the University of Sulaimani and Bochum. Contact: sonnenberg@evh-bochum.de

Analysis of the Results of the Bi-National Project from the Point of View of the Lecturers

Cinur Ghaderi

Abstract

A special feature in the research design of the CoBoSUnin project was a focus group discussion of the project team at the end of 2018, in which four core categories were identified: experiences and expectations, personal and professional learning processes, institutional change processes, and the assessment of the benefits, opportunities and risks of the bi-national cooperation project. The results after conducting a semantic content analysis are presented in the following article.

Keywords

International exchange • Intercultural learning • Lecturers´perspective • Focus group • Evaluation

1 Introduction

Within the framework of a structured focus group (Bär 2013, p. 155) the members of the project team were interviewed in terms of four main content categories. Specifically, the main content categories were: (a) Experiences and expectations, (b) Personal and technical learning and change processes, (c) Institutional change processes, (d) Evaluation of the usefulness, opportunities and risks of the

C. Ghaderi (✉)
Düsseldorf, Deutschland
E-Mail: ghaderi@evh-bochum.de

C. Ghaderi et al. (eds.), *Social Work at the Level of International Comparison*,
https://doi.org/10.1007/978-3-658-30394-5_7

bi-national cooperation project. Methodically, focus groups prove to be an elaborate but effective method for evaluating a complex cooperation context such as that of the CoBoSUnin project, which is why they were also carried out as part of the evaluation. The special feature is the active design of the content by the respondents, since there were four core questions related to the main categories, but no prefabricated items and these are only addressed by their articulations. This leads to a high relevance of the results of focus groups compared to questionnaire surveys. The statements were recorded, transcribed and subjected to a semantic content analysis. In the following, the results are sorted according to the main categories. The group interview was held on November 12, 2018 in Bochum with five members of the project team. In the following, the participants of the Focus Group are coded as P = Participant 1 to 5.

Pre-experiences and Expectations The first main category dealt with the previous experiences and, if necessary, the associated expectations of the work in the project. These previous experiences in international contexts were very different and vary from no experience up to 18 years of continuous experience, accordingly the expectations were varied. The Kurdish colleagues used the word *'dream'*[1] and *'the dreams transferred to reality'*,[2] especially based on the experiences of other international contacts that were not sustainable (*Because many people visited us and promised so many things...specially on international level. But they come and take some photos and...after this you don't see them ever again*[3]). Another general paraphrase was *'experience'*, which led to development, expansion and added value at different levels. Concrete learning and development processes will be identified on the basis of the new experience.

2 Personal and Technical Learning and Change Processes

Personal Development and Maturation Processes Learning takes place primarily through new experiences that allow differentiation (*You imagine some pictures or situations. But when you see them in real life you discover the detail*[4]). Through

[1] P 1: 1; P 2: 2; P 3: 3; total of 12 citations.

[2] P 1: 2.

[3] Ibid.

[4] P 4: 7.

access to other spaces, international mobility allows you to develop your own self (*I get more awareness*[5]), by looking at yourself from a different perspective (*The difference has opened my eyes*[6]). One respondent formulated, *This project looks like a mirror to see myself. Like an introduction theory if you want to see yourself and from the others.*[7] Another respondent confirms with similar words, *That's a real mirror if you ask the people from other countries about your own...while you are explaining there are so insides about your own actions and ideas.*[8]

There was much to be observed: that the handling of time and organization can vary, that age does not have to be an obstacle to development and that there can be no advance in the international context without a common language, usually English. (*I learned that I have to start a new life and I have to learn English. The age is no problem.*[9]).

While the German colleagues learned that development is also possible without permanent exhaustion and self-exploitation, a Kurdish colleague says: '*By comparison, I've seen how actively you work, despite all your fatigue. We were in a depressive political phase. And that gave me the drive to just say again: Okay... the exchange has given me strength*'.[10] Another respondent formulates similarly with the words, '*When I see you at the first time how optimistic you are that totally changed my life...You are so optimistic after the experiences of the Second World War, you took me to a museum for the Second World War. How people write something to be more optimistic...to lose that bad experience from war. I learned from this perspective to be more optimistic...So from this it was a big step that changed me.*'[11] Here, the international exchange and debate seems to have had positive effects, even in the sense of psychological hygiene. The prerequisite for all learning processes and active participation in the project is, as was pointed out repeatedly, openness and curiosity.

Profession-related Competence Enhancement Specialist, methodological, conceptual and scientific learning processes are mentioned several times.

---

[5] P 5: 11.
[6] P 2: 8.
[7] P 1: 10.
[8] P 3: 17.
[9] P 1: 10.
[10] P 2: 7.
[11] P 1: 11.

The concrete curriculum and the skills in teaching are changed and improved; new didactic competences are acquired, which are described with 'enjoyable and animated teaching'[12] and learning; the extended understanding of oneself and meaning motivates and, instead of blunt knowledge transfer, 'enthusiasm'[13] is added.

Intercultural and Transcultural Competence Development Distance from regional, linguistic, cultural and political points of view is seen as a challenge, but above all as a gain: by *'rethinking concepts and develop methods to learn and to develop intercultural competences'*,[14] which, in a regional comparison, would not be possible to a similar extent. *'It is very important to reflect your own methods in the process and that's easier if you have a totally different perspective then just comparing it from one local area'*.[15] Learning by comparisons and with a foreign or outside view of one's own self and context continues to educate. It allows learning from and through the different structure of the different higher education system and political system that affects the framework conditions of social work (welfare state aspects, curriculum content, communication, etc.). At the same time, not only are intercultural differences crystallized, but also transcultural similarities of the themes of social work. Over time, a professional collegiality and closeness develops (*'We became a family. We come clear and clear and now we make our international perspective about this project'*[16]; *'opportunity to make a friendship and professional relationship'*).[17]

This includes understanding the importance of knowledge (*'I learned politics and society and history is very important'*[18]; *'I even more now think that a background to know something about the history of the country you will visit is very, very important. And in addition, the actual political situation'*[19]). The most unpleasant social blunder[20] situation that led to this finding was the question of a German student in the plenum, *'Ahh, please, can you tell who is Saddam?'*.[21]

[12] P 2: 8.
[13] P 2: 7.
[14] P 3: 5.
[15] P 3: 17.
[16] P 1: 2.
[17] P 2: 11.
[18] P 5: 12.
[19] P 3: 8.
[20] German word: ‚Fettnäpfchen'.
[21] P 3: 9.

One learning experience was that people become strategically or unintentionally representatives of their group or institution (*'skills to develop is...being a representative, I learned to represent the German university in another country. That was quite new for me.'*).[22]

Learning Effects Through Duration of the Project The key factor in development is time and energy, considering the duration of the project. Short-term visits could not have produced the effects and results by far (*'I benefit much...on the scientific level,...and specially because it's such a long cooperation...I never experienced a cooperation that stay so long in an international level...and I think this is a very 'wertvoll' [valuable] and a fact that we have this and with this and have some dreams for the future.'*[23]). This longevity and activity of the team with visible results influenced the assessment that this is not about *'dreams'*, *'not just hope, but there is a transformation'*,[24] that plans can be developed and implemented (*'I hope more...I have idea about postgraduate and PhD for cooperation between the two universities'*).[25]

Another factor is that, in self-monitoring one's own development, further steps and an increase in self-confidence and self-confidence are possible (*'I compare myself about the travels, every case I change, have more skills, get to know me better and learn about it; make better teaching, my relationship with students and lecturers changed'*).[26]

Expanded Possibilities and Areas of Action Through International Mobility and Networking The certificates, the learning of the English language, the proof of international cooperation experiences: these have all yielded further benefits for the participating lecturers in Kurdistan. This makes them attractive to organizations operating internationally in Kurdistan, gives them expert status for specific topics and enables them to take on assignments that they previously did not receive as 'locals' (*'So many international organizations, said...you participated so much and in my CV it's not local, you are international and that makes me to participate. Making some research, working with UN agency totally changes our life...That's*

[22] P 3: 8.
[23] P 3: 5.
[24] P 1: 2.
[25] P 4: 3.
[26] P 2: 11.

not diplomatic speech, that's the reality.'[27]), i.e., the local connection to the international labor market has improved, which clearly leads to competitive ideas among colleagues in a politically fragile country where the self-evident nature of monthly salaries has long since become a gamble.

The visibility as experts with know-how and international experience leads to a domino effect, so that the participants of the project in each case – locally, binationally and, partly, internationally – were perceived and/or recognized and their professional networking increased. The latter also applies to lecturers in Germany, as their perception as experts increases and inquiries, for example, they were invited to give lectures.

Institutional Change Processes The question of the institutional change processes, according to which a project of this kind triggers a structural change in an institution such as a university, was answered in a differentiated way. At the level of the university management and the students, the project was instigated and supported, while at the collegiate level the reactions were ambivalent between interest, admiration and competition and envy. These reaction patterns were similar in both countries.

On a content level, the activities of the project led to changes in modules or new modules, and in Kurdistan for the implementation of completely new modules (*'Academically you can see our colloquium is changing'*).[28] The changed teaching is verifiable formally on the one hand, and informally through the teachers on the other. From their point of view, the participating lecturers have learned a lot, which would also benefit the students (*'We learned about skills, ...I put it totally in my workshops'*[29]: *'The students' perspective, I think...that was very good for them and special experiences and still we implemented the topic. So, I think they will have experiences for seminars like 'social work in crisis region' and we can develop more seminars to participate them'*[30]).

---

[27] P 1: 14.

[28] P 1: 10.

[29] Ibid.

[30] P 3: 15.

3 Assessment of the Usefulness, Opportunities and Risks

The evaluation of the possibilities, limitations and usefulness of such international collaborations, using the example of the experiences with the CoBoSUnin project, was the last category on which the project team expressed itself in the context of the focus group.

'I think it's more than sense. It's necessary for all...universities.'[31] Thus, one of the respondents argues and justifies the sensitivity on the one hand with globalization, on the other hand with the fact that development is only possible through intercultural relationships and cooperation (*'If you don't have any knowledge about the other society, about the academic level, how you can progress yourself?'*).[32] At the same time, the alienated view from the outside is not enough, local knowledge is just as relevant (*'Make a balance between the local and the global and the international experience'*).[33] The opportunities for international dialogue are seen in the following: *'Opens your thinking and you will get impulses'*[34] and this leads one *'to develop social work in a more global sense'*.[35] In addition, meaningfulness and opportunities can be seen in the profits: conference, publications, professional exchange of one country in the pioneering phase and one with a long history of social work.

The following points are assessed as risks: (a) projects of short duration, as they are not sustainable; (*'Just a short cooperation and visit and there is no sustainability'*),[36] (b) issues of financial support and attention to Euro-centrism (*'We got funded of a German or Euro-centered finance...good balance in processes'*[37]; *'Where the financial support is coming from because is always a political question and what the financier wants to have. Because they have conditions and then the teams have conditions'*)[38]; (c) language (*'Language can be a challenge'*)[39] and (d) the possible deficiency of inter- and transcultural competences.

---

[31] P 1: 17.

[32] Ibid.

[33] P 4: 18.

[34] P 3: 17.

[35] P 3: 18.

[36] Ibid.

[37] P 5: 18.

[38] Ibid.

[39] P 3: 18.

4 Concluding Thoughts

The results collected here are in part identical to those of Kruse (2018, pp. 80). Thus, the effects and returns are manifold, direct or indirect, in relation to the travelers involved or also to the fields of work and structures of social work (ibid, p. 88). Based on Thomas et al. (2007, p. 129), they can be differentiated between the mosaic effect, the domino effect, the turning point effect and the nice-to-have effect as a 'pattern of biographical integration'. Domino and turning point effects were observed among the respondents.

The researchers divide the effects into self-related, intercultural and sector-specific, action-oriented competences (ibid, pp. 133–140; Kruse 2018, p. 89). The role of distance, which has been dealt with more geographically and culturally here, and contributes 'to gain a new view of one's own self, to reflect implicit assessments of attitudes of systems' (ibid, p. 92) is supplemented by the aspect of time-out in the country of origin, and thus 'self-care, psychological hygiene and, to some extent, burn-out-prevention' (ibid, p. 90).

A typical development, which was still in its infancy at the time of the survey, and which is now becoming clearer, is the further development of knowledge in further international cooperation and projects and the increased joint commitment to specific issues of social work, in this case critical knowledge production of social work in the Kurdistan Region in Iraq and social work in post-war and conflict regions.

References

Bär, G. (2013). Wissenschaftliche Begleitung, formative Evaluation und partizipative Forschung. *Prävention und Gesundheitsförderung, 8*, 155–162. https://doi.org/10.1007/s11553-013-0397-y

Kruse, E. (2018). „Erst der Vergleich öffnet … die Augen". Internationaler Austausch in der Sozialen Arbeit. In Wagner et al. (Hrsg.), *Handbuch Internationale Soziale Arbeit* (S. 80–97). Beltz-Juventa.

Thomas, A., Chang, C., & Abt, H. (2007). *Erlebnisse, die verändern. Langzeitwirkungen der Teilnahme an internationalen Jugendbegegnungen*. Göttingen: Vandenhoeck & Ruprecht.

Cinur Ghaderi Prof. Dr., Professor of Psychology in the Faculty of Social Work at the Protestant University of Applied Sciences (EvH RWL Bochum). She is Vice-President for Research, Transfer and Internationalization. After her post-graduate education in psychological psychotherapy (behavioral therapy), she worked in the "Psychosocial Centre for refugees" (PSZ) in Düsseldorf. She received her PhD at the faculty of Social Sciences of the

Ruhr University Bochum. She is a member of the steering committee of DTPPP (transcultural psychiatry, psychotherapy and psychosomatics). Main academic interests: International Social Work, Refugee Studies, Transcultural Psychotherapy, Psychotrauma, Identity, Diversity and Gender. She is the initiator of the DAAD-cooperation project CoBoSUnin 2016–2019 between the University of Sulaimani and Bochum. Contact: ghaderi@evh-bochum.de

Challenges in International Cooperation—Reflections on the Development and Research Project CoBoSUnin

Kristin Sonnenberg and Lisa Marie Dünnebacke

Abstract

In this chapter we will reflect upon the *CoBoSUnin* research project (Cooperation between Bochum and Sulaimani Universities nowadays) from the perspective of two German project members without any experience in the Middle East. A special focus is laid on questions of safety and stability in instable regions. We report as *profisor u mamostai kari komaliayeti* (professor and scientific staff for Social Work Studies) in Germany. We will introduce the main challenges divided into a section on 'safety and reliability in instable regions' and a section on 'supposed secureness is getting unsafe'. We will finish with a third part introducing the solutions found for these challenges within the project.

Keywords

Instable regions • Challenges • International cooperation • Higher education

K. Sonnenberg (✉)
Bonn, Germany
E-Mail: sonnenberg@evh-bochum.de

L. M. Dünnebacke
Schmallenberg, Germany
E-Mail: l.duennebacke@outlook.com

C. Ghaderi et al. (eds.), *Social Work at the Level of International Comparison*,
https://doi.org/10.1007/978-3-658-30394-5_8

1 Challenges Part 1: Safety and Reliability in Instable Regions

At the beginning of the project, there were a lot of practical questions about travelling for the first time to Kurdistan-Iraq and about whether we could suppose it to be a secure travel:

- How can we apply internally at the university? How do we get insurance for overseas? Where can we fly from? Can we travel directly or with transit flights? Do we need a visa and, if so, how can we get it? Who could provide support? And will we be given permission to fly? Is Kurdistan-Iraq a secure region?

The answer concerning security can be found in the official evaluation of the German Ministry of Foreign Affairs. In 2016, at the time of the first application for the project, there was—and there still is—an official warning regarding travel to the Kurdistan Region of Iraq. In 2016, the recommendation form within our university was to meet in Turkey in case of trouble. Because of political changes in Turkey, however, that option did not last long. Things became dangerous for scientific cooperation. As a university, we still have a restriction on travelling to Turkey.

As an example of changing conditions, and of where supposed and experienced safety changed, we can refer to the visa processes and the flights accessible during the four years of the project. In 2016/2017, direct flights from Düsseldorf to Slemani were conducted only with a guest visa at the Kurdish airport, and this was our standard procedure for three of the trips. In September 2017, the Referendum was conducted for an independent Kurdish state. One of the reactions of the central government of Iraq was to issue a set of restrictions for the Kurdish Region. Part of this involved the cancellation of all international flights from Kurdistan to the outside world. Luckily, we caught the very last flight from Sulaymaniyah International Airport back to Düsseldorf. In 2018 there were no direct flights anymore. Added to this, an official visa process was introduced with the embassy and the central government in Baghdad. We nearly did not fly, due to political circumstances as described above. We got permission just one week before travelling. In 2019, direct flights with a guest visa were once again possible.

A second aspect was gaining knowledge and the question of what information to trust. What picture did we gain? What did we think about the information? Is it true? In 2015 and 2016, the pictures we got from the media in Germany included burning oil fields and destroyed cities, tanks and armed military, ISIS fighting (Islamic State of Iraq and Syria also known as IS or Daesh). The reaction of families, friends and colleagues was one of anxiety, worries and doubts about travelling. Eager to start our project, we sought further information. We decided to believe the firsthand information given by our Kurdish colleagues and to trust our partners and their expert views on the region. They assured us we could travel safely and be in no danger with them in the Kurdish Region of Iraq. They told us it was one of the safest regions in Iraq.

2 Challenges Part 2: Supposed Secureness is Getting Unsafe

One example we mentioned already is connected to the Independence Referendum of 2017. This showed that political stability can change very fast. This is due to the dependency on the central government in Baghdad, which has a lot of power over the Kurdish Region and might introduce restrictions like cancelling all international flights. A second important power relation is the pay system and the control and distribution of wages for state-related jobs. In 2014/2015 the Kurdish regional government declared that it wanted to sell the oil independently and as a result the central government cut the budget of the Kurdish Region.[1] This is a good example to show the effects of political influence, because the wages changed a lot within the four years from 2016 until now. They ranged from 70% every three months to 10% irregular payment and no payment at all to phases of stability and 100% wages and back again to financial crisis with no payment or irregular payment.

Comparable to the system of the federal states in Germany, the Ministry of Education in Erbil, the capital of the Kurdish Region in Iraq, is responsible at the federal level. Just as in Germany, political influence is a given factor with regard to persons in important positions such as the presidency. This could be a person who is eager to develop studies in terms of content or it could be that these are important strategic political administrative positions. This would seem to have a more marked effect in states with fragile political structures. The effects can hit the structure and content or even the very existence of studies.

Within our bi-national team, and especially for us as observers with our external German perspective, we asked ourselves:

[1] For example see report by Dmitry Zhdannikov (2015): Exclusive: How Kurdistan bypassed Baghdad and sold oil on global markets. Reuters. November 17, 20,152:46 PM; https://www.reuters.com/article/us-iraq-kurdistan-oil-idUSKCN0T61HH20151117. Accessed 21 October 2020.

- From a lecturer's perspective: Working without wages—Would I do it? Could I do it or would I need another source of income?
- From a student's perspective the question arises: Will there be lectures today? Should I go to university?
- Imagine not getting paid for your work. What would university look like? How would you estimate your motivation?
- Imagine a situation in which the central government of your country or, more precisely, a certain political party has the power to decide at any moment to close your university or to close your faculty.
- Imagine you have developed an excellent curriculum, which is acknowledged by the Ministry of Education, and other universities in your country follow your example.
- Imagine you are part of a project that, against all expectations, lasts longer than a year and will end with a joint international conference and a publication.
- It is all possible.

These questions refer to concrete situations, challenges and framework condition that our Kurdish colleagues faced during the project. As a next step, we now introduce a few solutions we developed with which to continue cooperative work in spite of challenged stability and secureness.

3 Solutions Part 1: Trust, Reliability and Sustainability

We are very happy—and this is indeed a special situation—that the project had a duration of four years. Looking back, the first year was successful in building confidence and trust in each other and laid the ground for our joint cooperation. The first steps included the initiation phase, for example the inclusion of deans and presidencies. Both parties were convinced that this is more than an exotic adventure. The second phase in year 2–3 aimed at reliable working structures. Even in crisis situations (e.g. no wages, no visa, no direct flights, protests and demonstrations), the project continued, because both partners had something they wanted to go for. At the practical level we set up cooperative structures between students and lecturers from both countries. The last phase in the fourth year was planned for laying a sustainable foundation. This means strengthening local players by including them in the International Conference in October 2019, Slemani, Kurdistan Region of Iraq.

A second focus was widening the cooperation by involving more staff members of the Faculty of Social Work and other social sciences. We prepared the international conference together, a lot of lecturers and researchers offered lectures or workshops, and a conference paper will be published. The lecturers of the Social Work Faculty are editors (all project members) and authors (everybody was invited) of this publication. Another special outcome is the first textbook for Social Work Studies in the Kurdish language Sorani.

4 Solutions Part 2: Fragmentary Solutions

If we reflect on the question of why we have been successful, there are three important points we identified and recommend as a strategy:

- Seek factual and pragmatic solutions.
- Keep a high level of flexibility and uncertainty in mind in planning.
- Seek strategic solutions.

To give examples, we always thoroughly prepared the weekly schedules of the meetings we held two to three times a year. In the end, however, they changed a lot due to external influences. We learned to act pragmatically and flexibly and changed the plans to conform with what was possible. Sometimes in the space of a day or just within minutes.

If you have to include different players such as colleagues, NGOs, local networks and institutions, this can be realized at different levels. Within the project, we provided workshops and training, concentrating, for instance, on counseling methods, which is one module within the BA Social Work Studies in both countries that we wanted to work on. Our Kurdish colleagues were asked for lectures, workshops and cooperation within the region. This leads to wider networks. At the level of BA Social Work Studies in both countries, a new curriculum was confirmed by the Ministry of Education. Modules of international and intercultural social work were influenced, as well as the structure and content of internships.

Not to forget, at its core the project aimed at reflecting and developing the education of students in both countries. This is to prepare them for dealing with situations of ambiguity as well as social and political crises. In this sense the project was successful, especially in its facilitation of hope and motivation.

Kristin Sonnenberg, Prof. Dr., Professor of Social Work at the Protestant University of Applied Sciences Bochum. She studied Social Pedagogy in Germany, completed an M.A. in Comparative European Social Studies at the University of North London and her PhD at the University of Cologne in Germany 2004 in the Faculty of Educational Science. She is a qualified psychodrama trainer. Since 2011 she is specialized in the field of methods and conceptualizing social work. Her main research projects are social inclusion of people with disabilities and international social work. She is member of the German Association of Social Workers (DGSA). Since 2016 she has been head of the BA Social Work Studies and, together with Prof. Ghaderi, she was leader of the DAAD cooperation project CoBoSUnin 2016–2019 between the University of Sulaimani and Bochum. Contact: sonnenberg@evh-bochum.de

Lisa Marie Dünnebacke, M.A., B.A. in German Philology and Comparative Education' (2010); M.A. in Social Inclusion (2014). From February 2017 to December 2019 she was scientific associate and lecturer at the EvH, Bochum, and a freelance Social Justice and Diversity trainer. Since January 2020 she has been Head of Education in the Martinswerk e.V. Dorlar child and youth service near Schmallenberg in the Upper Sauerland District, parallel to which she has been preparing her PhD thesis [projected thematic focal point: masculinity constructions in Kurdistan-Iraq]; Contact: l.duennebacke@outlook.com

Part III Teaching Social Work

Teaching Social Work in Germany

Kristin Sonnenberg

Abstract

The aim of this article is to give an overview about teaching social work in Germany. It starts with a small historical approach to the beginnings of teaching professional social work in general and more specifically at the EvH. After this, the aims and structure of the studies will be introduced, followed by the standard curriculum. For Germany, this is based on European, national and professional guidelines and standards of education. This includes core topics or recommended modules and different levels of education, starting from the BA level (academic education). In a final section, current challenges will be considered.

Keywords

Teaching • Social work • University • History

1 The History of Teaching Social Work …

1.1 … in Germany

As there is a variety of publications on the history of social work and teaching it in Germany, this chapter gives a summary of the major points that have been explored by a range of writers. In Europe and North America, three women are

K. Sonnenberg (✉)
Bonn, Germany
E-Mail: sonnenberg@evh-bochum.de

C. Ghaderi et al. (eds.), *Social Work at the Level of International Comparison*,
https://doi.org/10.1007/978-3-658-30394-5_9

important in pioneering work at the national and international level: Alice Salomon, Mary Richmond and Jane Addams. They travelled a lot, exchanged views, developed concepts by crossing borders. Within the history of social work in Germany, Alice Salomon laid the groundwork of the professional education, theory, methods and practice of professional social work: 'In 1908 she transformed the annual classes of the 'Groups' into the first German regular school of social work and became president and teacher of the school. In 1909 she became Corresponding Secretary of the International Council of Women (ICW) and was from now on in contact with the leading women in many different nations like Jane Addams, Lady Aberdeen, etc. (Salomon 1936).' (Kuhlmann 2008, p. 130). This first school of social work was founded in Berlin. After a hundred years of history, the University of Applied Sciences in Berlin still honors this, as it is named after Alice Salomon. In Germany, two world wars influenced the development of social work. After the first of these, the professionalization of social work was intensified. Salomon was very active in promoting the profession as Kuhlmann describes it, naming some of her most important roles and publications:

> '(…) Salomon's work proved crucial for the formation of the profession of social work in Germany: she founded and became president of the National Association of Schools of Social Work (1917–1933), she founded and became president of the 'Academy for Social and Pedagogical work of Women', the first post graduate school for social work (1929–1933). During this time she wrote many textbooks for social work, for example 'Introduction to Welfare Work' (Salomon 1921), 'Introduction to German Society: economics, state, social life' (Salomon 1922), 'Social Diagnosis' (Salomon 1926a), 'Social Therapy' (Salomon and Wronsky 1926b), 'Education for Social Work' (Salomon 1927). In the early thirties she started a family research project about the economic and social value of the work of women in the family (Salomon 1930a). In 1928 Salomon was asked to take over the chair of the division on social work education during the International Congress of Social Work in Paris.' (ibid.)

Social work until World War II can be described as follows:

> 'In Salomon's concept of social work understanding of the social conditions of the underprivileged class is crucial. Knowing about the unjust economic system social work can no longer be a kind of charity but has to be defined as a human right. In contrast to other theoretical approaches of that time in Germany, which defined social problems as being purely of an educational nature (Nohl 1919) or as a question of a personal lack of the abilities to adapt (Klumker 1918) Salomon emphasises the responsibility of the economical and political system' (Kuhlmann 2008, p. 132)

To react to these social problems, Salomon developed an approach of teaching social work that included two different sets of methods or areas of responsibility, material and personal. Material tasks can be finding and arranging of money, creating a network for relief actions and changes within the environments, in the sense of adapting the 'external circumstances to the needs of the client' (p. 134). Personal tasks are empathy, professional distance and empowerment, a very central assumption is that 'the main method to change the lives of clients is to encourage and enforce their will, to 'free their energy' (Salomon 1926a, p. 5) best by help for self-help.' (Kuhlmann 2008, p. 135). After World War II, these ideas were re-imported from other countries such as the US, because German scientist had to flee from Germany, they were killed in concentration camps, and the social welfare state was abolished for most of the clients and actors. Many of Salomon's central ideas are still to be found in recent curricula of social work studies.

1.2 ... at the Protestant University of Applied Sciences Bochum

The Protestant University of Applied Sciences in Bochum (EvH) was established in 1971. According to Kuhlmann,[1] it has four predecessor institutions. The *first* was a curative education course from Bethel initially as a postgraduate course, the *second* was the Social Work Social Women's School of the Westphalian Women's Aid in Bielefeld, Gelsenkirchen and Bochum, which had existed since 1927 and was officially recognized as a welfare school in 1928. Margarete Cordemann was the director until 1954, followed by Sigrid Willemsem. The *third* was the social education department, social pedagogy, which originated in diaconia Kaiserswerth in Düsseldorf, a Protestant charitable organization in Germany that had been active in the social, health and educational sectors since it was founded in 1836 by Pastor Theodor Fliedner and his wife Friederike.[2] Unmarried women could learn a profession in nursing and educational work there. At the same time, they lived together as deaconesses and developed a strong community of faith, life and service.[3] As of 1947, there had been a seminar for youth leaders, which in 1966 became a vocational school (college) for social pedagogy with a three-year

---

[1] Prof. Kuhlmann is an educational scientist at EvH. Together with her colleague Prof. Franke-Meyer she conducts historical research for preparing the jubilee of 50 years University of Applied Sciences Bochum in 2021. The information I refer to, are from the first steps of this research.

[2] https://www.kaiserswerther-diakonie.de/de/ueber-die-kaiserswerther-diakonie/ueber-die-kaiserswerther-diakonie.html, accessed April 7, 2020.

[3] https://www.fliedner-fachhochschule.de/die-hochschule/ihre-hochschule-aus-guten-gru enden/geschichte/, accessed April 7, 2020.

training course. The *fourth* predecessor institution was the department of community pedagogy that also derived from Düsseldorf. From 1961 onwards, there was also a seminar for catechetics and parish services in the building in Bochum, at that time still known as the Evangelical Social School Gelsenkirchen/Bochum.

All these were united in 1971 to form the Protestant University of Applied Sciences Bochum (EvH) with different departments and courses of study. The EvH is the largest protestant institution of higher education in Germany. At present, there are more than 2400 students registered and pursuing qualification for professions in the social and healthcare sectors, church educational work and diaconia. Approximately 1400 of them are taking a BA in Social Work. The studies begin twice a year in the winter and summer semesters with around 200 new students, or a total of 400 each year. The EvH is a state-accredited university of the protestant churches in Rhineland, Westphalia and Lippe. It participates in the Protestant educational mission and at the same time knows how to assign itself bindingly to the public education system. Its teaching, further education and research is geared to the problems and needs of the social and health care system, the social welfare service and church education work. In 2007 and 2008, five Bachelor's and two consecutive Master's programs were introduced at the EvH RWL. One of them is the BA Social Work, which is the successor to the Diploma Studies of Social Work.

2 Current Scientific Implementation and Framing Conditions

The BA Social Work study program enables graduates to practice professionally in the vocational field of social work. This includes relevant scientific basic knowledge, methodology, theories and models. The program comprises a systematic foundation of knowledge about societal contexts, patterns of human behavior, development and perception of people in current social environments. It includes an understanding of professional ethics, enabling the graduates to practice in a socially responsible, reflective and value-oriented way. Graduates have a wide scope of knowledge and abilities which enable them to work in a variety of sectors within the field of social work, and to evaluate and reflect this on the basis of their academic education. The studies train skills and abilities in communication, self-reflection and creativity, as well as presentation techniques. The official duration of this full time program, the standard period of study, is three years and leads to 180 credit points (ECTS). The study program includes practice placements of 100 days, which are supervised by teaching staff. The access requirements to study BA Social Work at EvH Bochum are a German General Higher Education Entrance Qualification or Advanced Technical College Entrance Qualification or comparable qualifications gained in other countries, playschool teacher examination and sufficient specific vocational experience. Students gain a first higher education degree of professional qualification. The Bachelor's degree is a professional qualification for entry to leading functions in social institution. The Bachelor's degree provides entitlement to enter a consecutive MA program.

The program requirements and qualification profile of the graduates are in line with the guidelines of the Standing Conference of the Ministers of Education and Cultural Affairs of the federal states of Germany (KMK), the BA course in Social Work aims to provide a broad foundation of specialized knowledge, to enable the student to acquire professional competence in social work practice and to develop method skills both in the field of overall key qualifications (such as project management or empirical social research) and in the field of soft skills (such as self-management or teamwork abilities). The central skills and fields of knowledge to be conveyed by this course can be summarized as follows (Tab. 1).

Table 1 BA Social Work Competence Matrix (own representation based on the modul manual of Social Work at the EvH RWL Bochum)

BA Social Work: Competence Matrix	
Professional Competence	
Knowledge	**Skills**
Familiarity with the latest theoretical and empirical interdisciplinary research. A critical understanding of theories, principles and methods referred to in the BA course. A multi-dimensional knowledge of the field of social work practice and related areas	A wide range of methods to deal with complex aspects of research and social work practice. The ability to face unknown or uncertain demands of intervention responsibly and with accountability
Personal Competence	
Social Competence	**Individual Competences**
Using available professional skills for social work practice. Working productively in interdisciplinary teams, shaping efficient work processes in leading positions, and achieving responsible outcomes. Working in expert committees to analyze complex problems, striving to develop a common solution and supporting it assertively	A critical multi-perspective assessment of self-acquired knowledge and its application on social work practice. Engagement in setting targets for learning and working processes and defining these constructively. Critical self-reflection and profound evaluation of the results of learning and work processes

The curriculum of this BA course is divided into five module blocks. The course begins with the foundation modules 1.1–1.6 in the first and second semesters. In line with the professional profile of Social Work, these modules focus on the acquisition of professionally appropriate research-based foundations in terms of core knowledge and of fundamental understanding. In the third and fourth semester, the focus turns to social work practice. The relevant modules 2.1–2.2 (practice placement/ field studies) serve to provide an introduction to specific work situations so that students can acquire key professional skills. After having become familiar with professional practice, the students in the third module block focus on interdisciplinary demands. They explore options for multi-perspective interventions, studying generalist modules on social care management and law, education and culture, counseling and treatment as well as the intercultural and international dimension of social work (modules 3.1–3.4). The fourth module block covers professional know-how and contextual skills as well as skills of intervention and evaluation which are the basis for professional work practice tailored to clients' needs. The modules 4.1–4.8 focus on concrete fields of work practice. Finally, in the fifth module block, students have the opportunity to learn ultimate key skills through critical academic study (BA thesis). These are prerequisite for the development of a deep sense of professional identity and for a successful career start.

An exemplary study plan can be seen in Tab. 2. Within a counseling context, alternative study plans can be developed that are adapted to the circumstances of the students.

Table 2 Exemplary Study Plan, Version Starting in Winter Term 2020/21 (own representation based on the modul manual of Social Work at the EvH RWL Bochum)

No	Module	Semester/ Credits (ECTS)					
		1	2	3	4	5	6
Module Block 1: Foundation							
1.1	Introduction to scientific work and methods of empirical social research *3 seminars/ 6 h*	6					
1.2	Introduction to the basics of social work *5 seminars/ 10 h*	12					
1.3	Human and social science basics *4 seminars/ 8 h*	12					
1.4	Politics/ law/ social management *5 seminars/ 10 h*		12				
1.5	Ethics *2 seminars/ 5 h*	6					
1.6	Arts education and media literacy *3 seminars/ 8 h*		12				

(continued)

Table 2 (continued)

No	Module	Semester/ Credits (ECTS)					
		1	2	3	4	5	6
Module Block 2: Principles of social work practice							
2.1	Practice phase and reflection *1 seminar/ 2 h, 100 days of internship*			36			
2.2	Professional action/ practical workshop *2 seminars/ 4 h*			6			
Module Block 3: Fields of interdisciplinary intervention							
3.1	Social management/ law *4 seminars/ 8 h*			12			
3.2	Education, training and culture *4 seminars 8 h*			12			
3.3	Counseling, support, pastoral care *4 seminars/ 8 h*			12			
3.4	Intercultural and International Social Work *4 seminars/ 8 h*				12		

(continued)

Table 2 (continued)

No	Module	Semester/ Credits (ECTS)					
		1	2	3	4	5	6
Module Block 4: Settings of social work practice = compulsory elective learning area (*2×3 seminars/ 2×6 h)*							
4.1	Child and youth welfare					6	6
4.2	People in the second half of life						
4.3	Addressees of social work in social problem situations						
4.4	Health, disability, diversity						
4.5	Criminology and assistance to delinquents						
4.6	Social and professional policy and representation of interests						
4.7	Diaconal work						
4.8	Church community education (approaches and concepts)						

(continued)

Table 2 (continued)

No	Module	Semester/ Credits (ECTS)					
		1	2	3	4	5	6
4.9	Church community education (target groups)						
Module Block 5: Professional identity in academic study and social work practice							
5	Bachelor Thesis *2 seminars/ 4 h*					18	
	Total credit points	30	30	30	30	30	30
	Total study hours	22	25	2	20	16	16
	Total examinations	3	3	1	3	2	3

3 Objectives, Plan of the Department

The contents of the course of studies as well as the forms of teaching and learning follow objectives that are based on the concretizing EvH guidelines. These are, for example: an understanding of education, which integrates professional skills, ethical, political and aesthetic reflection and personality development; the Christian image of man as a gift and task for shaping individual and social humanity; diversity, inclusion, interculturality and internationality as dimensions of the professional self-image; scientific orientation and scientific pluralism as well as the linking of teaching and research and the development of theory and practice and communication and cooperation, participation and systematic evaluation as well as continuous quality improvement.

The higher education development plan is of supplementary relevance for the design of the study program. Strategic objectives are laid down for a period of four years and are part of the university development plan, and they are also linked to the vision and mission statement. The current period lasts from 2017 until 2021. These form the framework for the objectives of the study programs of the university. For the Social Work degree program these are:

- reflection on the relationship between theory and practice and the theoretical location of the understanding of the profession in the course of studies
- evaluation and further development of practical support
- intensification of existing cooperation with practice, with the aim of conducting more local/regional excursions and internships
- reflection on the self-conception of the core subjects of social work in relation to the reference sciences
- reaction to current social developments, e.g. in the field of social work and the social sciences
- strengthening of existing competences in teaching and research on diversity and inclusion, taking into account aesthetic education
- international orientation of studies

4 Challenges of the Social Work Departments

In describing the more recent past, there were important developments starting in the 1990s. At this time, a relatively new topic was approached and was critically discussed in Western Europe: User involvement and quality management within the social service sector. Firstly, quality management was introduced as a control mechanism with the aim of achieving better quality. Secondly, there was a need to evaluate users' perspectives on social services, following new laws. But user participation was achieved in a relatively indirect way. There was an explanation or broader development to be discovered in Germany and UK connected to the introduction of quality management, namely so-called *neoliberalism* and *consumerism*. At this time in Great Britain and the United States, a phenomenon arose called the *McDonaldization of Social Work*, in other words a tendency towards standardization—Everywhere you go, you will get the same services—and it was very critically observed.

Around 2010, there was a rise of the *case management* method as a more technical approach, focusing on control rather than on a broad resource-emphasis method for the client in his or her living environment. This method was broadly implemented in Germany, and it has many positive aspects, but there is a need for critical reflection as well concerning, for example, the misuse of words such as *responsibility* and *empowerment* to defend restrictions arising from the state's withdrawal from offering social support to vulnerable people.

Present social work theories focus, for example, on human rights and empowerment. One example is Hans Thiersch, a German professor of educational science. He developed a certain way of approaching clients focusing on their living environment. The key idea is that subjective well-being and individual constructions of life have to be recognized and valued. The client is seen as an expert for his or her life. This started in the 1980s, and continues until now. Another theory that is discussed is social work as a human rights profession, deriving from Silvia Staub-Bernasconi, a Swiss professor with a systemic approach to social work. This is politically influenced by the current implementation of the Convention on the Rights of Persons with Disabilities from the year 2006 that was ratified by Germany in 2008. This shows the demand of developing participative methods, in practice and research, for all countries that ratified the convention. It strengthens social work as a human rights profession and delivers new impulses for social work. The possibilities of broad user-involvement and participation, in the field of living and social inclusion for example, using new media such as computers and internet are new and important research fields. Research is to be intersectional and should include participatory approaches. For the social work professions, this means an even stronger focus on what is stated within the international definition of social work. It means a consistent way of realizing social justice. At the same time, ideas have been forthcoming on evidence-based practice, activating concepts and on the state reducing support in times of financial crisis and cutbacks, all of which will challenge social work and welfare states in the next decades.

Current topics in Germany are a lack of skilled employees and educated professionals, especially in the care and youth sectors.

At the EvH, we try to promote professionalism and academic training. We offer two Master's degree courses and participate in programs for a PhD in Social Work. In Germany, only universities have the right to offer PhD courses. The universities of applied sciences have fought successfully for cooperation in some states and have been successful in obtaining the right to offer PhD courses independently in one state.

As a result of the Bologna process, the study program has been reduced from four years plus an additional supervised year for state acknowledgment to three years of studies in many European countries. Most of the universities and universities of applied sciences in Germany joined the process. This is an ongoing challenge, because it reduces the time to study. The practical fields, mainly state-run agencies, sometimes offer mentoring programs for those beginning in working life.

New financing programs are challenging teaching and education. The universities of applied sciences experience the ambivalence between high quality education and the money they *earn* for fast and in-time educational processes. In Germany, an increasing number of private universities are offering BA studies in social work, and there might be more competition to get students in the following years, which follows the paradigm of a mainly economical focus.

Reference

Kuhlmann, C. (2008). Alice Salomon. *Social Work & Society, 6*(1), 128–141. https://www.iassw-aiets.org/wp-content/uploads/2017/07/Alice-Salomon-Germany-President-1929-1946.pdf. Accessed 7 April 2020.

Kristin Sonnenberg, Prof. Dr., Professor of Social Work at the Protestant University of Applied Sciences Bochum. She studied Social Pedagogy in Germany, completed a M.A. in Comparative European Social Studies at the University of North London and her PhD at the University of Cologne in Germany 2004 in the Faculty of Educational Science. She is a qualified psychodrama trainer. Since 2011 she is specialized in the field of methods and conceptualizing social work. Her main research projects are social inclusion of people with disabilities and international social work. She is member of the German Association of Social Workers (DGSA). Since 2016 she has been head of the BA Social Work Studies and, together with Prof. Ghaderi, she was leader of the DAAD cooperation project CoBoSUnin 2016–2019 between the University of Sulaimani and Bochum. Contact: sonnenberg@evh-bochum.de

Teaching Social Work in the Kurdistan Region of Iraq

Luqman Saleh Karim and Cinur Ghaderi

Abstract

The history of teaching social work at the universities in the Kurdistan Region of Iraq is relatively new. The beginnings go back to the years 2006/2007 at the University of Salahaddin in Erbil (USE). A short time later, the department of social work was opened in 2014/2015 at the University of Sulaimani (UoS). Swedish and German universities, UNICEF and DAAD organizations supported both departments. Currently, these are the only two universities that offer this subject in the Kurdistan Region. At the University of Dohuk (UoD), social work is integrated into the course curriculum as part of sociology. However, there is no separate BA program in social work. In Iraq, the degree program is also offered in Baghdad. This chapter seeks to reveal the history of the emergence of the departments and their vision and mission, as well as the opportunities and challenges that social work faces. At the same time, it also details the social work curriculum and its objectives. At the end of this chapter, some questions are raised so that more follow-up can be done in the future.

Keywords

Social work • Curriculum • Challenge • University • Teaching • Kurdistan

L. S. Karim (✉)
Slemani, Iraq
E-Mail: loqman.karim@univsul.edu.iq

C. Ghaderi
Düsseldorf, Germany
E-Mail: ghaderi@evh-bochum.de

C. Ghaderi et al. (eds.), *Social Work at the Level of International Comparison*,
https://doi.org/10.1007/978-3-658-30394-5_10

1 Introduction

Caring for others is a part of human history from the age of antiquity until today. Others can mean various people. They can be family or relatives such as father, mother, sister, children and acquaintances. They can also be people we do not know, but for whom we care as our human duty, such as caring for infirm and elderly people, weak and marginalized people in society. The brief to care for unknown people is a part of the religious and social tradition and culture of most societies in the world (Kanie 2016, pp. 176–177).

The turning point in the development from charity work to a scientific profession was the emergence of social work as a scientific and ethical profession or craft. Historically, the year 1917 is referred to as the birth year of social work, when Mary Richmond wrote her book 'Social Diagnosis', in which the functions of social work were identified (Fahmi 2013, p. 14). Social work in the Kurdistan Region first appeared and was established at the Salahaddin University in Erbil in the educational year 2006–2007.[1] The second university to establish a social work program was the Sulaimani University (see Fig. 1) in 2014.[2]

Before this, there was no scientific department under the name of social work, but some social work subjects were studied in sociology lessons and lectures. The department of sociology was first opened in 1976 at the University of Sulaimani.[3]

It should be mentioned that, for a long time, family members and family structures supported people in need in a variety of ways—without the term volunteer and without the academic profession of social work. Later, graduates of other disciplines, such as sociology or psychology practiced social work as social researchers or 'Tuejari Kolamayati',[4] and compensated the need for social work in society. Over the past two decades, there has been a metamorphosis of traditional support structures. The risk of living in a society constantly at war and in conflict creates the need for change, and social work seems to be an attempt to handle

[1] Hamad, Shvan Ismael, Head of the Social Work Department, Salahaddin University. Interview (March 8, 2020).

[2] https://hum.univsul.edu.iq/HUM-Depts/social-work Accessed: March 19, 2020.

[3] In 2010 the Department of Sociology was opened at the University in Dohuk and recently there have been efforts to give more weight to social work within sociology, especially in the higher semesters. (Interview with Muhammad Saeed Al-Barwari, Head of the Department of Sociology, University of Dohuk; 5 July, 2021).

[4] Social analyst would be the word-by-word translation, but it is the common word for social worker.

Fig. 1 Department of Social Work at the University in Sulaimani: Building from the outside (left) and inside (right)

these challenges locally. At the same time, social work offers links to international practices and social work knowledge systems in a globalized world (Ghaderi and Saleh Karim 2019, p. 176).

2 Social Work at the University of Sulaimani

For the purpose of composing a suitable vision and mission for social work, the commission of developing programs worked by cooperating with the scientific commission of the department in making policies for the social work department as follows:

The department is to offer services in various sectors of the society, as well as being backed up with a scientific, professional, ethical and practical background for the purpose of raising the level of life quality, especially for those with special needs and people who are expected to be vulnerable. Generally, it can be said that the most important characteristics of the social work department are the following points:

- *Being practical*: most of the lectures which are taught are based on current social needs and foundations.
- *Being scientific and professional*: the department works on the skills and identity of social work and has its own professional limitation.
- *Being ethical*: the social work department differs from other departments, as it works on ethics and ethical codes with students, clients and social foundations.

- *Being current and realistic*: the department works on the essential and current needs of Kurdish society.

According to the department, it is possible that humanities education plays a practical role in reducing the sufferance of individuals, families and society, and in progressing its foundations. The lectures in this department are also composed on the same principle; meaning that it has a humanitarian viewpoint for family and social problems. In spite of being practical, it is also central and academic; in other words, it intends to show its offers based on a scientific and professional principle and avoid practicing theoretical abstraction, which fails to take the reality and needs of individuals, families and society into consideration. For the previous purpose—if psychology is more active at the level of the individual and sociology at the level of the society—it is also a function of social work to connect this gap between the individual and society and to offer services on the basis of a high quality and a perfect fit. At the same time, social work becomes a real advocate for minorities and for vulnerable groups and people in society.

3 Objectives of the Department

The strategies and policies of the department focus on academic aspects and their implementation in society. The objective of establishing the department was to demonstrate the practical role of academic science in solving problems and developing society, as can be seen from the following points:

- Preparing and training students through the development of knowledge, skills and ethics that are compatible with social action at the present day.
- Training students practically and supervising them in various basics such as jurisdiction, social reform, schools, social care, consultant centers, shelters, and local and international organizations concerned with humanitarian issues in order to give them a practical foundation in their professions.
- Providing advisory and social services for society, especially for people who currently need these services.
- Trying to compose a general social policy and developing different sectors of society, especially the educational sector.
- Directing graduation research towards the needs and current problems of Kurdish society and considering the awareness in regional and universal changes, especially in social work aspects.

- Participating in programs and work related with social work through the participation of lecturers directly in creating and composing the programs of research, practice, consulting with social foundations, and in both the private and the public sector.
- Activating and developing Master's and doctoral degrees in higher education.

Social development should be achieved through creating various links between the social work department and various service offices and foundations, in both governmental and non-governmental sectors, through linking the programs and curriculum to the current and long-term needs of society.

It is worthy of notice that the study of social work was originally organized on a yearly basis. However, in 2020, the Ministry of Higher Education decided that studies at universities should generally shift from a yearly organization to semesters, as is the case in western countries, and in order to be oriented towards the Bologna Process. This means that it starts in the first stage, and all four stages will change in accordance with the Bologna Process over the next four years. It has currently passed through the process, as follows (Tab. 1 and 2).

Stages 2 to 4 are still organized on a yearly basis, as follows, but over the next three years, these stages will be adapted to the Bologna Process and will be offered on a semester basis (Tab. 3).

It is worth mentioning that, for the first time in the Kurdistan Region, the social work department opened scholarships for Master's and doctoral studies in 2020. In the educational year 2020, a doctoral study program is available in partnership with the Protestant University of Applied Sciences in Bochum, Germany.

The number of the social work department students in Salahaddin University is 292 (Hamad 2020),[5] and there are 366 students at the University of Sulaimani (Ghafur 2020, 2021),[6] most of whom are women with a percentage rate of 82%. There are 15 lecturers, five assistant professors, five teachers and five assistant teachers in the social work department of the University of Sulaimani.

Graduate students of the social work department work as social workers in reformatory foundations, consultant centers, psychological hospitals, shelters, violence confrontation directorates, social care, schools and educational foundations, local and international humanitarian organizations, the courts, etc.

---

[5] Hamad, Shvan Ismael, Head of Social Work Department, Salahaddin University. Interview (March 8, 2020).

[6] Ghafur, Rizgar, Head of Social Work Department at the University of Sulaimani. Interview / Personal Communication. Accessed: March 15, 2020 and April 27, 2021.

Table 1 The First Semester (own representation based on the module manual of Social Work at the UoS)

No	Discipline\ Module	Notation	Code	First Semester (16 weeks)						ECTS
				No. of Hours per Week				Final Evaluation		
					Practice	LAB	Project	Exam	Continuous Evaluation	
1	**University Work Environment**	DU	– —	2	3	0	2	☐	☐	**4**
2	**Kurdistan Society**	DU	– —	2	0	0	3	☐	☐	**3**
3	**English Language (Reading + Writing)**	CD	– —	2	3	2	3	☐	☐	**6**
4	**Social Work Concepts**	FD	– —	4	0	0	4	☐	☐	**5**
5	**Introduction to Social Work**	FD	– —	2	4	0	4	☐	☐	**6**
6	**Introduction to Psychology**	FD	– —	2	4	0	4	☐	☐	**6**
Total per Week:				14	14	2	20			**30**

Table 2 The Second Semester (own representation based on the module manual of Social Work at the UoS)

No	Discipline / Module	Notation	Code	Second Semester (16 weeks)						ECTS
				No. of Hours per Week				Final Evaluation		
				Theory	Practice	LAB	Project	Exam	Continuous Evaluation	
1	**Professional Skills**	DU	– –-	2	3	0	2	☐	☐	**4**
2	**English Language (Listening + Speaking)**	CD	– –-	2	3	2	3	☐	☐	**6**
3	**Physical Education**	DU	– –-	2	3	0	0	☐	☐	**3**
4	**Computer Skills (Word, Excel, Power Point)**	CD	– –-	2	3	2	3	☐	☐	**6**
5	**Introduction to Sociology**	FD	– –-	3	3	0	4	☐	☐	**6**
6	**Social Problems**	FD	– –-	3	3	0	3	☐	☐	**5**
Total per Week:				14	18	4	15			**30**

Table 3 Social Work Module at the University of Sulaimani (own representation based on the module manual of Social Work at the UoS)

Social Work Module, University of Sulaimani			
Stages	No	Modules	Unit
Stage Two	1	Quantitative Methods	3
	2	Social Problems (in English)	3
	3	Wellbeing and Social Policy	2
	4	Case Work	3
	5	Family and Child in Social Work	3
	6	Social Statistics	2
	7	Law and Ethics in Social Work	3
	8	Psychology	2
Stage Three	1	Qualitative Methods	3
	2	Medical Social Work	2
	3	Professional Skills	3
	4	Gender	3
	5	Aesthetic Education	2
	6	Group Social Work	3
	7	Scientific Research Design	3
	8	Internship	3
Stage Four	1	Social Work Theories	3
	2	International Social Work	2
	3	Social Work in Rehabilitation Institutions	2
	4	School Social Work	2
	5	Counseling	3
	6	Graduation Research (Student Project)	2
	7	Internship	3
	8	Management in Social Work	2

As a result of globalization and the opening of the Kurdistan Region to the world as of the1990s, local and international organizations came to the Kurdistan Region, bringing with them a broad historical background and good experience of social work. According to Muslih Irwani,[7] they were a contributory factor towards opening the social work department at Salahaddin University—for example, the UNICEF agency of the UN supported the department financially and provided necessary funding. At the same time, the social work department of Salahaddin University was supported by Sweden's Dalarna University (Liedgren 2015), and the social work department of the University of Sulaimani has been supported by the German Protestant University of Applied Sciences in Bochum.

The international dialogue concerning diverse approaches to social work was fruitful for the development of social work in Kurdistan in this pioneering phase. International mobility and exchange programs enabled students and lecturers of the social work department of Sulaimani to participate in special social work training and workshops in Germany. As a result, some modules, such as International Social Work and Aesthetic Education, were added.

4 Challenges of Social Work Departments

Despite the fact that the social work departments have somehow developed and gained recognition in society, at the same time there are some challenges facing the development of social work in the Kurdistan Region of Iraq. One of the important points is that social work is situated between the individual and society (Adams et al. 2009, p. 35). It seems like this science has socially no specific limit, and some people think social work is sociology or psychology. The reason for this lack of recognition of this science has to do with its new appearance in the Kurdistan Region.

Additionally, for the Ministry of Higher Education and other relevant formal parties, social work does not own its job description. Although it has been made clear that social work has its own vision and mission, the relevant ministries' vision is not clear for this new department, and this has given rise to the fact that the professional function of social workers is a kind of mixture between sociology and psychology. Besides, until now, graduate students of the sociology and psychology departments have worked as social workers in most of the foundations in the Kurdistan Region. However, the respective professional limits of social work, psychology and sociology have been separated. A reason for the lack of a job description might be that, until now, there is no professional association of social work. However, there is a general union of human scientists, which comes

[7] Irwani, Muslih, Assistant Professor at the Social Work Department at the Salahaddin University. Interview (September 5, 2019).

historically from a combination of interest groups of social scientists with the psychologists in the year 1994 (Wali 2020),[8] and has nearly 4000 members. Based on the title 'Kurdistan Sociologist and Psychologist Association', it is clear that this association is only for sociologists and psychologists. Social workers have the opportunity to join and become a member. Forming one's own union presupposes formally that there are a certain number of social workers; this numerical criterion is currently not fulfilled. In terms of content, such an initiative has hitherto been regarded as a federation or similar not yet formed.

Another challenge is the teaching of theory–practice transfer and, respectively, cooperation with fields of practice. The current situation is that the social work department at the University of Sulaimani provides two days a week for field and practical training. This internship is in the third stage and it is located in schools (Ghafur 2020)[9]; in the fourth stage it is directed towards local organizations. Meanwhile, at the social work department of Salahaddin University, practical training is done in both the third and the fourth stage (Hamad 2020).[10] However, internship experience is new in these departments and organizations, and the relevant parties are not as helpful as required, thus the students, who form the main component of the profession, face obstacles and insufficiency.

In summary, it can be said that it would be a forward-looking task for teaching and the professionalization of social work: a) to remain in international dialogue with the social work scientific community, b) to establish a professional association that represents the interests of social work in the Kurdistan Region of Iraq, that initiates important debates on teaching, and that strengthens regional networking and, c) finally, the strengthening of cooperation and exchange with institutions in fields of practice is important.

References

Adams, R., Dominelli, L. Payne, M. (Eds.) (2009). Social Work: Themes, Issues and Critical Debates, Palgrave Macmillan, Third ed., Springer Nature.

Fahmi, M. S. (2013). *General Practitioner of Social Work, Practical Areas*. Alexandria: The Modern University Office.

[8] Wali, Jaza Hama Salih, Head of Kurdistan Sociologists and Psychologists Union. Interview / Personal Communication. (August 21, 2020).

[9] Ghafur, Rizgar, Head of Social work Department, University of Sulaimani. Interview / Personal Communication. (March 15, 2020).

[10] Hamad, Shvan Ismael, Head of the Social Work Department, Salahaddin University. Interview (March 8, 2020).

Ghaderi, C., & Saleh Karim, L. (2019). Social work with refugees in Kurdistan Region in Iraq. In: M. Pfaller-Rott, A. Kállay, D. Böhler. (Eds.) Social Work with Refugees. Ostrava: European Research Institute for Social Work (ERIS) Monographs. Vol. 5 , pp. 163–184.

Kanie, M. W. (2016). *Mrov u Karamat*. Teheran: Andesha Cultural and Artistic Center.

Liedgren, P. (2015). Teaching social work in Iraqi Kurdistan as a Swede, Transfer of teaching styles. *International Social Work, 58*(I), 175–185. The author's 2012 reprints and permissions: isw.sagepup.com.

LUQMAN SALEH KARIM, Ass. Prof., Assistant Professor in the Social Work Department. He holds a PhD in Social Work from the University of Sulaimani, Kurdistan Region of Iraq. He was head of the Social Work Department from 2014–2017. He is a researcher and has conducted a large body of academic and organizational research on gender-based violence, environment policy, honor killing, child marriage, GBV assessments of needs, impact evaluation and COVID-19. He also worked with the United Nations Population Fund (UN-FPA) and the Women's Refugee Commission (WRC) as a research consultant from 2018-2019, and as a child marriage research co-investigator in the Johns Hopkins University (USA); from 2016-2019 he was a University of Sulaimani coordinator of the DAAD cooperation project CoBoSUnin between the University of Sulaimani and the University of Applied Sciences in Bochum. Currently he works as lecturer at the University of Sulaimani, as a supervisor in the Khanzad women's organization, and as a research consultant for the Civil Development Organization (CDO). Contact: loqman.karim@univsul.edu.iq

Cinur Ghaderi, Prof. Dr., Professor of Psychology in the Faculty of Social Work at the Protestant University of Applied Sciences (EvH RWL Bochum). She is Vice-President for Research, Transfer and Internationalization. After her post-graduate education in psychological psychotherapy (behavioral therapy), she worked in the "Psychosocial Centre for refugees" (PSZ) in Düsseldorf. She received her PhD at the faculty of Social Sciences of the Ruhr University Bochum. She is a member of the steering committee of DTPPP (transcultural psychiatry, psycho-therapy and psychosomatics). Main academic interests: International Social Work, Refugee Studies, Transcultural Psychotherapy, Psychotrauma, Identity, Diversity and Gender. She is the initiator of the DAAD-cooperation project CoBoSUnin 2016–2019 between the University of Sulaimani and Bochum. Contact: ghaderi@evh-bochum.de

Part IV Topics of Social Work in Teaching and Practice: Professional Identity, Ethics, Counseling, Aesthetical Education, Gender, Teaching Meets Practice

Professional Identity in Social Work

Kristin Sonnenberg and Fraidoon Arif Saeed

Abstract

This chapter introduces the term 'professional identity' in social work. This is done by means of a clarification of basic professional theoretical framings as well as by giving examples from different perspectives on social work: the scientific level, including the academic discourse, associations of social work, the educational level with the perspectives of lecturers and students.

Keywords

Professional identity • Social work • Self-concept • Societal recognition • Perception

1 Introduction

Professional identity is the concept which describes how we perceive ourselves within our occupational context and how we communicate this to others (Neary 2014). Taking a broad definition as a starting point, a professional identity is the meaning or set of meanings that individuals use to describe how they perceive themselves in a professional context. It contributes to their identity, which

K. Sonnenberg (✉)
Bonn, Germany
E-Mail: sonnenberg@evh-bochum.de

F. Arif Saeed
Slemani, Iraq
E-Mail: fraidoon.saeed@univsul.edu.iq

C. Ghaderi et al. (eds.), *Social Work at the Level of International Comparison*,
https://doi.org/10.1007/978-3-658-30394-5_11

includes a self-concept. Different theoretical concepts contribute to and define professional identity in different ways, and more concretely. Professional identity can also be thought of in subjective terms, whereby individuals come to identify themselves as social workers (Webb 2017, p. 12).

2 The Perspective Within the Academic Discourse—Profession Theories

The first set of central theoretical approaches about professional identity derives from sociology, social psychology and social work theory. The main difference can be seen in the differentiation between the structure of a profession (social status, standards, independency, and code of ethics) and a practice-based perspective (competences, codes of conduct). There have been different sociological theories since the 1970s that debate the definition of 'profession theory' and whether social work meets the standards of being a profession or discipline. It is important to realize a dependency on laws and social policy regulations, as for other professions as well. At the same time, the associations of social work clearly define a political mandate that empowers to fight against unjust regulations or power structures within society. The latter perspective of practice-based professionalism demands the reflective abilities of the practitioners to reflect upon knowledge bases, such as theoretical and practical knowledge or competing theoretical approaches, and to use this to analyze situations and cases. Furthermore, the direct communication with the client is important, it is necessary to include societal factors and to respect participatory approaches with clients to support their autonomy. This theory derives from Dewe and Otto (2011).

A second theoretical impulse that can be discussed are psychological theories about identity. For instance, Keupp points out that social workers need a flexible identity. By this, he means that experiences that influence the self-concept of persons include part identities from work, family and free time, and are continuously in a process. Furthermore, societal context factors influence the biography and behavioral patterns of social workers (Keupp 2006). There is interconnectedness towards humans, society and nature, within which the individual analyses, reflects and develops his or her identity.

A third theory from social work explains the professional identity as a combination of being open-minded and being capable of a reasoned opinion. This open and flexible identity of social workers is considered as a strength if they learn to deal with this ambiguity (Kleve 2011).

A fourth theory focuses on the social workers being a tool themselves (von Spiegel 2011). With competences based on theoretical knowledge, methods and techniques (professional skills) as well as attitudes, but especially with social and self-competences the person enters reflexive processes that lead to self-assessment and self-development (Heiner 2004, 2016). Associations for social work can lay down competence profiles for social workers.

These theoretical approaches are derived from a German-speaking discourse. There are similar discussions in English-speaking countries. These theories have to be carefully examined to assess whether they are fitting for the cultural and societal context in Kurdistan-Iraq, and other important approaches from the theoretical discourse about the professional identity of social workers have to be added.

3 The Perspective within Education and Studies of Social Work

Gray (2001) explains that professional identity is 'understanding and having a sense of pride in one's profession (…) essential both for one's own internal satisfaction with one's chosen career and for the continued societal recognition of the profession' (p. 12). Professional identity is socially constructed as an individual and social activity that is constantly renegotiated through time, space, materials, relationships, and through person's bodily experiences (Moorhead 2017, p. 13).

Wiles (2017) explored the construction of social work identity among students pursuing a degree in social work. The qualitative study outlined three approaches that fostered students' development of professional identity: (a) supporting desired professional traits, (b) connections to a collective identity, and (c) promoting the student's internal professional identity process (Humphreys et al. 2019).

Professional identity has two interconnected components: the interpersonal, which relates to the culture, knowledge, skills, values and beliefs of a profession that the individual has acquired, and the intrapersonal which considers the individual's perception of themselves in the context of their profession (Tsakissiris 2016, p. 26).

Professional identity develops over time. Professional identity was not described as a fixed concept; rather, it was affected by a multitude of factors and experiences that accumulate over time (Alves and Gazzola 2011, p. 198). Professional identity formation does not end with graduation. A professional identity changes over time, as people mature as practitioners and change their positions within and outside of the field of practice (Trede and McEwen 2012).

4 The Perspective of the Social Work Profession in Social Work Associations

The most widely accepted definition of social work is the International Federation of Social Work's global definition:

> 'Social work is a practice-based profession and an academic discipline that promotes social change and development, social cohesion, and the empowerment and liberation of people. Principles of social justice, human rights, collective responsibility and respect for diversities are central to social work. Underpinned by theories of social work, social sciences, humanities and indigenous knowledge, social work engages people and structures to address life challenges and enhance wellbeing.' (IFSW and IASSW 2014)

Social work professional identity is defined as the internationalization of knowledge, skills, professional norms, behaviors, values and the mission of social work, and the development of a commitment to work at micro, mezzo and macro levels of practice with a focus on social justice (Adams et al. 2006; Bogo et al. 1993).

Social work is a broad field that encompasses micro-practice, mezzo and macro-practice so that it can feel as if it lacks a unified professional identity. In this regard, we try to answer some questions, such as: What are the basic values and concepts of social work that define the profession, and how can these values and concepts help social workers, social work students and researchers in identifying themselves and position themselves as professionals?

The professional identity of social work need not be inextricably linked to specific organizational structures. Rather, professional identity should be based more on core values and principles in order to distinguish the nature of the social worker's contribution from that of individuals working within other agencies and to protect against the threat of boundary erosion as the result of development in other professions. Issues of recruitment and retention to social work are inextricably linked to the issue of professional identity (Asquith et al. 2005, p. 39).

Professional identity is not a stable entity; it is an ongoing process of interpretation and customization which is shaped by contextual workplace factors. In this respect, identity formation is viewed as more interactive and more problematic than the relatively straightforward adoption of the role or category of 'professional social worker' (Webb 2015, p. 3).

The past decade has seen a growing interest in social workers' professional identity. For students, it is increasingly viewed as an important outcome of qualifying education, to be developed and maintained throughout their social work careers. Being clear and confident about identity is considered to improve social workers' contribution in working with other professionals. A strong, positive sense of professional identity is said to bolster social workers' resilience to stress (Wiles 2017, p. 35).

Professional identity, when linked with the concept of 'professionalism', has become bound up with the regulation of practitioners and the avoidance of 'unprofessional' behavior. These are very often laid down in codes of conduct, to avoid malpractice and give a guideline for orientation in difficult decision-making.

Professional identity formation can act negatively and may not necessarily be a good thing when the possibility of organizational coercion comes into the frame. Workplace organizations exert influence on individual practitioners in part through identity and identification but also through the regulation of professional conduct (Webb 2015, p. 7).

5 The Importance of Professional Identity

Why is professional identity becoming a 'matter' in social work? The reason for its mattering is because professional identity affects not only how practitioners identify themselves, but it also affects how practitioners are recognized by the out-group including other professions, service users, and the public. Moreover, the formation of professional identity in social work is closely connected with various concepts and issues such as work performance, commitment, resilience, and job satisfaction as well as recruitment and retention (Park 2018, p. 1).

Professional identity can be impacted by a range of factors, and it is important to be able to connect with what social work means to one, and then gain further experience (Moorhead 2017, p. 400).

Professional identity is important for social workers; social workers should be able to demonstrate the principles of social work through professional judgment, decision making and actions within a framework of professional accountability. Professional identity was perceived as an important part of early-career experiences and participants greatly appreciated opportunities to critically reflect on it. Their motivations to participate support international literature from Kearns and McArdle (2012) and Campanini et al. (2012) who found exploring and maintaining a social work professional identity was an important dimension of early career experiences, and that newly qualified social workers appreciated opportunities to do so (Wiles 2017, p. 35).

A professional identity is an important cognitive mechanism that affects workers' attitudes, effect and behavior in work settings and beyond. As such, understanding how professionals think about themselves has been the focus of many past research studies (Caza and Creary 2016, p. 4).

6 Challenges From Other Human Professions

Social workers typically work with the most complex cases where either medical or psychological interventions don't tend to work, or social factors such as poverty, poor housing or ineffective social networks are predominant. The effect of evidence-based practice in mental health services is that social workers are increasingly being appointed on their ability to deliver psychological interventions rather than their ability to solve social problems. According to IFSW, 'Social workers challenge discrimination, which includes but is not limited to age, capacity, civil status, class, culture, ethnicity, gender, gender identity, language, nationality (or lack thereof), opinions, other physical characteristics, physical or mental abilities, political beliefs, poverty, race, relationship status, religion, sex, sexual orientation, socioeconomic status, spiritual beliefs, or family structure' (IFSW and IASSW 2018).

Forming a professional identity is a complex and long process which is full of challenges and problems. This process takes place in a culturally specific context. Many factors are involved: personal, social, cultural, political, professional, global, etc. (Ivanova and Mincane 2016).

Divergence in relation to social work professional identity is historical, and dates to settlement houses and charity organizations as we debated the role of social work in society; the professions' lack of ability to agree on and articulate our role impacted the development of professional identity in social work students (Pullen Sansfacon and Crete 2016, pp. 767–779). Social work is a diverse profession, serving varied populations at multiple levels of practice, and while this is considered the strength of the profession, this diversity contributes to a lack of direction or 'lack of commonly recognized symbols' (Loseke and Cahill 1986, p. 255).

These challenges lead to the significance of developing, teaching and living a certain professional identity that has a clear(er) difference over against other human sciences and professions. With the newly introduced Social Work Studies in Kurdistan-Iraq, but also as an ongoing process in Germany, with scientific debates and professional training and experiences in working life with other social workers, a professional identity can be further developed. The international and national social work associations have the role to support this on different levels as discussed already above. It is the psycho-social focus with regard to complex and multi-level problems at individual, family or group level, while taking into consideration context and societal factors that mark the unique task of social workers.

References

Adams, K., Hean, S., Sturgis, P., & Macleod Clark, J. M. (2006). Investigating the factors influencing professional identity of first-year health and social care students. *Learning in Health and Social Care, 5*(2), 55–68. https://doi.org/10.1111/j.1473-6861.2006.00119.x.

Alves, S., & Gazzola, N. (2011). Professional Identity: A Qualitative Inquiry of Experienced Counsellors. *Canadian Journal of Counselling and Psychotherapy, 45*(3),189–207. Retrieved from https://cjc-rcc.ucalgary.ca/article/view/59317

Asquith, S., Clark, C., & Waterhouse, L. (Eds.). (2005). The Role of the Social Worker in the 21st Century — A Literature Review. Published on The Scottish Executive website in December 2005. UK Web Archive, UKWA: https://www.webarchive.org.uk/wayback/archive/20170701074158/ http://www.gov.scot/Publications/2005/12/1994633/46368. Accessed 12 Mar 2020.

Bogo, M., Raphael, D., & Roberts, R. (1993). Interests, activities and self-identification among social work students: Toward a definition of social work identity. *Journal of Social Work Education, 29*(3), 279–292. https://doi.org/10.1080/10437797.1993.10778824.

Campanini, A., Frost, L. & Höjer, S. (2012). Educating the new practitioner: The building of professional Identities in European Social Work. https://www.researchgate.net, Accessed 30 Mar 2020.

Caza, B. B., & Creary, S. J. (2016). The construction of professional identity [Electronic version]. Retrieved from Cornell University, SHA School site: https://scholarship.sha.cornell.edu/articles/878. Accessed 22 Mar 2020.

Dewe, B., & Otto, H.-U. (2011). Professionalität. In H. U. Otto & H. Thiersch (Eds.), *Handbuch Soziale Arbeit* (4th ed., pp. 1143–1153). München: Ernst Reinhardt.

Gray, N. D. (2001). *The relationship of supervisor traits to the professional development and satisfaction with the supervisor of post-master's degree counselors seeking state licensure (Unpublished doctoral dissertation).* University of New Orleans: New Orlean.

Heiner, M. (2004). *Professionalität in der Sozialen Arbeit*. Stuttgart: Kohlhammer.

Heiner, M. (2016). *Kompetent handeln in der Sozialen Arbeit* (2nd ed.). Ernst Reinhardt: München.

IFSW & IASSW. (2014). Global Definition of Social Work. https://www.ifsw.org/what-is-social-work/global-definition-of-social-work/. Accessed 16 Jan 2020.

IFSW & IASSW. (2018). Global Social Work Statement of Ethical Principles. Long version, April 27, 2018. https://www.ifsw.org/wp-content/uploads/2018/07/Global-Social-Work-Statement-of-Ethical-Principles-IASSW-27-April-2018-1.pdf. Accessed 22 Mar 2020.

Ivanova, I., & Skara-Mincane, R. (2016). Development of Professional Identity during Teacher's Practice. https://core.ac.uk/download/pdf/82407832.pdf. Accessed 30 Mar 2020.

Kearns, S. & McArdle, K. (2012). 'Doing it right?'– accessing the narratives of identity of newly qualified social workers through the lens of resilience: 'I am, I have, I can'. *Child*

& Family Social Work 17(4) https://doi.org/10.1111/j.1365-2206.2011.00792.x https://www.researchgate.net, Accessed 30 Mar 2020.

Keupp, H., et al. (Eds.). (2006). *Identitätsrekonstruktionen Das Patchwork der Identitäten in der Spätmoderne* (3rd ed.). Rowohlt: Hamburg.

Kleve, H. (2011). *Aufgestellte Unterschiede. Systemische Aufstellung und Tetralemma in der Sozialen Arbeit.* Carl-Auer Verlag: Heidelberg.

Lopez-Humphreys, M., Teater, B., & Dawson, B. A. (2019). Exploring the Professional Identity of Social Work Academics https://www.researchgate.net/publication/332896874_Exploring_the_Professional_Identity_of_Social_Work_Academics/citations

Loseke, D. R., & Cahill, S. E. (1986). Actors in Search of a Character: Student Social Workers' Quest for Professional Identity. *Symbolic Interaction, 9*(2) 245–258. JSTOR, https://www.jstor.org/stable/10.1525/si.1986.9.2.245?seq=1. Accessed 20 Mar 2020.

Moorhead, B. (2017). The Lived Experience of Professional Identity: A Year-Long Study with Newly Qualified Social Workers. https://researchoutput.csu.edu.au/ws/portalfiles/portal/13512079/BMoorhead_Final_Thesis.pdf

Neary, S. (2014). Professional identity: What I call myself defines who I am. *Career Matters, 3*, 14–15. https://derby.openrepository.com/handle/10545/324124. Accessed 26 Mar 2020.

Park, L. S.-C. (2018). Professional identity and social work [Book Review] [online]. *Aotearoa New Zealand Social Work, 30*(1), 71–72. https://search.informit.com.au/documentSummary;dn=656059676036684;res=IELHSS ISSN: 2463–4131. Accessed 21 Mar 2020.

Pullen Sansfaçon, A., & Crête, J. (2016). Identity development among social workers, from training to practice: Results from a three-year qualitative longitudinal study. *Social Work Education, 35*(7), 767–779. https://doi.org/10.1080/02615479.2016.1211097.

Trede, F., & McEwen, C. (2012). Developing a critical professional identity: Engaging self in practice. In J. Higgs, R. Barnett, S. Billett, M. Hutchings, & F. Trede (Eds.). Practice-based education: Perspectives and strategies (Vol. 6, pp. 27–40). Sense Publishers.

Tsakissiris, J. (2016). The role of professional identity & self-interest in career choices in the emerging ICT workforce. Availability: https://www.semanticscholar.org/paper/The-role-of-professional-identity-%26-self-interest-Tsakissiris/480f54207454898aba23fb49ee1bfdc9a965177e. Accessed 27 Mar 2020.

von Spiegel, H. (2011). *Methodisches Handeln in der Sozialen Arbeit*. Stuttgart: UTB.

Webb, S. A. (Ed.). (2017). Professional identity and social work. Routledge: London. ISBN 978-1-138-23443-7, p. 246, paperback, NZD69.97

Webb, S. A. (2015). Professional identity and social work. https://www.chester.ac.uk/sites/files/chester/WEBB.pdf. Accessed 12 Mar 2020.

Wiles, F. (2017). What is professional identity and how do social workers acquire it? In S. A. Webb (Ed.), *Professional Identity and Social Work* (pp. 35–50). London: Routledge Academic.

Kristin Sonnenberg, Prof. Dr., Professor of Social Work at the Protestant University of Applied Sciences Bochum. She studied Social Pedagogy in Germany, completed an M.A. in Comparative European Social Studies at the University of North London and her PhD at the University of Cologne in Germany 2004 in the Faculty of Educational Science. She is a qualified psychodrama trainer. Since 2011 she is specialized in the field of methods and conceptualizing social work. Her main research projects are social inclusion of people with disabilities and international social work. She is member of the German Association of Social Workers (DGSA). Since 2016 she has been head of the BA Social Work Studies and, together with Prof. Ghaderi, she was leader of the DAAD cooperation project CoBoSUnin 2016–2019 between the University of Sulaimani and Bochum. Contact: sonnenberg@evh-bochum.de

Fraidoon Arif Saeed, Social Worker and Assistance Lecturer in the Social Work Department at the University of Sulaimani. He studied B.A. Sociology/Authority and charisma, at the Salahaddin University, Erbil, Iraq (2007). He received his Master's degree in Social Work (MSW) in Social Development from the University of Bangalore, India (2012). He has wide experience from his voluntary work as a social worker for fourteen months from August 2011 until October 2012 at the Association of People with Disability (APD) in Bangalore, India. He worked as a Director of Media and University Spokesman at the Presidency Office of the University of Sulaimani (2014–2016). He participated in the DAAD-cooperation project CoBoSU in 2016–2019 between the University of Sulaimani and Bochum. Contact: fraidoon.saeed@univsul.edu.iq

Professional Identity of Teachers

Kwestan Ali Abdalla

Abstract

The aim of this chapter is to describe the requirements for successful teaching and the corresponding criteria for professional behavior. It illustrates the framing of theoretical assumptions, insights and examples from the BA Social Work lecturers at the University of Sulaimani, concerning the role, attitude and attributes for lecturers. These characteristics for successful teaching are outlined. Furthermore, this chapter explores why these qualifications are important, as well as the different levels of qualification, characteristics and willingness of the teachers. Finally, three steps of successful professional teaching are presented.

Keywords

Identity • Professional role • Successful teacher • Character • Qualification • Performance

1 Introduction to the Role and Abilities of Teachers

The term '*professional identity*' refers to the measurement of the relationship, practice and the training that individuals will be prepared for. Through them, the teacher can implement a certain professional role. The distinctive feature of this career is that involves a widened appendix of knowledge in scientific and

K. Ali Abdalla (✉)
Slemani, Iraq
E-Mail: Kwestan.abdulla@univsul.edu.iq

C. Ghaderi et al. (eds.), *Social Work at the Level of International Comparison*,
https://doi.org/10.1007/978-3-658-30394-5_12

academic study at the university as well as playing a special role in performing particular training, doing research, supporting the development of students' intellectual abilities and seeking and finding successful ways of producing success and awareness amongst them. This can be accomplished by bringing new interactive programs into the curriculum annually and listening to the needs and suggestions of the students.

Teachers should be qualified and capable in their profession. They should be ready to implement their career faithfully. They should act wisely when they face a question that they cannot answer directly. It is important to be in good health, safe and active. This has a great impact on their career. If these factors are not given, there might be a risk that the teachers will ignore their duties and avoid performing them efficiently.

In order to be trusted by the students and try to upgrade the level of the weak students to an intermediate level, they should not actively differentiate amongst the students.

Another important character is that teachers should be problem-solvers and help their students when they are in need of help. They should be aware of their students' social and economic condition and give them a helping hand when they need it. This will ensure the student that he or she is not alone and that there is someone who will support them and help to make better decisions. In this way, the teachers indirectly have a positive impact on the students' academic achievements.

Teachers should not engage or act violently under any circumstances since it only makes things more complicated and make students lose any interest in the subject. In addition, teachers should be patient in treating students and avoid getting angry. Being angry make teachers lose their characters and a big gap will be created between the teacher and the student. In contrast, acting in a simple and humble way, behaving as a friend and avoiding acting as a superior can be the marks of a successful teacher. This will let the teacher be successful in his/her career amongst the students and the other people. The students look to him/her as a role model.

Teachers should cooperate with the other co-teachers. If they would not, the educational objectives would be difficult to achieve. Furthermore, teachers should be able to direct the educational process towards a modern era as good education is not easy to accomplish, rather it requires skills and qualifications in order to educate a proper character. Students always look closely and observe the characteristics of a teacher's character; therefore, teachers should have trust and fully assign themselves to that particular profession. In addition, they should have sufficient confidence so that they can confront the students and avoid the excessive amount of criticism and humiliating the weak students for the sake of a slight piece of laughing. Conversely, teachers should encourage the students to pay attention to the lessons and be active. Sandelowski (2001, p. 230) discusses some characteristics of a qualified teacher. These are:

1. Authenticity: Having knowledge of their profession and subjective understanding and being capable of controlling the self.
2. Social support: Having critical thinking, doing scientific study and learning professionally for the entire life. Not only that, assessing the differences, advocating human rights and social justice. Finally, they should encourage social welfare and making moral decisions.
3. Qualification in teaching is a movable performance that the teacher practices with close consideration and continuity for this performance.

Professional identity includes a method of active teaching behavior to practice the specified objectives in which it performs by teaching through related rational responses, expressions and movements. All these responses should be tied and practiced with accuracy, speed and suitability to the circumstance of the teaching (Ali 2017, p. 51).

2 The Importance of Teachers' Qualification in Teaching

The success of education and teaching depends on some major factors. Not only are the curriculums, activities, buildings and teaching aids significant as well. However, the educational objectives cannot be achieved unless there is a qualified teacher for the subject with the teaching needs as well as the personal characteristics. This point can be explained in certain ways:

Simplifying the knowledge and the information for the students. This qualification depends on the capacity and the level of information of the teacher and the quality of the curriculum. The qualification of the teachers has a great impact in simplifying the information. Beforehand, it is necessary that the teacher has a deeper understanding of the teaching subject and the teaching materials.

Qualifying for a good performance and being active. When a person is qualified in his/her field, they can perform their tasks more easily and more professionally. In practicing it further, their capability in doing it will get better. A successful teacher will be noticed once s/he lets his/her students avoid doing careless activity, guides them in engaging with scientific matters, lessons, and seeing the outcome.

Selecting the teaching objectives and formulating the behavioral goals clearly. The objectives are selected based on knowledge, qualification and psychology.

And matching between the overall behavioral objectives and the teaching tools in upbringing the students should be taken into consideration.

Selecting the main headings of each lesson of the subjects. This subject includes the generalization of the concepts in each lesson of the same subject, selecting the teaching tools to achieve the objectives of the lesson, setting various activities for the individual differences, assigning the homework and the extracurricular activities and knowing the experience, information and the previous preference of the students (Al Obaidi 2017, p. 26).

Overall, the most important factor for a teacher is the ability to simplify the subjects and be selective in subject titles and objectives; of course, this can be possible when the teacher is qualified and has a good experience in teaching.

Concerning the levels of teachers' qualification when delivering the lessons, many of the related experts agree that the teaching qualification has some different levels including:

1. *Knowledge level*: That is, the information, the knowledge process and the mental ability and reflective qualification that they need. For the individual's behavioral performance in all the fields and the required activities, information, practice and theory are needed; of course, the qualification depends on the strategy of teaching and knowledge as well.
2. *Psychological level*: That is, the attitude, presence, desire, direction, value, belief and psychological behavior. In addition, this also extends into some other factors, such as the sensitivity of the individual, and the self-confidence and direction of the individual.
3. *Behavioral level*: That is, all the implemented action of an individual, which includes the psychological and practical qualification such as the technological and relevant tools and a physical movement. The ability to implement these qualifications depends on the previous achievements and the experiences as well as the qualification knowledge of the individuals.
4. *The productive level*: That is, the influence of performance and the practices and applicable parts of the previous qualifications of the students in the field. For applying this, there is a need to pay attention to the art program since these programs help the students to be more qualified.

The educational experts believe that the qualifications consist of the main parts such as: planning, execution and assessment (Abduljabar 2013, p. 112). The success of specialty and the level of performance of the action denote the suitability process of this act. Similarly, the successful lessons of any teacher can be seen in the performance of his or her qualification.

3 The Characteristics of a Successful Teacher

To identify a successful teacher there are some solid characters, which should be present. I highlighted the most important ones below:

Scientific qualification: The basic duty of teachers is that they should perform and present qualifications and skills to the students. There is no need to prove that the teachers must have full information and deliver it to the students clearly. In addition, it needs no proof that if somebody does not have something, s/he cannot give anything. Therefore, teachers cannot give information to the students if they will not take it easily.

Educational qualification: Scientific qualification alone is not enough, but it needs knowledge and a suitable educational method to deal with the students because the students are not machines to install a program on, but are human, they have a spirit, mind, body and anger. In every moment, they go through different psychological conditions and the teachers should deal with these various treatments. That is why teachers must have full information and use different educational methods.

Delivery qualification: As well as having full information about the subject and the educational method of behaving correctly, teachers must also have information about the ways of delivering methods to direct them and deliver excellent ideas to the students.

Teaching willingness: The most noticeable part of a successful teacher belongs to the teaching willingness and delivering the lesson. If the teacher does not love teaching and is not enthusiastic for his/her profession, they will not be successful. Another point of the human being is to feel the psychological comfortability and the greatness of his/her value, they should deliver useful information to the others (Al Obaidi 2017, p. 126).

The steps of succeeding for professional teachers: There are some important steps for professional teachers to follow in order to succeed. We mention some of them below:

1. The teaching method: No profession will be successful unless it is built on a healthy foundation. For delivering lessons, because it contains teaching and learning process and it has its own principles, some of them are related to the teachers, some others are related to the students and the rest are related to the teaching aids. All these principles can be found in educational psychology, sociology and social works.
2. The objectives of teaching: The objectives of teaching are two types: the specific and general objectives, whereby each one is related to the other. The

duration of the general objective lasts longer, it is related to the subject of study, and it extends almost up to two semesters of the educational year. The specific objective is only practiced for a lesson and the subject is specified. The commitment of the teachers to the teaching and education objectives is helpful to achieve the final objectives of the study, which was designed by the teaching policy.

3. Know the level of your students and consider their attitude and their age: When you enter the class for the first time, you will face an uncertain and unknown circumstance. However, their age, psychological status and passion are alike. Once you have information about this generation and their age, you can deal with them correctly. A successful teacher is the one who predicts different elements of his/her subject, prepares the subject, answers the questions, is ready to answer all the questions without being worried about it due to the fact that the teacher does not know the answer or any other reasons.

Generally, in order to present a successful class, the teacher should:

- Prepare students in the subject, state the importance of the objectives and the content of the subject of study, emphasize on the level of the knowledge of the students about the previous subject of study and give them time to do fast reviewing.
- Present a new subject; ask questions to the students so that s/he can collect information about their knowledge on the subject. Give them homework to do since the objective is to engage the students with reading and the school.
- The objective should be suitable and specified in giving ten English words, then, s/he will realize from the answers how many of them replied and how many of them found it difficult. By considering giving a right time, s/he can create a competition among them. The previous activity above will be suitable to make a reasonable competition between them. So, s/he can use it in his/her students' interests by taking the learning difference into consideration (Samin 2015, p. 23).

4 Conclusion

The process of education is, in every sense, one of the fundamental factors for development. No country can achieve sustainable economic development without substantial investments in human capital. Education enriches people's understanding of themselves and the world. It improves the quality of the lives of individuals in any society. To have successful educational institutions, it is vital to have qualified and creative teachers. Unfortunately, we as a Kurdish community until now have many barriers and obstacles in the process of education and teaching. This is why we need urgent actions in planning and developing a better curriculum to promote a qualified education in our institutions. For this, government, the ministry of education, principals, teachers and parents all have their role and need to step up to improve the process of education and develop our institutions.

References

Abduljabar, N. H. (2013). The assessment of the qualifications of the history teachers teaching in preparatory schools of Sulaimani city center, basic education college. Baghdad: Istazh Journal, Vol. 112

Al Obaidi, H. I. Sh. (2017). The modern strategy of teaching and evaluation. Amman: World of Modern Books, T8.

Ali, H. (2017). *Successful Teacher*. Erbil: Minara Printing House.

Samin, S. (2015). *The Characteristics of Successful Teacher*. Erbil: Chwarchra Printing.

Sandelowski, M. (2001). Real Qualitative Research Do No Count: The Use of Numbers in Qualitative Research. *Research in Nursing and Health, 24*(3), 230–240.

Kwestan Ali Abdalla, M.A., B.A in Sociology. Master's degree in Social Work at the University of Sulaimani (2012). Currently, she is doing PhD studies in General Sociology at the same university. She is a lecturer in Social Work in the Faculty of Social Sciences, University of Sulaimani. She has been a member of the Kurdistan Sociologist Association since 2005. She has carried out much research and has many publications in the field of social work and sociology. Her main academic and research interests are in the field of family, youth and adolescent education, international social work and developing education policies for schools, universities and associations. Contact: Kwestan.abdulla@univsul.edu.iq

Ethics and Ethical Values in Social Work and Their Meaning for International Social Work

Kristin Sonnenberg

Abstract

The chapter introduces a broad definition to ethics and values in professional social work and sums up the main theoretical approaches to lay the foundation of the understanding and knowledge of social work ethical values. Furthermore, key documents on an international level will be introduced and their function and meaning as guidelines discussed. At the end of this part, examples from the Middle East area that are members of IFSW (2019) and Kurdistan-Iraq are given with regard to social work values and professional status. As a conclusion, the relevance of shared values and reflection for everyday work within international social work will be summed up.

Keywords

Ethical values • Principles • Ethics • Social work • Codes of ethics

1 Why a Chapter on Ethics and Ethical Values?

Social work as a profession deals with complex situations and works with people who are excluded from various societal aspects. There is a need for critical and reflective thinking to prepare difficult decision-making in conflicting situations. It seems, that 'value commitments and ethical principles are at the core of social work' (Healy 2001, p. 101 in Banks 2012, p. 17). The study of social work ethics

K. Sonnenberg (✉)
Bonn, Germany
E-Mail: sonnenberg@evh-bochum.de

C. Ghaderi et al. (eds.), *Social Work at the Level of International Comparison*,
https://doi.org/10.1007/978-3-658-30394-5_13

can 'encourage critical thinking, reflection and reflexivity through exploring the nature of ethical problems and dilemmas in social work.' (Banks 2012, p. 14).

A knowledge of different theories and approaches enables professionals to see alternative ways of exploring and tackling problems. Sharing ideas about ethical values and guidelines can be a fruitful approach to reflect on social work in an international context. This chapter includes an understanding of social work values and ethics and its theoretical foundations. An ethical background to reflect practice and cooperation with a range of professions in the social welfare field is seen as a universal good. Taking into consideration that local and cultural circumstances differ within countries and contexts, Banks developed a situated ethics of social work or 'progressive social work ethics' (Banks 2012) that will be introduced here.[1]

In a second part an insight is given into the Global Definition of Social Work and the Global Statement of Social Work Ethical Principles published by the International Federation of Social Workers (IFSW) and the International Association of Schools of Social Work (IASSW). This is followed by the results of a small online research for those Middle East countries which are members of IFSW to find out if the international definition and ethical principles play a role within national associations of social work.

2 Social Work Ethical Values

A value-based attitude is a necessary foundation of professional action, because the inner will to reflect and the ability of critical reflection lead to a widening and reinforcement of the competences of action of social workers. It contributes to self-assurance and self-care of the practitioners.

Definition and terms: There is a wide range of values that can be referred to in the history of social work, e.g. spirituality; the influences of Christian (or other religious) values such as belief, love and trust; humanistic values that contribute to an understanding of dialogue-based education and subjective interpretation of reality; justice and social responsibility and economical values as framing conditions. To clarify the different terms of values and ethics, Banks suggests using the term 'ethics' and 'professional ethics' in a broad sense: 'Professional ethics concern matters of right and wrong conduct, good and bad qualities of character and the professional responsibilities attached to relationships in a work context.'

[1] For further discussion see the publication of Banks and Nohr 2012, that offers a broad selection of cases and commentaries of practicing social work ethics around the world.

(Banks 2012, p. 7). This definition contains three main aspects of ethics: conduct, character and responsibility in relationships.

As there are 180 different definitions of the term 'value' (according to Banks 2012, p. 7), 'values' and 'social work values' are used by her in a broad sense as well:

> '*Values* can be regarded as particular types of belief that people hold about what is regarded as worthy or valuable. The term 'social work values' refers to a range of beliefs about what is regarded as worthy or valuable in a social work context—general beliefs about the nature of the good society, general principles about how to achieve this through actions, and the desirable qualities or character traits of professional practitioners.' (ibid., p. 8)

This quote indicates that the values regarded as worthy have to be defined by the professionals and connected with the aim of a good society. This is a task for the community of social workers and the national and international associations they founded.

Different influences on values and powers: It is important to see the influence and interconnectedness of professional and personal values as well as the influence of societal values. Concerning the latter, politics and religion are two important sources of values that influence a society. Looking back on the Western history of social work, 'Religious foundations play a role in delivering social work (…). Social work with its origins in the late nineteenth-century Western Europe and North-America, is rooted in Judeo-Christian values' (Banks 2012, p. 10), such as individual duty. Later in the twentieth century the state took a greater role in providing welfare services. Banks gives an example that 'In some countries where religion is deeply intertwined with culture and law (for example countries where Islam is dominant), societal values will more explicitly reflect the prevailing religion' (ibid., p. 8).

For politics it can be positions such as liberalism or socialism, that are each connected to certain sets of values. 'One significant difference between religious and secular approaches to normative theories of ethics is, in religious ethics, the authority for the principles is derived from God or some other spiritual source. In secular ethics, it may be derived from reason, institution or cultural norms.' (ibid., p. 40). It is important to recognize the different sources of values within their regional context and their conflicting potential. They will, as described above, influence social work action and reflection in decision-making of the professionals involved.

One important argument in the current debate about accepted knowledge and power structures is to be sensitive and critical towards postcolonial developments:

> 'The export of western models of social work to many other countries across the world, and the dominance of western literature, has resulted in a social work practice (in some countries) that rests on an amalgam of different religious and secular values, deriving both from indigenous and external norms and cultures.' (Banks 2012, p. 10).

It is important to reflect on that and to understand what kind of mixture and interweaving influences developed and set the frame for social work practice. This is of special significance within international cooperation and marks one component, staff has to be aware of and open to learn during processes.

3 Different Approaches to Theories of Social Work Ethics[2]

There are two main theoretical approaches to social work ethics, those that focus on principles of action and those that pay more attention to the character of the moral agents and their relationship with each other. Banks argues there should be a progressive social work ethics as a third and new approach (2012). The principle-based approaches focus on ethical decision-making according to a set of principles, which could be conflicting (universal) rights such as self-determination and promotion of welfare. Central values are respect and autonomy. These are based on western philosophy and linked to the 1948 UN Universal Declaration of Human Rights. The assumption is that the individual is the fundamental unit in society, a focus shared by most of the literature on social work ethics and known as modern liberal principles. But:

> 'While presented as universal, these do not reflect the religious and cultural beliefs of people in many parts of the world where the extended family, tribe or community is the focus of attention and the notion of individual rights makes much less sense.' (Banks 2012, p. 41).

Other approaches such as radical or anti-oppressive ones based on quality of character and interpersonal relationships tend to fit better with more communal approaches to ethics.

[2] This chapter follows the structure of Banks and tries to summarize the main points. For a more detailed description of the theories and approaches and for further reading see Banks 2012.

3.1 Duty-Based Principles

The main reference point for modern deontological (duty-based) theories is the German philosopher Immanuel Kant (1724–1804). Based on the authority of reason, his ultimate principle is 'respect for persons' formulated as a categorical imperative. Good action is one that is done from a sense of duty. This approach lays down universal laws and principled autonomy (Banks 2012, p. 44). Human beings as rational and autonomous are free to make their own decisions and choices, they make the moral law and give it to themselves. Another contemporary German philosopher and social theorist Jürgen Habermas (*1929) developed the 'discourse ethic' as a formal system and a development of the Kantian ethics. It is based on universal principles of moral reasoning, enabling humans to reach consensus on generalizable maxims (Banks 2012, p. 44 referring to Habermas 1991). The American Catholic priest Felix Biestek also combines respect for persons with the social work relationships. His seven principles, developed for the first time in 1957, are: individualization, purposeful expression of feelings, controlled emotional involvement, acceptance, nonjudgmental attitude, service user self-determination and confidentiality (Biestek 1961 in Banks 2012, pp. 46 and 47). They can still be found within contemporary social work ethical principles (IFSW and IASSW 2018).

3.2 Utilitarian Principles

Utilitarian principles focus on promoting welfare and justice in society. There are many different concepts. The origins were developed by Jeremy Bentham (1748–1832) and John Stuart Mill (1806–1873): 'The basic idea of utilitarianism is that the right action is that which produces the greatest balance of good over evil—the principle of utility.' (Banks 2012, p. 50). Bentham defined good as happiness (sum of pleasure) and bad as unhappiness (sum of pains), this approach is called *hedonistic utilitarianism.* Mill claims that the good consists of more than happiness, e.g. virtue, knowledge, truth and beauty; this view is called *ideal utilitarianism.* Furthermore, there is *act* and *rule utilitarianism.* Similar to the Kantian approach, rules, such as principles, are e.g. truth-telling, not stealing, respecting autonomy.

Rules are not absolute, but utilitarians would test their efficacy against the consequences. Exceptions from rules are allowed if they lead to more utility (see Banks 2012, p. 50).[3]

3.3 Radical and Anti-Oppressive Principles

Since the 1970s, radical and anti-oppressive principles have followed commitments to emancipation and social justice:

> 'The radical social work approach acknowledged social workers' role as agents of social control on behalf of an oppressive state, and called on them to raise the consciousness of the people they worked with, to encourage collective action for social change and build alliances with working-class and trade union organizations.' (Banks 2012, pp. 53 and 54).

This movement encouraged social workers to change their roles and take a mandate for oppressed clients and against unjust structures within society. Influences on values of social work came with the feminist and anti-racist movements of the mid 1980s and added women and black perspectives, it '(…) identifies values such as equality, collectivism/community and social justice as central to emancipatory forms of social work.' (ibid., p. 54). This adds the criteria of collectivism and community and underlines the ideas of social justice. More precisely: 'Social justice is based on the idea of distributing resources in society according to need (as opposed to desert or merit), challenging existing power structures and oppressive institutions and actions.' (ibid., p. 54)[4]; alongside justice as fairness there is a political moment of questioning unjust power relations within society. These ideas can be found within the current ethical principles of the IFSW.

---

[3] Example: By *Bentham's* definition, everyone counts for one and no one for more than one; *Mill* argues that we should aim for the greatest good for the greatest number of people; these two principle conflict with each other (*utility and justice as fairness*) if, e.g. action 1 produces a large amount of good (happiness) for two people and none for eight; and action 2 produces slightly less total happiness, but distributed it equally between ten people (p. 51).

[4] The Social Work Action Network, www.socialworkfuture.org, places 'social justice' as a key value.

3.4 Character and Relation-Based Approaches

The character and relation-based approaches to ethics stress 'the importance of care, responsibility and relationships between particular people' (Banks 2012, p. xxi). They seem to fit better with non-western cultures. They were derived partly because representatives of these cultures criticized individual approaches as ignoring important features of the moral life and moral judgments, including character, motives and emotions of the moral agent. Furthermore, they fail to consider the context in which judgments are made and particular relationships and commitments people have to each other. The assumption that the individual is the basic unit does not reflect 'the actual norms and practices of many cultures in many parts of the world where the family and the community are primary' (Banks 2012, p. 69).[5]

Central within the *virtue-based approaches* is the importance of character. Its origin goes back to Aristotle [350 BCE]. Virtues generally include courage, integrity, honesty, truthfulness, loyalty, wisdom and kindness (Banks 2012, p. 72). These are relative to culture and role, and the consequence would be that the concept or meaning of a good social worker and of good is internal to the role of social worker, as defined by the community of practitioners. Virtues for social work found within the literature are (Banks 2012 pp. 74 and 75 with reference to Banks and Gallagher, 2009): professional wisdom, courage, respectfulness, care, trustworthiness, justice and professional integrity. All seven virtues are well explained, as in this example: 'Respectful social workers make use of the self in developing relationships and getting to know and understand the perspective of those people with whom they work' (ibid., p. 75).

Ethics of Care refer to caring relationships. Care represents connectedness as a key value, appealing to relationships and focusing on cooperation, communication, caring and relationship between persons. That could mean, e.g., within an African-centered paradigm 'a holistic view of the interconnectedness of all things, and the collective nature of identity' (Banks 2012, p. 79). An ethics of justice tends to represent the dominant mode of moral thinking that reflects the power structure in society (in the global North) and tends to marginalize and exclude the experience of women, black people, working class and other oppressed groups (ibid., with reference to Tronto 1993). Based on Tronto, there are four phases of care: caring about, taking care of, care giving and care receiving

[5] In her work Banks offers a well-structured table to contrast principle and character-based approaches, see 2012. p. 70.

and five elements of the ethics of care: attentiveness, responsibility, competence, responsiveness and the integrity of care (Banks 2012, p. 81).

Another relation-based approach is the ethics of proximity (Levinas), which focuses on responding to the call of the other. The relationship to the other is not reciprocal, but 'it is a readiness to give unconditionally and is non-negotiable' (Banks 2012, p. 83). There are more approaches recently discussed within the context of diversity, narrative and constructionism that could be summarized as postmodern ethics (e.g. Baumann).

3.5 Progressive Social Work Ethics: A Situated Ethics of Social Justice

Banks calls the variety of approaches a 'fragmentation of value' (2012, p. 87). There cannot be a ranking of values, but a concept of professional wisdom to capture the practical wisdom required by practitioners in professional contexts: 'It can be linked with the notion of the reflective and reflexive practitioner, requiring, among other things, the ability to learn from and reflect on experience, a sensitivity to people's feelings and situations, attentiveness to the features of situations and ability to reason' (ibid., p. 89). Professional ethics should include elements of principles, character, care and relationship, because principles provide a useful framework for discussing and analyzing ethical issues in professional practice. Not all people are always virtuous or have the capacity for it, therefore some rules are needed. However, it would not be desirable if there was a degeneration into a focus on rules that leads to a matter of learning and implementing rules rather than a process of critical and responsible reflection (ibid., p. 91). Banks suggests a situated ethics of social justice that includes a set of values for a progressive social work. This is based on Tronto's ideas of a political ethics of care, focused on human relationships in the context of structures of power and oppression. Preliminary values for a situated ethics of social justice for social work are: radical social justice, empathic solidarity, relational autonomy, collective responsibility and moral courage. (ibid., pp. 93 and 94). Especially in inter-professional contexts, it is important to be clear about the social work values to 'play a distinctive role that complements and sometimes challenges that of other professionals' (p. 95).

Considering the complex situations where social work is active, it seems convincing to follow the progressive approach, which is more flexible concerning situational factors, but at the same time sets basic principles and rules that are not open to discussion, such as social justice and human dignity. It encourages and demands an exchange and discussion within the teams and communities of social workers to reflect values and principles in specific contexts and relationships with a focus on the moral agent in relation to his or her environment.

4 Global Social Work Statement of Ethical Principles

A common form of writing down agreed values is a Code of Ethics. Most European countries, including Germany (DBSH[6] in 1974) and England (BASW[7] in 1975) introduced a code of ethics for social work. These codes are closely linked to the UN Convention of Human Rights and the Right of the Child. The current national codes are closely linked to the model of the International Federation of Social Work (IFSW).[8] Codes can include values, general key-principles, practice principles or even practical rules (Banks 2012, p. 109). In her latest work, Banks describes the functions of a code of ethics as protection of the clients, guidance for practitioners, enhancement of professional status, creating and maintaining professional identity and professional discipline and regulation (Banks 2012, p. 114).[9]

Around the turn of the twenty-first century, within social work a code was understood as a reference point for reflection, a 'map of the minefield of practice' (Payne 1996, p. 69) or as to fulfill the 'function of a lighthouse' (Clark 1999, p. 259). Serving orientation is seen as an element for professionalism with respect to specific ethical values (Banks 2012, p. 95). Codes can be the tool of reflection and enlighten the issues and controversies of practical dilemmas, which is indispensable within the context of the complexity and ambiguity of social work.

In recent social work literature, a range of principles from Kantian-utilitarian-radical approaches appear. Looking at the IFSW and IASSW statement, principles of human rights and social justice 'lie at the heart of social work' (Banks 2012, p. 60). Three basic principles generally occur in all kinds of codes of ethics (following Banks): (1) Respect for the dignity and worth of all human beings, (2) Promoting welfare of wellbeing, (3) Promoting social justice. Each one contains

[6] DBSH = German Professional Association for Social Workers and Social Pedagogues.

[7] BASW = British Association of Social Work.

[8] First version in 1976 (Baum 1996, p. 18).

[9] Her earlier works list four functions, the last one listed above is new, see Banks 1995, pp. 73–89; Banks 1998, p. 221.

a cluster of sub-principles. The feature and emphasis of social justice distinguishes social work from other caring professions (ibid., p. 65):

> 'Social workers require, therefore, not only a good understanding of the concepts and principles of social justice, human dignity and welfare, but also the confidence, commitment, motivation and skills to put these principles into practice in difficult and challenging contexts.' (ibid.).

These principles are found within the agreed global definition of social work in 2014:

> 'Social work is a practice-based profession and an academic discipline that promotes social change and development, social cohesion, and the empowerment and liberation of people. Principles of social justice, human rights, collective responsibility and respect for diversities are central to social work.' (IFSW and IASSW, 2014).

The newest version of the Global Social Work Statement of Ethical Principles from the IFSW was published in 2018 (IFSW and IASSW 2018). The three core principles at the very beginning are: (1) Recognition of the inherent dignity of humanity, (2) Promoting human rights, and (3) Promoting social justice. The nine principles are: (1) Dignity of humanity, (2) Human rights, (3) Social justice, (4) Right to self-determination, (5) Right to participation, (6) Confidentiality, privacy, (7) People as whole persons, (8) Technology and social media and (9) Professional integrity. As mentioned above, a strong link can be seen towards the Global Definition of Social Work.

Examples for human rights and social justice: Looking at the descriptions, social work has a political mandate on different levels that matches with the radical approach outlined above, to empower people and fight for excluded persons. Within the last quoted paragraph, collective responsibility is mentioned as well as a hint towards the relationships within communities, which could be a hint for the situated approach, taking into consideration the interconnectedness of human beings (and nature):

> Promoting human rights:
>
> '2.2. Social workers respect and defend the human rights principle of indivisibility, and promote all civil, political, economic, social, cultural and environmental rights.
>
> 2.3. Recognizing that culture sometimes serves as a disguise to violate human rights, social workers serve as cultural mediators to enable consensus building, find an appropriate balance between competing human rights, and to advocate for the rights of

> marginalized, stigmatized, excluded, exploited and oppressed individuals and groups of persons.
>
> 2.4. Social workers recognize that human rights need to coexist alongside collective responsibility, understanding that individual human rights can only be realized on a day-to-day basis if people take responsibility for each other and the environment, and if they work towards creating reciprocal relationships within communities.' (IFSW and IASSW 2018)

With respect to international social work, a special meaning can be found in paragraph 2.3 describing the task of a social worker to *serve as cultural mediators*. This seems to be a necessary and significant point within international social work. The *collective responsibility and reciprocal relationships within communities* (2.4) are named as coexisting with human rights. Within international social work, it underlines respectful and reflective critical awareness at local levels, with regard to common global standards or orientation.

4.1 Members of IFSW and the Connection with the Code of Ethics

The IFSW is structured into five regions and follows the continents Africa, Asia and Pacific, Latin America and Caribbean, Europe and North America. The Middle East is represented within the Asian and Pacific Region that has member organizations from 28 countries. At the moment there are listed: Bahrain, Iran, Lebanon, Kuwait, Palestine and Yemen. Germany belongs to the European Region, Kurdistan-Iraq to the Asian and Pacific Region. Out of the 178 members on the homepage, 23 National Codes of Ethics of Social Work are presented by IFSW member organizations. The member organization from Germany is called the German Professional Association for Social Work (Deutscher Berufsverband für Soziale Arbeit e.V., DBSH) and published the latest code of professional ethics for social workers in 2014 (DBSH). It is only accessible in German. Kurdistan-Iraq is not a member of the IFSW, because no association of social workers has been founded so far.

In the following Tab. 1, an overview is given concerning the associations of social work and national code of ethics for the Middle East members. These countries are non-Western and may have another orientation within a set of values. This is only a starting point and can be further researched in the future.

Table 1 Overview of the members from the Middle East within IFSW (own table based at the information found at IFSW and own research)

Association	Information	Code of Ethics
Bahrain Sociologists' Society	No more information given by IFSW Own research: It is possible to study an BA in Sociology at the University of Bahrain, College of Arts	*No social work as a profession, therefore no code of ethics found*
Iran Association of Social Workers l انجمنمددکاراناجتماعیایران	Established: 1961 Joined IFSW: 2012	Iranian Social workers' manifesto (oath), from 1978
Lebanese Association of Social Workers	No more information given by IFSW Own research[a]: Social Workers' Syndicate established under number 1/41 from the Ministry of Labor on February 1, 1997	Values and Principles of Social Workers' Syndicate
Kuwait Association of Social Workers	No more information given by IFSW Following the given links to facebook and twitter: Established in 1967[b], no more information given in English language	*No Code of Ethics found*

(continued)

As can be seen in Tab. 1, Iran, Lebanon and Palestine have associations for social workers and concerning ethical principles they offer information in English. In Iran they have an 'Iranian Social workers' manifesto' (oath) since 1978, in Lebanon they have written down 'Values and Principles of Social Workers' Syndicate', in Palestine it is the 'Palestinian Code of Ethics and Regulatory Policies'. For Kuwait the information is not accessible in English. It can be further researched in Arabic. Some countries do have interdisciplinary associations or possibilities for social workers to join other professional societies such as the Bahrain Sociologists' Society or the Yemen Association of Sociologists, Social

Table 1 (continued)

Association	Information	Code of Ethics
Palestinian Union of Social Workers and Psychologists نقابةالأخصائيينالإجتماعيينوالنفسيينالفلسطينية	Number of members: 9000 Established: 1997 Joined IFSW: 2006 Abstract describing the Union	Palestinian Code of Ethics and Regulatory Policies
Yemen Association of Social Workers	No more information given by IFSW Facebook: Yemen Association of Sociologists, Social Workers and Psychologists	*No Code of Ethics found*

Own representation in social media, facebook: [a]https://www.facebook.com/pages/category/Cause/Social-Workers-Syndicate-in-Lebanon-210432256016003/, accessed: September 2, 2019.
Own representation in social media, facebook: [b]https://www.facebook.com/pg/aswkuwait/about/?ref=page_internal, accessed: September 2, 2019.

Workers and Psychologists. In Palestine it is a Union of Social Workers and Psychologists. This is similar to Kurdistan-Iraq, where social workers can join the associations of sociologists or psychologists.[10]

Following the basic information given at the IFSW and due to my online research looking for the name of the associations found at IFSW, the following result can be added.

Bahrain Sociologists' Society: The Bahrain Sociologists' Society is part of Bahrain Social Watch Coalition. This organisation is composed of Bahrain Transparency, Bahrain Human Rights Society, Bahraini Women's Renaissance Society, Awal Women Society and Sociologists Society Best.[11] The BA of Sociology is located at the University of Bahrain, College of Arts. A short English description of the study program informs about learning outcomes:

[10] The profession itself is still in a pioneer phase since the introduction of the social work studies in 2014/15 in Slemani. The first BA *Social Work* studies in Iraqi-Kurdistan were established at the University of Salahadin in Erbil in 2008/09, see Ghaderi and Saleh Karim 2019, p. 177). At other universities, social work is part of sociology, e.g. at the University of Dohuk (see UoD 2019).

[11] https://www.socialwatch.org/node/831, accessed: October 7, 2019.

> '17: An understanding of social groups in various societies in terms of differences in socio-cultural resources and outcomes. 18: An understanding of the characteristics of contemporary societies and their international contexts and the ability to discuss the differences between Middle Eastern and Western societies, and between the developed and less developed world. 19: An understanding of some of the challenges that globalization poses to contemporary societies and ways of life. 20: An understanding of the social and ethical implications of sociological research findings and of social policies.'[12]

The information given here could be linked to social work within a broader understanding, it is here clearly a part of sociology. Only a small hint for ethical implications of research is given. Values are not explicitly named.

Lebanese Association of Social Workers: The Lebanese Association of Social Workers aims at influence within the Arab and international world. Objectives are to: 'Strengthen the status and role of the union in Lebanon and the Arab and international world, Organize the administrative entity of the union, Strengthen the social work profession in the Lebanese society and protect the rights of professionals.'[13] Concerning a code of ethics, the following information had been found: '*Values and Principles of Social Workers' Syndicate*: social responsibility, cultural diversity, social responsibility, excellence and creativity, transparency and accountability, equality and social justice'.[14] Some of them match with the IFSW statements, some seem to differ. That could be further analyzed and discussed with social workers from Lebanon. The three core criteria Banks suggests partly seem to be relevant: social justice is mentioned at the end of the list, human rights can be found on the website under 'activities', but the promotion of welfare could not be found explicitly. In another context the information was found that Lebanon is listed as a member of 'The International Association for Social Work with Groups (IASWG), Inc. [which] is the premier international association for social workers and allied helping professionals engaged in group work'.[15] This might be a hint for the promotion of welfare.

---

[12] https://www.uob.edu.bh/en/index.php/colleges/college-of-arts/social-sciences/102-ba-in-sociology, accessed: October 7, 2019.

[13] https://www.facebook.com/pages/category/Cause/Social-Workers-Syndicate-in-Lebanon-210432256016003/, accessed 08.10.2019.

[14] ibid. Lebanon facebook page, 'social responsibility' is listed twice within the original source.

[15] https://www.iaswg.org/

Iraqi-Kurdistan – ethical principles: In 2016 the 'Social Researchers' Conduct Regulations in the Juvenile Judicial System' was introduced.[16] The conduct is based on the Global Social Work Statement of Ethical Principles (IFSW) that was discussed in the field of social work in prisons. It is described as a 'set of rules and guidelines of behaviors to regulate the relationship between social workers and juveniles. This is for the sake of commitment to the professional boundaries and best compliance by the social workers on the one hand, and to ensure juveniles' rights and achieving the best interest of children in Kurdistan Region on the other' (Saed 2016 p. 1). These guidelines are not to identify details of daily work, but are:

> '(...) some main principles to set the researchers' relationship especially in those fields where confrontations can be found between the researchers' values and culture and the cases they see. They are also to offer help for making decisions professionally in order to avoid conflict of interest. These regulations have made (to an extent) the main principles of universal declaration of children rights a source to deal with juveniles: which are children's best interest, desegregation, and involvement for the sake of survival and growth of children.' (ibid.)

As basic principles of social work the following are named and later explained in detail: Respecting and applying human rights principles and social justice; Respecting human integrities; Respecting professional tangibility and Working according to professional skills. A strong link is set towards the rights of the juvenile in participating during the processes (UN Children's Rights Act 1989). The persons addressed are called 'the researchers', (syndicate of) sociologists and universities (Departments of Social Affairs, Sociology, Psychology). Social work as a special profession is not listed yet, whereas the area of social work within the juvenile judicial system is well described. B.A. Social workers can start their working life in this area.

4.2 Ethics in International Social Work—Final remarks

Independent from a specific context, situation or country, there will be a discussion about the relationship between universalism and particularity in ethics. Banks' suggestion of a progressive situated ethics approach that tries to combine different approaches and develops them further could be very fruitful and should

[16] Paper prepared by Salah Sedeeq Saeed Director of Access to Justice Program, Erbil Office, 2016, unpublished pdf version.

be discussed with social workers and within social work associations. Within international cooperation projects, critical thinking about different theories enables responsible decision-making and could be used in workshops to have a joint ground for discussions. The publication by Banks and Nohr (2012) offers a rich selection of cases from all over the world that can be used for further reflection.

It is important to think and connect this discussion to other discourses such as the postcolonial theory within current international social work.

To sum up, a shared value base can strengthen the profession in different ways: Guidance in difficult situations (conflicts, dilemmas), establish the professional status and identity at global and local level, enable and support reflective skills for high quality social work in accordance with human dignity and social justice. In practice there has to be a way of integrating agreed standards and local conditions. Exchanging ideas and issues can widen one's own understanding of difficult ethical decision-making. International comparison might lead to common grounds when different countries choose the same international values and principles such as the international definition of social work or the global ethics for social work. An ethical background to reflect practice and cooperation with a range of professions in the social welfare field is seen as a universal good. How these universal principles may be applied in local and cultural circumstances is an important discourse and should be further discussed in the future.

References

Banks, S. (1995). *Ethics and Values in Social Work*. London: Macmillan.

Banks, S. (1998). Professional Ethics in Social Work – What Future? *British Journal of Social Work, 28,* 213–231.

Banks, S. (2012). *Ethics and Values in Social Work* (4th ed.). Palgrave: London.

Banks, S., & Nohr, K. (Eds.). (2012). *Practising Social Work ethics around the world. Cases and commentaries*. Routlegde: Oxon.

Baum, H. (1996). *Ethik Sozialer Berufe. (Ethics of the social professions)*. München: Schöningh.

Clark, C. (1999). Observing the lighthouse. From theory to institutions in social work ethics. *European Journal of Social Work, 2*(3), 259–270.

DBSH (Eds.). (2014). Berufsethik des DBSH. https://www.dbsh.de/fileadmin/redaktionell/pdf/Sozialpolitik/DBSH-Berufsethik-2015-02-08.pdf. Accessed 12 Dec 2019.

Ghaderi, C., & Saleh Karim, L. (2019). Social Work with refugees in Kurdistan Region in Iraq. In M. Pfaller-Rott, A. Kallay, & D. Böhler (Eds.), *Social Work with migrants and refugees* (pp. 163–185). Ostrava: University of Ostrava.

IASSW & IFSW (2004). Global Standards for Social Work Education and Training. https://www.-aiets.org/global-standards-for-social-work-education-and-training/. Accessed 14 Oct 2019.

IFSW & IASSW (2014). Global Definition of Social Work. https://www.ifsw.org/what-is-social-work/global-definition-of-social-work/. Accessed 27 Aug 2019.

IFSW & IASSW (2018). Global Social Work Statement of Ethical Principles. Long version, 27.04.2018. https://www.ifsw.org/wp-content/uploads/2018/07/Global-Social-Work-Statement-of-Ethical-Principles-IASSW-27-April-2018-1.pdf, Accessed 27 Aug 2019.

Payne, M. (1996). *What is professional Social Work?* Birmingham: Venture Press.

Kristin Sonnenberg, Prof. Dr., Professor of Social Work at the Protestant University of Applied Sciences Bochum. She studied Social Pedagogy in Germany, completed an M.A. in Comparative European Social Studies at the University of North London and her PhD at the University of Cologne in Germany 2004 in the Faculty of Educational Science. She is a qualified psychodrama trainer. Since 2011 she is specialized in the field of methods and conceptualizing social work. Her main research projects are social inclusion of people with disabilities and international social work. She is member of the German Association of Social Workers (DGSA). Since 2016 she has been head of the BA Social Work Studies and, together with Prof. Ghaderi, she was leader of the DAAD cooperation project CoBoSUnin 2016–2019 between the University of Sulaimani and Bochum. Contact: sonnenberg@evh-bochum.de

The Ethics of Social Work in Kurdistan—the Curriculum Implementation on the Local Level

Chro Mohammed Faraj

Abstract

In Kurdistan, the roots of social work or helping people in need and life improvement are a unit and an integral part of Kurdish society, but academically and professionally it is new. Its aim is a completion of *full social services* in the most qualified way. The social work profession is proportional according to the need and resources to offer services to all categories of society through institutions. Ethics and Values are the reflection and combination of the academic preparation from university (knowledge, skill, ethic and value, process), society's culture, norms, values, religion, policy, law, and human rights, and the policy of the institutions or the organizations.

The aim of this chapter is to present a description and explanation of the ethical practice of social work in Kurdistan. The chapter includes a general overview about social work, the social work departments at universities, the meaning of ethics and its different levels in social work, practicing ethics within social work, and ethical roles and responsibilities according to clients, colleagues, institutions, society, practitioners, and the profession of social work.

Keywords

Social work • Social service • Departments of Social Work • Social Work Curriculum and Implementation • Ethic definition • Ethic structure • Ethical levels • Ethical roles • Ethical responsibilities

C. Mohammed Faraj (✉)
Slemani, Kurdistan Region, Iraq
E-Mail: chro.faraj@univsul.edu.iq

C. Ghaderi et al. (eds.), *Social Work at the Level of International Comparison*,
https://doi.org/10.1007/978-3-658-30394-5_14

1 General Overview of Social Work in Kurdistan

The main aim of social work as a scientific discipline and a practice-based profession is to help people in need and enhance their well-being. In other words, social work tries to improve the quality of life, promotes social change, development, and the empowerment of people. In Kurdistan, social work roots or helping people in need and life improvement is a unit and integral part of Kurdish society. It is new in its academic and professional form. Social work in Kurdistan is a practice-based profession that works appropriately in reality in a way that can benefit society, by using the theoretical approaches of sociology, psychology and pedagogy in the social context. In a way that completes other professional roles of other sciences or specialties, in another meaning: social work is the completion of *full social services.*

The necessity for establishing social work in Kurdistan is due to increase social problems of society as a result of the ongoing development and the complexity of modern life, and the effects of war and the ravages that lead to the disruption of human life in all aspects of society, and also because of ongoing developments of the sciences. On the base of the availability of possibilities (material and non-material resources) and the development of academic, scientific, and professional social studies, and also because of the great importance of care and protection policy, the Kurdistan Regional Government tries to provide services and necessary assistance for special need categories and for all citizens in general as well, to help those in need and gain well-being. The field of social work includes all categories of society, regardless to people's *race*, *gender*, *age*, *religion*, and *political interest*, and it includes all kinds of institutions and organizations (governmental and non-governmental or local and global) like welfare, education, special need, medical, reform, court, etc.

The social work application framework in reality has three levels: *micro-individual (personal frame), mezzo-small group (social frame), macro-society (public frame).* The role of social work occupation and the social work practitioners' right and duty is organized formally according to the type, the nature, the policy, and the kind of services of the institution or organization include formal writing. The formal writing includes the working guides, and the instructions of the social work practitioner like, in the kindergarten and the schools, and include the professional roles and the responsibilities of social work practitioner like in the juvenile laws.

2 Definition and Implementation of Ethics Within the Curriculum of Social Work Studies

In Kurdistan region, the establishment of social work as a scientific-academic field began for the first time in 2007. There are two scientific departments of social work in Kurdistan region; one of them belongs to the Salahaddin University in Erbil, within the College of Arts. BA studies and training started for the first time in the academic year 2008–2009. The other one belongs to the University of Sulaimani (UoS), within the College of Humanities. BA studies and training started for the first time in the academic year 2014–2015. Social work at UoS is established first for the academic year 2012–2013 as a dependent part of sociology. At that time, social work was introduced as a test, and the students could study their last two academic years (third & fourth grade) of sociology in social work specialty, according to their choice after finishing second grade successfully. But their professional titles were the same as the graduations of sociology which is a *Social Researcher (procedure social researches)*. The scientific title of the graduates of the department of social work after graduation is *Social Worker (practice social work)*. Both departments of social work have continuous theory–practice based learning and training included within the four years of studies.

Within the concrete curriculum of social work, ethics and values of social work will be studied in stage two and its title is 'Laws and ethics in social work', with three units of the module, and three hours in a week. The subject focuses on the laws, ethics and values regarding social work in the Kurdistan region. The subject is studied in Kurdish language. The methods of teaching include lecturing and preparing reports, seminars and doing exams. The course lectures consist of basic knowledge and the laws, ethics and values regarding social work in general and particularly the laws, ethics and values of social work presence in Kurdistan. The main aim of this subject is to teach the students the laws in general and particularly juvenile, personal, and family laws in Kurdistan region, and the ethics and values in practicing social work in Kurdistan region.

3 The Context of Ethics in Social Work

Ethic refer to the informal rules that define what types of behavior are appropriate and what types of behavior are inappropriate (Barsky 2010, p. 3) and what is good, right, and how one ought to behave in regard to other individuals and society as a whole (Tjeltveit 2005, p. 16). In social work, ethic is a system of moral principles and perceptions about right versus wrong and the resulting philosophy of conduct that is practiced by an individual, group, profession, or culture (Barker 1995, p. 106). The main ethics of social work that are implemented in reality are derived from its philosophy (each human has worth and dignity), principles (acceptance, individuality, non-judgmentalism, objectivity, self-determination, confidentiality) and values (social life, service, and justice) (NASW 2017, pp. 5 and 7). Professional ethics identify, draw and affect the nature and the framework of professional intervention and helping processes particularly in making decisions or decision-making process (e.g. how to perform and offer social services through social work by its practitioners). In other words: ethics concern the way social work is practiced, organized, managed and planned (Hugman and Smith 2001, p. 2). The ethics can be derived according to the main levels of social work practice like as follows:

A. Micro ethic toward individual (e.g. social work practitioner, clients).
B. Mezzo ethic toward small groups (e.g. family of client, colleague, institution or organization).
C. Macro ethic toward large group (e.g. community, society).

The basics of professional ethics in practicing social work are an unwritten system. The ethics of social work consists in accordance with the rights and duties of the practitioner according to the type of institution or organization. It is based on accepted beliefs and morals that affect, organize, direct, and control behavior. The ethics reflect the combination of three main resources together:

- Academic preparation from university (knowledge, skill, ethic and value, process).
- Society's culture, norm, value, religion, policy, law, and human rights.
- The policy of the institutions or the organizations.

4 Practicing Ethics within Social Work—Six Different Parts

The center point of social work is the client. Ethics in practicing social work can be explained by including six parts, which are: client, colleagues, institution, and the practitioner of social work, society and the profession of social work. All these parts are related, interconnected and complete each other, they are not independent and they affect and reflect each other (Fig. 1).

Fig. 1 Ethic implementations in social work (author's own)

(1) *Ethical responsibilities according to the client:* The client can be an individual, a family or a group of people that need social services. The client is the center point of social work because social workers focus on clients and manage material (physical, financial) and non-material (human, information) resources available in the clients' environment (social context) to change the clients state to a better state (fulfill the need of solving problem or obtain quality of life or gain well-being) and this through the process of professional intervention. Ethical implementation in practicing social work regarding clients has three direction:

1. Client as a person (combination of biological and psychological and social aspects).
2. Client as a member of a group or a member of his/her family.
3. Client as a member of his/her community and his/her society.

Ethical responsibilities according to social work practitioners include the following main points:

1. As the main aim: develop the client's situation to a better and promote well-being individually, socially, and publicly.
2. The practitioner has professional permission (academic certificate) that allows his/her academically and scientifically to apply the profession in reality.
3. Identification of social work: What are the possibilities and restraints for social work, what are the ways of working, and the possible consequences to

the client and other parties that are involved in the client's situation or condition (problem), in addition to laws, the institution's policy and the availability of resources.

4. Provision of services to client only in the professional context from the beginning to the end of the helping process, respect sensitive boundaries (personal, social, public) of the client and other parties that are involved in the client's condition and life (personal, and social environment).
5. Respect and promotion of the right of client to self-determination and assist him/her in his/her situation or condition, to identify and clarify his/her goals (the practitioner is the guiding spirit).
6. Protection of the information and the records of the client and the client's condition and other parties of the client's condition (the records should be documented in the client's files), and respect the client's privacy and confidentiality, and disclose the client's information when needed and appropriate, according to the client's agreement and consent, or the parties that are involved in the client's condition.
7. Commitment to the client and the society's culture, values, norms, and rules. And by that the awareness to understand and respect the diversity of the culture as a plural society (race, gender, age, marital states, religion, political belief, immigration status, social condition, mental or physical ability and condition).
8. Protection of the client's interests to the greatest extent possible, and also the other parties of the client's condition or problem, for example: family member, husband or wife as a couple, friend, co-worker, relative, etc.
9. Protection of the right (written-law and also unwritten-law) of the client and other parties of the client's condition and take responsible steps to safeguard their rights all together. In other words, the practitioner should not take the side of one party against another party or vice versa.
10. Avoiding abandoning and ensure the continuity of the social work services according to the client's needs and requirement and preferences, and also refer the client to other professionals when other services are required or needed.

(2) *Ethical responsibilities according to colleagues*: Colleagues are those employees and employers who work with social workers directly in the institution of work. They are social workers or have a different specialty. Social worker works with the colleagues as a staff or as a team to obtain the institution's goal together. The ethical implementation in practicing social work regarding colleagues has three directions:

1. Practitioner as an independent professional to the colleagues.
2. Practitioner as a professional member with colleagues (work as a team).
3. Practitioner as a professional member with colleagues of the institution.

And ethical responsibilities of social work practitioner include the following main points:

1. Respect: build a professional relationship and treat colleagues and employees with respect.
2. Confidentiality: respect confidential information that is shared by colleagues.
3. Obligation, solidarity, and collaboration: work assistance, participation, and cooperation with colleagues or different specialties and professions in a team framework, and maintaining the privacy or confidentiality of multi-professional teamwork while practicing social work.
4. Consult, dispute: avoid a dispute with colleagues and employees, and seeking the advice and counsel of colleagues in different specialties and knowledge and expertise as needed regarding the client's condition or situation to achieve the purpose of the helping process.
5. Interference: protect and maintain the privacy, confidentiality, and independence of social work, and not allow others to interfere with the working way in the field of social work- (identify work limits).

(3) *Ethical responsibilities according to institutions*: Institutions can be public or private, local or global organizations that are found to offer a certain service to particular persons in need (client) and in which social workers work with other employees. The kind of institution includes the social worker's institution and any other institutions that is involved in the client cases. Ethical implementation in practicing social work regarding institutions has three directions;

1. Institution, which has its own structure.
2. Institution with other institutions.
3. Institution, which is a unit of society.

Moreover, social work practitioners, ethical responsibilities include the following main points:

1. Commitment: ensure commitment to the institution's policy and instruction.
2. Resource: offer services to the client according to the availability of the institution's ability and competence.

3. Improvement: work to improve the institution's role in society as a unit that works with other institutions through improving the role of social work in the institution.
4. Organize: participate or engage by organize the activities of institution inside or outside the institution.

(4) *Ethical responsibilities according to the society:* Society is a social unit that contains the case of a client and the institution that the social worker works in. Alternatively, it is a social context that includes material and non-material resources with regard to a client. Ethical implementation in practicing social work regarding society has three directions;

1. Society as a resource of practice in reality.
2. Society as a resource of maintenance of practice in reality.
3. Society as a resource to prove and develop practice in reality.

And the social work practitioner, ethical responsibilities include the following main points:

1. Respect: regard clients as a basic unit in the society, so respect and maintain society's culture, value, norm, economic, religion, and politics.
2. Reality: building a social framework in reality, so that the helping process or provision of social services should be appropriate with the environment that the client lives in.
3. Welfare or well-being: promotion and enhancement welfare or well-being of the individual, group, and society locally and globally, obtain life needs with the aim of improvement and development.

(5) *Ethical responsibilities according to practitioner him-/herself*: A practitioner is a person that practices social work and manages the client's cases and offers social services directly to a client to help him/her to fulfill a need, solve a problem and restore stability and gain well-being or quality of life. The ethical implementation in practicing social work regarding the practitioner him/her has three direction:

1. Practitioner as a person him-/herself (personal, social, and public).
2. Practitioner as a professional.
3. Practitioner as a member in the society.

And the social work practitioner, ethical responsibilities include the following main points:

1. Personal, social, and public: draw a line between profession and personal life, updating personal life continuously, and maintain social life as a member of family and a society.
2. Professional: improve and update as social work practitioner contentiously through participation in academic courses and training and work as a supervisor and a trainer.
3. Reflection: being an active member personally, socially, and publicly in the society, reflecting society in the practice and in the social work regarding offering social services.

(6) *Ethical responsibilities according to the profession of social work:* Social work as a profession promotes social change, problem-solving in human relationships and empowerment, and liberates people to enhance their well-being. Utilizing theories of human behavior and social systems, social work intervenes at the points where people interact with their environment. Principles of human rights and social justice are fundamental to social work (Lymbery and Postle 2007, p. 3). Ethical implementation in practicing social work regarding the profession of social work has three direction:

1. Social work as an independent profession.
2. Social work as a complement of other professions.
3. Social work as a profession of society.

And social work practitioners, ethical responsibilities include the following main points:

1. Independence: enhance, maintain, and develop the profession of social work with its own background of knowledge, value, ethic, skill, and process.
2. Integrate: participate and share knowledge, value, ethic, skill, and process of social work with other professions to enhance and improve human well-being.
3. Reflect: social work reflects the society in practice, which differs from society to society.

5 Conclusions

Although social work or helping people in need is an integral part of Kurdish society, it is new as a professional form. The social work profession in Kurdistan is an imperative necessity like in any other community and society, and it is appropriate or convenient according to the need and the availability of material and non-material resources of society to offer services to all categories of Kurdish society and all Kurdistan citizens. In Kurdistan generally, social work fields (education, research, practice), and its ethics and values are organized according to international social work and according to Kurdish society (social context and needs). Success is the relative issue that includes quantitative and qualitative measures and is constantly changing according to availability. In general, the success of social work practice and its professional ethics, in particular, depends on the extent of commitment and is related to the development of social work and the development of the society in general and its accompanying problems and crisis.

References

Barker, R. L. (1995). *The social work dictionary* (3rd ed.). USA: Library of Congress Cataloging-in-Publication Data.

Barsky, A. E. (2010). *Ethics and values in social work*. New York: Oxford University Press.

Hugman, R., & Smith, D. (2001). *Ethical issues in social work*. U.K.: Taylor & Francis e-Library.

Lymbery, M., & Postle, K. (2007). *Social work a companion to learning* (1st ed.). Britain: SAGE publications.

NASW (2017). Code of Ethics of the National Association of Social Workers. PDF, NASW, U.S.A.

Parrott, L. (2010). *Values and Ethics In Practicing Social Work* (2nd ed.). U.K.: Learning Matters.

Tjeltveit, A. C. (2005). *Ethics and values in Psychotherapy*. U.K.: Taylor & Francis e-Library.

Chro Mohammed Faraj, Lecturer in Social Science, B.A. in Sociology (2008), M.A. in Social Work (2014) at the Department of Sociology, College of Humanities, University of Sulaimani in Slemani, Kurdistan Region of Iraq, where she also worked as an Assistant Researcher and Researcher (2009–2011), as Assistant Lecturer in the Unit of Higher Studies (2014–2015), and as Assistant Lecturer (2015), and Lecturer (2018). Contact: chro.faraj@univsul.edu.iq

Importance of Integration and Implementation of Psycho-Social Counseling in Social Work

Cinur Ghaderi

Abstract

The meaning of integrating and implementing psycho-social counseling as an intervention method within social work will be introduced in this chapter. This includes the differentiation between counseling in everyday life and in a professional context, the reflection of theoretical and methodical approaches as well as the consideration of historical and sociocultural circumstances. These multifactorial conditions frame the requirements of counseling skills in teaching and in practice.

Keywords

Counseling • International dialog • Teaching • Social work • Germany • Kurdistan

Counseling, counselling, Rawejkari, Beratung … not even the choice of the word is arbitrary, each one has its own history, a context, a connotation. Even the American (counseling) and the British (counselling) expressions are different. In the German-speaking area, the anglicism 'counseling' represents a history and marks a novel discourse concerning the German term 'Beratung'.

In the Kurdish-speaking language area in Iraq, the term 'counseling' reflects a historic turn in academic teaching after the disempowerment and downfall of Saddam Hussein and the increasing influence and presence of international organizations and forces on the education and job policies. In everyday life there is

C. Ghaderi (✉)
Düsseldorf, Germany
E-Mail: ghaderi@evh-bochum.de

C. Ghaderi et al. (eds.), *Social Work at the Level of International Comparison*,
https://doi.org/10.1007/978-3-658-30394-5_15

a difference to be made between the term 'Nasihat', borrowed from the Arabic language, and the cultural tradition implying seniors giving advice to 'juniors' or hierarchically higher persons giving instructions to subordinates. This act of directing instruction is enshrined in broad sections of society as a traditional habit, and advice-takers are not averse to this practice per se, as it is also associated with well-meaning caring. In that everyday practice, the distribution of power and the question of who is in possession of the right to give advice or of moral authority is predetermined according to social status. Increasingly, instead of the Arabic term 'Nasihat', the Kurdish term 'Amojgari' is used. This connotes less the hierarchical position of the interaction partners and puts the 'giving of advice' in the foreground.

Additionally, 'Rawejkari' (ڕاوێژکاری) is common, which can be translated as 'consulting' and is rather associated with a conversation between equal parties. The term 'Rawejkari' is also used in professional contexts, generally in specified combinations like 'Rawejkari komalayati' (social counseling), 'Rawejkari daruni' (psychological counseling) and 'Rawejkari yasaii' (legal counseling).

Whether it is 'Rawejkari', 'Beratung' or 'counseling' in the practice of social work—all these terms make demands on being a form of professional counseling and different from everyday counseling.

Professional counseling is more than mere helping and informing. It also comprises *process regulation and/or management.* The asymmetric distribution of knowledge and, respectively, the equal distribution of different knowledge, are constitutive for professional counseling. Moreover, the possible existing hazard of open and concealed misuse of power through this partial asymmetry is relevant for professional counseling.

In contrast to information brokering, counseling is a problem-focused cooperation process, which, in contrast to psychotherapy, represents help for generally healthy people. It deals with problems outside of the individual and considers the complexity as well as diversity of problem causes. The impacts of counseling can thereby vary: preventive, rehabilitative, curative, informative and encouraging with respect to developments (Beushausen 2016, p. 7).

Counseling is a *trans-professional* and a *profession-specific method,* which shows commonalities and differences to other professions and theory traditions. Besides social work education science, (American) counseling psychology and psychotherapy are considered as further psycho-social counseling disciplines (ibid., p. 29).

Profiling as a profession-specific method and the delimitation of other disciplines is a historical part of the professionalization debate with regard to social work and also the genesis of social work science, which has to ask itself: What makes counseling special as a profession within social work?

According to Wolf-Rainer Wendt und Hans Thiersch, who are amongst the most prominent representatives of social work in the German-speaking area, the problem-centered cooperation (Wendt 2000) and the help for self-help within the fields of life (Thiersch 1991) are fundamental determinants of social-work counseling. Both emphasize the solidary character of counseling. Wendt points out: 'It is about solidarity in practice [...]. Counseling [...] happens in interaction with people, who work together on the solution of problems (Wendt 2000, p. 97). And Thiersch underlines that 'Counseling can always be interpreted as a solidarity which is directed towards changes of lifeworld' (Thiersch 1977, p. 119).

According to Thiersch, the precondition for solidarity action is an enlightenment process which is, however, only possible beyond the paternalistic practice of either the traditional or ideology-critical version (see Stender 2013, p. 100).

This term for counseling, which emphasizes participation and help for self-help, is tied to historical roots of specific social-work counseling, which is notably coined by Alice Salomon. In the view of Salomon, the arising and stabilization of social problems are not unilaterally due to psychological circumstances of needy people but are also due to causative, social factors. For their treatment, Salomon therefore called on social anamnesis and diagnosis, which have to focus on changes concerning the person as well as the environment. For her, the art of helping was to find empathic and creative solutions with the intention of help for self-help in the individual case:

> 'The goal of anyone who feels for other people should be to promote their development, to increase their power, to strengthen their character—and this goal can be best achieved if a person solves his difficulties on his own.' (Salomon 1926; cited by Neuffer 1990, p. 33)

The term 'counseling' was replaced by the term 'individual case help'.

There was a break in this development of counseling during the period of National Socialism in Germany. Counseling was instrumentalized for the National Socialist state objectives:

> 'Primarily racist and eugenic selection tasks were assigned to the educational and marital counseling offices (e.g. with regard to the avoidance of so-called 'mixed marriages') and vocational counseling centers helped to implement banned occupations for women, Jews, etc.' (Sickendiek and Nestmann 2018, p. 221)

After 1945, counseling facilities were established in the FRG[1] and, over time, a sophisticated counseling system was increasingly developed, because according to the social welfare model, the legislator defined counseling as an obligatory task of social services. 'In the GDR,[2] the idea of solving social problems in the course of the socialist development of society did not lead to the establishment of widely available counseling. Only under the umbrella of the churches, individual counseling services could be realized.' (ibid., p. 222).

In the 1980s, social work became politicized and, after a wave of therapeutization, it was looking for something independent, something that could counter the increasingly psychotherapeutically oriented practice of social work. In the search for an independent definition of counseling within social work, the expert discussion has for some time dominated the relationship between social work and psychotherapy and also the question of whether these are to be regarded as different or identical forms of action. The notion of counseling within social work is therefore largely established as a term to make social work counseling recognizable as such.

Nevertheless, demarcation discourses and clarifications remain inadequate, since counseling itself can be categorized as a trans-professional method. What is relatively new is that psychosocial counseling in German-speaking countries is discussed as an independent discipline and profession (Gregusch 2016, p. 37). In German-speaking countries, 'counseling' is now used as a term in addition to the German term 'Beratung' and there are degree programs in 'Psychosoziale Beratung und Counseling'. Meanwhile a differentiating counseling sector has been established (educational counseling, family and marriage counseling, sexual counseling, student counseling, youth counseling, drug counseling, women's counseling, counseling for refugees, etc.).

In the English literature on the subject, John McLeod is considered as a prominent thinker of counseling approaches. In his comprehensive manual, McLeod (2004, 2011) describes the historical and cultural origins of the emergence and development of counseling from the origins of psychiatry at the beginning of the eighteenth century, which he sees as a turning point in the construction of mental illness. He embeds the development of psychotherapy and counseling in the social development of the last two centuries: the secularization (and medicalization) of mental disorders, industrialization and urbanization, scientification and de-traditionalization are mentioned as just a few of the social trends leading to psychotherapy and counseling as forms of psychosocial problem-solving and

[1] Federal Republic of Germany.

[2] German Democratic Republic.

healing. He sees Sigmund Freud and Carl Rogers as two key figures in the development of psychotherapy and counseling. He also describes behavioral-cognitive, person-centered, systemic, feminist and narrative approaches.

As mentioned, the new counseling discourse - Counseling - aims to overcome the limitation of counseling by informing or practicing 'small psychotherapy'. The term counseling represents a self-understanding of counseling as an independent interdisciplinary scientific research, education and practice area with the postulate that psychosocial counseling is a scientifically based and contextual paradigm. Contextual means that the entire life circumstances of individuals and groups in a dramatically changed world are considered. It takes into account the economic, ecological, cultural and other dimensions of life of those seeking advice.

Counseling is not just a transdisciplinary and profession-specific method of intervention, rather it is a communicative resource-activating activity which can be theoretically and methodically highly divergent, even in its orientation. These divergences are reflected in professional theoretical discourses, for example, in the discourse of a subject or of a topic of orientation towards the client and expert, additionally in the discourse of dialogue vs. diagnosis. Counselors integrate different professional roles (social technologist, evaluator, interpreter, dialogist) in a wide variance of consulting approaches like person-centered, systemic-constructivist, solution-oriented and life-world-oriented. All counseling approaches have in common that they can be reconstructed as problem-solving processes. The different weighting and the type of processing make their respective specificity.[3] In all approaches, the counseling follows not only a communicative understanding, it also follows a knowledge and value-controlled logic (Gregusch 2016, p. 341). Counseling skills require work on the relationship and process-problem-solving and action orientation.

In this variance of methods, how can counseling skills be mediated, which are neither oriented to fashionable concepts nor subject to any unsystematic eclecticism or asserts absolute validity claims? Allen E. Ivey calls the 'three powers of counseling' the most influential approaches: the psychodynamic theory, the cognitive-behavioristic theory and the existential-humanistic theory (Ertel and Schulz 2019, p. 1). In this, the awareness of the person in charge of situational, contextual, inequality-generating and socio-cultural aspects becomes more

[3] The specialization of the person-centered approach is according to the tradition of Rogers in the explication (self-exploration) of the existing description and evaluation knowledge of the clients; the specificity of the systemic-constructivist approach in the preferred use of the confrontational method. The solution-oriented approach has a clear focus on evaluation, targeting, intervention and evaluation knowledge. The life-world-oriented approach is methodically oriented on the person-centered approach.

important. This can be the gender relation, the life situation of minorities or an awareness of the importance of family and community with many groups (ibid., p. 27). At the same time, consultation requires much more communicative and interactive reflection, because uncertainty is not only due to precarious life situations. With the reduction of the welfare system, the entry of neoliberal policy models and the increasing individualization, pluralization and disorientation in the course of modernization, counseling institutions are being confronted more and more with the middle-class clientele, who are confronted with a loss of status and security (Engel et al. 2018, p. 91).

It would be desirable to acquire these trans-professional counseling skills on the basis of a biopsychosocial-cultural view in a basic education (e.g. social work study). In order to learn the counseling skills, students and practitioners need a variety of personal and specific-methodical skills.

These are high expectations, because in times of growing uncertainty and confusion in a changing world with increasing demands for flexibility, counseling is about managing everyday life and supporting people in stressful situations without taking responsibility for their actions. Complex social changes like mobility and migration (refugees) lead to more diversity and increase the importance of modern counseling approaches. These modern counseling approaches should have a sensitivity to the interconnection of personal problems and socio-cultural contexts and to the fact that cultural groups have their own ideas of the meaning of helping people with emotional and psychological problems (e.g. between autonomy vs. collective involvement). These transformed perceptions have spawned a new discussion, especially in English-language literature, which defines 'counseling as a culture-bound theoretical, conceptual, and practice-oriented field' (ibid., p. 88). A critical reflection of one's own dominant cultural gender-discrimination, racist or ethnocentric ideas of counselors is very important.

Counseling is a central aid form that is always integrated into the social demands of its time. In the last few decades, counseling has had to react to a variety of social cultural needs. Diversity, economization and medialization are the major challenges.

Counseling reacts to these social developments, which are reflected in areas of conflict and new offers. To this area of conflict belongs, for example, counseling between self-optimization and self-determination, between case-specific and social context, between everyday-counseling and professional-counseling, between trust and manipulation and resources and deficits (ibid, p. 83). Due to the technical developments and communicative conditions of the Internet, in the last decades the medialization of consulting has been given a central role in addition to the traditional form of personal counseling. The knowledge of modern neurobiology of psychology contributes to the professionalization of counseling as a social technique. The optimization with economization logic is reflected critically.

Counseling is also politics. It deals with power processes and disadvantaged clients, it empowers and emancipates the clients and at the same time, counseling itself is not a power-free space. The employment of power in relationships and the power in information is necessary. This relationship is embedded in institutional, legal and sociopolitical conditions.

This reflective discussion cannot be ignored. The attitude of the counseled person is directly reflected in the physical attitude and it influences the habitus of the professional in the counseling work.

There are questions arising in studies about the role of theory, the role of values and about ethics (see chapters in Part IV on Ethics),[4] and, in counseling practice, about the role of self-awareness, the development of a professional habitus, scientific awareness and the role of supervision.

As a place of education, the universities respond to these complex demands in the study of social work. The University of Suleimani's own response is described by Niyan Namiq Sabir (see next chapter). Through reflection in the context of practical guidance and by means of teachers who teach the breadth of theoretical positions, the EvH RWL is looking for a way to integrate the specific module 'Counseling in Professional Contexts' and the topic in general into the cross-section of teaching. In-depth courses are available in the person-centered and systemic approaches.

References

Engel, F., Nestmann, F., & Sickendiek, U. (Eds.). (2013). Das Handbuch der Beratung 3: Neue Beratungswelten - Fortschritte und Kontroversen. DGVT, 2013.

Engel, F., Nestmann, F., & Sickendiek, U. (2018). Beratung: alte Selbstverständnisse und neue Entwicklungen. In S. Rietmann & M. Sawatzki (Eds.), *Zukunft der Beratung. Von der Verhaltens- zu der Verhältnisorientierung. Reihe Soziale Arbeit als Wohlfahrtsproduktion* (Vol. 11, pp. 83–115). Wiesbaden: Springer.

Ertelt, B.-J., & Schulz, W. E. (2019). *Handbuch Beratungskompetenz* (4th ed.). Wiesbaden: Springer Gabler.

German Association for Counseling e. V. (DGfB) (n.d.). Das Beratungsverständnis der DGfB. www.dachverband-beratung.de/dokumente/Beratung.pdf. Accessed 13 Mar 2019.

[4] The German Association for Consulting, founded in 2004, has formulated a comprehensive 'consulting concept'. It involves socio-political developments into a clear professional conception of counseling (DGfB, no date).

Gregusch, P. (2016). Auf dem Weg zu einem Selbstverständnis von Beratung in der sozialen Arbeit. socialnet Verlag.

Beushausen, J. (2016). *Beratung lernen*. Opladen: Verlag Barbara Budrich.

McLeod, J. (2004). *Counseling - Eine Einführung in Beratung*. Tübingen: Dgvt-Verlag.

McLeod, J. (2011). *An introduction to counseling*. Buckingham: Open Univ. Press.

Neuffer, M. (1990). *Die Kunst des Helfens. Geschichte der Sozialen Einzelhilfe in Deutschland*. Weinheim: Beltz.

Sickendiek, U., & Nestmann, F. (2018). Beratung in kritischen Lebenssituationen. In G. Graßhoff, A. Renker, & W. Schröer (Eds.), *Soziale Arbeit. Eine elementare Einführung* (pp. 217–237). Wiesbaden: Springer VS.

Stender, W. (2013). Modelle kritischer Handlungswissenschaft. Silvia Staub-Bernasconi, Timm Kunstreich und Hans Thiersch im Vergleich. In W. Stender & D. Kröger (Eds.), *Soziale Arbeit als kritische Handlungswissenschaft* (pp. 95–121). Hannover: Blumhardt Verlagpp.

Thiersch, H. (1977). Kritik und Handeln. Interaktionistische Aspekte der Sozialpädagogik. Neuwied/Darmstadt: Luchterhand.

Thiersh, H. (1991). Soziale Beratung. In M. Beck, G. Brückner, & H. .U. Thiel (Eds.), *Psychosoziale Beratung. Klient/inn/en – Helfer/inn/en – Institutionen* (pp. 23–34). Tübingen: Dgvt.

Thiersch, H. (2007). Lebensweltorientierte Soziale Beratung. In F. Nestmann, F. Engel, & U. Sickendiek (Eds.), *Ansätze, Methoden und Felder Das Handbuch der Beratung* (Vol. 2, pp. 699–710). Tübingen: Dgvt.

Wendt, W. R. (2000). Rat finden in Kooperation Die Soziale Arbeit braucht einen eigenständigen Begriff von Beratung. *Blätter der Wohlfahrtspflege, 147*(5+6), 97–99.

Cinur Ghaderi, Prof. Dr., Professor of Psychology in the Faculty of Social Work at the Protestant University of Applied Sciences (EvH RWL Bochum). She is Vice-President for Research, Transfer and Internationalization. After her post-graduate education in psychological psychotherapy (behavioral therapy), she worked in the "Psychosocial Centre for refugees" (PSZ) in Düsseldorf. She received her PhD at the faculty of Social Sciences of the Ruhr University Bochum. She is a member of the steering committee of DTPPP (transcultural psychiatry, psychotherapy and psychosomatics). Main academic interests: International Social Work, Refugee Studies, Transcultural Psychotherapy, Psychotrauma, Identity, Diversity and Gender. She is the initiator of the DAAD-cooperation project CoBoSUnin 2016-2019 between the University of Sulaimani and Bochum. Contact: ghaderi@evh-bochum.de

The Realization and Changes in the Teaching of Counseling at the University of Sulaimani

Niyan Namiq Sabir

Abstract

In this chapter, 'Counseling' will be presented as an academic subject, taught in the Department of Social Work as a result of increasing human needs all over the world—in both developing and advanced countries—for helping people to be able to solve their daily social problems, rather than other problems that cause complications, such as economic, political and other current issues.

Beyond students' need to gain knowledge, skills and practice to become a professional social worker in the future, the process of teaching the subject of 'Counseling' is characterized by its diversity of various modern educational techniques that are used in order to create a successful teaching process.

Keywords

Counseling • Theories • Social work • Teaching

1 Introduction

Counseling is a kind of applied social science that has contributed to growth and development in various sciences such as psychology, sociology, education, economics and philosophy. It is the backbone of social service, because it deals with issues that concern the individual and his or her daily problems, whether they are psychological, social or emotional. The family as well is one of the

N. N. Sabir (✉)
Slemani, Iraq
E-Mail: nian.sabir@univsul.edu.iq

C. Ghaderi et al. (eds.), *Social Work at the Level of International Comparison*,
https://doi.org/10.1007/978-3-658-30394-5_16

social institutions that has its positions and disputes that require the intervention of a specialized professional. Furthermore, its relationships within the community need professional intervention, too. These topics and other topics within the scope of counseling are included in this module in the Social Work Department. These reasons encouraged me to write in this field. We also felt the need of the students to learn about counseling as a specialty that can help them in performing their work in the future.

Since the profession of social work is like other professions that are accompanied by continuous change according to the social changes facing society and the task of keeping pace with this change, it needs knowledge in this field in order to control what it faces from situations or life problems that need to be resolved.

2 Counseling as a New Module

The Social Work Department was established and it took on its role as a separate department in the 2014–2015 academic year. The influx of students was weak in the beginning, due to the fact that social service is a new field that was not previously present in the University of Sulaimani—despite its presence at the University of Salahaddin in Erbil three years earlier, as of 2010–2011.

The process of building curricula and academic subjects was done by looking at the curricula of universities that preceded us in this field, such as the University of Baghdad, Mansoura University in Egypt and Salahaddin University in Erbil.

Within the cooperation project (CoBoSUnin) between the Protestant University of Applied Sciences in Bochum, Germany and the University of Sulaimani, counseling has been put into the fourth-year curriculum with three hours per week over two semesters and is taught in English.

The situation of counseling faces some difficulties and challenges.

3 Difficulties and Challenges

The first challenge: Counseling is a new subject and the students do not have a solid background of knowledge and information on which they can base. The reason is due to the fact that the students have studied one subject in the field of psychology in the second year as an introduction or basic principle. It is necessary but not sufficient, but it requires integration by studying other subjects such as growth psychology and individual differences and mental health in order for the student to be able to possess a broad base of supportive knowledge that they can rely on. Counseling as a module is not taught in any other department at the University of Sulaimani, due to the lack of a psychology department. The Social Work Department is therefore the first department that teaches this module.

The second challenge is teaching the module in the English language. There is a ministerial order at all stages that some subjects should be taught in English, but the mother tongue of all students without exception is Kurdish.

In the first semester, the following topics are studied:

1. History of Counseling
2. Definition of Counseling
3. Aims of Counseling
4. Principles of Counseling
5. Roles of Counselor

As for the second semester, the following topics are studied:

6. Theories of Counseling
   - Psychoanalytic Theory
   - Reality Theory
   - Person Centered Theory
7. Counseling Tools
8. Counseling Aspects
9. Counseling Skills

The lectures are given for three hours per week, with two hours for theoretical instruction and one hour for training in the first semester, and this then switches to one hour for theory teaching and two hours for practice (i.e. converting theories into indicative positions).

For teaching counseling, we depend on the American Counseling Association (ACA) and the British Association for Counselling and Psychotherapy (BACP) definition and principles that fit with the nature of the Kurdish society for the reason that they are common for societies all over the world.

4 Methods of Teaching & Importance of Theories

Counseling has been taught in the Department of Social Work at the University of Sulaimani since 2017 in the fourth year of studies, and it still continues. The teaching of the subject uses suitable methods of teaching according to the educational situation, which differs between theoretical and applied topics. The teaching methods for theoretical topics are lectures and debates with advance preparation. This is a teaching method which provides a summary of the previous lecture at the beginning of the current lecture, in order to combine the two articles, and group discussions. The practical topics, on the other hand, need different methods of teaching like role play, small group work and brainstorming. Furthermore, we use critical thinking in teaching both theoretical and practical topics.

We teach the three main theory approaches in counseling, that are: psychoanalytic, cognitive behavioral and humanistic. We choose one theory from each approach as a sample of therapy techniques.

We teach our students that 'There is no perfect or magic theory that you can always use, but you should choose the most suitable theory that fits the situation'.

First, we chose Sigmund Freud for psychoanalytic therapy. The aim of using this theory is to identify the relationship between past experiences in an individual's life—especially in early childhood—and the emergence of psychological problems and disorders and how to deal with them (Ala Addin 2013).

The second approach is reality therapy as represented by William Glaser, a cognitive and behavioral approach. The aim of using this theory is to identify the effect of reality on people's lives, according to which people should be able to adapt to present situations without thinking about past experiences (Abu Asaad and Al-Azaida 2015).

Last but not least is the client-centered therapy by Carl Rogers, a humanistic approach. The aim of using this theory is to explain that the most important target of counseling is protecting the unity of people's personalities by creating a balance among their various selves (Al-Asmi 2015).

In order to clarify these topics, some techniques should be used that we already use for teaching theoretical parts of the module, like diagrams and images, while animations and short movies are present in the practical part.

After teaching theories, the students should identify the possible methods of counseling that might be used for contacting the client, one-on-one counseling by appointment or walk-in or by telephone or in-home counseling (Abdul Hadi and Al-Azzeh 2004). Nowadays, there is online counseling which might decrease the negative sides of other tools.

Of course, choosing any method depends on the characteristics of the client and the type of problem. Achieving this aim needs tools for collecting data which might be, for example, observation or interview or questionnaire, or it might need more than one tool (Abdel Moneim 1996). Finally, students should have information about the classification of counseling fields in order to make right decisions to identify the client's problem within the field of counseling personal, family, education, economy, or vocation (Zahran 1990).

Finally, counseling as one of the social work aspects needs a variety of skills such as: a genuine interest in others, self-reflection, the ability to listen on multiple levels, accessibility, authenticity, flexibility and a sense of humor (Zahran 1998).

5 Impact of Students' Social Background

The students' social background has its effects on their personality, which can be observed in thinking and behavior, since the majority of them are from a rural and clan social background. This background and the methods of socialization that they were brought up with, have repercussions on the quality of their dealings with life situations, including their response and acceptance of the new and uncommon. Social service as a new science and specialization is one such example. On the other hand, there is the effect of specifically religious extremism. Following a scientific definition, extremism is related to the English word dogmatism,[1] that is, dogmatic rigidity and mental closure. Extremism in this sense is a closed method of thinking characterized by the inability to accept or tolerate any beliefs that differ from those of the person or group (Ahmed 1990).

So, the students believe in some myths that they use as a traditional counseling, which contradicts the logic that they have learned from people who, under cover of religion, perform acts of shame and sorcery. So, dealing with this type of students is not comfortable or easy. But all societies have their own sayings and idioms that can be used for supporting the counseling process.

6 Conclusions

1. Counseling is one of the most important modules in preparing a program to create a professional social worker.
2. Students in the Social Work Department have problems with studying counseling in the English language. It would be better if they could study it in their own language, which is their mother tongue Kurdish.
3. Studying counseling is important on both theoretical and practical sides, but practice for life problems should cover the biggest part of the module.

[1] Dogmatism is a Greek word for intolerance or the intolerance of a particular idea by a group without accepting a debate on it or coming up with any evidence that invalidates it rigidity.

4. The social background of the students has its effect on their comprehension of counseling.

References

Abdel Moneim, A. (1996). *Guidance, psychological, social and educational counseling*. Gaza, Palestine: Mansour Publishing and Distribution House.

Abdul Hadi, J. E., & Al-Azzeh, S. H. (2004). *Principles of guidance and counseling*. Amman: Dar Al Thaqafa Library for Publishing and Distribution.

Abu Asaad, A. A., & Al-Azaida, R. A. (2015). *Modern methods of psychological and educational counseling* (2nd ed.). Amman: Debono Center for Thinking Education.

Ahmed, S. N. (1990). *Religion in Arab society*. Beirut: Center for Arab Unity Studies, Arab Society for Sociology.

Ala Addin, J. M. (2013). *Counseling theories, psychoanalytic and behavioral*. Amman: Al-Ahliya publishing.

Al-Asmi, R. N. (2015). *Client-centered counseling between experience and self-concept*. Amman: Al-Aasar publishing house.

Zahran, H. A. (1998). Psychological counseling and educational guidance. Fourth Edition. Qairo: niansabirunivsuleduiq.

NIYAN NAMIQ SABIR, Prof. Dr., Professor in the Social Work Department/College of Humanities at the University of Sulamani. She has a PhD in Philosophy of Education, an M.A. in Education and a Bachelor in Education and Psychology from Baghdad. She worked in Baghdad, Libya and Yemen. Since 2004 she has been working at the University of Sulaimani. From 2011–2015 she participated in the Delphi program of capacity building with the University of Bristol and she is one of the founders of the Gender and Violence Study Centre. From 2016–2019 she participated in the CoBoSUnin project with the Protestant University of Applied Sciences in Bochum. She has worked with most of the NGOs in Slemani. She taught and supervised MA & PhD students. She has about 20 published research articles in international, Arabic and local scientific journals. Contact: nian.sabir@univsul.edu.iq

Counseling Processes–Experiences as Trainer in a Workshop of the CoBoSUnin Project

Hildegard Mogge-Grotjahn

Abstract

In teaching and learning ‘counseling’ in the context of social work, the separation of theory and practice should be relinquished in favor of a systematic connection of cognitive and emotional processes. The teachers with their professional and counseling competence place themselves at the disposal of the students as ‘model’.

Regarding the gender dimension in counseling processes, there is a distinction between counseling situations that are directly connected to the gender of the persons seeking advice (e.g. pregnancy, sexualized violence, sexual orientations) and the fact that, in all professional—as well as in private—communication, the gendered dimensions of identity always resonate, in other words, these are permanent processes of ‘doing gender’.

Keywords

Counseling • Supervision • Gender • Social work • Training

As part of the CoBoSUnin project, I was asked to hold a workshop from 26 to 28 July 2018 at the Protestant University Bochum on the subject of *Counseling/Supervision/Gender*. While I had occasionally heard of the existence of this project, I had not dealt with it in any detail until then. I was informed about the political situation in Northern Iraq only from reading newspapers. The way in which the Kurdish colleagues at the University of Sulaimani had managed to

H. Mogge-Grotjahn (✉)
Bochum, Germany
E-Mail: mogge-grotjahn@gmx.de

C. Ghaderi et al. (eds.), *Social Work at the Level of International Comparison*,
https://doi.org/10.1007/978-3-658-30394-5_17

establish a Faculty of Social Work under hardly conceivable conditions inspired me with a kind of diffuse admiration and, upon deliberation, also raised the question of what I would be able to offer them at all. During preparatory talks with the project supervisor, my anticipation, curiosity and trust in the project increased. I decided not to attempt to offer something 'special' to the workshop participants, but to transmit what had become important to me, both theoretically and practically, due to my long-term counseling practice and teaching experience and, apart from this, trust in the exchange with the participants.

In preparation for the workshop, I drew up a handout summarizing the theoretical foundations of counseling that is sensitive to gender and oriented towards the idea of human nature as transmitted by humanistic psychology as well as addressing the framework conditions of counseling settings. In my view, it is essential to focus on counseling processes offered by social workers to the various addressees in different fields of social work. Additional priorities were the opportunities of counseling/supervision for the social workers themselves and finally the question of how counseling may be taught and learned ('learning by doing'). My preparatory considerations focused on an analysis of the ideas of human nature underlying the different counseling concepts, as these shape the attitude with which the professional counselors face their clients. I intended to design the practical exercises in the workshop in such a way that they would contribute to the self-awareness and reflection of the counselors beyond the familiarization and application of individual methods.

The most important elements of the counseling work I advocate are:

- The assumption that individuals are basically 'good'.
- The assumption that individuals are capable of learning and developing at each age.
- The assumption that individuals carry in themselves the resources and abilities needed to cope with and shape their respective life situations.
- The conclusion that counselors should face their clients with appreciation and empathy, giving personal assistance and support to them so that they may find their own solutions for the respective problems.

Questions that were completely open for me were:

- How culture-specific these basic considerations are?
- On the basis of which theories and ideas of human nature the participants in the workshop shape their counseling and teaching activities?

- Whether and how aspects of gender-sensitive counseling work would be capable of being thematized or how culture-specific the perceptions and constructions of gender would be?

Regarding the importance of the gender dimension in counseling processes, I made a distinction in the handout between counseling situations that are directly connected to the gender of the persons seeking advice (e.g. pregnancy, sexualized violence, sexual orientations) and the fact that, in all professional—as well as in private—communication, the gendered dimensions of identity always resonate, in other words, these are permanent processes of 'doing gender'.

Prior to the beginning of the workshop, positive as well as negative expectations, wishes and fears became clear to me.

My negative expectations and fears were:

- That my language skills would not be sufficient to express everything that was important to me precisely and sophisticatedly.
- That the language skills of the guests would not be sufficient to enable an effective exchange.
- That the guests and I would remain strange to each other, not so much because of linguistic hurdles, but rather due to the cultural and professional impediments.
- That the guests would not go along with the many interactive and practical exercises on counseling processes.

Nonetheless, I looked forward to the opportunity to have open and interesting encounters with individuals from a society that was so far completely alien to me.

My positive expectations and wishes were:

- That I would succeed in passing on some of what I feel particularly strongly about with regard to counseling and supervision processes (including the theme of gender).
- That I would get suggestions and impulses for the further development of my own counseling and teaching activities.
- That I would be on the same wavelength, both professionally and personally, with my (former) German colleagues.
- That there would be enough support within the group to overcome linguistic hurdles.
- That a genuine exchange would be achieved in the course of three days.

None of my negative expectations materialized, quite the contrary: On the very first day of the workshop, a rapport among all those attending arose, enabling an exchange between the Kurdish guests and the German participants, but also between the guests and the locals among themselves. The guests courageously engaged in all exercises and contributed subjects to them that were in part very personal. An increasing pleasure in trying out different counseling methods and in designing counseling processes developed, combined with a productive balance between cognitive and emotional proportions of the common learning process.

I experienced the course of the workshop as great encouragement to trust the processes that (may) arise both in me as instructor and in the participants during training courses, workshops, teaching and learning sessions. Even though the professional, content-related and didactic-methodical preparation remains essential, the concept determined in advance or a certain approach must not necessarily be adhered to. The existing culture-specific imprint of the idea of human nature, the understanding of femininity and masculinity and the construction of gender may be thematized free from fear and prejudice, if encounter and exchange are characterized by the very appreciative and empathetic attitude that is constitutive for successful counseling processes. Theory and practice—more precisely, cognition and emotion—must be systematically related to one another and be conveyed by the same persons.

It seems to me that the challenges connected with the transmission of counseling know-how and the mentoring of trainee social workers on their way to developing their counseling personality are not really different in Germany and Kurdistan. On the one hand, it is important to grant higher significance than before to the subjects of 'Counseling / Supervision' and 'Gender', when incorporated into teaching in the various courses of studies, and in this context to admit as many opportunities as possible to practice counseling methods and techniques as well as to reflect personal attitudes. On the other hand, and above all, the separation of theory and practice that is common both here and there should be relinquished in favor of a systematic connection of cognitive and emotional processes, whereby the teachers with their professional and counseling competence place themselves at the disposal of the students as 'model'.

It was my privilege to encourage such a 'co-productive' learning process with some impulses during the three days of the workshop and then experience it increasingly as a reciprocal event sustained jointly by all participants. For this, I thank the guests without whose professional competence, personal commitment and willingness to get involved in evocative shared experiences this workshop could not have succeeded.

Hildegard Mogge-Grotjahn, Prof. Dr., Professor of Sociology at the Protestant University of Applied Sciences Bochum from 1992 until 2017. She was Vice-President for Research, Transfer and Further Education (1999–2003 and 2007–2011). She studied Sociology, Political Sciences and Pedagogy at the University of Konstanz (1972–1974) and the University of Marburg (1974–1977). She worked in various research and education institutes and received her PhD at the University of Gießen in Germany in 1990. Main academic interests: poverty and social inequality; identity, diversity and gender studies; migration. She is qualified coach and advisor and works as a freelancer. Contact: mogge-grotjahn@gmx.de

Fine Arts Meet Social Work, from First Observations to Realization

Luqman Saleh Karim

Abstract

We may define social work as a science that performs its profession based on professionalism, ethics and skills in various areas of society; others think social work is not only a science that has its own ethics or skills, but is also an art. Art can fulfil its duty besides science and ethics in social work. As science and ethics are both inseparable aspects of the professional life, it can thus be said that art plays a significant role in society, especially art which has a relationship with social work.

The purpose of this research is to create an approach in which art executes its duty in social work. This art is meant objectively and intends to serve in this area. It is also related to a person's view of life with its inferences and consequences and to the social phenomena of daily life. The article aims to reveal the importance of art in social work, operating together as a package, in the Iraqi Kurdistan region. The research concludes with some questions so that readers can follow up on the subject to get more information and understand it more fully. Finally, it can be said that this subject works on the parallelism and balanced working of the two faculties of rationality and imagination so as to achieve a balanced approach which relates to both rationality and senses.

Keywords

Fine arts • Aesthetic • Education • Edutainment • Social work

L. S. Karim (✉)
Slemani, Iraq
E-Mail: loqman.karim@univsul.edu.iq

C. Ghaderi et al. (eds.), *Social Work at the Level of International Comparison*,
https://doi.org/10.1007/978-3-658-30394-5_18

1 What is Art?

The word 'ars' in ancient Latin, similar to the word 'techne' in ancient Greek, means profession (craft) or any other skills and specialization in craft, such as carpentry, smithery or paramedics. Greeks and Romans did not believe as we do that art differs from craft. They even initially regarded and saw the art of poetry, 'ars poetica', as being similar to carpentry and other crafts. The word 'ars' in ancient Latin meant 'craft'. Plato and Aristotle regarded art, especially the art of poetry, as a kind of craft. Plato talked about poetry as craft. He also attributed benefit to professional art (Mirawdeli 2005, p. 169).

The word 'art' in medieval Latin is the same as in Old English, because the word derived from ancient Latin. It meant learning of any kind of book information, such as grammar, logic and astronomy. In Shakespeare's era, art had the same meaning until the Renaissance era, first in Italy, then in other parts of the world, it had its previous meaning 'means craft'. The artists of the Renaissance, similar to the ancient world, regarded themselves as craftsmen. In the seventeenth century, people began to separate the problems and concepts of aesthetics from the techniques and philosophy of craft. In the eighteenth century, this separation reached the level of drawing lines between fine arts and useful arts. In the nineteenth century, this definition of fine arts was abandoned and the individual word 'arts' means 'art' was used. Since then, the separation between art and craft was theoretically attained. The essence of the word 'art' in the Kurdish language is related to the words 'hunari' and 'hunar' which, in spoken language, are each used for describing the achieving of a kind of intelligence and unusual necessary awareness. Nowadays in the world, the word 'art' involves all fine arts. The history of art is the history of human invention in **painting**, **sculpture**, music, literature, theatre and other activities (Mirawdeli 2005, p. 16).

The Italian idealist philosopher Bendetto Croce prefers art to metaphysics and science. Science keeps us apart from individuality and reality in a world of pure mathematics, but art reaches to the special person and unique fact, meaning soul. Knowledge has two forms, it is either intuitive knowledge or logical knowledge through imagination or the brain, individual knowledge or universal knowledge, knowledge of things or theories between them, knowledge of image or knowledge of concepts. If we reveal all activities of the soul, we will see that art is the foundation on which the great edifice of the soul stands. As Hegel explained, art is the first stage of soul expression because intuitive knowledge is art material, and it always comes before the logics of philosophy and science (Mirawdeli 2005, p. 106).

Aesthetics is a branch of philosophy and the explanation of the concept of 'aesthetics' is linked to the appearance of art's duties. 'The word (aesthesis) in Greek means dealing or working with sensation' (Nasr 2017, p. 492). Therefore, aesthetic experimentation is a kind of worldliness; aesthetics, as a human aesthetic relation to the world and as the essence and development of rules of art and the role of art, deals with social changes. The German philosopher Alexander Gottlieb Baumgarten was the first person to use the concept of aesthetics in a book written in 1735. In that book, he talks about artistic taste and its components (Mirawdeli 2005, p. 12). The motivation or power, which draws and motivates us to that kind of book, is called aesthetics or aesthetic sense. A person in prehistoric times had an artistic sense, even though the characteristics of his life were distinguished by brutality, but he also had artistic masterpieces in his life that were worthy of reference (Mirawdeli 2005, p. 123).

2 The Place of Art in Social Work

There are some factors that strengthen the importance of the arts in social work, such as: *delight of function.* In a summary of the history of art, of its meaning and directions, we reach the conclusion that art and craft were separated in the course of historical developments. Aesthetic feeling emerged from the work process, in the sense of human work to create material to provide life requirements and needs. For example, in olden days, craftsmen had a direct psychological and physical relationship with their crafts. The German psychologist Karl Bühler talks about the term *delight of function* which he used to teach people to entertain from their works. When the enjoyment that humans gain from working or the function of their work is not simply in providing their needs, but lies in the result of something that is made and in the creative ability, this has a crucial role in the learning process. The famous Italian physician and educator Maria Montessori observed that children can be educated in a playful way, but they cannot be taught. Many researches have proven that people learn things which are persuasive and satisfactory (Fromm 2008, pp. 47–48). Engendering delight of function in social work makes social workers not only see their crafts as task and duty, but also make an internal power in their ability among social workers can perform his job or duty perfectly and likes his craft. This thought brings entertainment and education together to form what is called *edutainment.*

- *Avoiding psychological burnout:* when a social worker is dealing with his/her clients on a daily basis, this might cause him/her to face burnout. Art can help us to express and use the power due to the calm and quiet status in our body, and the zest, which we get from art, is only the zest of using the extra powers. In other words, art can help the clients, for example, if we ask a sad or gloomy person to draw his/her situation in a portrait or write a verse about it, the person will feel better because instead of falling deeper into his/her sadness or melancholy, s/he changes to an objective status and comes out little by little.

- *Through art and aesthetics, a new worldview can be revealed to students of the social work department.* A multidimensional conception will be a catalyst for social work to provide a multidimensional analysis and interpretation of social phenomena. Here, we can say that aesthetics and art have an effective propensity in society. The images can deeply affect human feelings. James Baker, the US Secretary of State, talking about his experience, recalls: 'In my time, many important things have happened, such as the fall of the Berlin Wall, the desolation of Socialist state countries' systems and some other events, but nothing affected me as much as the mass exodus and departure of the Kurds, especially when I saw the children laying on snow, immediately I could not stop myself and return to the embassy, I directly spoke with the president in the plane and told him we should help and save them' (Jalal 2017, p. 183). On 7th March 1991, James Baker flew in a plane over a Kurds' camp in Turkey. What he saw had a strong influence on him and the US ambassador in Turkey, Morton Abramowitz, wrote that the trip is regarded as some of the most important moments in the history of humanitarian cooperation and collaboration (Jalal 2017, p. 189). It can be said that this case is an example of the influence of the image and the viewer on international opinion, and then on how to make a decision regarding preserving the Kurds from the attacks of the central government at that time.
- Art and aesthetics help students to have balanced views, depending on both their faculty of rationality and their imagination, and committing some levels of renewability, hypersensitivity, self-recognizing and life-recognizing based on education and art. Mathematical subjects should make human beings love poetry, and poetry should awake humans to universal scientific secrets. Unless science warns humans of their existence, unless it tells them that they are sensitive creatures or organisms, that apart from brains they also have hearts, in spite of thinking, they love (Wahab 2014, p. 69) human beings cannot step successfully towards development and righteous education. To do so would be to miss the important parallel between education and human rights principles, which focus on an education that shall be directed to the full development of the human personality and to the strengthening of the respect for human rights and fundamental freedoms. [Education] shall promote understanding,

tolerance and friendship among all nations (Universal Declaration of Human Rights, Article 26, No. 2).

This balanced view means that the main purpose of a learning process is to deepen and widen the learning view to life (Wahab 2014, p. 47). The process frees the student from being a container to keep information in. Paulo Freire calls the whole process in education 'the banking concept of education, meaning dealing with education as it is done with banks' (Freire 2015 p. 175). The duty of the brain is not only for saving, but also for solving or 'processing' data, information and various experiences which are collected through different sensors to create many rational examples (Wahab 2014 p. 226). During the opening ceremony of the Visva-Bharati University which he founded, Rabindranath Tagore said, 'Our education should be suitable or appropriate to our economic, rational, aesthetic, social and spiritual life' (Jahanbegloo 2005 p. 66). The existence of art with social work and their working together secure the suitability of education and art with various areas of life.

3 Art and Social Work, an Example in the Kurdistan Region

In 1979, the University of Sulaimani asked Dr. Kamal Mirawdeli[1] to write a book on 'The Philosophy of Aesthetics and Art' as part of the process of establishing a department of 'Kurdology' and providing references for the department. Generally, this subject did not involve Kurdology in order to be studied by departments of Sulaimani University, and aesthetic philosophy had been studied only in the College of Arts. The subject does not exist at the College of Humanitarian Sciences. As the Department of Social Work at the University of Sulaimani and working with the Protestant University of Applied Sciences in Bochum, Germany, we travelled to visit them in Germany. At the Bochum University, two things attracted our attention. The first one was a silent room. On one hand, I observed that the noise of teaching at our universities prevented us savoring or being interested in silence and listening to the inner voice which gives an experience of the artistic life. On the other hand, we noted that at the Department of Social Work

[1] Dr. Kamal Mirawdeli, a prominent Kurdish writer, academic, political analyst, author and poet, presidential candidate of Iraq's Kurdistan Region elections, July 2009. A senior contributing writer for Ekurd.net. https://ekurd.net/author/kamal-mirawdeli

in the University in Bochum, there is an effective course called Aesthetic Education, which is taught by Professor Dr. Helene Skladny. One of the beauties of this course is how it connects social work to museums and works of art. During the four years we have been visiting Germany, we saw four art exhibitions in Bochum museums.

Aesthetic Education has a significant position and effect among the students. After visiting exhibitions and having deep discussion in CoBoSUnin, Professor Helene Skladny visited the Department of Social Work at the University of Sulaimani and helped the department by adding and developing a course of Educational Aesthetics in the Department of Social Work at the University of Sulaimani. It is worth noting that in the workshop, Helene Skladny shed light on the quality of the research of aesthetics, aesthetic experience, self-awareness, orientation towards tradition and culture, theories of aesthetics and many other subjects. In 2015, a module called Aesthetic Education appeared, which is taught two hours a week at the third stage of the Social Work department. The importance of this lecture is that it not only works in one aspect and area of life, but also tries continuously to find the theories that joins the different worldviews together, thus it can be said that Educational Aesthetics is the mutual space that has no hesitation to enter all aspects of daily life and finds various networks of life to give an analytical interpretation.

Although this module works scientifically, it is not concerned with the delusive walls or obstacles created between sciences, and which prevent the sciences from working on transporting 'the whole vision' of human beings. This course believes that human beings are more than machines and more than their individual constitutive parts. The human being is a holistic unit, gifted with logic and rationality, but at the same time full of humanitarian sense and feeling, of imagination and motivated power of imagination, and Aesthetic Education therefore works on finding relations and realizing the problems, addressing rationalization and the faculty of imagination at the same time. If science works on 'focus', aesthetics works more on 'meditation'. Meditation is to work on the gap between concepts not focusing on them, thus this course works in the space which lies between aesthetics and education.

4 Course Objective—The Module of Aesthetic Education

There were two main objectives behind adding this module at the Department of Social Work in the College of Humanitarian Sciences at the University of Sulaimani:

First: Knowledgeable objectives, 'Knowledge and understanding':

- Revealing quantity and quality aesthetic education for students.
- Revealing the importance of aesthetic education in the currently changing world, listening to students to show their opinions and thoughts.
- Conjoining an aesthetic sense to education, meaning: how we can create an aesthetic sense through education, at the same time how to make an aesthetic sense an educational method.
- Reviving the faculty of imagination with the faculty of rationality, meaning: joining brain and heart, thus making humans more perfect and giving people a broad worldview.
- Working on art and art experience as a method to express problems, ideas and messages of the Social Work Department.
- Empowering the students and giving them the idea of how they can empower their clients in a positive way.

Second: Behavioral objectives

- Encourage the students to contribute in the process of education through experimenting with information, not only accumulating information.
- Improving and increasing skills in positive critique and how to evaluate others' opinions.
- Training students on how to deal with problems in society and how to understand the different ways of expressing daily life.
- Students are encouraged, trained and exercised to make links with students of other departments, such as Sociology, Psychology, Fine Arts and Art Education to work on 'mutual work projects'.
- Students are trained and exercised to analyze, discuss and question educational and art works with a logic and critical view.

It is worth mentioning that, in this module, students made an album of photos. Each student contributes an attractive photo that s/he had taken by herself or himself. Some of the students work on a theatre play that can be on social phenomena or a special play on the philosophy of different educations. A group of students prepare some reports on the method of righteous education. And some lecture days are specialized to show some family and social films and discuss them. A team of students hold seminars in the courses, and in some cases, teachers arrange the lecture and present some aesthetic subjects achieving dialogue among the students.

References

Freire, P. (2015). *Pedagogy of the Oppressed*. (trans: Mohammed Sleman, J.). Iraq: Sardam Publishing House.

Fromm, E. (2008). *In the Name of Life*. 4th Ed. (trans: Barzinji, A.) Sulaymaniyah: Chawder Institution.

Jahanbegloo, R. (2005). *Tagore and Human Conscience*. (trans: Hama Gharib, Y.). Erbil: Mukryan Publishing House.

Jalal, M. (2017). *From Youth to Republic House*. 2nd Ed. Prepared by Salah Rashid. Kairo Publishing.

Mirawdeli, K. (2005). *Philosophy of Aesthetics and Art*. 2nd Ed. Qania Publishing House.

Nasr, S. H. (2017). In search of Sacred. Renwen Centre.

Wahab, A. A. (2014). *Swimming Against Common Idea. Education from Critic Viewpoint*. Sulaymaniyah: Kairo Publishing.

LUQMAN SALEH KARIM, Ass. Prof., Assistant Professor in the Social Work Department. He holds a PhD in Social Work from the University of Sulaimani, Kurdistan Region of Iraq. He was head of the Social Work Department from 2014–2017. He is a researcher and has conducted a large body of academic and organizational research on gender-based violence, environment policy, honor killing, child marriage, GBV assessments of needs, impact evaluation and COVID-19. He also worked with the United Nations Population Fund (UNFPA) and the Women's Refugee Commission (WRC) as a research consultant from 2018–2019, and as a child marriage research co-investigator in the Johns Hopkins University (USA); from 2016–2019 he was a University of Sulaimani coordinator of the DAAD cooperation project CoBoSUnin between the University of Sulaimani and the University of Applied Sciences in Bochum. Currently he works as lecturer at the University of Sulaimani, as a supervisor in the Khanzad women's organization, and as a research consultant for the Civil Development Organization (CDO). Contact: loqman.karim@univsul.edu.iq

Where Language Fails, the Image Begins—Aesthetic Education and Social Work: Insights into the Cooperation Between Bochum and Slemani

Helene Skladny

Abstract

The following discourse deals with the significance of aesthetic education as part of the study of social work. Based on insights into the workshop activities of the CoBoSUnin project, possible perspectives, approaches and suggestions for professional practice are presented.

Keywords

Aesthetic education • Social work

1 Introduction and Context

For what do we need aesthetic education in studies of social work? I am often asked this question. As a rule, I answer: First, because this is an elementary part of human life. We grasp the world not only with our mind, but with our senses. Each human being possesses creativity, imagination and sensual expressiveness. All this is no luxury for privileged citizens. It is a means of life. And secondly: '*Where language fails, the image begins*', as the contemporary German artist Günther Uecker said. We communicate not only with a logical language in order to understand the complexity of our life. At all times and all places, people have created diverse forms of expression for this communication, as for example dance, music, theatre, poems, stories, buildings, objects, painting and others.

H. Skladny (✉)
Bochum, Germany
E-Mail: skladny@evh-bochum.de

C. Ghaderi et al. (eds.), *Social Work at the Level of International Comparison*,
https://doi.org/10.1007/978-3-658-30394-5_19

What strength this language contains, how it can build bridges between people and what all this has to do with social work—this is the subject of my discourse.

I was asked to provide insight into my subject area aesthetic education to a group of university teachers and students from Slemani. At first, they could not connect this subject with the study of social work. My presentation comprised a selection of different student projects which were in part created in cooperation with the Bochum Museum of Art. It involved, among others, the cultural participation of people with dementia as well as a participative photo project performed with refugees who had come to Germany. The guests from Iraq looked at my presentation with interest and asked critical questions. Then a lively exchange about images started a discussion, for example, of the question of what kind of images about people with a flight history prevail in our respective social systems and how we can work with these images in teaching. An intensive exchange began, continuing up to this day. In the evening, I invited the academics to a vernissage in the Museum of Art. We exchanged views about the pieces of art and our impressions and no longer needed an interpreter for this.

I met the group for a second time at a small exhibition on the subject 'homeland', emerging from a seminar in cooperation with Cinur Ghaderi. Students were given the assignment to do research on this subject from a scientific-theoretical as well as an aesthetical perspective. Photo walls and diverse display cases could be viewed. First, the students were to express in images what homeland means to them. Secondly, people from other countries of origin were to be given the opportunity to reproduce their perception of 'homeland' by means of photos, pictures and objects. Here, initial practical ideas emerged for the implementation of an aesthetic research project in Slemani. One year later, I was already able to gain an insight into this work. Students had arranged medial images from their everyday world to reflect themselves and their study situation. The results were exhibited and then documented in an exhibition catalogue. This catalogue was sent to me from Slemani to Bochum. I could 'read' these images, immerse myself in them and associatively sense the situation and thoughts of the students.

2 Insights from the Workshop in Slemani in 2017

The focus of the workshop was on three topics of aesthetic education:

1. *What is an 'aesthetic experience'?*
   First, participants were given the assignment to describe a personal aesthetic-sensual experience. It was their choice whether they had had this experience

through an encounter with a work of art, a piece of music or similar. Moreover, they could report about a receptive aesthetic experience as well as about any gained during an active creative process. What exactly is the peculiarity of these aesthetic experiences? The mutual exchange was interesting. The following were mentioned among others: visiting an opera, reading a book, listening to a specific piece of music or the painting of a picture in childhood. Common basic experiences were detected in the different descriptions, such as the feeling of presence and liveliness, the experience of an intensive perception differing from everyday perception, as well as a changed feeling of time and space. It was crucial here that these experiences were considered by all participants to be important for their own development. With regard to the study and practice of social work, it could be noted: Aesthetic education has the task to create framework conditions for aesthetic experiences activating, in a broad sense, manifold dimensions of being human. The following points are decisive in this connection:

Aesthetic experience ...

- is sensual
- is playful
- is free of use
- is a feeling of timelessness
- is not distant, but involved
- is not static, but rather a 'flow'
- sometimes it is ecstatic
- it is 'in this moment', here and now
- it is pure perception, not reflection

2. *Aesthetic research as instrument of social work*

Following the project 'homeland', I presented a sequence from a seminar which I had held in Bochum in collaboration with the sociologist Hildegard Mogge-Grotjahn. It dealt with the analysis of social gender roles which were examined by means of images of men and women as conveyed by media. In this part of the seminar, methods of aesthetic research were to be applied exclusively. Work tool was a large pool of collected media images. Within the scope of the seminar, these were arranged, re-explained, evaluated and re-interpreted. Part of this research was then put up for disposition in our workshop leading to multifaceted discussions in the group. The meaning of the work with images could be transferred to different areas of social work. It was noted that heightened attention and a readiness to adopt even unusual perspectives are the precondition for this. All this can be tried out in seminars with students by means of different topics.

3. *Social work and contemporary art*
   The third part dealt with the common observation of contemporary art. For this purpose, I had brought along works by the photographer Akam Shex Hadi born in Slemani in 1985. The black-and-white pictures offered an occasion for intensive discussions about human images, emotions and atmospheres. This block focused on a confrontation with works of the International Exhibition of Contemporary Art that takes place biannually in Venice. Two positions of Iraqi art: 'Wounded Water': Six Iraqi artists interpret the theme of water (2011) and 'Archaic': Works by eight Iraqi artists and Francis Alŷs (2017) were presented by me, then viewed and interpreted together with the group. Reflection concentrated on the specific artistic gestalt language which opens up spaces for interpretation and experiences and enabling intercultural communication. Thereafter I presented Anne Imhof's artistic work 'Faust' of the German pavilion created in 2017. What was to be seen was a monumental building traversed by thick glass bottoms and with high metal fences and dog kennels installed in front of it. By common exchange of the visual experiences, associations and interpretations, the themes 'power and powerlessness', 'arbitrariness and violence', 'opposition and freedom' could jointly be opened up: themes which are evident for social work in all countries.

3 Conclusions—The Role of Aesthetic Education in Social Work

In conclusion, I would like to summarize the meaning of aesthetic education as part of social work as follows: The major project of aesthetic education is an active and receptive understanding and practice of art. Art understood as a form that comes from aesthetic experience, containing all dimensions of sensual human possibilities: visual art, music, performing arts, theatre, literature, etc. The aim of aesthetic education is to deal with art forms in order to act out or to retrieve the potentials of aesthetic experiences. Therefore, aesthetic education is a necessary part of social practice grounded on the anthropological assumption that human beings are creative beings. Social work in this regard is one way of social practice under the conditions of exclusion and the disclosure of social equality. The role of aesthetic education in social work is to act out the principles of aesthetic experience under these conditions. It is not its major goal to use art as a means to 'aestheticize' these conditions in order to make them bearable or to instrumentalize art for the ends of social mending, even if these effects be part of it. But if these goals are the premise for the role art plays in social work, this would mean to impose on art a use it does not carry in itself, because art unfolds its inherent potential if it is free from these goals, even if art is in its effects very political. Rather, art in social work functions without being functional, as is true of art in general. For this reason, it is a very important task of aesthetic education in social work to protect aesthetic processes from the alienation of being useful. In this way aesthetic education contributes to empowerment under the conditions of exclusion, because it gives room for the freedom of play, self-awareness and self-esteem. In order to be very aware of this aim, our understanding and training of, with, and through art in aesthetic education has to be methodologically very critical.

If we encounter an object of art, we therefore have to be conscious of several specific modes which help to qualify these encounters as aesthetic experiences.

1. We have to make sure that there is room for sense perception in this encounter. That means: it is not sufficient to shape this encounter only in a cognitive way. We have to explore methods of seeing, hearing, touching, etc. as a sensual way of understanding.
2. The aspects of freedom, play and creativity in the production of an art form do correspond to the freedom, play and creativity of their perception and so-called 'understanding'. There cannot be just one correct interpretation. Rather, the constant change of standpoints and modes of perception is an apt way of encountering objects of art.
3. Everyone can contribute to this democracy of perception which does not mean that there are people with longer training in this perception from which others can benefit.
4. Encountering an art form means to experience oneself in relation to it, i.e. being involved in a process, so that this art form with its specific language can appear to me, reveal itself, can speak to me, with me.

Every participant of processes in aesthetic education can possibly learn principles of social practice which are essential for the encounters between human beings. In social work, dealing with art offers the possibility to discover aesthetics as a basic category of anthropology to the professional and the client at the same time. This means precisely that no reality of exclusion can be seen as a disruption from the potentials of creativity, which always can be explored through processes of art within social work. Because this work is not goal-orientated, it allows the experience of 'empowerment', because the source of creativity cannot be destroyed, no matter how hard the conditions of exclusion might be. And: Because initially utility is not aimed at in aesthetic experience, it can be a realm in which the aspects of failure, exclusion, poverty, self-doubts and so on possibly come to light, reveal themselves, appearing in the process or being mirrored in forms of art which are perceived. For the professional training of social workers, we need a professional training of an active and receptive means of dealing with art.

Helene Skladny, Prof. Dr., Professor of Social Work (aesthetic education) at the Protestant University of Applied Sciences Bochum. She studied Art Education, Protestant Theology and German. Her main research projects are the relationship between art and social work. She is specialized in methods of: art mediation, museum pedagogy, project work, neighborhood management, early funding and aesthetic research. In 2017 she held a workshop on 'aesthetic education' in connection with the DAAD cooperation project CoBoSUnin in Sulaimani. Over the past few years, she has organized exhibitions with students in cooperation with the Kunstmuseum Bochum (Bochum Museum of Art). Contact: skladny@evh-bochum.de

Gender—A Topic for Social Work and in Higher Education in the Kurdistan Region of Iraq

Cinur Ghaderi

Abstract

Gender is relevant at the interactional, institutional and societal level. Social work can hardly be thought of without addressing the omnipresent cross-sectional topic of gender: a subject studied primarily by women, in which questions are predominantly active and which addresses social issues that occur in a variety of gendered ways, such as phenomena of violence. Gender-based violence, for example, is subject to a clear gender bias. In this article, the significance of gender in social work is first described, then related to the CoBoSUnin binational project and thus classified as a dimension of higher education policy issues. This classification takes into account the relevant gender discourses and gender norms, which in this case are outlined with a focus on the Kurdistan Region of Iraq.

Keywords

Gender • Social work • Teaching • Higher education • Knowledge production

1 Introduction

With the introduction of the analysis category gender, gender studies strive to change common forms of knowledge production—and higher education is a place of knowledge generation and knowledge transfer. Taking the category of gender

C. Ghaderi (✉)
Düsseldorf, Germany
E-Mail: ghaderi@evh-bochum.de

C. Ghaderi et al. (eds.), *Social Work at the Level of International Comparison*,
https://doi.org/10.1007/978-3-658-30394-5_20

into account makes it possible to grasp the historical, political, social and cultural gender-relevant processes and gender constructions in all their complexity and contradictions and to examine existing relationships of power, violence and domination. Gender analyses make it possible to identify gender norms and their consequences: for example, at the micro level for concrete interactions in counselling interviews, at the meso level for institutions such as universities, and at the macro level, taking into account the overall social and political context. The following section will therefore look at gender from these three perspectives.

2 Gender Perspectives in Social Work—Fundamental Relevance for Professional Interactions

The idea that social work is a gender-specific profession is not new (Perry and Cree 2003), but it is still relevant. Dealing with gender issues remains indispensable for social work. 'Social problems and concepts of action in social work are linked to social conceptions of gender; thus violence and delinquency are associated with masculinity, neglect of young children with femininity, or more precisely with failing motherhood' (Ehlert 2012, p. 5).

Gender as a social category permeates our lives and our identity. Our self-image, our behavior, our living conditions and our intrapsychic perceptions are interwoven with gender stereotypes. The social assignment to a gender writes the texture of subjectivity down to its unconscious layers. The normative pressure to identify oneself as 'female' or 'male' in the course of socialization tempts adaptation or evokes resistance (Becker-Schmidt 2018, p. 77). It is now also undisputed that *gender is a principle of social organization* that is effective in structuring of social fabric. The typification of gender is linked to hierarchical gender relations based on complementary role attributions, gender-specific division of labor, and different evaluations of masculinities and femininities (ibid.).

Gender flows into the understanding of the profession and into professional action in the field of social work. Moreover, social work not only reflects the gender order that becomes visible in the occupational fields and social issues, but is—in the sense of 'doing gender'—itself part of it. For the teaching, research and practice of social work, it is therefore necessary to reflect on 'gender' aspects. On the individual level, this means for social work that professionals refer to their addressees as women, men or diverse and are perceived by them as women, men or diverse. The professionals can hardly escape the attributions themselves, but their knowledge of these gender issues is noticeable in their attitudes and actions.

If they have gender knowledge, they can competently use this knowledge strategically in the sense of problem solving, depending on the situation and framework, by focusing or dis-focusing the gender difference mark, by tone of voice, humor, clothing, by official formal or semi-private appearance, etc. Gender knowledge implies a gender-theoretical perspective of recognition, which means, for example, to understand gender-based violence as a symbolic social expression and not to classify it in a shortened, psychologizing or individualizing way. On an institutional level, this means that the help and support services provided by social work always respond to social gender and the associated attributions. At the societal level, this implies that social work is confronted with specific life and problem situations and with structural discrimination. In addition, the entire field of care work and social work has female connotations in society, so that social work is perceived as a typically female profession.

In the meantime, 'gender competence' has become an important professional feature in social work (Böllert and Karsunky 2008). Gender competence can be defined as 'knowledge about the emergence and social construction of gender roles and gender relations ('doing gender'), the ability to reflect on (one's own) gender role images and to apply gender (gender diversity) as an analytical category in the professional and organizational context' (ibid., p. 7). The prerequisites for gender competence are therefore awareness and sensitivity to gender-related aspects of one's own field of action as well as self-reflection with regard to one's own gender role and with regard to personal attitudes and assumptions regarding the conception of gender relations.

But people do not experience things solely on the basis of their gender, but together with other socially constructed identities such as social class, ethnicity, race, sexuality and disability. Therefore, gender-sensitive teaching is based on conveying this intersectionality in teaching and practice. The intersectional approach takes into account how the combination of different types of inequality (sexism, classism, racism, homophobia, and anti-disability) produces specific forms of discrimination or privilege (Crenshaw, 1991; Ghaderi and Lenz 2011).

3 Gender in Social Work—Anchored in the CoBoSUnin Project as Part of the Efforts in Higher Education

As outlined above, gender sensitivity is important because there is hardly any field of social work practice in which gender does not influence social experiences, perceptions and the way people process reality. Even so-called objective science and its teaching is not gender neutral, as long as knowledge, especially socially useful knowledge, is a field of power. Therefore, there was agreement among all participants of the CoBoSUnin project regarding the question that gender is a relevant category for social work and accordingly that gender-reflexive approaches are indispensable for the qualification of bachelor and master's students of social work. The curricula at both cooperating universities include modules on the 'gender issue' (see further contributions in this section). Subsequently, a core element of the project concept was the topic of gender; it was selected as a focus for further training and workshops (see contribution by Mogge-Grothjahn), for visits to Bochum and Slemani (shelter, women's shelter, women's prison, men's association, Khanzad, Pro Familia, etc.). A master's thesis was devoted to gender structures (Dünnebacke 2019).

Strictly speaking, the preoccupation with gender in the teaching of social work had already started before the project started: 'Successful living with regard to gender'—the first cooperative bi-national teaching in the context of the CoBoSUnin project 2015—was dedicated to this topic.[1] The course dealt with gender order from a global perspective. The question was asked: When has a life including the gender perspective been successful? Which cultural orders of gender relations can be observed in different contexts? Where are the chances for a successful life limited? What phenomena of violence and inequality related to gender relations can be observed? How do gender policies reflect the everyday routines of social practice? Where does this happen in fields of social work?

One focus was the Kurdistan Region of Iraq, where, similar to Germany, predominantly young women study social work and are active in the fields of social work, such as schools, prisons, women's shelters and NGOs. An intensive dialogue developed between students and the guest lecturer Dr. Saleh Karim. When asked by the students about the successful life in his city and his university, he answered with the following picture: In the seminar rooms, he observed that those attending the seminar took chairs and moved them according to their needs. Teachers and students sit on the same level in the room and speak, sometimes in a circle. In his university, which is newly built and very beautiful, the tables and chairs are fixed to the floor. You can sit on them, but you cannot change their position. This already symbolizes the given social order on which individuals can sit. The students there could only move themselves on these fixed chairs. Concepts of normality of a 'successful life' differ. The ideal of self-realization and autonomy is only possible to a very limited extent. Rather it is a question

[1] International conference, held at the EvH in Bochum from November 2–5, 2015, see also: https://duepublico2.uni-due.de/receive/duepublico_mods_00072446 (Accessed November 11, 20).

of making creative arrangements with the given limitations, in order to create space for individual opportunities. Explicit legal norms and implicit cultural guiding values form a clear hegemonic structure of gender orders. The coexistence is clearly overshadowed by gender inequalities.

4 Gender Inequalities at Universities in the Kurdistan Region in Iraq?

At the level of universities, there is no legal or political basis for gender discrimination in the Kurdistan Region of Iraq (KRI). Barriers to access to higher education are more likely to be coupled with conservative norm concepts. 'There are gender-specific issues that deserve attention. Women's ability to engage in research is seriously undermined by child care and domestic responsibilities, as well as lack of encouragement and mentoring. There is a perception of systematic bias towards men in opportunities for professional development' (Al-Ali 2013).

A politically important step was the decision of the KRI government that all universities should establish gender centers and include gender studies in their curricula. This decision was not only met with approval, but teachers had to contend with a great deal of resistance, including from conservative students and lecturers. There was and is also strong resistance from Islamic scholars against the use of the term 'gender'.[2]

5 A Look at Gender Issues in KRI

Without a doubt, gender and gender-based violence are one of the key issues that have been moving politics and society in KRI since 1991. Since the fall of the Baath regime (1968–2003), gender-oriented civil society organizations have formed, women's organizations have become active, and new freedoms have arisen to express one's own opinions and to put traditional gender constructions up for discussion for readjustment. Gender relations are undergoing a transformation

---

[2] For example, in the Kurdish parliament in 2010 there was a scuffle between the Ministry of Youth and Education and the Ministry of Religious Affairs over the term 'gender', which assessed this term as reprehensible and 'incitement to immorality' and therefore demanded it should even be banned. After a negotiation process in the committee for 'Law and Religious Affairs' a joint declaration was reached in which 'gender' could be used again as a term with reference to appeasing additional definitions (see Ghaderi 2014: 177).

process that is structured by the ideology of honor, the influence of Sharia in legislation, secular articulations and civil society movements, women's organizations, and international non-governmental organizations. However, women have continued to be marginalized at the level of political representation and participation, discriminated against at the legal level, and gender-based violence has remained an explosive phenomenon.

These findings were not surprising, since the basic norms of gender relations have remained in place in the post-Saddam era: concepts of honor and patriarchal models and, accordingly, a male-dominated society. In other words, violence is by no means reducible to that of individual men against individual women, but is embedded in the structure of society. Political developments have even reinforced religious models through the Islamization of society, which is reflected in particular in the legal aspects.

The forms of violence have changed or, above all, they have become more visible. Examples are: domestic violence, honor killings, increasing suicides, forced marriages, genital mutilation or subtle symbolic violence. The visibility is also related to the fact that 'In Iraqi Kurdistan, there are initiatives that aim to raise awareness of the problems which have resulted from the Kurdish patriarchalism that deprives women of personal autonomy and violates their basic rights' (Kurpiewska-Korbut 2018, p. 137). Gender-based violence is therefore the subject of research, media coverage, numerous events and everyday discussions. A paradox of identity politics becomes obvious: on the one hand, gender equity is 'according to many Kurdish intellectuals, … an integral part of Kurdish culture and often is a point of contention or ideological war being fought with Islamic extremists' (Kurpiewska-Korbut 2018, p. 138), on the other hand, annual statistics show a continuous increase in gender-based violence. The Kurdish regional government reacted to the high numbers of gender-based violence with gender equality policy measures and, in particular, in 2011, with the adoption of a law to combat domestic violence[3] based on the understanding of domestic violence as 'any act, speech or threat that can physically, sexually or psychologically harm a person in the household and deprive them of their freedom and liberties'. For

[3] Iraq: Act of Combating Domestic Violence in the Kurdistan Region of Iraq (Law No. 8 of 2011), June 21, 2011, available at: https://www.refworld.org/docid/5b2911044.html (accessed November 14, 2020).

more effective implementation, the Kurdish regional government has issued a by-law,[4] on the basis of which the *High Committees of Combatting Violence against Women and Families* was established.

In other words, there are improvements on the legal level, but on the one hand there are examples of existing Iraqi laws that are not compatible with the CEDAW Convention on the Rights of Women (keyword polygamy; early marriage), and on the other hand these laws are difficult to implement in practice, for example in cases of marital rape, genital mutilation or the protection of LGBT+ people from discrimination. In theory, they can be reported, but in practice they are difficult to implement. The British-Iraqi gender researcher Nadja Al-Ali accounts for this among other things with the fact that 'Family or tribal mediation continue to be the preferred means of dealing with violence, instead of seeking police intervention and the judgements of courts. Moreover, neither the police nor the judiciary is well-trained to deal with gender sensitive issues, and they often reproduce conservative and misogynistic gender norms and family values' (Al-Ali 2019, p. 20). Furthermore, consanguine marriage practices promote familial to tribal systems of loyalty that cut the authority of the state and slow down the diversity necessary for the formation of civil society structures and the dismantling of hierarchies.

Gender analyses include overall political considerations, and it should at least be mentioned that the negotiation processes on the political power relations in KRI are also conducted on the basis of gendered guiding norms. The above-mentioned laws on the elimination of GBV strengthen gender equity, while at the same time they are political instruments to present themselves 'as more democratic and progressive' than the rest of Iraq 'especially vis-à-vis the international donor and political community' (Al-Ali 2019, p. 20).

KRI activists are far more successful in influencing government legislation on gender issues than their counterparts in central and southern Iraq.[5] However, politically, the government continued to take an ambivalent stance on gender issues. 'Government officials argue that their priority has to be security and stability as opposed to women's rights, stating that 'the KRG has only limited economic and institutional capacity to implement and monitor new laws and regulations to improve the position of women' (Al-Ali 2013, p. 20). The neglect of gender

[4] The By-Law of High Committee of Combating Violence Against Women And Family In Kurdistan Region Governorates of Iraq; https://www.ekrg.org/files/pdf/by-law_highcommittee_combat_violence_against_women_English.pdf (accessed November 15, 2020).

[5] For example, an initiative against the draft law that would allow religious courts throughout Iraq to allow girls from the age of nine to marry. See 'Kurdish activists denounce Iraq's child marriage bill' https://www.rudaw.net/english/kurdistan/121120174 (accessed November 15, 2020).

issues can be observed not least in the fragile financing of gender-relevant places: Employers in social work are primarily international NGOs. A research study by Choman Hardi (2019) presents the marginalization of the interests of some women's organizations in the context of the humanitarian crisis of the Islamic state (IS). The result is an ambivalent relationship between the NGOs working to promote gender equality in Kurdistan Region Iraq and the women's organizations, some of which are dependent on these funds. This relationship is ambivalent because it both empowers and disempowers. In an increasingly competitive world, NGOs struggle for funding and to meet the demands of donors. Even participatory approaches cannot ignore the objectives of the funders. 'With changing funding trends, the focus of NGOs changes and their projects turn into short-term fixes for larger problems' (ibid., p. 14). There is no doubt that NGOs play a role in the direction in which normative changes in relation to gender are initiated in the short term through projects. 'While funders rightly argue that bringing about long-term change is the responsibility of the government' (ibid., p. 14).

At the universities, for example in Slemani, the financial security of the gender research centers is linked to international cooperation (see Gender Equality Center at UoS[6] and The Center of Gender and Development Studies at AUIS[7]). This structuring does not remain without lasting influence on the objectives and possibilities of social work.

Gender norms are not static, and so it remains to be observed how they are transformed in a conflict region that is not at rest and is repeatedly involved in wars. In this concise elaboration, the influence of the threat posed by the so-called Islamic state since 2014 was mentioned—a war that is highly relevant from a gender perspective, also fought through the instrumentalization of gender concepts. Significantly, a conference organized by Nazand Begikhani bore the title: 'Kurdish Woman on the Frontline: Between Victimhood, Representation, Political Participation and the Fight Against Terrorism'.[8] Not least the fate of the children born of war-time rape and their mothers in the context of IS violence forced a confrontation with existing gender norms: 'The existence of these children raises human rights and ethical-normative questions about the orientation points for society and law. Should they focus on origin and paternal line, or the perspective of human rights and children? This painful subject, these forms of violence should not be reduced to a rupture or break in civilisation, but must be perceived as a continuity

[6] Gender Equality Center at the University of Sulaimani: https://gec.univsul.edu.iq/home

[7] See: https://auis.edu.krd/CGDS/ (accessed November 15, 2020).

[8] See: http://www.bris.ac.uk/sps/events/2015/womens-conference-2015.html (accessed November 15, 2020).

of violence in society. For only normative gender orders that already exist prepare the ground for the legitimation of sexualized violence in the context of war and are to be read in this sense as a continuity of existing conditions' (see Ghaderi 2021).

The New Men's Movements also went unmentioned. Wars and conflicts influence gender norms: a young student explained to me that he wanted his wife to study and be financially independent, because if he died in a conflict or war in the region, she would be lost. Love and care for her meant that she would have to survive at any time alone, possibly with children. The demand for changed gender norms that relieve men of their 'breadwinner status obligations' is certainly also a pragmatic response to the permanently fragile economic situation and political instability.

6 Common Challenge: Gender Equity

A look back and forward: The relevance of gender in social work was emphasized at the beginning, gender as a topic in university teaching and in this bi-national project, and the situation in KRI was outlined from a gender perspective.

The project, in the context of which this article and the present book were written, primarily addressed the situation in the Kurdish-Iraqi region and university context. Certainly, there would also be important findings on gender in social work and at universities and society in Germany. There one would have encountered sometimes convergences and sometimes divergences if other inequalities had been mentioned, such as the pay gap.

These forms of transcultural dialogues, especially on gender issues, require a high degree of reflexivity. It is a challenge to hear empirical facts about gender inequalities without evaluating or hierarchizing them. In communicative acts it can be tempting to culturalize or relativize, to homogenize or individualize. Not only with regard to gender, but also with regard to the culture of others (also with regard to other intersectional structural categories), mindfulness and knowledge of the so-called 'hidden curriculum' is necessary. This refers to the unspoken, implicit socially and culturally communicated messages. The hidden curriculum should be conscious. It not only gives signals on a bi-national level, but also within the respective society. Thus, the conservative gender norms primarily function to control women and girls in their movement and mobility. International university cooperation irritates this norm in a productive way, because it enables physical mobility, initiates intellectual movement through dialogues and opens up new access to knowledge beyond territorial borders by softening digital paywalls, for example when students are temporarily given access to publications of the host university.

There are learning lessons from the university dialogue on gender: Gender issues are complex. Time and again, there was a perception of different gender norms in relation to body, sexuality, mobility. The dialogue and analysis of the respective contextual conditions beyond culturalist assumptions continued. Gender competence means knowledge of histories and contexts. Competence is connected with competition and is not free of rivalry in the contest of values and 'legitimate' feelings and positions for the 'right way' in gender issues. The discernment and recognition of different realities enable dialogue. Social work may thus have to perform a balancing act between accepting religious or cultural traditions and promoting a change in social values and gender democracy. In practice, this requires an accepting attitude (patriarchal family constellations) to gain access to addressees at all. Nonetheless, in the recognition of cultural difference, gender inequality as a source of conflict and violence cannot be ignored and its significance can be played down in cultural relativism. For this reason, Ilse Lenz argues that social difference, with its core of gender difference, should not be allowed to merge with cultural difference and thus allow a culturalist legitimation of evident inhumanity (Lenz, 2010). And humanism, being human, according to Ilse Lenz is always gendered. She takes up the male-dominated model that defines women and non-European peoples as 'others' with the ironic title: 'All men shall become sisters?' (ibid., p. 373). From a global perspective, different global currents can be identified with regard to gender relations at present; in those who stand for the opening of gender relations, another current that wants to settle the conflict ('all is achieved') and one that is striving for closure and hierarchical reorganization. The latter can lead to an explosive mixture of ethnocentrism and sexism, in which women's human rights are restricted (e.g. PEGIDA; ISIS, Boko Haram).

Gender relations cannot be discussed without inequality relations. Therefore, despite all historical and current differences, similarities in the KRI and in Germany could be identified, and intersectional interdependencies lead to similar phenomena: Migrant women from poorer countries meet the demand for care work (care chain); refugee and migration movements influence gender relations and lead to processes of opening and closing: Gender models function as markers of a nationally defined collective; an 'authentic' national identity is negotiated through them. Conservative and progressive forces in society argue and compete over 'who are we?' And: Islamic fundamentalism is being discussed, and parallel to this, there is a discussion about Islamophobia or about Westernization and Westophobia. It is worthwhile to discuss gender norms: one that reflects one's own positioning, one that goes beyond dichotomizations of familial-patriarchal and liberal-individualistic, of woman-man, and seeks a humanistic, human rights-based path. For gender justice is a core of democracy and universal human rights.

References

Al-Ali, N. (2013). The Challenges for Women Working at Iraqi Universities. In: MIRIP266, Spring 2013. https://merip.org/2013/03/the-challenges-for-women-workin-at-iraqi-universities

Al-Ali, Nadje. (2019). Feminist Dilemmas: How to Talk About Gender-Based Violence in Relation to the Middle East?. *Feminist Review*. 122. 16–31. https://doi.org/10.1177/0141778919849525.

Becker-Schmidt, R. (2018). Feministische Wissenschaft und Geschlechterforschung. In O. Decker (Eds.) *Sozialpsychologie und Sozialtheorie* (pp. 77–90). Wiesbaden: Springer VS. https://doi.org/10.1007/978-3-531-19564-3_6.

Böllert, K., & Karsunky, S. (2008). Genderkompetenz in der Sozialen. *Arbeit*. https://doi.org/10.1007/978-3-531-90916-5.

Crenshaw, K. (1991). Mapping the Margins: Intersectionality, Identity Politics, and Violence against Women of Color. *Stanford Law Review, 43*(6), 1241–1299. https://doi.org/10.2307/1229039.

Dünnebacke, L. M. (2019). Soziale Arbeit in Kurdistan-Irak und Deutschland – ein Vergleich am Beispiel von Genderstrukturen. Empirische Zugänge im internationalen Dialog. Genderstudies – Interdisziplinäre Schriftreihe zur Geschlechterforschung. Vol. 32. Hamburg: Kovac.

Ehlert, G. (2012). *Gender in der Sozialen Arbeit*. Frankfurt a. M: Wochenschau Verlag.

General Framework for Incorporating the Gender Framework in Higher Education Teaching (2019). https://www.aqu.cat/doc/doc_21331700_1.pdf

Ghaderi, C., & Lenz, I. (2011). Diversity, Gender, Intersektionalität: Von der modernen Gleichheitsrhetorik zu der geschlechter- egalisierenden Praxis. In E. Van Keuk, C. Ghaderi, L. Joksimovic, & D. David (Eds.), *Diversity – Transkulturelle Kompetenz in klinischen und sozialen Arbeitsfeldern* (pp. 117–133). Stuttgart: Kohlhammer.

Ghaderi, C. (2014). *Politische Identität – Ethnizität – Geschlecht. Selbstverortung politischer aktiver MigrantInnen*. Reihe: Studien zu Migrations- und Integrationspolitik. Wiesbaden: VS Verlag.

Ghaderi C. (2021) Children Born of Wartime Rapes – an Analysis from a Gender-Sensitive and Psychosocial Perspective. In: Sonnenberg K., Ghaderi C. (eds) Social Work in Post-War and Political Conflict Areas. Springer VS, Wiesbaden. https://doi.org/10.1007/978-3-658-32060-7_8.

Hardi, C. (2019). Gender Issues in the Context of a Humanitarian Crises. In: Centre for Woman and Peace. Research at London School of Economics, No. 21/2019.

Kurpiewska-Korbut R. (2018). The Socio-Political Role of Modern Kurdish Cultural Institutions. In J. Bocheńska (Ed.) *Rediscovering Kurdistan's Cultures and Identities. Palgrave*

Studies in Cultural Heritage and Conflict. Palgrave Macmillan: Cham. https://doi.org/10.1007/978-3-319-93088-6_3
Lenz, I. (2010). Differenzen der Humanität - die Perspektive der Geschlechterforschung. Alle Menschen werden Schwestern? Differenzen als Herausforderung an den Humanismus; pp. 373–407; DOI: https://doi.org/10.14361/transcript.9783839414149.373
Perry, R. W., & Cree, V. E. (2003). The changing gender profile of applicants to qualifying social work training in the UK. *Social Work Education, 22*(4), 375–383. https://doi.org/10.1080/02615470309144.
Pieck, N. (2018). Gender und Macht in der Sozialen Arbeit. *Sozial Extra, 42,* 31–35. https://doi.org/10.1007/s12054-018-0085-4.

Cinur Ghaderi , Prof. Dr., Professor of Psychology in the Faculty of Social Work at the Protestant University of Applied Sciences (EvH RWL Bochum). She is Vice-President for Research, Transfer and Internationalization. After her post-graduate education in psychological psychotherapy (behavioral therapy), she worked in the "Psychosocial Centre for refugees" (PSZ) in Düsseldorf. She received her PhD at the faculty of Social Sciences of the Ruhr University Bochum. She is a member of the steering committee of DTPPP (transcultural psychiatry, psychotherapy and psychosomatics). Main academic interests: International Social Work, Refugee Studies, Transcultural Psychotherapy, Psychotrauma, Identity, Diversity and Gender. She is the initiator of the DAAD-cooperation project CoBoSUnin 2016–2019 between the University of Sulaimani and Bochum. Contact: ghaderi@evh-bochum.de

Gender—Founders' Perspective

Niyan Namiq Sabir, Najat Mohamed Faraj,
and Jwan Bakhtiar Bahaulddin

Abstract

The first academic center in the Kurdistan Region of Iraq for the study of Gender and Violence was established at the University of Sulaimani (UoS) in 2011 as part of a cooperation project with the University of Bristol. The center has carried out a number of activities such as workshops and seminars inside and outside the university. Furthermore, a considerable amount of scientific research has been conducted by the lecturers who run the center on the topics of violence and gender in the various segments of society. The most important achievement of the center is adding *Gender and Violence* as an academic subject, first in the Sociology Department, and then in the Social Work Department. Nowadays it is a subject of teaching in all departments of the universities in the Kurdistan Region of Iraq.

Keywords

Gender • Violence • Center • University of Sulaimani

N. N. Sabir (✉) · N. Mohamed Faraj · J. Bakhtiar Bahaulddin
Slemani, Iraq
E-Mail: nian.sabir@univsul.edu.iq

N. Mohamed Faraj
E-Mail: najat.faraj@univsul.edu.iq

J. Bakhtiar Bahaulddin
E-Mail: jwan.bahaulddin@univsul.edu.iq

C. Ghaderi et al. (eds.), *Social Work at the Level of International Comparison*,
https://doi.org/10.1007/978-3-658-30394-5_21

1 Introduction

Kurdish society in Iraq is currently undergoing drastic transformation in many life aspects including many social, economic, and political changes. Especially since the downfall of the former regime of Saddam Hussein, Iraqi Kurdish society is experiencing an acute and often violent social struggle between conservation and modernization forces. Women and gender relations have been at the center of this transformation and struggle. While some mainly rural and tribal men fervently try to hold on to their patriarchal notions of women's roles and gender relation, the more urban-based population has been systematically resisting and challenging previously accepted gender norms and relations.

2 Establishment and Aims of the Project of the Gender and Violence Studies Center at the University of Sulaimani

The proposed project aims to introduce violence and gender studies to a selected group of Iraqi Kurdish academics based at the University of Sulaimani in the city of Slemani, first in order to establish a gender and social work course at the university focusing on violence and secondly to raise wider awareness amongst male and female members of staff of violence and gender issues within higher education and society. It is within higher education that prevailing gender norms and relations can be understood, challenged, and discussed in a constructive environment.

In April 2010, a delegation from Bristol University visited the University of Sulaimani. The delegation was composed of the director of the Centre for Gender and Violence Research (CGVR) at the University of Bristol and Dr. Nazand Begikhani, the coordinator of the project.

In November 2010, a conference was held at the University of Sulaimani for two purposes: (1) to promote the necessity of establishing the center of Gender and Violence studies in Kurdistan specifically at the University of Sulaimani and (2) to present new research on honor-based violence in Kurdistan and the UK.

On March 1, 2011, the Gender and Violence Study Center was established at the College of Humanities and Sociology Department according to the memorandum between the University of Bristol and University of Sulaimani and as part of the Delphi program of the British Council.

The aims of the Center are the following:

1. Developing the curriculum at the University of Sulaimani by opening gender courses for faculty members and students in the Department of Sociology.
2. Improving the quality of teaching and expanding its area in the department, by studying the concept of gender and violence and its theories in the departments of sociology and social work.
3. Developing the academic capabilities of students by conducting qualitative research on gender and violence in general and gender-based violence in particular.
4. Raising awareness about gender in general and gender-based violence in particular and expanding women's participation in higher education in the Kurdistan Region of Iraq.

3 The Activities of the Gender and Violence Study Center at the University of Sulaimani

The center was opened in April 2011. During the period from April 2011 to April 2012, several meetings were held between the University of Bristol and the University of Sulaimani in order to construct a useful program for gender at the University of Sulaimani.

In September 2011, the administrative members of the Gender and Violence Study Center at the University of Sulaimani (four faculty members of the Sociology Department, Dr. Najat Muhammad Faraj, Dr. Niyan Namiq Sabir, Dr. Jwan Bakhtyar Bahaadin and Dr. Paiman Abdulqadir Majeed) visited the United Kingdom as part of the capacity-building program of the British Council. They visited the University of Bristol, the British Parliament and many institutions and shelters, for example, for women survivors of domestic violence.

The most important point was adding *Gender and Violence* as a subject for second-year studies in the Sociology Department, taught in team teaching by the four administrative staff of the center.

During the first period of time from 2011–2012, a lot of activities took place in the center. For example, the administrative staff hosted two seminars for the British Consulate in Erbil in support of the center, they met the Minister of Culture and Youth, a Member of Parliament to clarify the domestic violence law, and the *High Committee of Women's Affairs* in Erbil in order to discuss the committee's cooperation with the center. They participated in the *16 Day's Campaign on Violence against Women* from November 25–December 10, with more than twenty seminars conducted by lecturers from a variety of colleges within the university.

During the second period from 2013–2014, the administrative staff participated in many conferences, workshops and seminars relating to gender and violence in Slemani and Erbil, but the focus lay on conducting and publishing several research findings in scientific journals. These researches are listed in the following overview.

1. **Psychological and Social Factors of Female Burning Suicide**
by Prof. Dr. Nizar Muhammed Amin, Dr. Najat Muhammed Faraj, Dr. Niyan Namiq Sabir, Dr. Jwan Bakhtiar Bahaddin and Dr. Paiman Abulqadr Majeed, published in the Journal of Adab / Mansura University, Egypt, vol. 55, September 2014.
The research aims to identify:

   - The most important psychological causes of burned women suicide.
   - The most important social reasons for the suicide of burned women suicide.
   - The relationship of psychological and social causes with the following variables: age, marital status, occupation, educational level.

   The research is descriptive and uses the social survey method. The research included all women who committed suicide by burning themselves and recorded their names in an Emergency Hospital in Slemani during research period lasting seven months, from February until September 2013. The total of the sample was 105 women, which was achieved (purposive sample) by interviewing all the women who burned and visited the Emergency Hospital during the seven months in which the data was collected.

The research reached the following findings:

1. The majority of suicides who had violence used against them was among married women who live in cities.
2. The high illiteracy rate among members of the research sample, spouses and parents.
3. The highest rate of suicide incidents for unmarried women is among female students.
4. The results of the research revealed that the divorced women who attempted or committed suicide by burning were in the prime of life.

5. Suicide was used as an attempt to intimidate and retaliate against those around.

The psychological causes of women's suicide by burning are poor psychological stability, loneliness, loss, frustration, and identity disorder.

As for the social reasons, these are summarized in the problems of married life, the low level of education of the members of the sample, husbands, and parents, the lack of awareness of the peculiarities of marital life, and the weak sense of responsibility among spouses.

2. **Social Security for Women Who Contributed to Social Mobility**, by Dr. Najat Muhammed Faraj, Published in the Journal of Koya University, Vol. 33, 2014.
3. **The Role of Family Upbringing in the Formation of the Concept of Non-Violence among Adolescents** by Dr. Niyan Namiq Sabir, published in the Journal of Education and Psychology of the University of Baghdad, vol. 127, 2016.
   The research aims to identify the level of family upbringing used with adolescents, identify the effects the concept of non-violence has, as well as identifying its relationship with some variables such as sex, age, and educational level of the parents, as well as presenting the correlation between upbringing styles and the concept of non-violence. The sample involved 150 students taken from six secondary schools in the center of Slemani for the academic year 2007–2008.
   The researcher used the descriptive analytical method and constructed two tools, the first for family upbringing styles consisting of 21 items, and the second for non-violence consisting of 28 items. The validity and reliability of the tools have been approved. The Pearson-Spearman correlation coefficient test and an analysis of variance were used as a means of statistical verification.
   The research found that the permissive pattern of family upbringing used with adolescents was 51.93%. An average ratio of 62.67% of teenagers was exposed to the concept of nonviolence, and females ranked higher in relation to the nonviolence concept compared to males as well as the 16–18 age group. The effect of the educational level of the mother is greater than that of the father in forming the concept of nonviolence. Finally, there is positive correlation between an antiauthoritarian attitude and the concept of nonviolence.

4. **Psychological and Social Problems for Women Who Remain from the Anfal Process**
   by Paiman Abulqadr Majeed, published in the Journal of Zanko at the University of Sulaimani, vol. 41, 2013.
5. **Occupational Violence Against Women in Educational Institutions**
   by Dr. Niyan Namiq Sabir and Paiman Abulqadr Majeed, published in the Journal of Education and Psychology at the University of Baghdad, vol. 112, 2015.
5. **The Social Status of Women in Shelters**
   by Dr. Najat Muhammed Faraj, published in the Journal of Zanko at the University of Sulaimani, vol. 45, 2014.

The research aimed to:

1. Understand the family, social, and psychological situation of the women's sheltered house.
2. Identify the social and psychological conditions inside the women's sheltered house.
3. This research is analytical and descriptive; the researcher used the social survey method.

Questionnaire, observation, interview, reports of social workers were used as tools of the research.

The research is about women who attended the sheltered house because they were in danger and threatened by their family or any male in their life. The period of the data collection was from August 1–November 1, 2013.

The three major reasons why these women chose the shelter are first social problems, second psychological problems, and third the economic status of the women.

1. Violence ranks first among the social problems that prompted the research sample to live in the sheltered house for threatened women, divorce comes second, rebellion against customs and social norms comes third, the misuse of mobile phones came fourth, and forced marriages came fifth. The sixth reason was cheating, polygamy and tribal differences.

2. The violence that the women in our sample faced inside their families is (ranked from most to least frequent) as follows: physical, psychological, verbal, economic, sexual, and educational violence.
3. Women inside the sheltered house suffered under the basic social and health services provided there. Mistreatment from the shelter employees is the most common problem that the women suffered from because they lack professional education background. The building itself is not suitable for living in and does not have any principles of privacy.

In this period the center was managed by Dr. Jwan B. Bahaddin:

During the third period from 2013–2016, the focus of the Gender and Violence Study Center was on conferences, training and seminars.

Conferences: The Gender and Violence Study Center held three international Conferences in cooperation with academic and governmental institutions and NGOs.

The first international conference (Women and Human Rights) was held on December 10, 2014.

This conference at the new University of Sulaimani campus was organized by the Gender and Violence Study Center of the UoS together with the Felsberg Institute for Education and Academic Research and with the cooperation of the University of Kirkuk and the Wadi crisis assistance organization.

The second international conference (Solidarity with Iraqi Women and Kurdish People in Facing Terrorism) was held at the Grand Millennium Hotel, Slemani from March 7–9, 2015. This conference was arranged by the Gender and Violence Study Center of the University of Sulaimani and the Stockholm Chamber of Commerce and Industry with the cooperation of the Slemani Governorate, the Ministry of Women's Affairs, and the Ministry of Women's Development and Family Affairs, Somalia.

The third international conference (Women's Issues and Gender Problems) was held at Tower Hall, Slemani from November 20–21, 2015, and was arranged by the Gender and Violence Study Center of the University of Sulaimani, and the Gender and Violence Research Centre of the University of Bristol with the cooperation of the Galawej cultural center.

Training: As a part of a cooperation agreement between the University of Sulaimani and UN agencies and NGOs, the Gender and Violence Study Center prepared training courses on gender and human rights perspectives in both the Slemani and Erbil governments.

1. Concepts of Human Rights (basics), Erbil, Iraq: medical staff of health centers in Erbil in July 2015, for medical staff with indirect contact with emergency cases.
2. Gender and Violence (advanced training), Slemani, Iraq: NGO staff (Zhyaninwe) in September 2015, for NGOs working with women's issues based on gender discrimination.
3. Concepts of Human Rights (basics), Slemani, Iraq: medical staff of health centers in Slemani, December 2015, for medical staff in direct contact with emergency cases.
4. Diagnosis of Battered Women, Slemani, Iraq: medical staff of pregnancy care centers, January 2016, for medical staff in direct contact with pregnant women.
5. Protection from Sexual Exploitation and Abuse (PSEA), awareness training, Slemani, October 2016, for IDP camp observers in Slemani.

Seminars: The Gender and Violence Study Center arranged two seminars in Slemani and Erbil:

1. Women and Globalization in Slemani at the UoS in November 2015, for all university staff and students.
2. Women and Terrorism in Erbil with cooperation of the Middle East Research Institute (MERI) in November 2015, for international NGOs in Erbil.

In this period, from December 2016 until July 2017, the center was managed by Dr. Basma M. Mustafa, during which time she participated in an intentional conference on research into *Gender, Religion and Social Policies in the Kurdistan Region.* From August 2017 until January 2018, the center was then managed by Dr. Zhiya. The main activities undertaken during this period included: participation in various seminars including an event on International Women's Day (March 8). Dr. Zhiya worked at the Gender Center from 2016 to 2018 as a member and/or as director of the center. Among the most important activities that were accomplished during these two years the following:

To begin with, we sought to recruit a male or female instructor with a Doctorate or Master's degree from each of the colleges within the university as representatives of the center in order to publicize the gender concept at the university level. They participated in weekly meetings that were organized to discuss how to present this issue and how to make it more popular among colleagues, instructors and employees in the universities.

Each delegation organized activities during the ceremonies on March 8 and on November 16 in their colleges, after which some young people of both genders were recruited to spread the activities of the center.

During this period, seminars and academic panels were organized together with other universities such as the Polytechnic University and governments authorities such as the Directorate to Combating Violence Against Women and Families, as well as with organizations in civil society addressing gender and violence with the aim of raising gender awareness.

Prizes were awarded to instructors of both genders who obtained Master's degrees or Doctorates on women in order to encourage them to undertake further activities on gender issues in the academic and scientific processes of higher education.

Relations were set up and links established to the American Corner at the University of Sulaimani, with whom joint activities were undertaken in the artistic field (watching movies) and in sports (a marathon between the youth of the university and the youth of refugee camps), each involving both genders. At the same time, we as a Gender Center were able to establish relations, internally or at an international level, with organizations and civil communities in the broad context of research on refugees in the Kurdistan Region.

In the period from 2018–2019, when the center was managed by Dr. Talar A. Amin, several activities were organized on International Women's Day (March 8).

In 2020, the name of the center was changed to *Gender Equality Center* and it was managed by the Ministry directly. At the same time, the experience of teaching gender became more generalized as a part of one of the subjects in the first semester in all departments of the colleges at the universities of Kurdistan.

4 Reflections

A decade ago, *gender* was a new term in Kurdish society, and the nature of our society and its character in tribalism made the process of proposing a concept that had never been known before so difficult. The acceptance of society was therefore almost impossible, with the result that it had to be presented in many seminars and workshops in order to introduce it and explain it in scientific ways that helped people understand its correct form and content. The concept was clarified in the Kurdistan Parliament and, after that, in many audio and visual media. These were the first steps and a prelude to raising the topic.

As for the university community, colleagues, and students, the acceptance process was not easier than in the community at large. The reaction was characterized by rebellion, lack of acceptance, and opposition. Therefore, it took a great effort to clarify it by means of instruction using accurate academic methods. But now, after these struggles, the topic of gender has become a subject taught in all departments in the university.

References

In order to write this chapter, the writers depended on:

- The memorandum between the Universities of Bristol and Sulaimani.
- The annual reports of the Gender and Violence Study Center at the University of Sulaimani.

Niyan Namiq Sabir, PhD, Professor in the Social Work Department/College of Humanities at the University of Sulaimani. She has a PhD in Philosophy of Education, an M.A. in Education and a Bachelor in Education and Psychology from Baghdad. She worked in Baghdad, Libya and Yemen. Since 2004 she has been working at the University of Sulaimani. From 2011–2015 she participated in the Delphi program of capacity building with the University of Bristol and she is one of the founders of the Gender and Violence Study Centre. From 2016–2019 she participated in the CoBoSUnin project with the Protestant University of Applied Sciences in Bochum. She has worked with most of the NGOs in Slemani. She taught and supervised MA & PhD students. She has about 20 published research articles in international, Arabic and local scientific journals. Contact: nian.sabir@univsul.edu.iq

Najat Mohamed Faraj, PhD, Professor in the Department of Sociology, College of Humanities, University of Sulaimani. She was associate dean of students for three years, head of the department for another three years, and as the head of the Postgraduate Student Department of the College of Humanities. She was awarded her PhD in Sociology Organization. She was one of the founders of the Gender and Violence Study Center in the Sociology Department and served for three years as a member of the center management. She is currently teaching Bachelor, Master's and PhD students as well as supervising research and participating in committees to discuss Master's and doctoral theses at the universities of the Kurdistan region. She has 12 scientific research papers published in scientific journals. Contact: najat.faraj@univsul.edu.iq

Jwan Bakhtiar Bahaulddin, PhD in Anthropology, Lecturer in the Sociology Dept., College of Humanities, University of Sulaimani. She is Senior Trainer in Gender Equality and General Policy Management at the Kurdistan Institute for Public Administration within the Ministry of Planning of the Kurdistan Regional Government, Senior Trainer in Religion Diversity at the ADYAN Foundation (Lebanon), and a member of the Advisory Committee of the Alliance of Iraqi Minorities. Contact: jwan.bahaulddin@univsul.edu.iq

Realization of Teaching Gender as a Subject in Kurdistan

Zhiya Abbas Qader

Abstract

This paper describes how the important topic of gender at the University of Sulaimani is implicated in the university's courses, and in particular in the Department of Social Work, and what core topics and objectives are addressed in teaching.

Keywords

Gender • Social work • Teaching

Gender is originally a Latin term to denote a biological distinction, i.e. differentiating human beings on a biological basis. However, once it became connected to sociology, its meaning was changed by attempts to differentiate human beings on the basis of their culture and social aspects. Ultimately, its meaning has thus changed into social gender.

There is no doubt that human beings differ in their bodies in terms of biology and physiology. This means that male and female are different from each other in terms of their physical components, particularly their sexual organ functions, hormones, chromosomes and genes. Furthermore, the elements mentioned are the major principles of gender difference. It is certainly the case that male-dominant social culture and socialization play a huge role in raising the generations of society in that culture, and they are the main defendants of that particular form of practice and existence. That is why they are far from wishing to eliminate

Z. Abbas Qader (✉)
Slemani, Iraq
E-Mail: zhiya.qader@univsul.edu.iq

C. Ghaderi et al. (eds.), *Social Work at the Level of International Comparison*,
https://doi.org/10.1007/978-3-658-30394-5_22

it. Nevertheless, the role of the society is neutral. At the same time, however, every male-dominant social culture and socialization is accused of creating gender differences in which females have been the major victims so far. Consequently, females have suffered a lot in terms of facing physical, psychological, verbal, cultural, political, economic, sexual and other forms of violence.

These differences are unquestionably to be found in all aspects of the community. If we start with social culture, for example, it is formulated and structured on the basis of the superiority of men and the inferiority of women. This is clearly to be seen in the behavior of individuals and in the practice of social relations. Moreover, if we look at the political field, we can easily notice that the participation of women is very low; conversely, men have dominated the political positions and take important decisions in that process, too. When it comes to the law, gender differences can be easily seen as well. As John Stuart Mill said, the inferiority and weakness of women in law can be easily noticed by whether that law is civil status law, personal status law, guardian law from divorce, labor law, penal or maternity law, etc. Mill believed that this mandatory inferiority of women is the biggest obstacle to the development process of a society. Therefore, absolute equality between male and female is the only solution (Huso 2009, p. 171).

Gender differences and distinctions can be also seen in economic aspects as well. When the majority of the employers are males and the employees are females, the distinction again exists and the type of jobs and the specialties are also controlled by men. Furthermore, other fields like religion, politics and business are all dominated by men, and this has constantly led to issues of the exploitation of women by their employers, etc.

As Charlotte Perkins Gilman has said, women work like men and contribute to increasing the income and products of the family, so why don't they have the same rights as men? Or, women do the household, so even if their job is not more important and valuable than men's, it is not less important than them, as the women raise children, educate them and prepare them for their role in society (Compiled Works 2005, p. 25).

Gender and Social Work

Despite the fact that gender is a new subject in Kurdistan, its scientific and academic emergence and appearance have been part of the University of Sulaimani since the first Center of Gender and Violence Studies was established there in 2011. Following that, it emerged as a topic in the Sociology Department of the said university. In implementing the shared project between the University of Sulaimani and the Protestant University of Applied Sciences in Bochum, Germany in 2016, one of the steps taken was to amend the curriculum of the University of Sulaimani by adding some new topics in the Social Work Department in the College of Humanities. One of the added topics was Gender. Since it was a contemporary topic, the main goal of it was to focus on social work, to solve current issues and to ensure social equality in society. There is thus a strong relation between the profession of social work and many of the themes that gender focuses on.

Since then, gender has become a main lesson for third-stage students, and it is taught three hours per week both theoretically and in practice. It is a controversial topic, as we referred to before, it is a new subject matter and its contents are very debatable. Further, it concentrates on some topics that are strongly tied to people's daily life. This is because of the fact that, although Kurdish society has changed a lot, still it is a male-dominated society and gender distinctions can be clearly seen in practice.

Moreover, in 2018, the Ministry of Higher Education and Scientific Research decided that gender must be taught as a subject in both the governmental and non-governmental universities and institutes in the Kurdistan Region. As a result, after implementing the Bologna Process in Kurdistan's universities, gender lessons were added to all first-year programs in all departments and colleges of the universities in the Kurdistan Region as part of a subject called 'Environment', within which gender is studied in both theory and practice for seven hours in two weeks.

The two most important objectives of this lesson are:

1. The knowledge aspect, which includes the following:
   A. Analyzing the term of gender and how it differs from sex and introducing related concepts.
   B. Interpreting the concept of gender based on related theoretical perspectives.
   C. Analyzing the process of gender classification.
   D. Showing the role of socialization in gender classification.
   E. Highlighting feminist movements and discussing their roles in the emergence of this concept.
   F. Discussing LGBTQI society.
   G. Discussing the concept of violence in general and violence based on gender.
2. The behavioral, which includes the following:
   H. Trying to bring about changes in the students' attitudes towards the concepts of men and women.
   I. Encouraging students to have a dialogue on gender differences and understand the challenges that face gender equality in Kurdish society.
   J. Involving students in the training so that they will understand much more about the topic.

K. Encouraging the students to start thinking critically so that they will be able to ask questions about the whole system of society.
L. In order to make changes in the culture of society, since the students are regarded as new generations, they will become parents of the future generation and educate them to avoid practicing the same culture as is currently prevalent. Attempts should be made to change the behavior of the students by teaching this subject.
M. This subject is of great help in creating the basis of much understanding between males and females about their differences. It also helps them accept each other's differences and build bridges to minimize the gaps between them. IN this sense, it also aids them for their daily lives.
N. The students are encouraged to address and deal with subjects relating to gender in their professional life as social work specialists by studying this subject.

References

Huso, I. M. (2009). Gender, Dimensions of Sociology and Culture. Dar Al Shruq Amman. Print T1.

Compiled Works of a Group of Researchers (2005). Male and Female Differences and Racial Discrimination). Translated by Mohammed Qadry Amara. No place of publishing. Print T1.

ZHIYA ABBAS QADER, Ass. Prof., Assistant Professor, Lecturer and since 2021 head of the Social Work Department, College of Humanities, University of Sulaimani. Her specialty and major is in gender. She was a member of the delegation of the social work department in the shared project between the University of Sulaimani and the University of Applied Sciences in Bochum, Germany. Furthermore, in 2017–2018, she was Director of Center for Gender and Development Studies at the University of Sulaimani. Since 2018, she has been in charge of the Higher Education Department at the College of Humanities, University of Sulaimani. She has thus researched widely on gender, violence, woman and LGBTQI with publications in academic journals. So far, she has participated actively in many international and local conferences. Moreover, she is Iraq Coordinator of the Arab Association for Research and Communication Sciences and she is a member of many local and international organizations. Finally, she has a great deal of interests in gender studies, violence and related matters. Contact: zhiya.qader@univsul.edu.iq.

Gender and Masculinity in Kurdistan in Transition—Some Images of Change

Kamil Basergan

Abstract

This article is an attempt on my part to write on 'Gender and masculinity among Kurds in Iraqi Kurdistan' in spite of a paucity of literature on the subject. I will present the goals of and the reasons for the foundation of the men's organization 'Kurdistan Men's Union' and of the club called 'Mr. Erbil'. I have incorporated sections of interviews with the chairmen and/or founding members of both organizations in the article. My day-to-day journalistic research, my trips to Kurdistan, and intensive contacts to the Kurdish men and their families also helped shape my own perspective on the subject.

Keywords

Gender • Masculinity • Kurds

1 Introduction

The subject of this paper is gender and masculinity. The approach I have taken to this subject has been that of a journalist, a social worker and a Kurdish male. Initially, I spent a long time seeking to locate information and academic and

---

Translation by James Brown.

K. Basergan (✉)
Düsseldorf, Germany
E-Mail: basergan@hotmail.com

C. Ghaderi et al. (eds.), *Social Work at the Level of International Comparison*,
https://doi.org/10.1007/978-3-658-30394-5_23

non-academic sources on gender and Kurdish men in Iraqi Kurdistan but, unfortunately, I was hardly able to find or get hold of any books or articles on the subject that might have been helpful for writing this article. In a second step, I sought to contact some experts in the field by phone and to interview them. However, this was largely to no avail since, with the exception of the two interview partners whose comments are integrated into this paper, they did not respond to my enquiries with regard to men's initiatives and activities in Kurdistan-Iraq in relation to gender. In my opinion, the reasons for this could lie, on the one hand, in the taboo on this topical social question in Kurdish society and, on the other, in my own geographical distance and the fact that I was not physically present.

Since my academic quest was not particularly fruitful, I then adopted a journalistic approach, using opinion polls, interviews and internet research. As a result, this paper should be read more as a collage or as essayistic in nature. And my own perspective also had some influence. In concrete terms: My information and prior knowledge consists of my day-to-day researches in various Kurdish media in Iraqi Kurdistan and conversations with a variety of players during my periodic trips to the region. There are many organizations in Iraqi Kurdistan that are dominated and led by men. But I was only able to find two that are purely men's organizations. These are 'Mr. Erbil' and the 'Kurdistan Men's Union'. I conducted an interview with Mr. Burhan Ali, Chairman of the 'Kurdistan Men's Union', in May 2018.[1]

On the whole, I detect a change as regards gender and masculinity, and I would like to illustrate this change with the aid of some images and facets: the 'Mr. Erbil' gentlemen's movement, the founding of the 'Kurdistan Men's Union' and the change in society that I have personally observed, experienced and researched.

2 'We Want a Change of Image'—The 'Mr. Erbil' Gentlemen's Movement

In February 2016, a few young men founded 'Mr. Erbil'. One of the founders is Ahmed Nauzad. In an interview for *Zeit Online* on 23 March 2017, Nauzad said, 'It's as if the people were paralyzed, many just hang around at home and are lethargic.' (Nauzad 2017, p. 1).

Nauzad and two of his friends wanted to take action against the miserable political and economic situation in Kurdistan-Iraq. To begin with, they scoured the

[1] The unpublished interview with the Chairman of the 'Kurdistan Men's Union' was conducted by Kamil Basergan in May 2018 and is abbreviated in the following as: Burhan Ali 2018.

social networks, teahouses and cafés in search of men who might fit in well with them. They should be men who are fashion conscious and able to tolerate other ethnicities, religions and persuasions. Together, they developed their own style of dress combining western and oriental influences. Their fashion style includes certain patterns and colors in their suits and shoes, as well as a style of clothing combination with colored breast pocket handkerchiefs. 'They take their inspiration from the Effendis, a group of former Kurdish landowners who wore trendy clothes and visited salons.' (ibid.)

The model for the group is a Gentlemen's Club from Italy, who describe themselves as follows: 'We are a couple of gents who cultivate manners, celebrate fashion, and love pleasure' (ibid. p.[2]).

In his interview for *Zeit Online*, Nauzad says that fashion is not the most important aspect of Mr. Erbil. It is a vehicle for transporting the real core message, which is: 'We want a change of image' (Nauzad 2017, p. 1). In other words, the founding of this organization is a reaction against the frustrating situation of young people in Iraqi Kurdistan, aimed at showing something positive as a model. In spite of long years of wars, conflicts, financial crises and threats from ISIS, there are also other sides to life. On September 13, 2019, in the course of my journalistic activities, I was able to interview Rawa Ali by phone, one of the founding members of Mr. Erbil. According to his statement, the club currently has 15 members. Despite a large number of enquiries, they initially want to keep membership numbers down to this size. The members are aged between 18–30, and they meet together regularly to discuss new fashion and to exchange views. Women are not eligible for membership of Mr. Erbil, but its members do advocate women's rights on social media. They have their own fashion line. Their fashion photos are published on social media. They also run a café, where the young people can meet.

In the above-mentioned interview on September 13, 2019 for the Kurdish radio program Bernama Kurdîon WDR Cosmo, Rawa Ali said in relation to the club's attitude to gender and masculinity:

> 'We are always being criticized and asked why we only have men as members. We are a handful of adolescent men who, from the very outset, shared similar opinions with regard to respecting women's rights and gender. And so, we wanted to be an example for the youth, and we seek to exercise our influence in this area. At the same time, our dream is for a Mrs. Erbil to be set up. So that Mrs. Erbil can emerge as well, parallel to Mr. Erbil, and we can work together. As the young class in our society, our take on

[2] Gentlemen's Club from Italy: https://www.gents-club-germany.de/business-influencer/, accessed October 10, 2019.

> the subject of gender is equality between women and men, and this is something we openly advocate. We have also been working in this direction. As young people, we want to try to improve the role of women and, rather than obstructing them, to value their contribution and to be proud of them.' (Rawa Ali 2019)[3]

The 'Mr. Erbil' initiative would appear to be addressed more to the upper class, but as a reaction to the situation up until now, it is, for this group at least, a move against the mood of lethargy.

3 Only Image or Fundamental? Data, Statistics and the Men's Union Movement

To what extent are there changes beyond the picture that 'Mr. Erbil' seeks to paint? What relevant statistics and laws can be called into play? This and other questions formed part of the interview I conducted in May 2018 with Burhan Ali, Chairman of the 'Kurdistan Men's Union' that was founded in 2009. What picture of the situation of Kurdish men does he paint? What was the reason for the Kurdish men to organize themselves? He had this to say on the idea behind the founding of the organization:

> 'The idea to found the Kurdish Men's Union came about in the period between 2003 and 2005, that is, after the overthrow of the Saddam Hussein regime. We, as Kurds, had previously been a society that was cut off from the world at large and from the Iraqi government on account of the double embargo. There was a fair degree of activity on the question of human rights here, in spite of the fratricidal war that was waged from 1994–1998 between the two major Kurdish parties, the Patriotic Union Kurdistan (PUK) and the Democratic Party Kurdistan (DPK). There was work being done on women's rights, and this deserves to be acknowledged. In comparison to the rest of Iraq, the personal rights of the individual were improved and reformed. But after the overthrow of the Iraqi government and the opening of Kurdistan to Iraq and to the world, a number of reports were published between 2003–2005, in particular the annual reports on violence and murder. With reference to women's rights and human rights, we noticed a difference between Kurdistan over against Central and Southern Iraq…then we examined the statistics. We discovered that more people, including many women, were murdered on a regular basis in Central and Southern Iraq, but that these cases were not recorded. We therefore came to the conclusion that there is violence against women and murders of women in Kurdistan, but not more so than in the rest of Iraq.' (Burhan Ali 2018).

[3] Interview with Rawa Ali conducted on September 13, 2019 by Kamil Basergan for WDR Cosmo's Bernama Kurdî, abbreviated in the following as: Rawa Ali 2019.

A probable explanation for this state of affairs is: These reports and statistics were published by women's rights and human rights organizations. Since the NGOs in the rest of Iraq did not immediately take up their work after the overthrow of Saddam Hussein and there was a considerable time lap until they did, it was not possible to register all acts of violence and there is a high dark figure of unrecorded cases. For that reason, acts of violence against women in Iraqi Kurdistan, which were registered in the statistics, are more numerous than in the rest of Iraq.

These observations led to further considerations and further steps, which he expanded on as follows:

> 'At the same time, we appreciated that the Kurdish men, in contrast to other men in the Near East, suffer not only from social and religious problems, but also from national problems. They are so preoccupied with this that they are incapable of perceiving or appreciating social changes. And so, we realized that a center is necessary, first and foremost to embolden the men and raise their awareness and wokeness (Hoshyarkrdnawa), so as to enable them mentally and emotionally to appreciate the developments and changes in society and to cope with them. We realized that, without an organization or an association, we would not be taken seriously. That was why we founded the Kurdish Men's Union. To start with, there were only fifteen of us, including lawyers, doctors, imams and men from many other professions and social classes.' (Burhan Ali 2018).

The founding of the Kurdish Men's Union was officially announced on March 27, 2007 in the newspaper *Awene*. In 2009, it was officially approved by the Ministry of the Interior:

> 'Starting from then, we set about raising men's awareness (Hoshyarkrdnawa), for that was our goal. Before that, because the official bodies were unprepared and unsuited, people turned to the women's associations and organizations to solve women's problems. Since violence against women exists, so too there are men who are sometimes victims of cultural and social values, and since there was no center to which such concerns might be addressed, we had to open up and take on these cases. Since then, we have become the port of call for taking on and dealing with men's problems.' (Burhan Ali 2018).

These problems include, for example, the problem of older men being evicted from their homes. Some suffer from violence at the hands of their own children and are forced to move out of their homes for their own safety. During the financial crisis, some men were under pressure as 'breadwinners' to meet their families' wishes or to make maintenance payments, in spite of having neither wages nor money.

In the meantime, the Kurdistan Men's Union has 7,500 members and is represented in several towns and villages in Iraqi Kurdistan. It is a port of call for those men who have family problems or private problems. According to its Chairman, Burhan Ali, the organization seeks '(…) to offer the men legal and social support as well as liaising between them and their families in order to find a solution to their issues and their problems.' (Burhan Ali 2018).

Burhan Ali draws attention to the fact that men also suffer from the violence structures in families and in society, referring to a statistical survey of the Kurdistan Men's Union of July 31, 2017. This includes, as is shown in Tab. 1 below, the incidence of suicides amongst men and violence against men for the towns of Erbil, Slemani, Duhok, Kirkuk and Halabja.

When the law on violence against women was passed by the Kurdish parliament, the Kurdistan Men's Union felt there was a gap in the legislation, according to its Chairman Burhan Ali. They have therefore set themselves the goal of making some proposals and suggesting projects for men's rights:

> 'There was the issue of the right of access. Men were disadvantaged by this. In this society, we are not in favor of the separation of families, but developments are leading to an increased number of family separations. According to Ministry of the Interior statistics, there were ca. 45,000 divorces in the Kurdistan region of Iraq between 2010 and 2017, with 71,000 children affected. In terms of the old Iraqi legislation on the right of access dating from 1959–1960, the parent who does not live together with a child is only allowed to see the child for two hours within the space of two weeks. If the child lives with the mother, the father will only see his child for two hours every fortnight, and vice-versa. As part of a project, we proposed to parliament that the child should live with its other parent for at least two days per week. Thankfully, a decision was reached in favor of 24 hours per week. The parents are only allowed to see their children on the premises of an organization, and they are not allowed to take their children outside due to the risk of abduction.' (Burhan Ali 2018).

These two examples of the Kurdistan Men's Union and Mr. Erbil show that there are many social problems that cannot be resolved by the men's organizations alone, but which all parties must take seriously and attempt to resolve—the state, politics, the family, the individual, etc. In my view, the commitment shown by both organizations is to be welcomed. There may be differing views on the contents and objectives of their work, but I see the fact that they had the confidence to assert themselves as providing a platform for an open discussion and presentation of the social problems in Kurdish society.

Table 1 Overview of suicides amongst men and acts of violence against men for the towns of Erbil, Slemani, Duhok, Kirkuk and Halabja, internal statistic of the Kurdistan Men's Union from July 31, 2017 and January 2nd, 2021. (https://www.awene.com/detail?article=41094, Accessed: January 7, 2021)

Year	Cases	Murders	Suicides	Eviction of older men from their homes	Unfaithfulness/ adultery	Physical violence	Interference of relatives in marital relations	Emotional or sexual pressure	Control of wages	Obstructed right of access
2015	526	6	69	29	53	8	167	44	14	211
2016	583	8	70	36	56	13	182	48	17	231
2017	614	5	74	41	61	13	192	45	11	251
2018	558	5	115							
2019	545	5	84							
2020	553	8	91	37	52	11	197	20	9	227

4 Personal Impressions and Reflections

I wish to begin by drawing a comparison between the process of gender and Kurdish men and that of the struggle and demands of Kurdish women and girls for their rights. These consist, specifically, of the demands of Kurdish women for their rights and their position, their opposition against violence towards women and girls, the setting up of women's shelters as safe spaces, all of which were fought for and achieved by committed women and their organizations. Neither at the individual level, nor at the level of the family or of society, has a convincing and plausible solution to and acceptance of these gender issues in families and in society yet been found.

In my view, if we regard the problems facing women and girls in Iraqi Kurdistan as one side of the coin, it holds true that, as long as we fail to make any substantial progress on that side, we will still be at the very beginning of the process on the other side of the coin (meaning gender and Kurdish men). For interaction between the genders, between women and men, is relational, it is based on interdependence and is mutually permeated. But even this very simple correlation has not yet been appreciated in everyday life, and everyone still thinks one-sidedly of gender issues as being the concerns of women and girls. In my opinion, specific consideration of gender and masculinity still requires a great deal of patience in order for progress to be made.

At the same time, it would be mistaken to view the processes of human rights in general or in particular and specifically in gender relations in South Kurdistan from a Eurocentric perspective and with a Eurocentric attitude. In saying this, I mean that all steps and developments against violence towards women and men, and for equality in gender relations or the achievement of legal equality between the sexes, can be hampered by wars, conflicts, persecution, political unrest and systematic oppression by the state, all of which can slow processes down. Consequently, any comparison with developments in Europe is invalid, since different circumstances pertain for the goals and processes being pursued and they should not be judged by European standards. Instead, respect from outside is called for with regard to the specific or particular means of bringing about change.

Religion and traditional or social values could be further factors that impact on what progress is made on women's and girls' rights, men's rights, children's rights, or the rights of dissenters. In recent years, tolerance towards ethnic and religious minorities has come to be valued less in Iraq, in my opinion, as a result the polarization of religions that has taken place, especially in the early years of the new millennium. For that very reason, the tolerance shown by Mr. Erbil towards all religions and minorities is particularly to be welcomed in the present situation, and it is vitally important as a positive example.

At this point, it is important to mention that, after the second Gulf War in 1991 and the liberation of the Kurdish territories in Iraq, a number of activists and human rights and women's rights organizations undertook what was like a kind of revolution, writing and campaigning against and in response to everyday violence towards women and girls and advocating their rights in Iraqi Kurdistan. These activities were welcomed and supported from the very outset by several international NGOs. Now, even after 28 years, no-one can maintain that the problems have been resolved. But, in my assessment, in spite of a thousand obstacles placed in their paths, and in spite of threats and honor killings, the hard work and struggle of these individuals and organizations has at least influenced Kurdish society and individual Kurdish men, however minimally, to reflect on the issue. The work of these organizations has thus touched a sore point, highlighting the injustice towards Kurdish women and girls.

The most important aspect of this development is that it means social and everyday problems constantly were and continue to be the subject of discussion. That is to say, it remains a live issue that is discussed in society and by individuals. The awareness (Hoshyari - هۆشیاری) of the individual in Kurdish society plays a role here and whether or not they assume an attitude of gender justice in this change process, an attitude that leads to clear words and actions.

The arduous struggle and the work that has been done for the rights of women and girls in the past years has directly and indirectly influenced Kurdish men and gender relations. This can influence the conservative attitude they still have or lead to a more open approach towards the social problems and conflicts that have shaped Kurdish society for many years, and from which especially women and girls suffer hugely. A decisive factor will be whether these changes and developments in how they think and act enable Kurdish men to relinquish their power over the traditional structures of the freedom of the individual in the family and in society. For Kurdish society is a male-dominated society, and a positive change amongst men towards the rights of women and girls is decisive for advancing the process of gender justice in Iraqi Kurdistan. Naturally, this must happen in measured steps, persuasively, and with the support of the women so that a stable change can take place in families and in society.

Consequently, Kurdish men have, in my opinion, a key role to play in gender justice, in order to open many doors and to seek means to resolve many longstanding problems. As I see it, one half of Kurdish society, namely the women, have been campaigning for years for their rights and many have paid for that struggle with their lives. On the question of equal rights and gender in Kurdish society, it is therefore up to the men to decide whether they wish to advance this process side by side with the women or whether they decide against doing so.

If we regard gender justice and the development of the role of Kurdish men in Iraqi Kurdistan as a process, I believe that that process has only now begun, openly or covertly, for some individuals. In Kurdish society, this is a decision that requires courage, self-confidence and strength in order to openly take practical steps in all areas of everyday life, in the family and at work. In my opinion, the following are factors that could have an influence on this decision and on the men themselves: strength of character, social and professional status, whether or not they are open to influences from family and social structures or from their friends, confidence in making decisions although criticism and rejection from their environment is likely. Education could, but need not, also have a role to play.

Life situation and environment naturally have a major influence on a person's mental and physical perception. Gender, expectations, and 'duties' towards family, society, religion, friends, etc. have a major role to play in this.

I am of the opinion that the role of Kurdish men with regard to their gender role must at least be subdivided into two groups, namely intentional and unintentional. By intentional I mean that they consciously assume their role as guardians of their family, women and 'honor' and manage that role according to their attitudes and moods so as not to lose their "masculinity" and not to lose face. We then have the other group of Kurdish men who want to have no part in this guardian role. This group relinquishes a role and an expectation which many of them had neither chosen nor feel happy with, namely that of guardians of honor. Education, environment, friends, urban or rural life are a variety of factors that could influence the process of gender equality in the minds of many men.

For me, the question remains open as to what the future will hold: Will the dominant traditional and conservative type be replaced by a gender justice type, or will these heterogeneous images of masculinity continue to exist parallel to each other? When and how will the Kurdish male reinvent or redefine himself?

References

Ali, R. (2019). Mr. Erbil, WDR-Cosmo Bernama Kurdîon September 13, 2019. Accessed 7 Oct 2019.

Nauzad, A. (2017). "Die Dandys von Erbil", Zeit Online on March 23, 2017. https://www.zeit.de/gesellschaft/zeitgeschehen/2017-03/irak-kurden-hipster-dandy-mrerbil. Accessed 14 Nov 2018.

Ali, B. (2018). Personal Interview with the Chairman of the 'Kurdistan Men's Union' was conducted by Kamil Basergan in May 2018 in Slemani.

Kamil Basergan Diploma in Social Work, systemic consultant, freelance journalist. Since 2009 he has been working with young refugees and migrants at the Youth Migration Service of Diaconia Düsseldorf in Germany. He studied Social Work at the Protestant University of Applied Sciences in Bochum. Since 1993 he has worked as a freelance journalist for the Kurdish-language program 'bernama kurdi' at a German radio station (WDR, West German Broadcasting, Cosmo). Contact: basergan@hotmail.com

'Rahenani Maidani'—the Kurdish Version of Social Work Internships at UoS

Chro Mohammed Faraj

Abstract

In this chapter, generally, I will describe the internship education of social work university students in Kurdistan. The chapter includes the introduction, the definition, the objective, the structure, the procedures, and the instructions.

Keywords

Internship • Supervision • Evaluation

1 Introduction and Definition of Social Work Internships in Kurdistan

In Kurdistan, in the departments of social work, the internship has been built and designed according to academic quality and local and international standards of social work and social service theoretically and practically. An internship is a learning experience that involves receiving academic creditor learning at an approved institutional site, agency, institution, or organization, with supervision for a specific period of time (Sweitze and King 2009, p. 3). The internship supplements students' formal education, and introduces them to the work application in society. Internships represent the central form of instruction and learning within social work studies to socialize its students to perform the role of practitioners. It provides a real-life experience in a social work setting where student social workers

C. Mohammed Faraj (✉)
Slemani, Kurdistan Region, Iraq
E-Mail: chro.faraj@univsul.edu.iq

C. Ghaderi et al. (eds.), *Social Work at the Level of International Comparison*,
https://doi.org/10.1007/978-3-658-30394-5_24

are placed and can practice their skills (Kirst-Ashman 2010, p. 27). Internships teach students the application of classroom learning, theories, and experiences to professional settings (Encyclopedia of Education 2004, p. 1325). An internship contains the process of transformation of learning between the classroom and the field of social work, which helps students to connect their learning with the field of social work (Hessenauer 2011, pp. 58–59). Through the internship, university students take on temporary roles as workers in an organization and reflect on these experiences in an academic setting (Green 1997, p. 9). Synonyms of internship are: cooperative education, practicum, externship, apprenticeship, article-ship, field practice, field training, field placement, or fieldwork.

2 The Objective of Internship

In general, the internship enables students to undertake learning and becoming a reflective social worker, through:

- Providing the opportunity to work in a professional setting within the reality of institutional life.
- Integrating what has been learned in and out of the classroom, and developing a reciprocal relationship between theories and practices critically, and becoming dynamic in the teaching–learning process of field instruction.
- Developing a sense of commitment to the profession of social work and to integrate knowledge, feeling and doing aspects of social work education.
- Recognizing and understanding the diversity roles of social work practice according to the types of the institutions and organizations.
- Gaining exercise to analyze the effects of social welfare policy on programs and services.
- Evaluating social work practice interventions and processes.
- Developing research questions in relation to practice efforts.

Like as follows:

1. *Knowledge*: Knowledge about:
    1.1. The system and the structure of social work in a specific institution.
    1.2. General social work practice in a specific institution.
    1.3. Practice and policy issues regarding social services in a specific institution.

   1.4. Professional role of the practitioner of social service in a specific institution.
2. *Skills*: Learning and developing basic professional skills that include the following aspects:
   1.1. The system and the structure of social work in a specific institution.
   2.2. Development of the collaborative ability to work in teams.
   2.3. Development of the ability to supervise.
   2.4. Development and enhancement of interpersonal and intrapersonal attributes regarding the social work role.
3. *Values*: Identifying and recognizing the values and ethics of social services in general which include the following points:
   3.1. Enhancement and appreciation of values and ethics of social work in general and clients and institutions particularly.
   3.2. Enhancement and appreciation of rights and duties regarding organizations and systems include clients and professional practitioners of social services and other staff.
   3.3. Appreciation and respect for individuals, groups and organizations in the society.
   3.4. Appreciation and respect for individual's privacy and self-determination.
4. *Processes*: Identifying, recognizing and practicing the processes of social services in general and developing social work interventions which include the following aspects:
   4.1. Apply an institution's instructions and obligations as a student and a social worker within an institution (a student becomes a part of the institution during the internship).
   4.2. Participation with a professional practitioner in social services of the institution according to the availability of resources.
   4.3. Applying social work methods on the levels of the individual, group, community or at the institution level.
   4.4. Organizing activities in the institution such as interviews, seminars, reports, questionnaires, and researches within professional interventions.

3 The Structure of the Internship

As a training field, an internship is a basic theme (the main subject); it is taught as one of the main themes throughout the academic year of the bachelor's degree. The internship is studied in two stages; stage three and stage four, it has three units with 100 degrees. The students of the stages study internship three hours continuously from 9:00 am to 12:00 pm on one specific day per week throughout both semesters within a pre-limited teaching schedule. The procedures and the instructions are like as follows:

3.1 Classification of Students

At the beginning of the new academic year, students of stage three and stage four divide into small groups. Each group contains five to ten students. Each group is supervised by a lecturer of the department of social work and the lecturers of each stage are supervised by an organizer teacher from the department.

3.2 Agreement of the Internship

At the beginning of the internship, the department contacts the institutions through the lecturers, and a formal agreement is made between the departments of social work and the institution for a fixed period, where students (interns) train in the institution and the institution agrees to mentor and teaches the students. Many companies go on to hire their successful intern through the practitioner of social work of the institution.

3.3 Organizations and Institutions of the Internship

The department and the lecturers of the department identify the institutions (a placement or a site) of the internship through coordination between the institutions and the university in advance. The institutions include every governmental and non-governmental organization and international institutions that provide social and psychological services by their professional members. The institutions include nursery, kindergarten, school (public and private), hospital or medical center (physical and mental), social reform, social welfare, labor, the court (the personal state court, the family court, the juvenile court, and the criminal court), the organizations like civil society organization, family and violence organization, and shelter, etc.

3.4 Program of the Internship

The program of the internship is planned by the lecturers of the department of social work in advance, and the lecturers themselves are making an appropriate modification, and the program of the internship is proportional according to the following determinants:

1. The educational needs and requirements of the social work students.
2. The availability of resources.
3. The permissions and facilities of the institutions.
4. The type of services of the institutions.
5. The policy of the institution.
6. The mechanisms of the work of social work practitione in the institutions.
7. Pre-limited time of internship in the institutions.

3.5 Supervisor Instructions

Although the internship is managed by the department of social work in general, its supervising process is performed through the consolidation of the three sides. First, the supervision of the organizing teacher; each stage (third stage and fourth stage) has the organizing teacher that supervises other lecturers of internships regarding the formal or official procedures in general. Second, the supervision of the lecturer; each group of students of the internship has a lecturer that supervises a certain group inside the department and the institution as well during the internship process. Third, the supervision of the institution; every institution that participates in internship processes has its own professional member or practitioner that offers social or psychological services according to his or her specialty, and the professional coordinate with the lecturer during the internship to implement the internship program inside the institution that she or he works.

3.6 Commitment and Practical Application of the Students

During the internship, the student performs as a student and as a social worker together, with the commitments or obligations and requirements that implemented like any other themes or subjects during the semesters. At the institutions and during the internship, students within groups practice the following implementations:

1. In the beginning, upon entering the organization or the institution, students are introduced to the structure, the policy, the type of services available of the institution, and the social and the psychological professional roles.
2. Students will become a part of the institution and a part of a professional teams with the social and psychological professionals or practitioners and this as a student and as a professional exerciser with the determination of the student's duties and rights at the institution in relation to the internship.
3. Students participate appropriately in the days of the internship with social and psychological practitioners. Students record notes about what they do and what they learn each day of the internship like information and their observation during the internship period.
4. Students allow preparing and presenting activities in the institution such as a seminar, report and questionnaire regarding the internship according to the agency's permission and the availability of time and resources.
5. At the end of the internship, students prepare a research or a paper about the internship.

3.7 Evaluation of the Students

As the main theme and like any other subject, each student of the internship that includes the students of stage three and the students of stage four will be evaluated at the end of the academic year. The students evaluate according to his or her commitment towards his or her duties and activities in the frame of an internship. Each student evaluated by the evaluation form that is pre-build and designed by the department of social work. A student's degree of the internship is (100) degree over one academic year. The degree is divided by a supervisor lecturer in the department. The institution's supervisor evaluates each student with (30) degree and a supervisor lecturer evaluates each student with (70) degree at the end of the internship. A student does not pass if his or her average degree at the end of the one academic year is less than (50) degree and his or her level is weak, and a student passes with (50) degree.

4 Evaluation of the Chapter

In Kurdistan, social work education is new in its academic form and so is the social work internship. An internship for social work university students is an utmost necessity tool that supplements their formal education. The internship has achieved the level that needs more support and work for the sake of accomplishment and development, particularly to rebuild the programs of the internship that I mentioned before, for example: introduce a guidebook to social work university students and the announcement of a formal contract and coordination permanently between the departments of social work and the institutions to facilitate internship.

References

Encyclopedia of education (2004). Second Edition. U.S.A: Macmillan Reference.

Green, M. E. (1997). *Internship success*. USA: Ntc contemporary.

Hessenauer, S. L. (2011). *From classroom to workplace: becoming a Social Worker*. Chicago: Loyola University.

Kirst-Ashman, K. K. (2010). *Introduction to Social Work & social welfare* (3rd ed.). USA: Brooks\cole Cengage learning.

Sweitze, H. F., & King, M. A. (2009). *The successful internship* (3rd ed.). USA: Brooks\cole Cengage learning.

Chro Mohammed Faraj Lecturer in Social Science, B.A. in Sociology (2008), M.A. in Social Work (2014) at the Department of Sociology, College of Humanities, University of Sulaimani in Slemani, Kurdistan Region of Iraq, where she also worked as an Assistant Researcher and Researcher (2009–2011), as Assistant Lecturer in the Unit of Higher Studies (2014–2015), and as Assistant Lecturer (2015), and Lecturer (2018). Contact: chro.faraj@univsul.edu.iq

'Praxisbegleitung'—the German System of Social Work Internships at EvH

Frank Fechter, Tobias Klug, and Kristin Sonnenberg

Abstract

The article describes the legal ground of practical phases in studies of social work in Germany as a condition to entering a licensed profession. The main topics are the structure of practical phases in the study of social work, the concept to achieve professional and personal competences and the main methods with which to reach these aims. Criteria to frame the internship are mentioned as well as the aims and the philosophy of practical phases.

Keywords

Internship • Practical phase • Training • Professionalism • Attitude • Learning • Experiences

1 Introduction

In Germany, the studies of social work contain a practical phase of at least 100 working days within an institution or service, dealing with some kind of social problems and having social workers as employees. This internship is framed by a

F. Fechter (✉) · T. Klug · K. Sonnenberg
Bochum, Germany
E-Mail: fechter@evh-bochum.de

T. Klug
E-Mail: klug@evh-bochum.de

K. Sonnenberg
E-Mail: sonnenberg@evh-bochum.de

C. Ghaderi et al. (eds.), *Social Work at the Level of International Comparison*,
https://doi.org/10.1007/978-3-658-30394-5_25

law and lays the ground for obtaining recognition by the state. This is obligatory to work in state agencies such as state-run youth welfare services, child protection units, social welfare offices and law services.

The practical phase is placed in study year two, after the students have finished the basic modules of social work (methods, practical fields, history and theory) as well as the basic modules of human sciences (such as education, sociology and psychology, health) and the introduction to law, management, politics and aesthetical education.

2 Structure, Concept and Methods

During the practical phase, the students work four days at their placements, where practitioners guide them. One day a week they join a seminar at the university, where a reflection of experiences is realized. These courses are conducted by teachers who have an education in social work or social pedagogy and have special training in supervision. What is fundamental here is that the places of learning—university and professional practice—must be understood as equivalent places of learning in the study program. The 100 days of practical experience must be conducted at two different working places. At the end, the students have to write a report to show their competences.

After studying the module, the students should have reached the following aims and gained certain competences:

a) *Professional competences*, such as knowledge and understanding of organizational structures, processes, professional action and decision-making, life world and living environments of the clients, framework conditions for working in the chosen working fields and social service agencies. They should learn methods and means for professional action, get to know and identify different approaches to action, examine scientific theories in their jobs and reflect and document their own action.
b) *Personal competences*, such as social and personal competences. This means they should learn to interact in a professional way with clients, build up relationships, based on communicative and cooperative skills as well as the ability to solve conflicts and develop empathy. Another important competence is working in a team of colleagues and to understand institutional backgrounds and conceptions. Concerning their personal competence, they should further develop awareness and reflective skills to master a professional habitus and personality.

The seminar is held on a weekly basis (90 min per unit) or fortnightly (180 min). The group consists of 12 students. The main method is group supervision and reflection, such as counseling with colleagues and intervision. The cases worked on are brought by the students from their practical experiences. This is done to deepen their skills of reflection and to support role development. The teachers apply a set of methods that support the learning process of the students such as experience orientated learning.

3 Quality Standards

The coordinators of internships at the EvH developed a paper called 'Quality Standards of a Successful Internship: 10 Criteria for a Successful Internship' (internal document: Fechter and Klug 2017, see appendix) to lay down certain criteria that frame the internships. They are structured at the three levels of preparation ('before the internship'), the duration, and the reflection phase after having finished the practical phase. A few criteria shall be emphasized here by way of example. Before the internship there should be a definition of aims and tasks to plan. There are two reasons for this. One is to find the right working place according to the expectations and the second is to evaluate the aims afterwards, to evaluate a realization of expectations and demands and to find the right working place. The coordinators and lecturers at EvH recommend an interview between the student and the practical institution, exchanging views about expectations, demands, aims and tasks of the internship. Framing conditions are core criteria for a successful internship. These are, for example, nomination of a supervisor and contact person at the university for obligatory preparation courses, visitations during the internship, etc., and also within the institution there has to be a nomination of a mentor and a substitute, creation of a timetable and fixed dates, definition of tasks and working steps, laying down fixed dates for interviews between student and mentor. These have to be realized during the internship. The following criteria shall secure this (used as a checklist):

- Delegation of responsibilities and clearly defined tasks of the intern
- If possible, preparation of a self-developed project
- Full introduction of tasks and detailed explanations
- If possible, participation in advanced education/training

It is within the responsibility of the institutional mentor to supervise the intern by taking care of the intern's interests, being available for all questions and giving feedback on a regular basis.

After the internship, all actors should evaluate the internship. For the students, this means a reflection on the competences gained, which is part of the internship report. A final internship certificate needs to be stamped and signed by the extern and intern mentor. Additionally, the students should request a qualified, written certificate with detailed declaration of duration and aims of the internship as well as tasks and performance rating of the intern, including an assessment of professional and meta-professional competences.

4 Aims and Philosophy

To sum up, it can be said that the study of social work is a hybrid study: Two different learning locations, each with a different systematic rationale, are interlinked in training future competent employees in the fields of social work. The basic goal of the practical phase is to get to know social work with its aims and tasks. Three specific goals can be identified:

1) *Promotion of professional identity*
An important point for the development of a professional identity is getting to know and learning how to work in the field of tension between society, institutions and client expectations. It is about recognizing these tensions and being able to move and position oneself within them. These tensions cannot be simulated in seminars. A professional identity that knows how to deal with these political, social and personal tensions cannot be acquired solely through book knowledge or discussions about the theory of professionalization. This is known as a tolerance for ambiguity. It means on the one hand to balance against and reassess tensions, and on the other hand to bear and resist them. For the development of a professional identity, practical experience is necessary. For the development of a professional identity—in the sense of a methodical self—re-assurance necessitates substantial practical experiences during the study to achieve a higher level of awareness for individual professional correlations.
2) *Promotion of professional competence*
The main focus here is testing the means and methods of specialist action. The methods and theories learned are tested in professional practice. To what

extent do they help with practical decisions? Are they helping to move safely in the professional field as a social worker?

3) *Promotion of reflection competence*
Social work takes place wherever there is an encounter between social workers and clients. This entails a special feature that social work has in common with all occupations and activities that are intended to serve the development of social behavior of individuals and social groups: The most important tool at your disposal is your own personality. Working with people places special demands on self-reflection—of the social worker him, or herself—which is the 'tool' in these relationships and working processes.

A major challenge is that your own personality and conflict potentials necessarily come into contact with the challenges of the clients. The resulting dynamics require the ability to reflect as a principle of professional regulation. To work out these dynamics and not just to describe them theoretically is a central point of the practical phase.

It is also about developing one's own self- and external perception, becoming aware of the values and norms on which one's own actions are based and being able to assess the consequences of one's own actions. Practical phases as study elements are therefore an enormous area of experience for social work activities and at the same time contain an intensive potential for reflection and processing.

Appendix

Quality Standards of Internships: 10 Criteria for a Successful Internship
By Frank Fechter, Tobias Klug, July 2017, ***EvH***

I. Before the Internship

1. **Definition of aims and tasks**
   - Realization of expectations and demands
     For students: What do I want to learn? What do I want to achieve?
       (e.g. development of social competences, preparing to enter the profession, getting to know potential employers)
     For institutions/companies: Which tasks is the student supposed to fulfil? What is my interest? (e.g. gaining junior staff)
     For universities: Which strategy of internships does the university/the course have? In which way is the internship integrated in the course?

- Interview between the student and the practical institution/company, exchanging views about expectations, demands, aims and tasks of the internship

2. **Organization of Supervision/guidance**
   - *For students and universities*: Nomination of a responsible person/supervisor and contact person for obligatory preparation courses, visitations during the internship, etc.
   - *For institutions/companies*: Nomination of a mentor and a substitute, creation of a timetable and fixed dates, definition of tasks and working steps, laying down of fixed dates for interviews between student and mentor
3. **Provision of necessary resources at the workplace**
   - Workplace, working appliances (e.g. desk, computer, etc.)
4. **Clarification of legal questions and duties**
   - Working hours, payment, discretion, insurance, credit of study
5. **Conclusion of a contract**
   - Between the institution, the student and the university
     Including at least the following:
     - Start and duration of the internship
     - Payment
     - Working hours
     - Training schedule, procedure and content of the internship, aims and evaluation

II. During the Internship

6. **Introduction of the intern and the institution/company**
   - Welcoming and introduction of the intern in the institution/company, introduction of colleagues and contact persons
   - Informing the intern about basic rules and necessary information
7. **Content and tasks of the internship**
   - Delegation of responsibilities and clearly defined tasks of the intern
   - If possible, preparation of a self-developed project
   - Full introduction of tasks and detailed explanations
   - If possible, participation in advanced education/training
8. **Supervision and support through the mentor**
   - Supervision of the intern through the mentor, by taking care of the intern's interests, being available for all questions and regular feedback

III. After the Internship

9. **Evaluation of the internship**
   - *For the institution/company*: detailed feedback and reflection of the internship drawing conclusions for further internships/further studies,
     final talk between the institution and the intern, final evaluation of feedback, chances of employment opportunities
   - *For students/interns*: reflection of the internship and the competences gained, preparation of an internship report
   - *For universities*: obligatory and established course, evaluation of the internship
10. **Creation of final internship certificate**
    - Qualified, written certificate with detailed declaration of duration and aims of the internship as well as tasks and performance rating of the intern, assessment of professional and meta-professional competences
    - Certificate needs to be stamped and signed by the intern's mentor.

Frank Fechter lecturer in Social Work and Internship; Representative for internship matters at the Protestant University of Applied Sciences Bochum. Diploma in Social Work and Diploma in Supervision. He is specialized in the field of Social Work in Outpatient Dispensing of Drugs and Alcohol. Contact: fechter@evh-bochum.de

Tobias Klug currently holds a position as lecturer of Social Work at the Protestant University of Applied Sciences in Bochum. He holds a diploma in Social Work and is also deacon, systemic educator and supervisor. Mr. Klug is specialized on the topics Youth and Youth Work, as well as on the coordination of internship programs within university courses and, in specific, the ongoing support of interns. Contact: klug@evh-bochum.de

Kristin Sonnenberg, Prof. Dr., Professor of Social Work at the Protestant University of Applied Sciences Bochum. She studied Social Pedagogy in Germany, completed an M.A. in Comparative European Social Studies at the University of North London and her PhD at the University of Cologne in Germany 2004 in the Faculty of Educational Science. She is a qualified psychodrama trainer. Since 2011 she is specialized in the field of methods and conceptualizing social work. Her main research projects are social inclusion of people with disabilities and international social work. She is member of the German Association of Social Workers (DGSA). Since 2016 she has been head of the BA Social Work Studies and, together with Prof. Ghaderi, she was leader of the DAAD cooperation project CoBoSUnin 2016–2019 between the University of Sulaimani and Bochum. Contact: sonnenberg@evh-bochum.de

Exchange of Experiences About the Practical Phases in the Study of Social Work—A Workshop Report

Frank Fechter and Tobias Klug

Abstract

The article formulates the contents and experiences of a bilateral workshop between the University of Sulaimani and the Protestant University of Applied Sciences in Bochum. The main questions are the different historical and theoretical backgrounds of Kurdish and German education of social workers, the concept and structure of the practical phases and especially an exchange about central aspects which have been skilled. Finally, an example of quality standards for the internship in Bochum was discussed.

Keywords

Study of social work • Internship • Practice and theory • Professional identity • Quality standards

1 Introduction

In July 2017, a workshop on the subject 'Internship' was carried out at the city of Bochum between teachers of the University of Applied Sciences Bochum (EvH) and the University of Sulaimani (UoS). This workshop was prepared by

F. Fechter (✉) · T. Klug
Bochum, Germany
E-Mail: fechter@evh-bochum.de

T. Klug
E-Mail: klug@evh-bochum.de

C. Ghaderi et al. (eds.), *Social Work at the Level of International Comparison*,
https://doi.org/10.1007/978-3-658-30394-5_26

the authors. This article will reflect on contents, results, personal expectations, experiences and observations.

Having been asked to present the current model of our university for the practical vocational study phase, we did not hesitate to say 'yes'. The idea for an exchange at a professional, political and interpersonal level with the colleagues and students from Kurdistan was extremely exciting and ambitious.

- How does a professional understanding and a study of social work develop during a time of social upheaval, such as currently prevails in the Kurdish autonomous region in Iraq?
- What role does social work play in building and developing civil society?
- What form does studying social work take in the region, and what are the fields of action and professions?

These were our questions that made us curious about the exchange.

2 Contents of the Workshop and Exchange about Central Aspects of the Internship

The workshop was started with an introduction to the different historical and theoretical reasons for implementing practical elements in the education of Kurdish and German social workers.

The construction, structure, organization (especially the ongoing challenge to respond flexibly on personal student requirements) of practical phases in both courses of study were intensively presented and discussed in the resulting 'Quality standards of a successful internship'.

In addition to the presentation of organizational processes during the practical phase, the discussion focused on a complex of topics, such as how practice and theory are interlocked and interdependent. The central question was how and where professional practice and theoretical parts of studies interact in such a way that they become relevant for the education of students and are meaningfully integrated into the overall framework of the study program.

Finally, we discussed an example of quality standards for the internships in Bochum, to reflect on criteria for a successful practical phase.

The structure of the German idea of conceptualizing internships is described in chapter 6.2. The important aspect concerning the two places of learning—university and professional practice—were discussed as equivalent places of learning in the study program. Another main point was developing a professional identity and attitude. This is most exciting in the context of Kurdistan-Iraq, where these aspects are currently being constituted and consolidated.

Professionalism in social work is made up of several dimensions and 'knowledge' is only one dimension. The dimensions of 'ability'—i.e. methods—and the development of one's own 'attitude' as a professional habitus in social work are equally important. The 'attitude' is the basis on which 'knowledge' and 'ability' dock and develop. Practical experience is required to develop and enhance a social work attitude. 'Attitude' cannot only be taught theoretically. For this purpose, further places of learning are needed which are in the professional field and are interlinked with studies during the practical phase. Practical experience is therefore an important opportunity for students to gain professional knowledge experience. A major challenge is that your own personality and conflict potentials necessarily come into contact with the challenges of the clients. The resulting dynamics requires the ability to reflect as a principle of professional regulation. To work out these dynamics and not just to describe them theoretically is a central point of the practical phase.

3 Impressions, Expectations and Reflection of the Experiences

In the exchange about the aspects mentioned here, it became clear that the study as well as the entire range of social work in Kurdistan is currently in its pioneer phase. The colleagues and students there accept this situation in a creative manner and are open to and highly interested in incorporating (new) ideas and elements for the organization and design of the practical phases in the social work course of studies and in transferring meaningful elements and aspects into their own university context.

Our expectations were that we would inform each other of the most relevant facts and, after that enter a professional exchange on the subject of 'internship' to bring up questions of a possible transfer of the EvH model to the UoS.

These expectations were exceeded by far, because the participants engaged in intensive and constructive discourse becoming inspired by essential questions and inputs on a high level, e.g. how to arrange the timeframe in student counseling or how to arrange the contacts to institutions / companies where students spend their internships. According to our observation, all actors were on the same footing in this process.

This means that a good understanding of professional skills and requirements was achieved by listening, inquiring, remaining open to what each member wanted to explain. This was not easy, because the agreed workshop language was English and not the mother tongue of the participants. In this way, mutual reassurance that we were each on the right way could be perceived. Of course, this expert discussion was positively promoted by providing enough space and time.

The constant changing of perspectives by questioning, explaining patterns of your everyday work, comparisons of work processes between the Kurdish colleagues and vice versa effectively led to an intensive reflection of our own development needs, e.g.: How does the EvH organize the study objective 'employability' considering what the modern working world 4.0 demands from the graduates?

4 Conclusion

All in all, this workshop was marked by an open-minded, friendly and pleasant working atmosphere, making it possible that the members could participate in a free and authentic discussion. These are good conditions for the further development of the CoBoSUnin project.

With regard to higher education in the German context, we asked ourselves whether social work shouldn't always have some kind of pioneer status. In order to perceive social development processes with their social challenges, it cannot see itself as complete. This means continuous further development for higher education.

We are grateful for the insight into the study of social work at the University of Sulaimani and the valuable and profitable exchange.

Frank Fechter lecturer in Social Work and Internship; Representative for internship matters at the Protestant University of Applied Sciences Bochum. Diploma in Social Work and Diploma in Supervision. He is specialized in the field of Social Work in Outpatient Dispensing of Drugs and Alcohol. Contact: fechter@evh-bochum.de

Tobias Klug currently holds a position as lecturer of Social Work at the Protestant University of Applied Sciences in Bochum. He holds a diploma in Social Work and is also deacon, systemic educator and supervisor. Mr. Klug is specialized on the topics Youth and Youth Work, as well as on the coordination of internship programs within university courses and, in specific, the ongoing support of interns. Contact: klug@evh-bochum.de

Part V Internationalization in Higher Education – Different Perspectives on Opportunities and Boundaries

Introduction to Internationalization in Higher Education—Different Perspectives on Opportunities and Boundaries

Cinur Ghaderi

Abstract

Perspectives on internationalization can vary depending on the point of view; they are guided by different motivations and interests. This polyphony of perspectives, which will be given space in the following chapters, is introduced here.

Keywords

Internationalization • Higher Education • Different Perspectives

Perspectives on internationalization can differ depending on position, and they are guided by multiple motivations and interests and playable depending on the instruments available. This polyphony of perspectives is to be given space in this chapter by being heard in its broad variance: the perspective of universities as educational institutions in general is outlined in the first part. On the one hand, it emphasizes the connection between the task of the internationalization of the global university community and the social-political responsibility for society and the global production of knowledge. The other contributions each share their professional perspective within the bi-national CoBoSUnin project. Renate Dietrich and Johannes Sczyrba describe the German-Iraqi Partnership Program, in which the CoBoSUnin project was funded, as an example of 'efforts towards nations in a transformative or crisis state', and they recognize it as positive with the words: 'an example of how a project can be successfully implemented in a challenging

C. Ghaderi (✉)
Düsseldorf, Germany
E-Mail: ghaderi@evh-bochum.de

C. Ghaderi et al. (eds.), *Social Work at the Level of International Comparison*,
https://doi.org/10.1007/978-3-658-30394-5_27

environment'. This is followed by contributions by Karzan Ghafur Khidir and Karen Bossow from the International Offices, who place the CoBoSUnin project in the history of the internationalization of their respective universities. These approaches from an institutional point of view are followed by descriptions and analyses by the teachers. In his contribution as a trainer in a workshop in the project, Thomas Eppenstein critically reflects on learning processes that cannot be thought of without 'power effects of the production, dissemination, and exchange of knowledge' and advocates a consistent dialogue and participatory orientation. With their contribution 'Teaching International Social Work', Kristin Sonnenberg and Luqman Saleh Karim introduce the specific BA/MA programs of the participating universities and explicitly focus on the potential of international and intercultural education through teaching. In the final part (Part VI Contributions From The Students' Perspective), students describe what they have learned and researched from their perspective of the internationalization of the university and the concrete project experience. This is complemented by a selection of posters that give an insight into the collaborative work of the students involved in the project (Shatw Farhad Hassan, Kale Jamal Hama Salih, Niklas Rokahr, Shnya Shwan Omer) and in a seminar in preparation for the conference, where they were presented. They give an insight into the BA topics of the Kurdish students, Aurfa Hassan Husen and Briska Mariwan Mustafa.

Cinur Ghaderi, Prof. Dr., Professor of Psychology in the Faculty of Social Work at the Protestant University of Applied Sciences (EvH RWL Bochum). She is Vice-President for Research, Transfer and Internationalization. After her post-graduate education in psychological psychotherapy (behavioral therapy), she worked in the "Psychosocial Centre for refugees" (PSZ) in Düsseldorf. She received her PhD at the faculty of Social Sciences of the Ruhr University Bochum. She is a member of the steering committee of DTPPP (transcultural psychiatry, psychotherapy and psychosomatics). Main academic interests: International Social Work, Refugee Studies, Transcultural Psychotherapy, Psychotrauma, Identity, Diversity and Gender. She is the initiator of the DAAD-cooperation project CoBoSUnin 2016–2019 between the University of Sulaimani and Bochum. Contact: ghaderi@evh-bochum.de

Internationalization in Higher Education—The Universities' Definitions, Motivations, Concepts, and Perspectives

Cinur Ghaderi

Abstract

The importance of internationalization has grown in recent years for universities due to changes in world politics and scientific policy. As a result, in an increasingly competitive environment, the tasks are now quantitatively and qualitatively greater than before, while, at the same time, the political and social expectations facing scientific institutions in their internationalization have also increased. One of the expectations universities face is that they should assume social responsibility for society. This article describes the internationalization of higher education as a diverse phenomenon. Universities face the challenge of operating within the global university community as actors with socio-political responsibility for society and as sites of global knowledge production.

Keywords

Internationalization • Higher education • Global production of knowledge

The internationalization of higher education is a new and diverse phenomenon of the past decades. The European research and education programs—in particular ERASMUS—have been the driving force behind a strategic approach to the internationalization of higher education not only in Europe but also globally. It goes without saying that this development has been influenced by the globalization of

C. Ghaderi (✉)
Düsseldorf, Germany
E-Mail: ghaderi@evh-bochum.de

C. Ghaderi et al. (eds.), *Social Work at the Level of International Comparison*,
https://doi.org/10.1007/978-3-658-30394-5_28

the economy, society and knowledge. This connection between internationalization and society is evident in a frequently quoted definition of internationalization by de Wit et al. (2015, p. 29) as 'the intentional process of integrating an international, intercultural or global dimension into the purpose, functions and delivery of post-secondary education, in order to enhance the quality of education and research for all students and staff, and to make a meaningful contribution to society'.

This definition makes it clear that internationalization is not an end in itself; changes in world and scientific policy have further strengthened the importance of international cooperation. Universities, as part of the global higher education community that wants to shape change, are in demand to assume social responsibility for society.[1] With the internationalization of the university, they are faced with the task of contributing to the current social challenges of this time, such as climate change, flight and migration, populism and radicalization, in order to strengthen the democratic foundations of society. Hardly any future-oriented university can escape its role as a co-creator of a globalized society and a global university community. This is why internationalization has become a central, institutionalized component of universities. Many universities, including the University of Sulaimani and the EvH RWL in Bochum, define internationalization as a core part of their positioning. The last time the EvH adopted the internationalization strategy in 2019 was to demonstrate this increase in importance that was given to this area. Internationalization is structurally anchored in a Senate Committee which was set up containing representation from all levels and status groups. Internationalization has also been designated as a core responsibility of the Rectorate, which it exercises via the Office of the Vice-Rectorate for Research, Transfer and International Affairs. Since 1996, the University of Sulaimani has taken steps towards internationalization, which has been expanded and professionalized over the years, most recently, among others, with participation in the DAAD-Tigris program.[2] The goal of internationalization is associated with numerous challenges and needs for action for universities, e.g.:

- to further structure and strengthen good international cooperation,
- to pursue a targeted language policy,

[1] https://www2.daad.de/der-daad/daad-aktuell/de/75937-durch-internationalisierung-der-hochschulen-den-wandel-mitgestalten/ (accessed on August 30, 2020).

[2] 'Transfer of Good Practices & Reinforcement of Internationalisation Strategies in Kurdistan' (TIGRIS), https://www.tigris-erasmusplus.eu/ (accessed on August 30, 2020).

- to expand the (blended-) mobility options for students, lecturers and administration,
- to consider how to combine sustainability and mobility,
- to interlock international and digital possibilities,
- to use digital media for the integration of international-intercultural perspectives in teaching,
- to promote/normalize diversity orientation and 'internationalization at home' (IAH),
- to strengthen the intercultural competence of all university members,
- to establish transnational educational offers, to internationalize curricula,
- to internationalize the area of transfer to local society and the regions of the partner universities abroad (Internationalization of Third Mission),
- to develop concepts in cooperation with crisis and conflict countries, especially when scientific freedom appears to be threatened
- and, last but not least, to promote the internationalization of research.

It is evident that the tasks of internationalization have increased in terms of quantity and quality in recent years and that political and social expectations regarding the internationalization of scientific institutions have increased. At the same time, the financial leeway available to universities for this important cross-cutting task is currently extremely limited. One question, therefore, is what real contribution universities can actually make through internationalization to major social problems such as climate change, refugees, radicalization, populism or securing democracy.

The International Higher Education for Society (IHES) study has set itself the goal of measuring precisely this potential by combining the two topics of internationalization and the social responsibility of universities. In concrete terms, it has to systematize the concept of International Higher Education for Society (IHES), i.e. internationalization for society, and to deliver a kind of classification based on practical examples of how universities can systematically integrate their social responsibility as part of their internationalization measures. In their research design, the researchers describe five definable steps in the development of Internationalization in Higher Education (IHE):

> 'Development 1: from individual activities (late 80 s) to systematic institutionalised comprehensive internationalisation
>
> Development 2: from individual 'nice-to-have' mobility experience to educating global citizens
>
> Development 3: the convergence of the concepts of internationalisation at home (IAH) and internationalisation of the curriculum (IOC)

> Development 4: from living on myths to fact-based accountability or: from input to output, outcome, and impact
>
> Development 5: from Anglo-western and European-centred internationalisation to a truly global approach and regional self-confidence' (Brandenburg et al. 2020, p. 14).

One result of the study is that although universities, students and researchers are part of society, society outside the university has so far rarely been directly involved in internationalization measures. The links between these two agendas (social engagement and internationalization) do not seem to be structured or systematic (ibid., p. 11). Although the researchers are optimistic that universities that intensely promoted their internationalization could also make important contributions to the positive development of the regional environment of their universities and the respective partner universities abroad by following the United Nations (UN) Sustainable Development Goals (SDGs) (ibid., p. 16), the gap between claim and reality is transparent. Currently and for the future, a work area of the said claim will be at the fifth level 'from Anglo-western and European-centred internationalisation to a truly global approach and regional self-confidence' (ibid., p. 14).

These demands on 'regional self-confidence' are embedded in a global 'business' of the internationalization of universities, which holds many opportunities and challenges for universities in the Global South. The promotion of cooperation opens and strengthens them, and it is subject to strong normative components, which may be a problem for academic institutions in smaller or poorer nations (Abbas et al. 2018). Scientists who are researching the internationalization of universities as a subject observe that conditions are changing in recent times. De Wit (2020). noted that low- and middle-income countries are becoming more active in focusing their national policies for internationalization on South-South cooperation in order to break through the 'westernized, largely Anglo-Saxon, and predominantly English-speaking paradigm' (ibid., p. 35). However, this path seems to be more difficult than expected. 'There is much copying of the western paradigm in focusing strongly on mobility, on reputation and branding, and on South-North relations. There is also little continuity in their national policies due to political and economic factors' (Brandenburg et al. 2020, p. 18).

The claim of a 'truly global approach' refers to, among other things, the globalization of knowledge, which is closely intertwined with historical, grown continuities and current economic and political contexts. In theory, universities as social spaces with transnational and transcultural knowledge are an adequate biotope for these planned changes and developments. In Europe, the internationalization of educational biographies is now the norm. This means that local students and researchers are internationally mobile. In addition, one third of all German students have a migration history, if international students are combined with those with a migration background (cf. Neusel and Wolter 2017, p. 10). Through international mobility and migration, universities become transnational institutions and places of transcultural knowledge with the aim of teaching universally. At the same time, this claim of a power of definition over knowledge is certainly to be critically questioned again and again and is to be contextualized in the de-colonial and de-universalist sense (Ghaderi and Ehret 2019, p. 151).

With the production of knowledge at German universities, questions about epistemic violence, which originates from science and contributes to the power gap between the Global South and the Global North, and the transfer of this knowledge to society, Darowska deals with the following:

> 'If the theory of knowledge examines the prerequisites of knowledge stocks and knowledge production, then its topic is also knowledge production at German universities. What knowledge that diffuses into other areas of higher education, media, education systems and social discourses is currently being generated, and what assumptions underlie its generation, is the overarching question.' (2019, p. 367)

Darowska argues for a decentralization of the knowledge production of Western modernity and for an exchange on certainties, as she argues: 'The universities contribute significantly to the shaping of the global order and are thus challenged to align their policies with human rights. Orientation towards human rights and global social justice should be the core principle of internationalisation' (ibid., p. 370). Social work can certainly follow this orientation from its understanding of the profession as a human rights profession; the implementation of internationalization at universities remains an ambivalent objective as a challenge rich in opportunities and as a competing cooperation between people and their institutions.[3]

[3] Or in the words of de Wit et al. (2017, p. 9): 'The regional, national and institutional cases from the emerging and developing world illustrate that higher education, in its international dimensions and efforts to become more internationalized, struggles between past colonial influences and current presence and related challenges, its social role, and the increasingly competitive environment universities have to operate in. In this complex context, regions, countries and institutions have to make choices that find the right balance between their local, national, regional and global roles'.

References

Abbas, S., Yousafzai, M. T., Khattak, A. (2018). Internationalization of Universities: Challenges, Threats and Opportunities for Third World Countries. https://www.researchgate.net/publication/322741171_Internationalization_of_Universities_Challenges_Threats_and_Opportunities_for_Third_World_Countries. Accessed 31 Aug 2020.

Brandenburg, U., de Wit, H., Jones, E., Leask, B., Drobner, A. (2020). Internationalisation in Higher Education for Society (IHES). Concept, current research and examples of good practice (DAAD Studies). Bonn: DAAD. https://www2.daad.de/medien/DAAD-aktuell/ihes_studie.pdf. Accessed 31 Aug 2020.

Darowska, L. (2019). Can epistemic silence be decolonised? Diversity, Menschenrechte, Feminismen. In L. Darowska (Ed.), *Diversity an der Universität. Diskriminierungskritische und intersektionale Perspektiven auf Chancengleichheit in der Hochschule* (pp. 323–379). Transcript: Beilefeld.

de Wit, H., Hunter, F., Rumbley, L., Howard, L., Egron-Polak, E. (2015). Internationalisation of Higher Education. Study requested by the European Parliament. Brussels: European Commission. https://www.europarl.europa.eu/studies. Accessed 31 Aug 2020.

de Wit, H., Gacel-Avila, J., Jones, E. (2017). Voices and perspectives on internationalization from the emerging and developing world, where are we heading? https://www.researchgate.net/publication/340351359_Voices_and_perspectives_on_internationalization_from_the_emerging_and_developing_world_where_are_we_heading. Accessed 31 Aug 2020.

de Wit, H. (2020). Internationalisation in Higher Education. International Journal of African Higher Education, 7(2). https://doi.org/10.6017/ijahe.v7i2.12891. Accessed 31 March 2021.

Ghaderi, C., & Ehret, R. (2019). Diversity und Fluchtmigration. Anforderungen an die Hochschulausbildung für Sozial- und Gesundheitsberufe. In L. Darowska (Ed.), *Diversity an der Universität. Diskriminierungskritische und intersektionale Perspektiven auf Chancengleichheit in der Hochschule* (pp. 151–178). Transcript: Beilefeld.

Neusel, A. (2012). Von der Internationalisierung der Hochschule zur transkulturellen Wissenschaft. In C. Cremer- & B. Jansen-Schulz (Eds.), *Von der Internationalisierung der Hochschule zur transkulturellen Wissenschaft* (pp. 41–61). Baden-Baden: Nomos.

Neusel, A., & Wolter, A. (2017). Einführung. Mobile Wissenschaft. Internationale Mobilität und Migration in der Hochschule (pp. 9–21). Campus: Frankfurt a. M.

Cinur Ghaderi Prof. Dr., Professor of Psychology in the Faculty of Social Work at the Protestant University of Applied Sciences (EvH RWL Bochum). She is Vice-President for Research, Transfer and Internationalization. After her post-graduate education in psychological psychotherapy (behavioral therapy), she worked in the "Psychosocial Centre for refugees" (PSZ) in Düsseldorf. She received her PhD at the faculty of Social Sciences of the Ruhr University Bochum. She is a member of the steering committee of DTPPP (transcultural psychiatry, psychotherapy and psychosomatics). Main academic interests: International

Social Work, Refugee Studies, Transcultural Psychotherapy, Psychotrauma, Identity, Diversity and Gender. She is the initiator of the DAAD-cooperation project CoBoSUnin 2016–2019 between the University of Sulaimani and Bochum. Contact: ghaderi@evh-bochum.de

The Directorate of International Academic Relations at the University of Sulaimani (UoS)

Karzan Ghafur Khidhir

Abstract

This chapter presents perspectives from the International Offices involved in the CoBoSUnin cooperation. For many years now, the University of Sulaimani has maintained international contacts to universities around the world. Things have changed and developed, cooperation programs started and ended, but some still exist and continued, even during the conflict with ISIS over the past few years. One of these is the cooperation with the Protestant University of Applied Sciences in Bochum.

Keywords

International Office • Abroad • Cooperation • Exchanges • Scholarships • International relations

The University of Sulaimani (UoS) was established in 1968. To begin with, the UoS consisted of only three colleges, but, over the following years, the number of the colleges increased as a result of growing demands for higher education in the country. In 1981, the former Iraqi regime closed the UoS and transferred it to the city of Erbil (Hawler). In 1992, the UoS was reestablished by the tremendous efforts and enthusiasm of many Kurdish intellectuals and academics and was officially reopened on November 14, 1992. Today the UoS includes 19 colleges, 92 departments and offers a wide range of undergraduate and postgraduate degree courses. The UoS offers a multidisciplinary curriculum, which covers all fields

K. Ghafur Khidhir (✉)
Slemani, Iraq
E-Mail: karzan.khidhir@univsul.edu.iq

C. Ghaderi et al. (eds.), *Social Work at the Level of International Comparison*,
https://doi.org/10.1007/978-3-658-30394-5_29

of studies from Medical Sciences to Applied Sciences, Agriculture, Engineering, Law, Commerce, Physical and Basic Education, Political Sciences, Languages and Humanities and Administration.

Towards the end of 1996, the Directorate of International Academic Relations was established. At first, the International Office was mostly used by postgraduate students who wanted to go abroad, especially to the United Kingdom or the United States of America. The Directorate was totally reorganized in 2004. When the government initiated the Human Capacity Development Program (HCDP), which is funded by the Ministry of Higher Education and Scientific Research of the Kurdistan Regional Government, many students wanted to join the international program. Since then, the International Office first became very well-known and very busy, although it has again become less busy due to ISIS war in the region and COVID19 outbreak. In spite of this, it still has its own media office, a magazine and a radio program showing the international activities of the UoS.

There have, in other words, been differing developments over time. The directorate currently assists students studying at universities abroad, prospective students willing to study at universities abroad and international students intending to take undergraduate or postgraduate courses at the UoS. For example, with time, we obtained an office specializing in the Erasmus program. We also have a small team of ten who manage the mobility of the students (incoming and outgoing); they assist with visa applications for international conferences or for those students who want to study abroad. Furthermore, we have a small team for the exchanges and the delegations who visit the UoS.

These days, many students are interested in studying abroad, especially if there is government funding. Most of the students are in search of individual scholarships in various parts of the whole world such as European scholarships under Erasmus or other European programs. We also have US scholarships and scholarships in Russia, Turkey and Hungary. The International Office also arranges, develops and manages relationships, twinning and collaboration with universities around the world and arranges conferences and workshops, joint PhD projects, split-site PhD programs, exchanges of postdoctoral fellows and other research collaboration. The UoS currently has more than 100 signed contracts of cooperation with universities around the world.

The CoBoSUnin project (Cooperation between Bochum and Sulaimani Universities nowadays) between the University of Sulaimani and the Protestant University of Applied Sciences in Bochum is one of the most active ones we have. There are many agreements and cooperation programs with universities around the world, but not all of them are active. Even in the last few years with the influence of ISIS, the cooperation between Bochum and the UoS has not stopped. We are looking forward to maintaining this cooperation with Bochum. To maintain this would mean to continue the modernization and internationalization of the Social Work study program in Kurdistan-Iraq, for example, through the joint development of new curricula or the introduction of new teaching methods and workshops such as happened in counseling and aesthetic education, etc. Furthermore, there is the possibility of dissertations in cooperation and other research which is also important for the practice of social work—in Germany and in Kurdistan-Iraq.

Karzan Ghafur Khidhir, Assistant Professor, PhD, Director of International Academic Relations and Media at the University of Sulaimani, Slemani, Kurdistan Region of Iraq. As manager of the International Office, he coordi-nates UoS joint projects with international partners around the world through various initiatives including DAAD and Erasmus programs. He provides assistance to students currently studying at universities abroad, prospective students willing to study at universities abroad, and international students intending to pursue undergraduate or postgraduate studies at the University of Sulaimani, arranging staff and student exchanges as well as arranging for delegation visits and facilitating other academic/cultural collaborations such as joint international symposia and conferences. As a Faculty member of the College of Science he teaches, does researches and supervises postgraduate students. Contact: karzan.khidhir@univsul.edu.iq

Internationalization at the EvH RWL and the Contribution of CoBoSUnin. An International Office Perspective

Karen Bossow

Abstract

At the Protestant University of Applied Sciences, Bochum, Germany (EvH), internationalization developed, as it did in other institutions, ranging from personal contacts to structural cooperation and the recent set-up of a strategy reflecting its profile. The development of personnel and international activities are outlined. The CoBoSUnin project represents a new step, a new challenge and an example of best practice in the internationalization of the EvH.

Keywords

Internationalization • International office • Administration • Personnel • Development plan • Study programme • Strategy for internationalization • Unjust global system • Intercultural and interreligious learning • DAAD funding

The Protestant University of Applied Sciences in Bochum, Germany (EvH RWL), founded in 1971, developed its international relations in accordance with the general development of internationalization in higher education institutions: It started with individual relations and reached the level of structural cooperation in the 1990s. At that time especially, a cooperation with Russia was started with a major effort and financial funding through the German Academic Exchange Service (DAAD) for building up a social work program in a partner university in Vologda. In the new millennium, other international cooperation programs were

K. Bossow (✉)
Bochum, Germany
E-Mail: bossow@evh-bochum.de

C. Ghaderi et al. (eds.), *Social Work at the Level of International Comparison*,
https://doi.org/10.1007/978-3-658-30394-5_30

set up and, besides relations in the European Erasmus program, there was a focus on Africa, especially South Africa, Tanzania and Uganda, as well as Brazil in South America. Students were encouraged to spend time abroad for studies or obligatory internships. Academic staff planned excursions into other countries with students and started small research projects.

A research assistant working for the rectorate was in charge of administrating the programs, applying for funding and organizing exchanges — besides his/her other tasks. In 2009, an international office was founded as a separate unit within the administration of the EvH and equipped with a co-worker on a half-time basis. Since then the structures have been developed. The working hours of the personnel were raised step by step to about 80% of a full-time position.

A working group on internationalization was introduced in 2010 for the coordination of the different activities, for developing common goals and strategies and for planning international events for the whole university. The information and financial support for students going abroad was widened. The number of international partners and the number of students going abroad increased. Two development plans of the EvH RWL have listed strategic aims and measures regarding internationalization. Three international conferences were held in 2011, 2013 and 2015. In 2017, an international study program was introduced, offering incoming students the opportunity to study in English, together with EvH students. It is therefore concurrently an instrument of internationalization at home. The focus is on social work and health professions in the context of culture and diversity, as the program is organized in cooperation with the Bochum University of Applied Health Sciences.

In 2017, a second (full-time) position was installed, mainly financed by the federal state of North-Rhine-Westphalia through the DAAD, with the task to inform, integrate and support refugees who are interested in studying.

A strategy for internationalization was developed and discussed in 2018 and adopted in January 2019.[1] It includes all groups of the institution and reflects its specific profile, based on its Christian values and its aim of contributing to a just and inclusive society. It understands internationality and interculturality as important dimensions of education in the field of social and health professions and diaconia. This requires a (self-)critical reflection of postcolonial structures and the history of mission. In its international cooperation, the EvH aims to contribute to a sustainable development, building on the principles of human rights.

[1] The strategy can be found on the EvH homepage at: https://www.evh-bochum.de/internationalisation-strategy.html. Accessed: March 11, 2020.

The cooperation between EvH RWL and the University of Sulaimani somehow shows the general development in fast motion: It started through the personal initiative of a professor, quickly reached the structural level and became an institutional cooperation, it received funding from the DAAD and contributed to building up the social work program in Slemani (just as in Russia in the 1990s) and included at least the whole social work program in Bochum, being open even for other study programs and departments.

At the same time, CoBoSUnin opened up a whole new chapter, starting with this special, acronymic name for the cooperation project. It is the first official cooperation of the EvH RWL in Asia and it is the first in an Arabic, Muslim country. Furthermore, the partner university is based in an autonomous region in a politically instable country amidst a region suffering from war, violence, terrorism, refugee migration and global geostrategic interests of different powers.

This context poses new challenges: the feasibility of the project depends on many outward factors which cannot be influenced and which make the protagonists dependent on political developments, e.g. they never know whether, how and when the next visas will be issued.

The politically unsafe situation also means that students may only be included very carefully in exchange activities. So far it has not been possible to send students from Bochum to Slemani for a semester or an internship abroad, as is done in other contexts. The other way around might also fail due to financial limitation, but also because young, single Iraqis would hardly get a visa for Germany, since they might be inclined to wish to stay here and ask for asylum.

These outer conditions demand endurance and a strong will not to give up, but to continue and develop the common work. The staff involved is highly dedicated and sensitive to withstand all obstacles and keep the spirit alive.

The cooperation makes us aware of our involvement in the unjust global system and teaches us about the hardships which our system of sealing-off means for people in other countries.

The cooperation started at a time when the so-called refugee crisis reached Europe and challenged its countries to integrate people from quite different cultural backgrounds. The intercultural learning taking place through this cooperation can directly help in social work with migrants and refugees in Germany who come from a similar cultural background. It can also contribute to an interreligious learning and dialogue between Muslims and Christians.

The opportunities and outcomes of the project are tremendous. This is to a large extent due to the fact that the DAAD funded not only the costs of travelling and staying abroad for meetings on both sides, but also of personnel, so that a research assistance could be employed on a 50% basis to administer the program and keep it running. Thanks to her, it worked almost independently of the International Office, where it might well just have been another one of many other programs. CoBoSUnin therefore gives a best practice example of international cooperation that strategically contributes to the internationalization of study programs on the one hand and of the higher education institution on the other hand.

Karen Bossow, Diploma in Social Pedagogy, Deacon. Since 2009, she has been working in the International Office at the Protestant University of Applied Sciences Bochum. She studied Social Pedagogy and Diaconia in Hamburg, Germany. Then she worked in various positions in the field of development education, intercultural learning, and ecumenical cooperation with the international mission society United Evangelical Mission, including student work in Tanzania for some years. She is a qualified Bibliodrama trainer and grief counsellor. Contact: bossow@evh-bochum.de

German Academic Exchange Service (DAAD) Perspective. Academic Cooperation With Iraq: Chances and Challenges

Renate Dieterich and Johannes Sczyrba

Abstract

The German Academic Exchange Service (DAAD) is the largest funding organization for the international exchange of students and researchers, and it supports the internationalization of German universities and assists developing countries in establishing effective universities. DAAD programs are offered worldwide. Some of these programs are developed to direct their efforts towards nations in a transformative or crisis state. The German-Iraqi Academic Partnerships program, which started in 2009, is an example of such a program. Projects within this program subsequently aim at supporting the development of the higher education landscape, they promote the development of sustainable and lasting structures at the Iraqi partner universities, improve teaching, and intensify the German-Iraqi academic network. Within this program, the CoBoSUnin project by the Protestant University of Applied Sciences in Bochum (EvH RWL) in cooperation with the University of Sulaimani (UoS) is an example of how a project can be successfully implemented in a challenging environment.

Keywords

R. Dieterich (✉) · J. Sczyrba
Bonn, Germany
E-Mail: dieterich@daad.de

J. Sczyrba
E-Mail: sczyrba@daad.de

C. Ghaderi et al. (eds.), *Social Work at the Level of International Comparison*,
https://doi.org/10.1007/978-3-658-30394-5_31

DAAD • CoBoSUnin • University of Applied Sciences in Bochum (EvH RWL) • University of Sulaimani (UoS) • Transnational education • Sustainability • Academic partnership • Social work • Academic cooperation • Project implementation

The German Academic Exchange Service (DAAD) is the world's largest funding organization for the international exchange of students and researchers. Since it was founded in 1925, around two million scholars in Germany and abroad have received DAAD funding. It is a registered association and its members are German institutions of higher education and student bodies. Its activities go far beyond simply awarding grants and scholarships. The DAAD supports the internationalization of German universities, promotes German studies and the German language abroad, assists developing countries in establishing effective universities and advises decision makers on matters of cultural, education and development policy.

Its budget is derived mainly from the federal funding for various ministries and its operating budget in 2019 totaled approximately 594 million EUR. The most important funding providers include the Federal Foreign Office – AA (35%), the Federal Ministry of Education and Research – BMBF (25%), the Federal Ministry for Economic Cooperation and Development – BMZ (10%) and the European Union – EU (23%). In 2019, the DAAD funded 145,659 people from all regions of the world – 50 percent of whom were women. 890 students, scholars and scientists were of Iraqi origin.

The DAAD stands for mobility and transnational education and its motto 'change by exchange' means to make people move – not as an end in itself, but with the ambitious goal of academic exchange in combination with scientific excellence. DAAD offers numerous programs for individual scholarships and project funding alike. Criteria for selection decisions are based on the principles of partnership, sustainability, transparency and quality. German universities have a say in deciding which partnerships and academics the DAAD should support. Independent selection committees comprised of German professors representing a variety of disciplines take the funding decisions based on the aforementioned transparent and academically substantiated criteria.

Many of the DAAD programs are offered worldwide. However, there are also numerous programs with a special regional focus. The DAAD is also committed to supporting transformation and crisis states with tailor-made offers. The promotion of the future knowledge elite and the establishment of new and lasting academic networks with foreign countries mean a lot for countries in transition.

An example of such a program is the German-Iraqi Academic Partnerships program. This started in 2009 with funding from the Federal Foreign Office (Auswärtiges Amt) and is offered on a yearly base. It allows funding of projects for a duration of up to four years. Central aim of the program is to support the development and expansion of the higher education landscape in Iraq. The German-Iraqi academic partnerships are intended to promote the formation of sustainable structures at the Iraqi partner universities. Projects shall focus on improving and developing teaching in the partner country and on intensifying academic contact between German and Iraqi higher education institutions. Since the start of the program, 28 projects have been funded, some of them for up to ten years. The program is open to all disciplines and the list of projects comprises cooperation from the fields of STEM (Science, Technology, Engineering, and Mathematics) as well as from social sciences and humanities. Projects put a particular focus on capacity building, curriculum development and the further intensification of the German-Iraqi academic network. But they are also encouraged to tackle the question of employability of graduates. This is of special importance for Iraqi universities given the fact that higher education in the country has traditionally been more theoretical than hands-on. The Iraqi economy is seriously affected by high rates of unemployment, especially among the younger generation. Iraq, which once had one of the best education systems of the Arab world, suffers until today from the political legacy of the Saddam Hussein era, the year-long international embargo policy, internal violence and, since 2014, from the brutal rule of so-called Islamic State forces in wider parts of the country. The Northern part of the country is just recovering from the destructive consequences of IS rule and the repercussion of its final defeat in 2017.

It is obvious that academic cooperation under such circumstances is far from the ordinary. Difficulties may range from technical problems to travel restrictions all the way to mental stress for some of the participants caused by the insecure situation and personal trauma. Things of everyday life often take much more time than in the industrialized countries and sometimes prevent the participants from actively getting involved in the cooperation. Among the regular occurring problems are power cuts, roadblocks, and financial problems at universities.

Projects in countries going through such uncertain times as Iraq must be planned even more carefully, since all sorts of problems may emerge due to the security situation, political developments or unforeseen regional developments. Academic partnerships, working under such difficult circumstances, need reliable structures, sound financial resources and, above all, mutual trust. Regular personal meetings of those responsible are essential in the strongly oral cultures of the Middle East. Also, cultural differences must be taken into account. Involving students in exchange projects with transformation states requires a particularly culture-sensitive preparation. Teaching methods differ as well as the structures of the higher education systems. Various opinions and purposes as well as interests and expectations of different parties have to be considered.

All this results in partially unknown variables. To a certain extent, these variables may be anticipated in planning the project. But they may still require a flexible response within the course of implementation.

In a workshop held by the DAAD, several prerequisites that are essential for a successful cooperation were defined by project managers: The basis for success is great commitment and motivation of the parties involved in the cooperation. To avoid irritation on any side, there should be unequivocal agreements that go beyond the objectives formulated in a Memorandum of Understanding (MoU). Defining roles and tasks within the project also helps to avoid misunderstandings, and it should become clear what expectations each partner has and what each side is able and willing to contribute to the project. This is not the least determined by the existing budget.

Another important factor is the exchange of visits to prepare the project. Those meetings help to clarify the specific situation on site of the partner institutions (teaching rooms, equipment, administration, organization, university system and curricula) and they support the development of mutual trust, understanding, and transparency. Such meetings also serve to maintain continuous contact and networking. In addition, they can be used for the transfer of knowledge and experience (e.g. summer or winter schools, workshops, and conferences).

Special features of each scientific discipline, structures of different higher education systems and different cultural contexts as well as goals, interests and expectations of multiple actors must be taken into account and brought together profitably for all sides. To meet this end, it generally has been found useful to plan with extra time for coordination and understanding and, if necessary, for moderating rounds. This measure also helps to get to know the structures of the higher education system of the partner country at the respective universities.

As for the *CoBoSUnin* project (*Co*operation between *Bo*chum and *S*ulaimani *Uni*versities *n*owadays), these elements that are essential for a successful cooperation mentioned above can be found. First steps were taken more than a year before the actual DAAD-funded project began. A meeting with the chancellor of the Iraqi partner university and the Director of the International Office as well as talks with the dean and lecturers of the departments of social work and psychology paved the way for the cooperation. All these preliminary talks proved to be helpful since they provided information on the university as such and on current issues of the university and the department and relevant scientific subjects at the time. During the first year, the dean and a professor were invited to take part in an international forum and the partners conducted a joint lecture.

During the following year, the initiation phase, the contact was intensified through telephone conferences, followed by exchange visits. The partners met on an equal footing and they agreed to continue the dialogues on the theory and practice of social work and to learn from each other. The contacts were intensified and were institutionalized through a five-year cooperation agreement with the aim of establishing and expanding a long-term partnership between the EvH RWL and the UoS.

Both universities are interested in the internationalization of teaching and research by means of transferring knowledge and competence. Therefore, it is their common aim to modernize the university training in the social work study program and to jointly develop new modules for the study courses. In the long term, the further development of teaching and research with an international and intercultural comparative perspective will be encouraged. On both sides, a special focus lies on hands-on measures to prepare the graduates as comprehensively as possible for their future jobs.

Based on workshops, interviews and the analysis of documents, the demands concerning the modernization and internationalization of the social work study program were determined in 2017. Subsequently, concepts and concrete measures for the modernization of the existing curriculum and for the promotion of young scientists were developed and implemented. The social work as a practical science degree program, with special consideration of social work as a human rights discipline, was established.

The next steps in 2018 include the implementation of an international and regional network in Kurdistan through meetings and further education as well as cooperative research work with various specialist groups. The aim is to expand the opportunities for students to practice and develop sustainable teaching materials and to publish publications. Not only staff from teaching, research and practice are involved, but also junior scientists and students as well as staff from university management in both countries.

The challenge will be to bring all sides together for the benefit of all actors. Still, problems might emerge that have not been considered and that the project partners may have no influence on. However, the DAAD is convinced that the determination and the commitment of the partners will guarantee that problems will be solved.

Renate Dieterich Dr., is currently director of the DAAD regional office in Tunisia. She was educated in Islamic Studies, Geography and Political Sciences at the universities of Bonn and Amman and received her doctoral degree from Bonn University with a dissertation on the process of democratic transition in Jordan since 1989. She has been working for the DAAD since 2007 in various positions and has been in charge as head of the section for funding programs for the Middle East and North Africa. Contact: dieterich@daad.de.

Johannes Sczyrba, PhD, is a team leader with the German Academic Exchange Service (DAAD) in the section Cooperation Projects in the Middle East, Asia, Africa and Latin America. He received his PhD in Comparative Literature from the University of Colorado Boulder, where he taught English literature, essay writing and German. Afterwards he worked as a press officer and later was a personal assistant to the 1st Vice President of the Freie Universität Berlin. From 2000 to 2009 he was a self-employed multimedia consultant. Since 2009 he has been working for the DAAD managing programs with Afghanistan, Iraq and Pakistan. Contact: sczyrba@daad.de.

Experiences as a Trainer in a Workshop of the CoBoSUnin Project

International and Intercultural Perspectives: Shared Perspectives?

Thomas Eppenstein

Abstract

The article reflects on social work issues in an international and intercultural perspective with reference to a dialog project between Kurdish and German students and teachers in the context of their cooperation. From what perspective can this succeed, if disparate motives and lines of tradition are involved? What was long predicated in intercultural educational theory as 'ideational realization of one's own culture' in the context of intercultural learning processes can also be evinced between internationally cooperating universities, insofar as they make critical allowance for the power effects of the production, dissemination, and exchange of knowledge. A critical appreciation of 'internationalization' in the light of existing power relations is therefore reflexive of the participants' own respective positioning and is consequently dialogical and participatory in orientation. In view of the effectuated dynamics of global society, 'glocal' internationalization strategies are called for that place the respective regional praxis in a broader global context.

Translation by James Brown

T. Eppenstein (✉)
Frankfurt, Germany
E-Mail: eppenstein@evh-bochum.de

C. Ghaderi et al. (eds.), *Social Work at the Level of International Comparison*,
https://doi.org/10.1007/978-3-658-30394-5_32

Keywords

Internationalization • Intercultural orientation • Comparative international perspective • International social work • Forms of knowledge • Decolonization • Glocal university

Is the perspective of 'internationalization' and 'intercultural orientation' an agenda that is generally shared by all universities, or is it divided respectively into different or even contrary motives and interpretations?

Agreement is often simply assumed rather than – as ought to be the case – first being examined and established in situations where diverse narratives and academic discourses are involved and it clearly becomes apparent that dialoguing with partners from abroad does not automatically lead to an awareness or understanding of each other's particular perspectives.

Classic motive strands for internationalization draw on (at least) seven lines of tradition, including compounds or an overlapping of them:

- Internationalization in the context of global aid and charity, usually religiously motivated.
- Internationalization in the context of labor movements and 'international movements', motivated as solidarity.
- Internationalization in the context of feminist or gender orientated concerns, motivated as mobilization.
- Internationalization as a consequence of diaspora migration, interconnectedness and networks among individual groups or institutions, motivated as the preservation and furtherance of cohesion.
- Internationalization as a consequence of globalization processes and worldwide economic interdependencies, motivated as acquisition of competencies.
- Internationalization in the context of international cooperation, e.g. in fields of research, motivated as development.
- Internationalization as a reaction to new global risks in the fields of the conservation of resources, environment, global health, sustainability, education, motivated as ethics of responsibility towards generations to come.

To an extent these respective perspectives have 'come of age' and internationalization seems increasingly indispensable, yet in that process the clarity and uniqueness of the respective rationales and perspectives are gradually disappearing since the motive strands outlined above no longer necessarily appear in isolation from each other, but occur in compound or overlapping manifestations.

The following notes based on experiencing the CoBoSUnin project demonstrate that controversies and a diversity of perspectives on the topic of internationalization and the intercultural agenda of a university can be constructively stimulated, especially in situations that demand communication to others of what is thought to be self-explanatory, thereby revealing how far from self-evident that essentially is. A productive twist is thus given to different experiences and positions: from the assumption that they primarily exist between binational partners to the realization that an ongoing need for discussion and clarification exists within one's own university.

Consent was quickly given to conducting a workshop on the subject of 'Social work in international and intercultural perspectives' in the course of the visit of a delegation of Kurdish students and teachers as part of a CoBoSUnin project in July 2017.

The partners from Slemani were keenly interested in setting up a corresponding curriculum for their own university and, to that end, the aim was to communicate, amongst other things, structures and teaching experience from the 'Intercultural and International Social Work' module at the EvH-RWL. No problem, it would seem: instantly recallable tried-and-tested structures, instantly recallable knowledge, but: The critique of that brand of educational hubris that seeks to communicate to others content of which it is impossible to know what parts are even compatible with these other persons' own dispositions, compels one to first communicate how – in this case from a (West) German perspective – one arrived oneself at what is being presented.

This triggered an unpremeditated twofold stimulus: Firstly, the question of how – in spite of all professional discipline and thematic focus – one can explain oneself, even over against international partners. Specific European motives and historical experiences are part of this, for example: exchange programs between Germany and France after the Second World War; qualification for the European Single Market; combinations of 'internationality at home' and 'outgoing exchanges' with regard to developments in migration society at home (labor migration, forced migration), the specifics of public discourses on belonging and forms of recognition and their influence on intercultural agendas, etc.

The other stimulus is the question as to how the 'internationalization' perspective can be further developed within the internal structures of one's own university.

This has given rise to intensive work on reformulating an appropriate independent conceptualization of the university that draws on a 'definition' of internationalization by the DAAD, which we also discussed with our Kurdish guests:

> 'Internationalization is a process of integrating an international, intercultural, and global dimension into the goals, functions, and delivery of higher education. As such it is a process of change—tailored to meet the individual needs and interests of each higher education entity. Consequently, there is no 'one size fits all' model of internationalization. Adopting a set of objectives and strategies that are 'in vogue' and for 'branding' purposes only negates the principle that each program, institution, or country needs to determine its individual approach to internationalization – based on its own clearly articulated rationales, goals, and expected outcomes.' (Knight 2015, p. 2).

In dialog with our Kurdish partners it became apparent that, even with the aim of being internationally compatible, an independent conceptual development that sets itself apart from the dominant motives and image cultivation of the international competition is nevertheless always possible.

However, motives and objectives for comparative international cognitive processes are not available from the outset, nor can these always be explicated as such: It is often precisely the unplanned, unintentional lessons that, ex post or retrospectively, prove to be significant (cp. as early as 1999: Demorgon).

Universities as places where knowledge is produced and communicated are discursively involved in asserting what is to be understood by the term 'knowledge' and which forms of knowledge are to be regarded as valuable as opposed to others.

Here – seen rather simplistically – two positions stand in opposition to each other:

To start with, 'knowledge', by its very nature and aspiration, is considered to be tendentially universal and international, not tied to any national boundaries, and committed solely to the strict requirements of academic integrity, verification, transparency, etc.

At other times, the focus is on the interplay of knowledge and power – such as in the reception of post-colonial theory in Germany – and exposes the problems of failed decolonization processes. In this context, de-universalization means questioning all such knowledge that is claimed to be universally valid.

This addresses the power effects of the production, communication and exchange, etc. of knowledge.

The internationality of knowledge, the internationality of scholarship and the internationality of scientific policy thus turn out to be entirely controversial areas.

The production and dissemination of 'knowledge' and 'forms of knowledge' are also affected in the wake of globalization processes.

Not only goods, commodities, services, and people migrate faster and more easily than ever before, knowledge does so too, and there are varyingly privileged forms of migration and migration routes that knowledge takes, indeed there are hierarchies of forms of knowledge.

A normative orientation should be guided by the precepts of human rights in the context of concepts of the good or successful life, defending a pluralistic structure of forms of knowledge in terms of education theory. The approach of academic analysis is not to inquire as to suitability, functionality and usability, but to take full account of the fundamental questionability of persisting circumstances.

A critical approach to understanding 'internationalization' in respect of existing power relations is therefore of necessity reflexive of the enquirer's own positioning and is consequently dialogical and participatory in orientation.

To what extent this ambitious program can actually be fulfilled is a question that can only be resolved empirically. For that to happen, exchanges between international cooperation partners are indispensable.

Approaches to and motives in intercultural education and internationalization may well differ accordingly when compared internationally, since they address themselves to different narratives and real historic manifestations, and these are not always readily comparable. With reference to social work, it is important to remember its beginnings as a means of dealing with the social question in Europe and so, generally speaking, it also ought to contribute towards dealing with modernization processes. So-called 'glocal' internationalization strategies are called for, given the pervasive global or universal dynamics, interdependencies and differentiation of transnational systemic relations, since such strategies seek responsibly to set each respective local praxis in an overall global context.

What, then, was the outcome of the workshop reflected on here by way of example, what resulted as 'tertium comparationis', as the 'third part of the comparison'?

There was an unexpected response to a satirical caricature from France (*«Le perchoir» in: Un autre monde, chez Fournier, Paris 1844*) by the illustrator and graphic artist Grandville (Jean-Ignace-Isidore Gérard, 1803–1847) that had initially only been incorporated as a didactical element in a supporting Power Point presentation on the subject. In the genre of so-called *homme-bête* illustrations, it features a juxtaposition of various animals and hybrids with human facial features and attitudes in a menagerie and, on the other side, human visitors in the shape of animals. The unambiguousness of who is observing whom, who is marveling at whom, is profoundly confused: The difference between human visitors and caged animals (all of them, incidentally, with wings) still remains visible and extant, but the mutual permeation of animalistic and human attributes must have been hugely unsettling for the self-perception of the up-and-coming middle-class intellectuals at the time of publication. Human superiority versus the dumbness of animals is ironically called into question. Evolutionary and apartheid theories are operational and, at the same time, challenged. The illustration is still suitable today for a critical discussion of racist world views and ethnopluralist identity politics, but also of a naive multiculturalism that enshrines diversity culturally and fails to recognize the dynamics of all culture. This image was seized upon as an invitation to discuss the present-day problems and options of multiethnic societies and the corresponding options for social professions and educational work in a binational dialog. Who is dealing with whom here? Who is presenting themselves, and how? How are they viewed? What dominance relations have crept in? It was surprising that this 173-year-old ironic illustration should offer opportunities for identification in binational dialog, allowing the participants henceforth to address their respective particular experiences transnationally in the context of theoretical considerations.

Some comments from the evaluation illustrate this: 'It was amazing the explanation of the caricature from 200 years for modern situation', or 'This can be helpful to create a lecture about international social work especially for stage one, to understand that the problem is in a lot of societies not only in Kurdistan.'

In a transnational perspective, the focus is moved from a comparative perspective oriented on nation-state patterns to one of overcoming a transnational illiteracy that is hitherto virtually incapable of apprehending or appreciating the dispositions of those who have to or are supposed to participate as spokespersons. In this process, 'transnational' means something more and something different than any respective supranational shared multiplicity, aiming far rather at an 'alphabetization' that is sensitive to difference vis-à-vis the diversity of voices in existing dominance relations.

International cooperation and international exchanges can therefore be useful as dialog forums and mediums for such transnational alphabetization, thus understood.

The workshop gave a foretaste of the notion that such a perspective is possible.

The question posed at the outset as to shared perspectivism can be answered in two respects: On the one hand, it is essential to acknowledge distinct and separate perspectives and not to assume that harmonizing them into a shared or joint 'us' is either appropriate or possible. Secondly, this is valid not only for international cooperation between binational partners, but equally well within pluralistically organized institutions, such as universities claim to be. Sharing out in the sense of separation is enhanced by a shared perspective in the sense of mutuality whenever and wherever efforts towards the intercultural communication (cp. Eppenstein and Kiesel 2008), understanding, and clarification of such particular perspectives bear fruit.

References

Demorgon, J. (1999). *Interkulturelle Erkundungen. Möglichkeiten und Grenzen einer interkulturellen Pädagogik*. Frankfurt a. M.
Eppenstein, T., & Kiesel, D. (2008). *Soziale Arbeit interkulturell*. Stuttgart: Kohlhammer.
Knight, J. (2015). Five truths about internationalization. *International Higher Education, 69,* 4–5. https://doi.org/10.6017/ihe.2012.69.8644.

Thomas Eppenstein, Prof. Dr., Professor of Education and Theories of Social Work in the Faculty of Social Work at the Protestant University of Applied Sciences (EvH RWL Bochum). He studied Social Education at the Johann Wolfgang Goethe University in Frankfurt/Main, worked for several years in an advice organization with migrants, and was awarded a doctorate for his work on intercultural competences in the theory of education in 2002. Member of the German Association for Educational Sciences (DGfE). Main fields of research and academic interests: Intercultural education and social work, global education, sustainable education, social inclusion and knowledge of change. Contact: eppenstein@evh-bochum.de

Teaching International Social Work – Perspectives of the Universities

Kristin Sonnenberg and Luqman Saleh Karim

Abstract

This chapter introduces the topic of internationalization as part of BA and MA studies at the University of Sulaimani (UoS) and the Protestant University of Applied Sciences (EvH) and a PhD program at the UoS. Both universities have specific modules on the topic of international social work. The structure, content and aim of the modules of both universities will be introduced. Both universities have internationalization strategies and international offices that support the universities at the institutional level. These topics are discussed in the other chapters on internationalization in higher education, on international and intercultural perspectives, and from the perspective of the international offices.

Keywords

International • Intercultural • Teaching • Modules

K. Sonnenberg (✉)
Bonn, Germany
E-Mail: sonnenberg@evh-bochum.de

L. S. Karim
Slemani, Iraq
E-Mail: loqman.karim@univsul.edu.iq

C. Ghaderi et al. (eds.), *Social Work at the Level of International Comparison*,
https://doi.org/10.1007/978-3-658-30394-5_33

1 International Modules at the EvH in Germany

The EvH in Bochum, Germany has several different BA and MA study programs. The BA Social Work and the MA Social Inclusion: Health Care and Education have been chosen to illustrate this topic in relation to social work.

Modules of the BA Social Work at the EvH in Bochum, Germany
The BA Social Work study program enables graduates to practice professionally in the vocational field of social work. This includes relevant scientific foundation knowledge, methodology, theories and models. This is a three-year full-time study program. It is structured around five levels of learning, and it contains 22 modules.[1] Four modules, one of which is 'Intercultural and international social work', fall within the category of 'Interdisciplinary fields of action'. The students are at the final stage of their course when they study this. The module offers four different lectures: intercultural education within a migration society; structural conditions of migration processes (legal, political, economic and ethnic-religious aspects), international social work and international comparative social work, practical fields and various theoretical concepts and theories (diversity, anti-racism) or approaches (migration, age, family, health, asylum). The lecturers offer a wide range of topics within these core themes. Examples of concrete titles of some of the lectures on international social work are:

- A cross cultural comparison: Roma life in Germany and Hungary
- Social work with youth and young adults – a German-Russian comparison
- Social work and social policy in international comparison
- Intercultural work and the arts
- Power structures within the context of international social work cultures
- Global music – musicmaking and youth culture in a globalized society
- Peace education through music? The role of music for integration and diversity
- Social work in regions of war and crisis, countries in processes of transformation

Some of the lectures are in English, but mostly the language used during the seminars is German. The EvH is a participant in the International Study Program[2]

[1] https://www.evh-bochum.de/social-work-ba.html, accessed February 13, 2020. The social work studies are described in more detail in Part III, chapter Teaching Social Work in Germany.

[2] https://www.evh-bochum.de/international-study-programme-2020.html, accessed: March 31, 2020.

of the Bochum universities. The overall qualification aim of this module is to gain competences and learning results in the area of cultural differences, different theoretical approaches to plurality, globalization and culture. The students should gain and train their competences in intercultural reflection and communication and learn new methods to act within intercultural practical fields. Students should, for example, develop a critical self-evaluation of attitudes and reflect upon concrete experiences.

Modules of the MA Social Inclusion: Health Care and Education
Graduates within the Master course in Social Inclusion gain scientifically-founded practice-oriented competences to analyze exclusion processes in society, especially concerning the fields of income, health, and education. This includes developing interdisciplinary concepts and strategies to overcome exclusion. During their module 'Intervention competence II', they deal with inclusive concepts and practical projects implemented on the national, transnational and international level.[3] The courses deal with international, transnational and intercultural programs to reduce poverty and inequality. Inclusive projects are visited at the local, regional, national or, if possible, international level. The overall qualification aim of this module is to gain competences and learning results in international comparative research, managing change, assessing and developing concepts with partners from practice, and reflecting upon experiences within international contacts.

2 International Aspects at the UoS in Kurdistan-Iraq

The University of Sulaimani (UoS) was first established in 1968 as the first university in the Kurdistan Region of Iraq, and it includes 19 colleges. Its students obtain BSc and BA degrees in various fields of study. At the university there is a Directorate of International Academic Relations which provides assistance to students currently studying at universities abroad, prospective students willing to study at universities abroad, international students intending to study undergraduate or postgraduate studies at UoS, arranges for staff and student exchanges, and arranges for delegation visits and university collaborations. For this purpose, there are many university partnerships with UoS throughout the world.[4] The social

[3] https://www.evh-bochum.de/social-inclusion.html, accessed: February 17, 2020.

[4] https://foreign.univsul.edu.iq/, accessed: March 29, 2020.

work department belongs to the College of Humanities which consists of the following departments: history, geography, sociology, media, archaeology, philosophy and social work.[5]

Social Work BA Study Program

The social work program at UoS is a four-year full-time program with 36 modules.[6] Study programs are changing now, year by year and step by step, following the Bologna Process, a process which started in 2020. The main language of these social work studies is Kurdish-Sorani, and some lectures are in English, including international social work focusing on the subjects listed below:

- Social work with internally displaced people and refugees in Kurdistan-Iraq and Germany
- Global warming and environment pollution
- International code of ethics
- Local and global issues, i.e. poverty, drug abuse, human trafficking
- Social work in post-conflict areas
- Networking and international organizations of social work
- International social work education

Master's Course Program

An MA in Social Work in accordance with the Bologna Process is being offered for the first time in Kurdistan-Iraq in the academic year 2020–2021. Completing the Master's degree will require two years. The MA curriculum includes English texts on social work, methodology, counselling, critical thinking, local gender or local social norms and their impact on gender-based violence (GBV), statistics, social organization, computer skills and international social work. The main language in the Master's degree is also Kurdish-Sorani, however the two modules *English texts on social work* and *International social work*, focusing more deeply on the international level of social work, will be taught in English.

PhD Course Program

The social work department at UoS launched a partnership with the Protestant University of Applied Sciences in Bochum, offering a PhD in social work for the

[5] https://hum.univsul.edu.iq/, accessed: March 29, 2020.

[6] The social work studies are described in more detail in Part III, chapter Teaching Social Work in the Kurdistan Region of Iraq.

first time in Kurdistan-Iraq. The prospect this offers will be a great opportunity for the UoS, especially in the stratification of its social work at the international level. The study program includes social work theories, personality theories, international gender, progressive statistics and supervision, and completing the PhD will require three years, starting with the academic year 2020–2021. The main module in the PhD program that relates directly to international social work is *International gender issues and inequality*, which concerns the global issue of gender norms and its impact on gender-based violence.

3 International Social Work in the Kurdistan Region of Iraq

After the Kurdish uprising of 1991 in Iraq and the mass exodus to escape the attacks of Saddam Hussein, one of the world's most brutal dictators (King 2014, p. 1), as well as the Alliance's defense of and support for Kurdistan and the declaration of a no-fly zone, Kurdistan first began holding elections in 1992. It has many features of a democratic government and has excellent relations with western countries (King 2014, p. 39), and these international links have led to political and cultural liberalization, including the growth of civil society and campaigns for human rights and expanded concepts of citizenship (Moghadam 2009, p. 128).

After the formation of local government in the Kurdistan Region in 1992, the University of Sulaimani opened again,[7] although a distinct and separate Department of Social Work was not established until 2014. In that year, the social work department was opened and, as part of the CoBoSUnin project, a lecture entitled 'International Social Work' was incorporated, drawing on the experience of the EvH in Bochum. The first encounter the Kurdish lecturers had with the topic was during a workshop on July 26, 2017 in Germany, presented by Professor Thomas Eppenstein and entitled 'Social Work in International and Intercultural Perspectives'. In 2018, Professor Ronald Lutz then visited the UoS to lead a workshop there. Currently, this module is implemented within the social work curriculum at the University of Sulaimani and is studied in English two hours a week in the fourth stage of social work studies. There are two main objectives:

[7] The University of Sulaimani was first founded in 1968 in the city of Slemani, but it was then closed down in 1981 due to the Kurds' revolutionary opposition to Saddam Hussein's regime. After the Kurdish uprising and the establishment of local government in the Kurdistan Region, it was opened once again in 1992.

1) The knowledge aim:
   - Presentation of what and how international social work is.
   - Presentation of the importance of international social work in the recent situation.
   - Establishing a link between local and global perspectives.
2) The behavioral aim:
   - Encouraging students to participate in learning processes.
   - Increasing skills for understanding global perspectives.

In this module, light is shed on local issues – such as poverty, crime, drugs, child labor and many more – and their relation to global issues. At the same time, it also highlights issues that suggest the world has become a global village, such as environmental concerns, issues of protecting human rights, developing society and many others besides. The module discusses the most important international organizations in the field of social work, and the students also present special seminars in group work.

References

King, D. E. (2014). *Kurdistan on the global stage*. New Jersey: Rutgers University Press.
Moghadam, V. M. (2009). *Globalization and social movements*. USA: Rowman and Littlefield.

Kristin Sonnenberg, Prof. Dr., Professor of Social Work at the Protestant University of Applied Sciences Bochum. She studied Social Pedagogy in Germany, completed an M.A. in Comparative European Social Studies at the University of North London and her PhD at the University of Cologne in Germany 2004 in the Faculty of Educational Science. She is a qualified psychodrama trainer. Since 2011 she is specialized in the field of methods and conceptualizing social work. Her main research projects are social inclusion of people with disabilities and international social work. She is member of the German Association of Social Workers (DGSA). Since 2016 she has been head of the BA Social Work Studies and, together with Prof. Ghaderi, she was leader of the DAAD cooperation project CoBoSUnin 2016–2019 between the University of Sulaimani and Bochum. Contact: sonnenberg@evh-bochum.de.

LUQMAN SALEH KARIM, Ass. Prof., Assistant Professor in the Social Work Department. He holds a PhD in Social Work from the University of Sulaimani, Kurdistan Region of Iraq. He was head of the Social Work Department from 2014–2017. He is a researcher and has conducted a large body of academic and organizational research on gender-based violence, environment policy, honor killing, child marriage, GBV assessments of needs, impact evaluation and COVID-19. He also worked with the United Nations Population Fund

(UNFPA) and the Women's Refugee Commission (WRC) as a research consultant from 2018 to 2019, and as a child marriage research co-investigator in the Johns Hopkins University (USA); from 2016 to 2019 he was a University of Sulaimani coordinator of the DAAD cooperation project CoBoSUnin between the University of Sulaimani and the University of Applied Sciences in Bochum. Currently he works as lecturer at the University of Sulaimani, as a supervisor in the Khanzad women's organization, and as a research consultant for the Civil Development Organization (CDO). Contact: loqman.karim@univsul.edu.iq.

Part VI Contributions from the Students' Perspective

Just Like In Germany, But Different

Jan Gerrit Weweler

Abstract

At first glance, the attempt to find similarities between social work in the Autonomous Region of Kurdistan and in Germany seems to be a difficult undertaking. On the one hand, Kurdistan has been through decades of war and has only recently established the social work program. On the other hand, Germany is a leading industrial nation worldwide and can draw on the knowledge of decades of practice and research in social work. During our study trip as part of the CoBoSUnin project and the associated visits to the Kurdish social work practice sites, however, we were able to learn that the identity of social work is based on far more than social, cultural and economic preconditions. The identity of social workers is – as became clear through the direct exchange with our Kurdish colleagues – also essentially determined by the professional self-image, the resulting attitude and the resulting communications.

Keywords

Prison • Women's shelter • Double mandate • Professionalism

During my research for the job interview as a student participant in the CoBoSUnin project, my initial curiosity about the Kurdistan Autonomous Region in Northern Iraq grew to a veritable enthusiasm. Much of the literature I used was about the effects of the last two Gulf Wars, the Iraq War and the fight against the

J. G. Weweler (✉)
Bochum, Germany
E-Mail: jan.gerrit.weweler@gmx.de

C. Ghaderi et al. (eds.), *Social Work at the Level of International Comparison*,
https://doi.org/10.1007/978-3-658-30394-5_34

Islamic State during the Syrian conflict. It was therefore difficult for me to imagine what social work in Northern Iraqi Kurdistan would look like under the war conditions there. In addition, I lacked the experience, openness and imagination to locate social work in a culture unknown to me.

When I thought about social work in Germany, first of all a lot of bureaucracy came to my mind. One writes mountains of reports, holds conferences, advises and helps within known political and legal frameworks and, as the basis for all of this – in spite of economization and the associated cutbacks – has a well-developed infrastructure and well-established aid systems compared to many other states. In addition, we in Germany can draw on the knowledge of decades of practice and research in the field of social work. In Kurdistan, on the other hand, at the time of our stay from April 21 to 28, 2016, there was not yet a single graduate of the still young social work and literature course of study who could be organized by professors for trips abroad.

At the time, my idea of social work in Kurdistan was basically very similar to the summary of the Kurds on site: Social work in Kurdistan did not exist until now and was something completely new. As I would like to show in the following section, the practical visits during our trip gave us a different picture.

During our visit to the Slemani prison, we were informed about the tasks of the practitioners employed there. Among other things, they are responsible for new inmates and the associated formalities, decide on early dismissals in the form of a social report and provide three months of aftercare for adolescents.

Our entire tour was marked by the authority of the prison director, which inhibited open exchange. Instead, the director insisted on a lecture that left little room for academic – let alone critical – discussions.

In retrospect, these statements point to a conflict between the restrictive institutional framework of the prison or the director as its deputy and the attitude of the practitioners, who obviously would have liked to reflect this context with us.

Even though the Kurdish practitioners may never have heard of the so-called double mandate consisting of help and control and its dilemma, this conflict seemed very familiar to me from my time as voluntary worker in a prison and the reports of the social workers employed there.

During our visit to the Comfort Centre for Women who are affected by violence, we learned that the concept originally only applied to women who suffered violence in families and institutions, but, due to the blatant needs and lack of alternatives, has now been extended to homeless women exposed to street violence and mentally ill women. While listening to the history of the center, analogies with the development of the women's shelters in Germany became clear, although this 'Kurdish women's shelter' was more like a prison. The building was surrounded by high walls and a total of 15 guards were employed, who surrounded the building day and night to protect the women and staff. The aim of the furnishing concept was to reintegrate the women into the families. This would be difficult because the relatives were hardly able to understand the situation. On the contrary: as soon as the women concerned filed a complaint with the police, they were considered outlaws in many cases. Often the women would give up because of that and return unconditionally to their families due to the lack of alternatives. Only a few could start a new life abroad with the help of NGOs.

In response to our question, the female director of the institution reported on the burdens that these desolate working conditions entail for the staff, who are often threatened themselves and usually conceal their actual field of work from their friends and acquaintances in order to avoid hostility. She also told us about networks that had developed out of the emergency situation and were used for regular supervision and working groups. In addition, the government has not paid any money for the staff for months, but the staff continued to appear for work without exception, which is currently not a matter of course in Kurdistan.

These two examples from the Kurdish practice sites are exemplary for many, in which the Kurds deeply impressed me with their will to help professionally and to alleviate systematically produced discrimination. The reports presented on the lack of state support and lack of social recognition prompted us to listen and to put on a discreet, approving smile and nod and confirm that all this was known to us from the practice of social work in Germany.

The social, cultural and economic preconditions may not even be comparable to some extent, but it was in some way exactly like in Germany, only different. The encounters in Kurdistan made clear to me that the road social work takes is determined by the resources of the professional actors themselves – their self-image, attitude and the resulting communications and actions.

Jan Gerrit Weweler B.A. Social Work (2011); M.A. Management in Private and Church-Based Social Welfare Organizations (2014). Since April 2019 head of the department for outpatient assisted living for people struggling with addiction at the crisis support organization Krisenhilfe e. V. Bochum, freelance sex educationist and systemic counselor; Contact: jan.gerrit.weweler@gmx.de

An Academic Journey to Germany as a Kurdish Student

Shatw Farhad Hassan

Abstract

This article is about the cooperation project between The University of Sulaimani and the Protestant University of Applied Sciences in Bochum. I participated in this project from 2016 to 2018 as a student and was interested by some of the places we visited.

Keywords

Kurdistan • Germany • Clients • Addicts • Methadone ambulance center • Pro-Familia counseling center

When I joined this project from 2016 until 2018, I was able to see many places I hadn't seen before. We visited Germany for the first time in 2016 for eleven days and again in 2017 for nine days. And so, I learned a lot during the course of this project. For me as a student, it was my first experience of travelling to another country and visiting many new places. I think this is so important for all social workers: to gain another perspective on problems, such as homelessness, addiction and refugee clients. Although I had the chance to extend my knowledge of other cultures, nations, religions, norms and values, and to compare and enter into a dialogue between the communities, I know that I learned from people who were working in specific social work fields, while they were talking about their experiences.

S. F. Hassan (✉)
Slemani, Iraq
E-Mail: shatooofarhad@gmail.com

C. Ghaderi et al. (eds.), *Social Work at the Level of International Comparison*,
https://doi.org/10.1007/978-3-658-30394-5_35

I think this project is very useful for us, because social work is a new field in our society, and we don't have enough information about it. It is important to know how to work in this field and what the difference is between a social worker, a psychologist and a sociologist.

During the trip to Germany, we had the opportunity to visit a few specific fields in which social workers are active and deal with their clients.

I want to write about two of the many places we visited that were particularly interesting for me. I chose these places, because we have no place like them in our society, although they are most important and necessary for each community.

The Methadone Ambulance Center

This center consists of three sections: (1) a room for giving methadone under precise control, (2) a special place for injecting and (3) an open hall to get together and meet other addicts. I was really surprised when I saw this center, because I hadn't seen anything like this before where they deal with addicts as patients and not as criminals such as in Iraq and Kurdistan. In Kurdistan and Iraq, they treat addicts like criminals, because they think these people are dangers for their society. They keep them out of the way and punish them, so they are not able to hurt and affect others. But I think the existence of this center is necessary, because it helps to collect addicts and drug users in one place and keeps them away from the streets and bars. It also can help those addicts to feel good and secure for not been ignored.

Pro-Familia Counseling Center

This center deals with topics like physical ailments, gender, HIV testing, pregnancy and aborting pregnancy. The main slogan of the center is love, body, sexuality. In my opinion, this was the most important place. It would be necessary to have a similar center in the Kurdistan Region to give knowledge and awareness for our teenagers and anyone who has a question about these topics. It could help us to reduce health and social problems.

I hope that this project will continue for a long time and so afford many students and staff awareness and give them knowledge through workshops, training and visiting such places, all of which is necessary for Kurdish staff.

So, I hope that, in the future, our society will understand more about the importance of social work as a great and necessary career for all fields, and of the real need for social workers to work in schools, hospitals, kindergartens, family centers and all places attending to clients and people who need help. And our government will hopefully build some center like the Pro-Familia counseling center and the methadone ambulance center, because I, as a student and social worker, have seen these places in Germany and I understand that our society needs these places to give more social service for the population.

Shatw Farhad Hassan Kurdish social worker graduated from the University of Sulaimani in 2017–2018. She is one of the students who participated in the project staged from 2016 to 2018 between the University of Applied Sciences in Bochum and the University of Sulaimani (CoBoSUnin), and she wrote her Bachelor's research on "The social worker's role in psychosocial support for cancer patients" between Germany and Kurdistan as part of this project. Contact: shatooofarhad@gmail.com.

Obstacles to Interviewing in an Intercultural Context

Julika Laura Rundnagel

Abstract

The article gives an insight into the experiences with conducting interviews for the bachelor thesis in an intercultural context, which in this case is the Autonomous Region of Kurdistan in Iraq. The focus is set on misunderstandings and obstacles during this process, like the language barrier or cultural differences, and the text gives recommendations on how to overcome them. It describes the preparation of the interviews as well as interesting moments and experiences during the conduct and includes some information about the methodology of expert interviews. Moreover, the author emphasizes the gain of applying intercultural research in the bachelor thesis.

Keywords

Interview • Bachelor thesis • Social research • Kurdistan • Intercultural • Misunderstanding

Leading a research interview for the first time is not easy – especially if the interview takes places in a distant country and in an unknown language. In my bachelor thesis on the subject of 'Professional Identity within the Studies of Social Work', I conducted three interviews with Kurdish experts from the Autonomous Region of Kurdistan in Iraq. The thesis discussed which ideas they have about professional identity in social work and how a professional practice with vulnerable youth in the Autonomous Region of Kurdistan could be realized. I therefore

J. L. Rundnagel (✉)
Velbert, Germany
E-Mail: julerund@outlook.de

C. Ghaderi et al. (eds.), *Social Work at the Level of International Comparison*,
https://doi.org/10.1007/978-3-658-30394-5_36

conducted an interview with a social worker in practice as well as a professor and a student of social work.

The appropriate interview method, a good structure for the interview guideline, the right questions and an adequate introduction and conclusion of the conversation are important elements of qualitative social research. In an *intercultural* context, the language barrier should also be considered, for example when the comprehension of the technical terms differs or when the culturally influenced communication patterns lead to misunderstandings. It could be something simple like the pronunciation, as happened in one interview, when, for example, the word 'law' is pronounced like 'low' and is only understood after asking five times. Thorough preparation is thus as important as openness and calmness while conducting the interview, so that a good communicative atmosphere can be created and linguistic misunderstandings can be dealt with.

The preparation of an *intercultural* research study includes different documents to fulfill legal requirements. Beforehand, declarations of consent, confidentiality and data privacy had to be created and translated to English, which was our lingua franca. These are the requirements of the German data protection law to carry out qualitative research. The preparation of the documents took almost the whole time before the research trip to Kurdistan, which was short anyway. Furthermore, I had chosen the abstract subject of 'professional identity', which is already hard to describe in German and which was a new area of expertise for me, so that I had to become acquainted with it first. The content could therefore not be prepared adequately before conducting the interview.

Furthermore, there was no material available about practice with 'vulnerable youth' in Kurdistan. There were several reasons for this: On the one hand, literature is difficult to obtain in this region, because there is no Amazon and also no postal service. Additionally, access to the internet is partly restricted, as there can be power failures from time to time for financial and political reasons, such as an oil crisis or the systematic isolation of the population from the outer world. On the other hand, the literature about the local practice would have been in Arabic or Kurdish, even the typography of which is unfamiliar to me, so that I couldn't use it. The lack of material should be reflected in the thesis and the research objective should be adjusted appropriately.

From my point of view, it is recommendable for *intercultural* research in a bachelor thesis to provide enough time *in advance* for orientation in the theoretical context. It also makes sense to choose a subject about which the researchers already have theoretical knowledge or which they have faced in practice. A better level of communication can thus be reached more easily.

During my research, I explored a new culture in a variety of ways and noticed at the same time that there are many similarities on the professional as well as on the personal level. For example, I shared the attitude of the student that society should be sensitized for dealing with vulnerable people, so that they don't have to experience so much rejection. During the first conversation with the interview partner from the practice of social work the encounter with religiousness was particularly impressive. She worked in a Muslim orientated consulting institution for girls and young women, where an exhibition of hijabs was being prepared at the time. Although the welcome was warm and friendly like everywhere in Kurdistan, I still felt uncomfortable. At first, I assumed this was because I wasn't wearing any head covering. But then I realized that I just was very nervous because I didn't know the type of institution, the language context was incomprehensible for me, and I was not used to the new and challenging practice of conducting interviews.

In spite of these difficulties, I gained an enriching insight into the attitudes of the interview partner during the conversation: For example, on the one hand she considered that young couples should meet secretly before marriage to figure out whether they would really fit together. On the other hand, the marriage covenant was the only relationship model which the expert from the practice seemed to accept. During another conversation, I learned that the attitudes would get mixed up on a macrosocial level in Kurdistan: There would be many modern and western influences, but also a lot of people would refocus on their tradition and religion.

Furthermore, a methodical trap became apparent in this interview: the length of the interview guideline. Three pages with approx. 20 questions and sub-questions per page would have exceeded the frame of one hour, so that it had to be reduced during the talk. Instead of planning too many questions in advance, more space should remain for spontaneous questions which appear during the course of conversation. For the chosen method, it was not necessary to comply exactly with the interview guide, because it is rather there to provide guidance. Hence in a bachelor thesis it makes sense to limit the questions to one or two pages and try different versions of the sequence in terms of content. This can possibly be tested with other students as an exercise for the researcher.

Even for my second conversation with the professor of social work, a prior discussion of the interview guideline would have been better. Misunderstandings thereby occurred, as there was – in contrast to the first interview – no translation from Sorani to German, but to English. This led to a different understanding of terms like *self-reflection* or *values*. Questions like 'What do you mean by this?' or 'What does this term mean to you?' would have led to more precise results. As I rarely asked such questions, the answers were rather general, which left much space for interpretation in the later evaluation, although quite a lot of references to the specific knowledge and the attitudes of the interview partners could be found.

All in all, I would advise interested students to have the courage to conduct intercultural interviews, even as early as in their bachelor thesis. Even though it initially involves a little more work and a bit of nervousness, the student researchers can gain a lot of exciting insights and new discoveries – and they can learn something about themselves and their own culture. Sufficient theoretical preparation and good time management are especially important in the process. Moreover, coming to an understanding with the interview partners on the meaning of complex terms is to be recommended. In my opinion, interviews can be conducted and evaluated successfully, in spite of all the obstacles, if the aspects mentioned are taken into consideration.

Julika Laura Rundnagel B.A. Social Work (2018). Since March 2017 caretaker in the open day care of a primary school at the Deutscher Paritätischer Wohlfahrtsverband social welfare organization in Wuppertal and since March 2018 studying for an M.A. in Social Inclusion at the EvH Bochum; Contact: julerund@outlook.de

Difference of Culture and Places

Kale Jamal Hamasalih

Abstract

Visiting similar places in different countries; the differences and common points between them.

Keywords

Student • Social worker • Cooperation project • Geriatric care center • Refugee camp

I was involved in this project for two years as a student from April 2016 until April 2018. We visited Germany for the first time in 2016 for eleven days and again in 2017 for nine days. This was a great journey and a great experience for me, and it was also useful for me as a social work student. It was a great process for me to see social work fields in two different countries, and to experience how people work in those fields, discovering what was common to them both and what the differences were between them, and to realize myself how to start working in the future.

I would like to talk about two important places that I have been to in both countries – in Germany and in Kurdistan-Iraq.

K. J. Hamasalih (✉)
Slemani, Iraq
E-Mail: kalejh@gmail.com

C. Ghaderi et al. (eds.), *Social Work at the Level of International Comparison*,
https://doi.org/10.1007/978-3-658-30394-5_37

1 A Diaconia-run Geriatric Care Center

There were 90 elderly people in this center, aged 48 and over, each of whom has his or her private room with bathroom. In this center, they take care of elderly people who have a physical illness and psychological instability, as well as those who are not able to live on their own or without the aid of others. We noted that there was a room for art and handicrafts and a social counselor.

We have a geriatric care center in Slemani too, but people who wish to stay at the center must be healthy and able to perform daily tasks like eating or taking a bath without any help. But still, there is a social worker and psychologist in the center to help them.

In my opinion, having a special place for older people is important, because somehow everyone is getting older in the course of time, but not everyone can stay with their family forever. So, having a place like this is useful – psychically and mentally – for those persons and especially for their personal safety and wellbeing.

I realized that the way of working on therapy in the diaconia center was very useful, and it is something we can use in the Slemani center to achieve better results, for example by focusing more on those technique and activities that could be used with elderly people, such as art therapy and animal therapy. These have positive effects such as encouraging socialization and communication with each other and lessening feelings of depression and anxiety.

2 A Refugee Camp

Another important place we visited was a refugee camp in the city of Düsseldorf. More than 290 refugees – 200 children and young people and 90 adults – live in this camp. It consists of six sections; each section has ten rooms, and each room is for one family.

We have a lot of refugee camps in Kurdistan too, because of the ISIS war and a lot of people stay in the camps, and every family have their own cabin or tent to stay in.

The structure of the camps in Kurdistan and Germany differs, because there are so many people at the camps in Kurdistan and the way of working is different somehow. But the most important thing is the role of social workers and their way working with refugees.

From my point of view, working as a social worker in a refugee camps in a war zone makes the process much more difficult, because people are not going to trust the social worker easily, or some of them don't even believe in working with someone else outside the family. Most of them don't have a plan for the future; they don't know if they are going back to their home land or till when they will stay in the camps and, besides all of this, domestic violence is happening inside the families, and that is why the social workers should be careful in deciding which techniques they should use in order to achieve better results with the refugees.

Generally, the whole project had a positive influence on me as a student, because after visiting these places, meeting many people, and collecting a lot of information in the field, it was much clearer for me to decide which field to work in after graduation. Because of that, I decided to work in a refugee camp for helping those families who need help in general, and women specifically for decreasing domestic violence.

Kale Jamal Hamasalih Kurdish social worker graduated from University of Sulaimani (2017–2018). She is one of the students who participated in the project staged from 2016 to 2018 between the Protestant University of Applied Sciences in Bochum and the University of Sulaimani (CoBoSUnin), and she wrote her Bachelor's research on "Migration of youth between reality and expectation" as part of the project. Contact: kalejh@gmail.com.

How International Can Social Work Be? Examples and Thoughts on Social Work in the Kurdistan Region of Iraq

Niklas Rokahr

Abstract

International social work is a major field of research within social work and social sciences. But how international can social work really be? International actors such as non-governmental organizations and cooperation projects can have a major influence on the studies and professional activities of local social workers. Both parties often benefit from international cooperation. But internationalization also harbors a certain risk potential – especially due to the dominance of the English language in teaching, research and practice.

Keywords

Internationalization • Non-governmental organizations • Finding identity • Professionalization • Lingua franca • Exchange of knowledge

I joined the cooperation project as a student assistant in March 2018 when the project was in its last stages and stayed until December 2019. In the beginning, the project, its structure and its implementations were not entirely accessible to me due to my lack of experience in such cooperation projects as well as the project's advanced progress. However, my understanding quickly changed during my stay at the University of Sulaimani in Northern Iraq/the Autonomous Region of Kurdistan.

Before, during, and especially following my stay, I thought in detail about how and if the students studying social work in Kurdistan-Iraq (KRI) could work in

N. Rokahr (✉)
Bochum, Germany
E-Mail: niklas.rokahr@posteo.de

C. Ghaderi et al. (eds.), *Social Work at the Level of International Comparison*,
https://doi.org/10.1007/978-3-658-30394-5_38

the field after successfully completing their studies. Within this context, I also asked myself to what extent internationalization can impact the study and practice of social work and whether the relatively young professional field of social work can establish itself as a part of society. Within the fields of social work, KRI mainly focuses on the work of psychologists and sociologists. As a professor of the cooperation project reported, due to the high activity of (international) nongovernmental organizations, associations and institutions, the students within social work create new vocational possibilities, in part on their own initiative, and can experience these options during the practical phases of their studies or through voluntary internships. In my opinion, the frequent work of (international) nongovernmental organizations and institutions in socially relevant areas, such as in work focused on refugees, poverty, and gender-based issues, are of importance for establishing a social worker's identity and, as a result, enabling him or her to develop social recognition and acceptance as professionally trained specialists. The social relevance of the previously mentioned social work fields can also be understood by the fact that a large part of the population is variously affected by issues like seeking refuge and facing poverty. In my opinion, the identity of prospective social workers is formed when what they have learned is applied to relevant fields, and their actions are then recognized (socially), allowing the students to independently create new employment opportunities. Thus, international cooperation projects also influence the studies and future professional opportunities, and under certain circumstances they may promote internationalization. Nevertheless, the activities of various international actors also offer the possibility of an exchange of knowledge and experience, which can promote both internationalization and professionalization.

Despite the visible advantages of these extensive occupational areas as well as the internationalization of social work by (international) nongovernmental organizations and cooperation projects, I regard the current developments of internationalization within education, specifically teaching, as problematic. Many of the social work lectures are conducted in English as it is the lingua franca, and the intention is to develop this further. In addition to my experiences that only a few of the students could speak or understand English at all and that the important contents of the lecture can be misunderstood or lost under these circumstances, in my opinion, teaching purely in English hinders prospective social workers from sufficiently finding their identity as well as their professionalization. In their future day-to-day practice as social workers, the students will mainly have contact with clients in their native language. Additionally, due to internationalization, research and corresponding publications that are in the native language and that are particularly important for the ongoing professionalization of social work in Kurdistan-Iraq will probably be lost.

By contrast, knowledge of the English language enables a transnational exchange as well as knowledge transfer between countries and professions. Potential danger may lie in noncritical adaptations of literature and other knowledge, as well as in the 'imposition' of international actors without taking local conditions into account.

Personally, the cooperation project between the Protestant University of Applied Sciences in Rhineland-Westphalia-Lippe and the University of Sulaimani represents a particularly important experience that also illustrates the enormous potential of the future of (international) social work. I can visualize an internationally oriented and transferrable social work as an important step towards professional recognition, provided that the respective national conditions and requirements do not fall victim to internationalization.

Niklas Rokahr B.A. Social Work (2019). From March 2018 to December 2019 student assistant at EvH Bochum, since January 2020 educational companion/social worker in secondary schools with Kirchenkreis Hamm e.V. Contact: niklas.rokahr@posteo.de.

The Role of Social Workers in Refugee Camps (A Comparison between the Refugee Camps of Kurdistan and Germany)

Shnya Shwan Omer

Supervised by Prof. Dr. Niyan Namiq Sabir, University of Sulaimani

Abstract

To show the importance of the job of a social worker regarding work with refugees. Social workers working in refugee camps have the task to help the refugees with their needs and working with vulnerable people regardless of ethnicity, age, status or any other condition.

Importance:

1. To show the importance of the job of a social worker regarding work with refugees. Social workers working in refugee camps have the task to help the refugees with their needs and working with vulnerable people regardless of ethnicity, age, status or any other condition.
2. To identify the competences, skills and knowledge that social workers need to have when they are working with clients. One of these importance skills is empathy. Empathy is a major reason people enter the profession. The social worker needs the ability to listen carefully and to get more information about body language. Social workers should have the ability to communicate effectively.

S. S. Omer (✉)
Slemani, Germany
E-Mail: shnyashwan97@gmail.com

C. Ghaderi et al. (eds.), *Social Work at the Level of International Comparison*,
https://doi.org/10.1007/978-3-658-30394-5_39

3. What are the differences of this job in two different societies, and in a cultural context? Social workers should have some details or facts about different cultures in a different society, and they should respect these differences and values. Their job is to help the refugees in the camps without difference when they need help in learning the language or studying or finding a job or finding a place to live.

Aims:

1. The role of social workers in Kurdistan camps.
2. The role of social workers in Germany camps.
3. The similarity between the role of social work in Kurdistan and Germany.
4. The differences between those social workers, when working with families and individuals.

Methods: Interviews, because of a lack of literature on the subject.

Sample: The sample for the BA interviews include nine interviews with social workers. One in Bochum, Germany, two in Düsseldorf, Germany, and the others in Slemani, Kurdistan.

Results: The research is not finished yet, but the researcher expects that the social workers working in refugee camps in Kurdistan or Germany do not have any differences in their goals or their aims, because they want to help refugees who are in need of help or need more information about the language and cultures or a place to stay, etc. Moreover, they also greatly love their jobs in both places. Social work is a new science in Kurdistan, so the German social workers have more experience in all fields of social work. Social workers in both places face challenges and difficulties in their work, and they still each have ideas of how to resolve those challenges and are looking for good ways to deal with them.

Shnya Shwan Omer studies B.A. Social Work at the University of Sulaimani. She is one of the students who participated in the project between the University of Applied Sciences in Bochum and the University of Sulaimani (CoBoSUnin). Contact: shnyashwan97@gmail.com.

Social Workers' Role in Psychosocial Support for Cancer Patients

Shatw Farhad Hassan

Supervised by Prof. Dr. Kristin Sonnenberg, Protestant University of Applied Sciences in Bochum

Prof. Dr. Niyan Namiq Sabir, University of Sulaimani

Importance: To present the importance of social workers in hospitals.

Aims:

1. To identify the role of social workers in supporting cancer patients.
2. To identify the importance of the existence of social workers in hospitals, either for patients or for the medical staff.
3. To identify expectations and needs of patients from social workers.
4. To compare the roles and tasks of social workers between Germany and the Kurdistan Region of Iraq.

Sample: Ten social workers: Three of them are working in hospitals in Germany and seven of them are working in Hiwa hospital in Slemani.

Methods: The research used the descriptive and comparison method.

Results:

S. Farhad Hassan (✉)
Slemani, Iraq
E-Mail: shatooofarhad@gmail.com

C. Ghaderi et al. (eds.), *Social Work at the Level of International Comparison*,
https://doi.org/10.1007/978-3-658-30394-5_40

1. There is no special rule for the social workers that work in hospitals to limit their tasks, responsibilities and the ways they treat the patients.
2. The number of social workers is less compared to the number of other staff of the hospital.
3. Most of the patients and their families feel disappointed and hopeless when they get to know about their disease, so they need psychosocial support, provided by social workers.
4. Communication and cooperation between social workers and the staff of the hospital is very important in order to help the patients in the best way possible.
5. The difference between social workers in Germany and Kurdistan is that in Germany, social workers have studied social work academically and they have expertise in the field. However, in Kurdistan the profession of social work is new, especially in hospitals, so psychologists and sociologists act in the role of social workers and work in the hospitals.
6. Having special hospitals for cancer patients in Kurdistan is very helpful for social workers, in order to treat the patients well. Meanwhile in Germany there is a special department for cancer patients in general hospitals.

Social workers have an important role in hospitals and they are a key help in the process of curing the patients, as well as the medical staff.

Shatw Farhad Hassan Kurdish social worker graduated from the University of Sulaimani in 2017–2018. She is one of the students who participated in the project staged from 2016 to 2018 between the University of Applied Sciences in Bochum and the University of Sulaimani (CoBoSUnin), and she wrote her Bachelor's research on "The social worker's role in psychosocial support for cancer patients" between Germany and Kurdistan as part of this project. Contact: shatooofarhad@gmail.com.

Migration of Youth Between Reality and Expectation

Kale Jamal Hamasalih

Supervised by Prof. Dr. Cinur Ghaderi, Protestant University of Applied Sciences in Bochum

Dr. Luqman S. Karim, University of Sulaimani

Importance: This is an international research program between Kurdistan and Germany, which is mostly composed of recommendations and suggestions that we concluded by practical field work.

Aims:

1. Clarification of migration phenomena
2. Focusing on reasons behind youth migration
3. Suggesting expectations and visions of the youth towards migration to European countries
4. Revealing the reality of the situation of those who migrated to Europe

Sample: Nine People were part of this research, six of them were from Slemani and three from Düsseldorf, Germany; eight of them were male and one female.

Method: The research used the descriptive and comparison method.

K. J. Hamasalih (✉)
Slemani, Iraq
E-Mail: kalejh@gmail.com

C. Ghaderi et al. (eds.), *Social Work at the Level of International Comparison*,
https://doi.org/10.1007/978-3-658-30394-5_41

Results:

1. Most young people suffer from a vague and uncertain future, due to a range of economic, political and social crises.
2. The existence of a clear percentage of unemployment is resulting in migration for the purpose of securing better living conditions.
3. Neglect of young people towards the poor conditions of the country and the lack of development of those conditions experienced by the country.
4. The psychological side of the young people and their instability and lack of sense of safety and reassurance due to lack of clarity of their future as an individual and of their country.
5. Young people do not attempt to repair existing conditions.
6. Lack of opportunities for young people to address the problems and create the opportunity to work and develop the country by the concerned authorities.
7. Young people despair of returning to the country because they believe that the situation will worsen again.
8. Of the three people who emigrated and later returned to their home country, two want to emigrate again.
9. The perception of these three people of the Western countries was true and the paradise they were waiting for.

Kale Jamal Hamasalih Kurdish social worker graduated from University of Sulaimani (2017–2018). She is one of the students who participated in the project staged from 2016 to 2018 between the Protestant University of Applied Sciences in Bochum and the University of Sulaimani (CoBoSUnin), and she wrote her Bachelor's research on "Migration of youth between reality and expectation" as part of the project. Contact: kalejh@gmail.com.

Social Work and Politics – The Perspective of the Students of Social Work in Relation to the Political Dimension of Social Work and its Mediation in Studies in the Autonomous Region Of Kurdistan

Niklas Rokahr

Supervised by Prof. Dr. Benjamin Benz and Prof. Dr. Kristin Sonnenberg

Protestant University of Applied Sciences in Bochum

Abstract

In what dimensions do politics find their way into the contents of the study of social work at the University of Sulaimani (UoS) in Kurdistan (Iraq)?

Questions:

1. In what dimensions do politics find their way into the contents of the study of social work at the University of Sulaimani (UoS) in Kurdistan (Iraq)?
2. How do students of UoS rate political social work and how do they perceive it?

Method: Empirical research in the form of a group discussion/focus group and a qualitative content analysis in category systems to evaluate the group discussion.

N. Rokahr (✉)
Bochum, Germany
E-Mail: niklas.rokahr@posteo.de

C. Ghaderi et al. (eds.), *Social Work at the Level of International Comparison*,
https://doi.org/10.1007/978-3-658-30394-5_42

Structure:

- A political, historical and financial overview of Iraq and Kurdistan (Iraq)
- Theoretical representation of political social work (policy, politics, polity, social policy, practical dimensions of working)
- Social work in Kurdistan (Iraq)

Results:
After evaluating the category system and the statements of the students, it can be stated that students tend to assess political social work as practicable and as necessary, even if they expressed some criticism about the (party) policy and the situation in Kurdistan (Iraq). The students assume that they can move institutions and ministries to more humanity and human rights. They described a political potential of social work, especially at the ministerial level. Statements refer to the Ministry of Education, the Ministry of Social Affairs and also to the Ministry of Finance.

The students described that there is no policy content in teaching during study in the curriculum. But the students showed an interest in political social work.

Niklas Rokahr B.A. Social Work (2019). From March 2018 to December 2019 student assistant at EvH Bochum, since January 2020 educational companion/social worker in secondary schools with Kirchenkreis Hamm e.V. Contact: niklas.rokahr@posteo.de.

Psychological and Social Effects of Female Sexual Abuse

Aurfa Hassan Husen

Supervised by Prof. Dr. Niyan Namiq Sabir
University of Sulaimani

Importance:
This research is a field research, which attempts to highlight and clarify the psychological and social effects of the topic that is known as sexual abuse of individuals in the community. This is a work to increase the understanding of the cases exposed to this shameful phenomenon and aims to look at and assess the status of personality when exposed to this type of abuse by friends and society.

Aims:
The aim of this research is to identify the psychological and social effects on the women who are exposed to this situation.

Methods:
The theory used in this research is the case theory, which works to emphasize the individuals who need such research and know their own problems.

A. Hassan Husen (✉)
Slemani, Iraq
E-Mail: aurfa.hassan2370@gmail.com

C. Ghaderi et al. (eds.), *Social Work at the Level of International Comparison*,
https://doi.org/10.1007/978-3-658-30394-5_43

Sample:
The sample of this research includes a number of victims who are exposed to such attacks and who are between the ages of nineteen and twenty-five years. Most cases are victims of attacks by people close to them.

Results:
The results of the research included wrong methods in dealing with females with respect to education in the family. Poverty, ignorance and confidence in the wrong people are the reasons for the occurrence of such crimes against the souls that cause many psychological and social problems, including fear of the opposite sex and a society in which men dominate women. The latter causes the female to be afraid of mentioning the things that happened to her.

Aurfa Hassan Husen studies B.A. Social Work at the University of Sulaimani. Contact: aurfa.hassan2370@gmail.com.

Social Problems of LGBT+ People in Kurdish Society

Briska Mariwan Mustafa

Supervised by Prof. Dr. Niyan Namiq Sabir
University of Sulaimani

Importance:
Theoretical importance: the main point of the theoretical importance is to highlight a new and sensitive subject that is forbidden in Kurdish society.

Practical importance: the practical section of the research lets the researchers observe the life of the LGBT+ people closely and evaluate their situation as caused by their social problems.

Aims:

1. To find out whether LGBT+ individuals, residing in Kurdish society, encounter social problems related with the social oppression.
2. To identify how LGBT+ people deal with the problems they encounter and, when they are not able to cope with such problems and move to other cities or countries, whether they are faced with the same kind of problems.
3. To find whether LGBT+ would have experienced the same social problems in their new places.
4. To analyze those problems that affected them.

B. Mariwan Mustafa (✉)
Slemani, Iraq
E-Mail: Briskasaied@gmail.com

C. Ghaderi et al. (eds.), *Social Work at the Level of International Comparison*,
https://doi.org/10.1007/978-3-658-30394-5_44

Method: This research used the case study method. The data was collected by interviews and observations.

Sample: The sample consists of five cases who visited the Rasan organization: two of them are gay, two of them are transgender, and one is bisexual.

Results:

1. Lack of acceptance is one of the biggest problems that they are facing, which is leading them to have another problem.
2. Lack of public education about different sexual identities is another problem.
3. Lack of support from the Ministry of Interior and lack of knowledge of how to deal with them.
4. They all dropped out of education (school, college, etc.) because of bullying from other people.
5. Because of being bullied, they are always afraid of being murdered, so they can't live a normal life as any other people.
6. They want to leave Kurdistan because they do not think that this is a safe place for them to live.

Briska Mariwan Mustafa studies B.A. Social Work at the University of Sulaimani. Contact: Briskasaied@gmail.com.

The manufacturer's authorised representative in the EU is Springer Nature Customer Service Centre GmbH, Europaplatz 3, 69115 Heidelberg, Germany. If you have any concerns regarding our products, please contact ProductSafety@springernature.com

Printed and bound by CPI Group (UK) Ltd, Croydon, CR0 4YY
30/09/2026
02225688-0004